Matatu

Matatu

*A History of Popular
Transportation in Nairobi*

KENDA MUTONGI

The University of Chicago Press   Chicago and London

The University of Chicago Press, Chicago 60637
The University of Chicago Press, Ltd., London
© 2017 by Kenda Mutongi
All rights reserved. No part of this book may be used or reproduced
in any manner whatsoever without written permission, except in the
case of brief quotations in critical articles and reviews. For more in-
formation, contact the University of Chicago Press, 1427 E. 60th St.,
Chicago, IL 60637.
Published 2017
Printed in the United States of America

26 25 24 23 22 21 20 19 18 17   1 2 3 4 5

ISBN-13: 978-0-226-13086-6 (cloth)
ISBN-13: 978-0-226-47139-6 (paper)
ISBN-13: 978-0-226-47142-6 (e-book)
DOI: 10.7208/chicago/9780226471426.001.0001

Library of Congress Cataloging-in-Publication Data

Names: Mutongi, Kenda, author.
Title: Matatu : a history of popular transportation in Nairobi / Kenda
    Mutongi.
Description: Chicago : The University of Chicago Press, 2017. |
    Includes bibliographical references and index.
Identifiers: LCCN 2016057140 | ISBN 9780226130866
    (cloth : alk. paper) | ISBN 9780226471396 (pbk. : alk. paper) |
    ISBN 9780226471426 (e-book)
Subjects: LCSH: Transportation—Kenya—Nairobi. | Minibuses—
    Kenya—Nairobi. | Local transit—Kenya—Nairobi. | Urban
    transportation policy—Kenya—Nairobi.
Classification: LCC HE283.5.Z7 N35 2017 | DDC 388.4096762/5—
    dc23 LC record available at https://lccn.loc.gov/2016057140

♾ This paper meets the requirements of ANSI/NISO Z39.48-1992
(Permanence of Paper).

Contents

To all the matatu workers and passengers

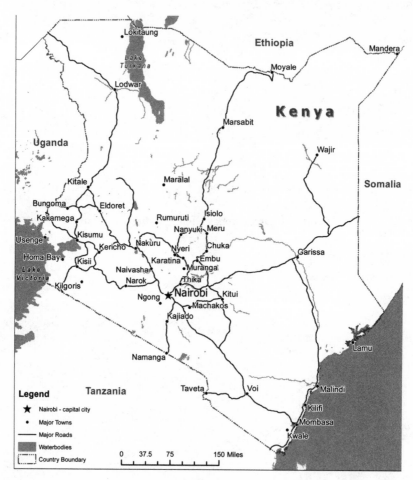

MAP 1   Kenya, 2016. Prepared by Sharron Macklin.

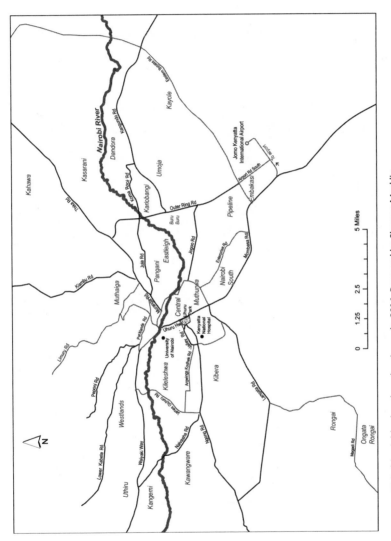

MAP 2 Nairobi neighborhoods and main roads, 2016. Prepared by Sharron Macklin.

PART ONE

Background

Matatu

Without its matatus, the city of Nairobi comes to a near standstill.[1] It happens some ten to fifteen times a year when matatu workers go on strike. Whenever they suspend their scramble through the streets, everything in the city slows down—the town center grows quiet, offices sit empty, stores close their doors, and the last lingering pedestrians are able to walk the sidewalks with ease. There are no commuter trains or trams, the traffic and poor road conditions make cycling impossible, and the government, regrettably, provides only a few irregular and ineffective buses. Since so few people can afford private cars, a majority of people have come to rely upon matatus, the privately owned minibuses that have engulfed the city over the past half a century. Unfortunately, the citizens of Nairobi have become used to the matatu strikes, used to waiting on dusty side roads and crowded street corners until, angry and out of patience, they abandon hope and either trudge home or hike into town. Whenever the city's moving mosaic of matatus comes to a stop, the forsaken commuters are once again reminded of just how much their lives depend on these flamboyant minibuses and the army of workers who operate them. Inevitably, the offices, cafés, and *dukas* begin to echo with resentment, and the muttered complaints of the stranded rise like bitter clouds of exhaust—"*tumeshindwa kabisa!*"

In other words, without the matatus Nairobi's commuters feel "completely defeated." The familiar phrase expresses more than simple frustration at the lack of transportation. It also reveals a sense of thwarted prospects,

FIGURE 1   Matatu workers' strike, May 9, 2012. Courtesy of the NMG, Nairobi

even a sense of national failure, at least to the extent to which the whole of the city and its economy have come to depend on these vehicles. To the uninitiated outsider, this sense of gloom can be baffling. Those unfamiliar with the city's culture tend to see matatus as little more than a noisy, garish way for residents to get about the city; at worst, they look at the encroaching chaos of matatus as if it were nothing better than a gang of venal marauders—strident, greedy, relentless— intent upon vanquishing the city with their custom-built coaches. But despite the ambivalence with which the matatus are viewed, the citizens of Nairobi have come to acknowledge, reluctantly, that they are instrumental to the city's success. It is unlikely that Nairobi's economy could survive without the overwhelming achievements of the matatu industry. Since the early 1960s, the matatu has provided transportation to at least 60 percent of the city's population, and the matatu industry has become the largest employer in the so-called popular economy by providing livelihoods to mechanics, touts, fee collectors, drivers, artists, and other associated businesses.[2] Even more significant is the fact that the matatu industry is the only major business in Kenya that has continued to be almost entirely locally owned and controlled; in other words, it has, from its beginnings, remained free from the influence of foreign aid or foreign aid workers.[3] The matatu industry is homegrown. The owners and workers are making it on their own, without foreign aid or government support, and despite subsidized competition, government interference, and systemic corruption. For several decades now, the matatu industry has provided a rare example of a highly profitable business that has turned out to be vital to the development of Nairobi and its identity—as the acclaimed Kenyan writer and activist Binyavanga Wainaina has remarked, "Matatus are Nairobi and Nairobi is matatus."[4]

In fact, matatus are so much a part of life in the city that it is no exaggeration to say that modern Nairobi could not have taken shape without the invention of these colorful contraptions. The two cannot be separated. They are too mutually dependent, too tightly intertwined. Not only is the motley stampede of transports inescapable to anyone on the street, but they have also, since independence, existed at the heart of the city's economy and its culture, politics, and street life. They have, over the past half century, provided the city with its circulatory system; they are its lifeblood. So, to understand the history of Nairobi and its rapid growth, we need to understand the history of the matatu; similarly, if we want to understand the triumph of the matatu, we need to understand the particular social, economic, cultural, and political history of postcolonial Nairobi.

This uneasy alliance of Nairobi and its matatus is the subject of this book. It is the story of the matatu industry as it unfolds within the larger historical contexts of the community and the nation, from its beginnings in the early 1960s through the authoritarian years of Daniel Arap Moi's presidency, and into the twenty-first century.[5] Given the industry's humble origins, as well as its ad hoc, opportunistic nature, the book is necessarily an ethnographic history, written from the perspective of the streets. The story of the matatu cannot be found anywhere else, anywhere but on the peripheries of society, on the rough streets and in dirty garages, and among the grease-stained entrepreneurs who tend to thrive outside the purview of bureaucrats and politicians—and all too often outside the law. And though the story may start around the margins of Nairobi, it does not end there. Eventually the history of the matatu will take everyone involved—the workers, the passengers, the police, the gangs, and the government—on a rough ride straight into the center of the city.

―――――

Matatu-like transportation is not unique to Kenya. The use of vehicles similar to matatus is an important phenomenon in most of the Global South. Called *pesero* in Mexico, *jeepney* in the Philippines, *tuk-tuk* in

Indonesia, *songthaew* in Thailand and Laos, *otobus* in Egypt, *combi* in South Africa, *dala dala* in Tanzania, *danfo* in Nigeria, *taxis-brousses* in Francophone Africa, they can be found throughout areas with uneven development, popular economies, and a large-scale need for public transportation. In Nairobi it became relatively commonplace to see a matatu on the roads right after Kenya achieved its independence from Britain. They could not have existed earlier. During colonial rule, Nairobi was meant to be a white-only city, and the idea of an African-owned vehicle bringing Africans into the city was not encouraged. Not only were major African business ventures generally discouraged, the movements of Africans were also vigilantly restricted.[6] Typically, the only Africans allowed to remain in the city center for more than brief visits were laborers performing menial work for Europeans, and most of these workers walked to their places of work. They had no choice. This changed significantly once racial restrictions were lifted after independence in 1963 and Africans could work and move about the city more freely. The effects of freedom were immediate, throughout the country. Straightaway Africans began migrating from the rural areas to the city in search of economic opportunity and excitement, and the majority of these new residents needed a way to get around the city and to get into the city from the rapidly growing suburbs. And so the matatu was invented.

The early matatus were ramshackle affairs (the name "matatu" derives from the Kikuyu word for "three," the three big ten-cent coins used to pay for a ride to the city). They were cobbled together "bit by bit, piece by piece," recalled one Nairobi resident who witnessed the birth of matatus in the early 1960s: "Matatu entrepreneurs scrounged old motor parts and carried them to garages on River Road. After weeks of hammering and tying pieces of wire, an earsplitting roar, accompanied by machine-gun-type backfiring, was heard, [then] huge mechanical monsters emerged from behind. After a long time, the engine fired and broke into a tremendous roar, and the turn-boys removed the stones that kept the wheels in place."[7] For the most part these enterprising businessmen were ambitious tinkerers who would recover and repair vehicles—cars, trucks, or buses; anything that could accommodate a few passengers and maintain fairly regular routes to and from the city. In the eyes of the authorities, however, these individual ventures were illegal. Since they had not been licensed by the new government they were deemed to be operating outside the law. But that did not matter to the passengers; they desperately needed transportation to and from the city center. In time the government grudgingly came to tolerate matatus as a necessary evil.

The private businesses lurched along unchecked, despite the government's grumbling, until 1973, when President Jomo Kenyatta abruptly declared matatus legal. The ruling was a surprise. Even more surprising was the fact that Kenyatta had declined to prescribe any restrictions, or require any form of licensing, on the matatus. It may have been a simple oversight. But by foregoing the chance to regulate the industry he gave the matatu owners de facto permission to explore the limits of laissez-faire capitalism.[8] Suddenly everybody wanted in on the action. Unfit vehicles in all states of disrepair began roaming the streets; even more dangerous was the recklessness with which drivers began to operate their rickety rattletraps—bouncing through potholed streets, reeling around corners, the drivers raced through the streets as fast as they could to get first crack at passengers who they then packed in so tightly that arms, legs, and backsides were left hanging out of doors and windows.[9]

The indifference to safety, along with the government's regulatory neglect, led to a predictable increase in accidents. In fact, they became so common that newspaper headlines routinely announced the tragedies with a weary shrug. Reporting became jaded: "Another horror matatu crash"; "twenty people perish in another matatu accident"; or, "matatus are a Black Hole of Calcutta." Not to be outdone by the newspapers' scoffing unconcern, the owners began emblazoning the sides of the minibuses with slogans that reveled in the matatu's perils: such slogans as "Coming for to Carry Me Home" or "See You in Heaven" announced the matatu's dangers with daring cockiness. Owners seemed to have no qualms at all about suggesting to passengers that their next destination might well be the next world. And the passengers, with places to go and no other way to get there, overlooked the odds of an accident.[10] If you hopped on a matatu and did not get where you were going, at the very least you would arrive in heaven. Either way, everyone would win.

While this kind of gallows humor no doubt invited a certain cavalier camaraderie, it did nothing to mitigate the risks of actually riding in a matatu. The increasing number of injuries and fatalities made it clear that something needed to be done to make the industry safer. In response to the crisis, President Moi passed a law in 1984 requiring that matatus be inspected and licensed. The new regulations had both good and bad consequences; while the new law clearly helped provide some oversight, it unfortunately ended up curtailing the business by shutting out many of the poorer matatu owners who lacked the means to meet the new safety requirements. The law also ended up helping the wealthier owners, who quickly began to consolidate their power by forming associations; on the other hand, this power grab had the beneficial effect of allowing matatu owners to organize itineraries and thus limit the chaotic overlapping of routes and reduce traffic congestion.[11]

By the early 1990s, then, the consolidation of operators, along with the corresponding decrease in competition and increased organization of routes, noticeably reduced reckless driving and improved safety. Unfortunately, the associations formed by the well-off owners began selfishly controlling the routes and exacting exorbitant parking fees and "goodwill payments," thus making it difficult for new owners to enter the business.[12] These exclusionary tactics meant that the entry of new owners into the business was no longer a matter of free market choices. Suddenly matatu startups encountered a barricade of byzantine negotiations with key stakeholders over a wide range of social, political, and economic variables—and passing through the barricade typically involved some kind of payoff. If you wanted to be on the streets, you had to be ready to offer a bribe.

As fewer and fewer owners managed to enter and survive the industry's consolidation, those who did quickly began to monopolize it. But as bad as this may seem, some of the consequences were beneficial. It was not long before the wealthier owners purchased safer and more comfortable vehicles.[13] By the late 1990s, instead of the old, overburdened jalopies, the streets soon entertained new Nissan, Toyota, and Isuzu minivans with ornate paint jobs, air conditioning, and lavish interiors with such luxuries as tinted windows, state-of-the-art sound systems, and eventually flat-screen TVs. Much better than splintery benches bolted to the bed of an old pickup. Still, despite the exclusionary tactics, despite the streamlined routes and all the added comforts, there remained the mad scramble for passengers. So, to lure passengers, matatu operators started to "trick out" their vehicles with blaring hip-hop and flamboyantly painted exteriors—from somber black to a Rubik's-Cube assortment of colors, or with airbrushed creations normally reserved for movie posters or street murals. Each matatu had to be unique. Particularly popular were the names and portraits of American hip-hop artists like Kanye West, Eminem, Ludacris, Jay-Z, or Snoop Dogg; sometimes they promoted political figures—there were predictable portraits of Barack Obama, that most honored child of Kenya (in one such image he is kissing his wife, Michelle), but you might also en-

FIGURE 2 September 2002. Courtesy of the Standard Group, Nairobi

counter such political absurdities as George Bush sitting beside Osama bin Laden. Regardless, the transformation of the matatu was profound. Just a few generations earlier matatu owners had been repurposing used parts to assemble simple vehicles that could carry a few passengers; now, a few decades after independence, they were adorning large, top-of-the-line vans with personalized artwork and high-tech accessories.[14]

Passengers also changed. They began to expect more creature comforts, and as the comfort improved, so did their behavior. Passengers began to cultivate a certain degree of matatu etiquette at the stops and in the parking lots. Now, more often than not, commuters lined up to board the fancy vehicles rather than jostling and shoving each other as they had done before, nor was there so much tiresome bickering over fares. But as the operators improved and regulated the matatu business, they also made it more enticing to the less disciplined elements of society. To put it another way, the success of the matatu began to attract parasites. By the mid-1990s criminal gangs, such as Mungiki, began to infiltrate the business and extort protection money from the operators, and their efforts were so successful that they eventually ended up becoming the self-appointed rulers of the matatu parking lots.[15] The government did little to curtail their power, and so the owners were left more or less helpless against the gangs' predations. In fact, as the gangs began to accumulate wealth and influence, prominent politicians began to hire them as political mercenaries to harass their opponents during elections.[16] It was becoming clear that if you could control the matatus, you could control Kenyan politics. The matatu had become a political weapon.

But not just for powerful politicians. During the 1990s and early 2000s, a new generation of young men (and occasionally women) began to enter the industry as drivers and conductors, and they managed to change the social and political landscape. This generation—I sometimes refer to them as "Generation Matatu"—came of age during a period of democratic reform and neoliberal economic policy. Educated but unemployed, many of these young workers had no other options than the matatu industry, and even if other employment had been available—as office clerks, for example—most of them could earn more money in matatus than in the jobs they had been trained for. Since the traditional path toward government employment had been largely closed off, many in this new generation came to believe that working in the popular economy was the only way forward—or at least the most lucrative. For Generation Matatu, success no longer meant landing a nine-to-five job in an office as it had in the 1960s; it meant becoming a self-reliant man or woman, fending for oneself in the popular economy by any means possible—much as the early matatu workers had done.

The benefits of matatu work were not just monetary. These new conductors and drivers—young and trendy, sporting the latest hip-hop fashions—became increasingly desirable boyfriends for young women in Nairobi, which naturally made matatus one of the most favored locations for secret rendezvous. Even young women from the upper middle classes, who might previously have preferred riding comfortably in their parents' cars, now began to ride in matatus with the poor and working classes. In a sense, then, matatu mobility made for mobility among the classes, and, as is typically the case, the proximity led to change. Before long, interactions on these vibrant, modernized matatus began to alter the forms of class and respectability in Nairobi, and perhaps even more significantly, these interactions began to increase political awareness—so much so that many members of Generation Matatu started to join Kenya's nascent democratic movement. Eventually, the young reformers took to the streets—often in the same matatus in which they rode or worked—to challenge the government and call for multiparty elections and economic change. Inspired and enabled by the independent and provocative matatu culture, this new generation of citizens turned the matatu into a highly charged, politicized space. In other words, the matatu became a weapon of the people, not just the politicians.[17]

―――――――

All told, the matatu's "creative, ambiguous, and malevolent" history offers important insights into the history of postcolonial Kenya.[18] Yet there are no historical studies of matatus. The two recent monographs on matatus, by Mbũgua wa Mũngai and by Meleckidzedeck Khayesi, Frederick Muyia Nafukho, and Joyce Kemuma, are, respectively, marvelous studies of literary aspects of the matatu, and of the general economic organization strategies of the industry, but they are not historical.[19] A detailed study of the matatu industry shows that despite the appreciable social, economic, and even political advances associated with the industry, its history has been one of exploitation, crime, violence, and corruption.[20] This sordid side of the industry cannot be ignored. Some of the problems were self-imposed, some were the fault of government neglect or dishonesty, and sometimes even the customers were complicit in the industry's illegal practices. At almost every turn, plans for improvements met with insurmountable obstacles. All this is to say that a thorough history of the matatu industry in Nairobi must also unravel the many social, economic, political, and personal trade-offs forced upon the city's residents who depended on the matatu. Sadly, and perhaps predictably, many of these trade-offs fell hardest upon the average commuters, the anxious matatu workers, or the struggling owners.

Yet what also emerges is the seldom-heard story of African economic creativity, resilience, and self-sufficiency, all of which figured into the matatu's success. Everyone involved—the oil-stained repairmen in the garages, the conductors squeezing bodies on board, the barking touts, the artists embellishing the vehicles with outlandish images, the bank managers offering loans, the women selling chapati in kiosks at the stations, even the policemen taking bribes from the drivers and the Mungiki extorting protection money—all of them hustled in and around the matatu industry to make a living in the exciting confusion of postcolonial Nairobi. To succeed in the matatu industry, it helped to be quick-witted, and to adopt a high-handed, customer-be-damned attitude; often this meant doing business with a compulsory cunning, and often it meant being a little less than scrupulous, or a little too keen to cut corners, or having a tendency to shade the truth to snatch that extra shilling or two.[21] The matatu industry was nothing if not resourceful. And at best, amid the compromises and chaos, the business of the matatu created a model of capitalistic enterprise that demonstrated to Kenyans that they could make it on their own and in their own country.

And it is not just Kenyans who are making it. Africans in other countries have succeeded just as well in businesses of their own, though there are few historical studies of indigenous businesses or industries in postcolonial Africa.[22] Unfortunately, the models of local large capital ventures have largely been ignored, and, as a result, our picture of African enterprise is incomplete.[23] Instead, historians have concentrated on studying "development" in Africa, typically with a focus on the role of foreign aid, NGOs, or foreign investors.[24] Regrettably, the familiar "development" model is often inadequate since it tends to constrain our thinking. All too often it traps us in an easy narrative of success and failure, or hope and despair, which always seems to be determined by some outside agent.[25] The real story is neither so simple nor so confining. We need to recognize and appreciate what the Africans themselves are doing with their economies as they take risks, create businesses, and accumulate capital.[26] On a very basic level, this book is about how informal businesses succeed and evolve, and how they are, over time, incorporated into regulated marketplaces. When we actually look at Africans' own businesses and their evolution, the narrative becomes more complicated, more interesting, and even more hopeful—despite the absence of beneficent benefactors from the NGOs, or the deus ex machina of foreign aid grants.[27] It is of course the case that indigenous businesses may initially involve disruptive, extralegal activity—activity that is often enabled by organized crime and political corruption.[28] But it is also the case that the consumer interests generally prevail, and that eventually the businesses do tend to become socially sanctioned and successfully regulated. Of course the road is never straight or without obstacles—certainly not for the owner of a matatu. What I hope to do in *Matatu* is to show how ordinary Kenyans have managed to make their self-made matatus into a thriving and sustaining industry.

––––––

While it may be surprising that so little attention has been given to the history of the matatu, it is even more surprising that scholars have largely ignored the history of postcolonial Nairobi—despite the fact that as a city with a population of more than four million people, Nairobi is representative of other major megacities of the Global South.[29] In fact, Luise White's *The Comforts of Home*, published twenty-five years ago, is the only book available on the history of Nairobi, and it focuses on the colonial period.[30] White uses prostitution as a lens through which to view the broader history of colonial Nairobi. In a similar way, I examine matatus as a means to analyze more fully the history of post-colonial Nairobi. By telling the story of the matatu from the vantage point of the streets and parking garages, I can show a great deal about how the matatu helped coalesce the city and the nation.[31] This broader scope is possible because there is simply no corner of the city, or of the city's recent history, that the matatu industry has not reached, and no corner of its culture, economy, and politics that it has not affected.[32] For better or for worse, the matatu is what moves Nairobi's people, politics, and economy. No matter who you are or how you travel, whether on foot or by bus or motorcade, you will encounter matatus. In this regard, matatus provide useful lessons in how to live in postcolonial Nairobi. But the lessons are sometimes the unwelcome kind. Riding in a matatu requires alertness. Pickpocketing, muggings, and sexual harassment are particularly common in and around matatus, so attentiveness to one's surroundings is necessary.[33] Indeed, to be a seasoned citizen of Nairobi requires such caution and vigilance.

But life is not always a hassle in this "city in the sun." Nairobi is a city that teaches its residents ways to survive against the odds, a city where the lines between good and bad often seem to blur, where ingenuity and resourcefulness are crucial—but so is a certain level of consideration for one's neighbors. Just when Nairobians seem on the point of despair, something shining seems always to relieve them, if not rescue them: the clean Iko toilets by the parking lots, the well-tended bougainvillea gardens lining the streets, the conductor who abandons his route to rush a pregnant woman to the nearest hospital, the spirited beat of hip-hop music. And if you look inside any matatu as it staggers down a Nairobi street, you are likely to see the poor or working class jostled alongside the middle class, or the Luo and the Luyia, the Kikuyu and the Kamba, all intermingled, all at the mercy of the drivers to whom they have entrusted their lives. The motley mix of passengers will see the same billboards and buildings, watch the same videos, listen to the same music, and witness the same passing crowds of pedestrians who, just like they, are now Nairobians. No doubt each passenger experiences the city in his or her own unique way, but by sharing their fates in boisterous matatus they share the same cosmopolitan experience, and at least for the moment they make Nairobi their city.[34] In this regard, *Matatu* tells the story of some of the ways in which matatu passengers learn to live together as Nairobians, as cosmopolitan citizens, to adjust, to bend the rules to help those worse off, to *kaa square*, "squeeze in" and make room for just one more in a crowded matatu.[35]

───────

To tell this story of the matatu and postcolonial Nairobi I have relied to a large extent upon newspapers, magazines, and interviews. There is good reason for this: almost all of the material lies outside formal government archives. In most cases the matatus' rough-and-ready operators were participating in a popular economy that made up its own rules and regulations as it struggled to survive. Whenever matatu operators came into contact with officialdom, problems tended to be resolved under the table or on the street with bribes or brickbats, and hence there are very few official sources to draw on. The history is not to be found in the government archives.

Newspapers, especially, provided a wealth of material. Over the past thirty years there has been an almost daily story or two concerning matatu accidents, gang violence, or bribery. Granted, some of the material is sensational, or driven by the need for drama, and a fair share of it is written in haste to meet a deadline or in response to its audience's bias. Much of the reporting is therefore contradictory or inconsistent, so I have had to weigh the evidence and assess the different angles and interpretations to arrive at a fittingly complex understanding of the matatu. And of course, the information I have gleaned from newspapers is supplemented by numerous interviews. Over the past ten years I have returned to Kenya for at least four or five weeks a year to conduct research and interview passengers, touts, drivers, owners, officials, former members of the Mungiki, and many others. Overall, I interviewed at least two hundred people in Nairobi and other parts of Kenya.

And finally, I have drawn upon social media for information on contemporary developments and viewpoints, and especially for matatu photographs. Kenya is awash in cell phones, and for the past decade people have been taking photos and posting them on blogs and Facebook with spendthrift abandon. In particular, I have found the "matatu culture" site on Facebook, and Wambururu's blog, to be useful for their currency and colorful commentary.[36] The Internet-based sources are a cultural phenomenon just as surely as any other text that is relevant to historical study, and in a sense the blogs and Facebook pages merely

extend the range of sources.[37] The fact that matatu culture is so avidly represented on the Internet is in many ways a reflection of the
intensely communicative aspect of the matatus, with their extravagant
airbrushed art, slogans, raucous music, and the constant social and political banter that echoes in their confines. You could perhaps say that
all along the purpose of the matatu has been to provide a social network that connects people to their city.

ONE

"The Only Way to Get There Was on Foot"

Before the matatu entered the scene in the early 1960s, transportation was woefully inadequate and mobility in Nairobi—at least for Africans—was limited. Most commuters journeyed to work on foot—a fact that did not escape the notice of the notorious writer/journalist (and Hemingway epigone) from North Carolina, Robert Ruark, who traveled extensively in Kenya between 1952 and 1958.[1] Ruark typically wrote with colorful conformity about the poor conditions of Africans, but he seemed unusually surprised by the amount of foot traffic clogging the city. Looking out the window of his comfortable motorcar as he was conveyed from the Eastleigh Airport to the Norfolk Hotel, he marveled at the "ceaseless, relentless stream of plodding people—people coming in from town or going out of town, crowding the sides of the roads on bicycles and afoot, on sway-backed burros and packed like shrimp in buses and lurching lorries. The women ever bear some burden on their backs—whether food, firewood, or a few pitiful belongings; their necks bow and the carrying strap creases their foreheads."[2] For Africans this kind of plodding was the customary means of getting around during most of the colonial period.[3] Before independence the layout of Nairobi had been primarily organized to meet the needs of the white population, with little thought given to the Africans' need for reliable transportation. The disregard was deliberate: the economy of the city had been organized so that the white population would reap most of the benefits, and the well-being of the Africans who worked for them was more or less a matter of indifference. Nor did the colonial officials encourage—or anticipate—any significant independent economic activity among the Africans, and predictably, they gave little consideration to potential African commerce or businesses. Early Nairobi was very much a racialized society: Africans were allowed in the city in order to serve the needs of the whites, and then they were expected to withdraw to their settlements on the city's unseen outskirts.[4] How they got back and forth was their own concern.

———

None of this is particularly remarkable given the nature of the city's origins, but it is useful to know how Nairobi came to exist if we are to understand its need for the matatu once the country gained its independence. Like so many African cities, it was founded in the context of late nineteenth-century European imperialism. Simply put, Nairobi was a city built to further the demands of Empire, and the racialized organization of mid-twentieth-century Nairobi was very much a consequence of its origins. According to the convoluted logic of the "Scramble for Africa," the British in eastern Africa required a way to get to Lake Victoria, the source of the Nile River, so that they could prevent France, Germany, or Belgium from tampering with the lake's water. Defending the lake would protect the water's flow into the Nile, which was considered essential for the security of the Suez Canal, which, in turn, was required to secure the passage to India. And so, presumably, the well-being of the Empire was contingent upon getting troops and supplies to a remote body of water in East Africa, and in order to safeguard the British claim to the region they needed a railway, from Mombasa to Kampala. After all, the Empire was at stake. This, at least, was the argument made in the 1890s by the British East Africa Company to persuade Parliament to finance the rail line (this, and altruistic assurances that it would hasten the end of the slave trade in eastern and central Africa).[5] The reasoning proved convincing: the railway was built, at the colossal cost of five million pounds.[6]

It was a huge investment, given that the land that now forms Kenya did not initially interest the British, despite the pressing concerns about the security of the Empire. And certainly the location of the future capital was not given much thought. Nairobi, or Enkare Nyirobi (which translates from the Masai language as "the place of cool waters"), was simply chosen as a rest stop, a place for the railway workers (most of whom were indentured laborers from India) to recuperate after an exhausting four years and three hundred miles away from the railway's origin in Mombasa.[7] The year was 1899. The work up to that point had been costly: not only was the labor exceptionally punishing, but also one out of every four workers fell prey to lions and other wild animals, and many more were killed by malaria. The mortality rate was even worse for the animals forced into service, as over half the horses and donkeys were killed by tsetse flies.[8] The improvised rest stop at Nairobi therefore provided a much-welcomed break for the railway workers and their overseers.

Still, Nairobi was not necessarily the ideal place for a rest stop. There was no geographical justification for its location. According to Ronald Preston, the railway's chief engineer, the site of the encampment was "a bleak, swampy stretch of soppy landscape, windswept, devoid of human habitation of any sort, the resort of thousands of animals of every species." It seemed to him nothing but a "barren wasteland."[9] Nevertheless, Nairobi's location, halfway between Mombasa and Kampala, was at least logistically justified, since the railway administrators were eager to settle down momentarily to rest and regroup before beginning the next half of the railroad. Over the next few months they began to set up shop: "Roads and bridges were constructed, houses and workshops built, turntables and station quarters erected, a water supply laid on, and a hundred and one other things done which go into the making of a railway township."[10] By the end of 1899, new headquarters had been built, and the "place of cool waters" quickly turned into a settlement. Still, it remained rather unassuming. Visitors to the area in 1903 described Nairobi as a "tin town" consisting of little more than a few corrugated iron houses. When the celebrated doctor/missionary Dr. Albert Cook (later Sir Albert Cook) revisited Nairobi in 1906, he remarked, "Where five years before there had been only long grass, we found the rudiments of a township in the shape of higgledy-piggledy arrangements of tin shanties."[11]

The lackluster tone of these early accounts was relatively short-lived as the virtues of Nairobi's location came to be appreciated by the more forward-looking visitors. Despite the rough-and-ready nature of its beginnings, the location benefited from a moderate climate, tempered by an altitude of 5,300 feet, and its gently irregular and open terrain. Eventually the site's unexpected advantages came to be seen as evidence of exceptional foresight, and it was not long before the Colonial Office began to play up the region's blessings and encourage white settlers to move to the area and establish farms. The arguments offered to potential settlers were not only about the pleasant situation, they were also political and economic, and racial. What could be more beneficial to the Empire than to have the land populated by white farmers employing African laborers to grow raw products for industries in Britain? Besides, the enormous cost of the railway could better be justified if it drew a significant number of white settlers to the area. This was, in fact, just what the Colonial Office wanted; throughout the first decade of the 1900s they made a concerted effort to convince white settlers to immigrate to Kenya.[12]

A few years later the short-lived Empire Marketing Board even fashioned a series of advertisements in the major British newspapers urging people to move to Kenya by heralding it, shamelessly, as a "white man's country."[13] Eager to establish a permanent settler colony, the board members did not hesitate to play up the advantages that Kenya offered. One Empire Marketing Board advertisement in the London *Times* was particularly effusive: "As one rides or marches through the valleys and across the wide plateaux of these uplands, braced by their delicious air, listening to the music of their streams and feasting their eyes upon their natural wealth and beauty," eventually "a sense of bewilderment overcomes the mind."[14] And just in case the country's beauty might prove a little too bewildering to future colonizers, the advertisements were careful to provide practical assurances that the land offered untapped riches, and that the "raw and naked lazy natives" were amiable, docile, and graciously awaiting the chance to be civilized by hard work on the Europeans' farms. It was even hinted that the future Kenya was a kind of undiscovered biblical paradise. It was, according to an advertisement in the London *Daily Telegraph*, "the land from which, men say, ages ago King Solomon's ships came sailing with their freight of rare and precious things, 'gold and ivory, apes and peacocks.'" The tracts of available land and the opportunities for wealth were apparently limitless, and now was the time for aspiring colonists to take advantage: "today it is British—and of all the tropical domains of the Empire none is richer in promise than this vast territory twenty times the size of England."[15]

None of this advertising included any reference to the needs or desires of the Africans. The railway line, like the emerging city, was geared toward serving the needs of colonizers and their empire; nonwhites were meant to exist invisibly in the background. This omission presumably facilitated the ads' success. Lured by the promise of privilege, white settlers began to move to the Kenya Highlands at a rapid pace—by 1909 there were 600 white settlers in and around Nairobi.[16] Most of these—including men like Lord Delamere, the Ewarts, the

Huxleys, Victor Hays, the Earl of Erroll, the Blixens, and many others—
were from vaguely aristocratic backgrounds, though more often than
not they were lazy philanderers looking to escape the stuffiness of
Europe's upper classes and live freely in the tropics without the constraints of their supposedly reputable backgrounds.[17] The other major
group of white settlers consisted of poorer immigrants (mostly Boers)
from South Africa, seeking better opportunities after their defeat in
the Second Anglo-Boer War.[18] Regardless of origin, white settlers were
given exclusive rights to the land between Machakos and Fort Ternan,
in what became known as the "white highlands."[19] They made the
most of their prerogatives; Nairobi became their little city, their private
playground in East Africa, and as rumors of the possibilities spread,
others naturally followed. Over the next few decades, white settlement
continued to climb steadily so that by the late 1950s there were about
3,000 white settlers in all of Kenya, among a total of 60,000 whites
(0.2 percent of the total Kenyan population). Of the total white population about 22,000 lived in and around Nairobi in 1957, a few years
before independence.[20]

———

Still, back in 1899, in the place of cool waters, the Kikuyu and Masai
began selling food and other necessities to the railway workers who
had settled in the encampment. As their business increased, they began
setting up makeshift homesteads on the outskirts of the railway settlement; soon other African groups started to join them—the Kamba, the
Swahili, and Somalis from the coast, who were passing through as casual traders along the railway line. As these traders stopped over in Nairobi many of them ended up establishing homes of their own on the
outskirts of the town, typically with names that indicated their coastal
origins—Pangani, Pumwani, Mji wa Mombasa, Masikini, Kaburini, and
Kileleshwa.[21] Then in 1912, the Colonial Office gave land in the area
now known as Kibera to some 400 retired Sudanese soldiers who had
helped the British in their original conquest of Kenya.[22] Until the 1920s
these were the main groups of Africans in and around Nairobi, residing
in about 200 self-constructed huts outside the city center.[23] Colonial
officials generally left them to themselves, interfering only when tribal
chiefs were sent in to collect taxes.[24] Except for the few who worked
as housekeepers and cooks for the Europeans, the vast majority of the
Africans' economic activity consisted of petty trade.[25]

During the years between World Wars I and II the number of Africans increased steadily. The steady growth was partly a consequence

of the number of white settlers moving into central Kenya and com-
mandeering land from the Kikuyu, thus forcing the landless to relocate in Nairobi and look for work. Many of the new immigrants also
set up small trades in food and other necessities, while others worked
as hawkers, tailors, and masons, or as manual laborers for the railway
company and for various government departments.[26] Most of these
menial workers earned only enough money for basic sustenance. There
was, however, another important group of Africans who settled in
Nairobi during the interwar years—the literate Africans employed by
the colonial government. Typically they worked in various lower-level
posts in the colonial bureaucracy or industries, though, like the menial
workers, even these educated clerks were paid only enough to take care
of their basic needs.[27] It was rare, if not impossible, to find a job that
paid well enough for anyone to acquire sufficient capital to invest in a
business that might, someday, reward them with a better than subsis-
tence income.

Most of these migrants were men, though a fair number of women
moved to Nairobi and managed to survive by pursuing livelihoods in
petty trade, brewing beer, or selling personal services.[28] Many of the
women were divorced, widowed, or barren, and Nairobi provided an
escape from the derision they often received in their rural communities. Altogether, then, by 1938 there were about 50,000 Africans in
Nairobi, living in estates on the eastern outskirts of the city—typically
in rudimentary settlements like Shauri Mwoyo, Eastleigh, Kaloleni,
Muthurwa, and Makongeni. And, as companies making footwear, textiles, and alcohol began to move into the industrial area in the city's
southeast corner after World War II, the number of migrants continued to rise, especially since these industries required both skilled and
semiskilled African workers. Over the next twenty years—between the
late 1930s and the late 1950s—the African population in and around
Nairobi more than doubled (to about 115,000 by 1957).[29] In response,
the Nairobi City Council began to build new houses, also in the eastern part of the city (in Ofafa, Starehe, Bahati, Gorofani, and Mbotela),
in order to accommodate some of the new workers, particularly those
who had managed to bring their families from the rural areas to live
with them.[30]

The one other significant group of people in colonial Nairobi was
the Indians. About 2,000 Indian ex-railway laborers had settled in the
outskirts of early Nairobi after their labor contracts had expired in the
early 1900s. Some were artisans who were contracted to build new
houses for the growing population of white settlers and administrators.

Many of them, however, set up bazaars and *dukas* (shops) on what are now the Accra and River Roads. There they sold basic supplies to fellow Indians as well as Africans in the nearby neighborhoods; these mercantile exchanges provided the main point of interaction between the Indians and the African populations.[31] By 1957 there were about 85,000 Asians in and around Nairobi, many of them having migrated from India or other parts of eastern Africa to set up businesses in Kenya. Because they often arrived with at least some capital, they were able to buy taxicabs for hire by foreign visitors or to open various retail businesses.[32]

———

From its inception, Nairobi was almost completely segregated along racial lines, though the segregation became more acute in the 1930s when more Africans began moving into the city. Despite the fact that the number of white inhabitants in Nairobi had also increased, the colonial government still felt the need to maintain their elevated status by instituting harsh "pass" laws, or Kipande laws, to restrict the movements of Africans. The pass laws made sure only those Africans who worked for Europeans could legally enter the city.[33] They also had the added benefit of facilitating the collection of taxes by colonial officials and helping them monitor the shifting migrant populations.[34] Ironically, the city that had been founded out of a need to cross the country was becoming a very restrictive place: travel throughout the city had become a privilege granted only to whites, and the Africans, if they were not hiking to and from work, were meant to stay put.[35]

Yet even if Africans had been allowed to move freely around the city, there was no way for them to do so—except by foot. For most of the colonial period, Nairobi had only one public bus system—the Kenya Bus Service (KBS), which had been introduced in 1934 by the London-based Overseas Transport Company (OTC). The two buses operated by the company served the needs of whites only, though eventually the number of buses was increased and a few were allowed to transport Africans. By the late 1950s there were about thirty buses, but still there were not nearly enough to meet the needs of all commuters in Nairobi, and even if there had been enough, the buses charged fares that were too high for many Africans to afford.[36] So the Africans continued to walk.

According to Priscilla Atieno, who lived in Nairobi in the early 1950s, "women walked, sometimes as far as fifteen miles long, carrying their luggage and children on their backs. You reached your destination tired, your feet aching, aaaiiih."[37] Atieno's experience was typical: she lived in Muthurwa on the eastern edge of the city with her four children and her husband, a mechanic at the Kenya Railways, in a tiny two-room concrete flat provided by the railway. If they wanted to go somewhere or move something, they had to walk—there was no other way to get around. And if the family wanted to get out of town—if, for instance, they wanted to visit their cousin in Pumwani, a village about ten miles distant—transportation simply did not exist. "The only way to get there was on foot," she said. "It was not easy."[38]

Listening to Atieno, I felt I was hearing something familiar, something I had always known but had forgotten or ignored. All around the city African men and women had once trooped through the dusty streets on their way to the market, or to work and back, dodging the animals and pushcarts, the carriages, and the noisy automobiles driven by whites. Occasionally one might encounter a plucky cyclist, always a man, threading his way through the crush of pedestrians. But what would most strike the visitor were the women dutifully walking everywhere, every day, lumbering under the load of the day's provisions with children strapped on their backs.[39] The large loads—up to 20 percent of their body weight—were usually supported by straps wrapped across the women's foreheads, straps pulled so hard upon their brows they carved permanent furrows.[40] "Your neck was in pain all the time," remembered Mary Mweneka, a trader in Nairobi in the 1950s. After years of carrying heavy loads, Mweneka said, some women ended up permanently bent with the posture of a humpback. "It was not a good life . . . we were just struggling because there was no other means of transportation. So what do you do?" Many women who lived in Nairobi in the 1950s also remembered their children's misery during the long walks to visit relatives in the villages. "We had no matatus then," Elizabeth Kamali said, "we just walked . . . the only way to get there was on foot. . . . See there were no matatus then to pick us up like we have now."[41]

Men walked too, of course, though at least men could ride bicycles if they could afford one, and occasionally you could have seen a well-dressed clerk riding to the office. Learning how to ride a bicycle was not a possibility for women, however, even for those who could afford one—according to Kamali, "bicycles were not for women, just for men. Women were not expected to ride bicycles." Occasionally a man might offer a woman a ride on the back of his bike, though such rides were not comfortable over any distance: "You had to cross your legs tight and wrap your dress around your legs tightly so that your legs were not exposed when the wind blew," said Kamali, "and then hold the back of the bicycle tightly so you did not fall off."[42] Since the roads were not paved, the rides were often bumpy, and the women were often in danger of falling off. It was simply easier for women to walk.

Those who did not have bikes used the KBS, but only after payday at the beginning of the month when they had a little more money in their pockets.[43] From the middle of the month onward, until the next payday, they usually walked to work or to shop. This too was not without expense since their shoes, a valued commodity, quickly wore out from walking on muddy, unpaved roads. Also, "in the dry months," recalled Moses Kamau, "you would arrive in the office with a shirt full of dust and sweat," and he turned out his shirt collar to demonstrate how the sweat ran from his armpits down his ribs as he walked.[44] "And yet," he told me, as a clerk, "you were supposed to look smart in the office . . . and respectable" if you wanted to avoid reprimands.[45]

So, all told, mobility for Africans was severely limited. In fact, their lives were purposely restricted by colonial policies that prohibited them from traveling efficiently from one point in Nairobi to another. And the consequences were clear: without a means of getting around there could be no getting ahead, just as there could be no getting ahead without a means of getting around. Without a reliable form of public transportation, the possibilities of attaining any kind of personal and political autonomy were kept limited, and any kind of major entrepreneurial activity among Africans was discouraged, if not made impossible. Without personal mobility there could be no economic mobility. In other words, as long as the mobility of Africans in and around the city was limited, so too was their upward mobility, and any social or economic aspirations the Africans might entertain were meant to remain merely pedestrian. This was to change, however, once Kenya achieved its political independence and Africans were no longer "kept in their place" by the obstructive policies of colonial officials.

PART TWO

Moving People, Building the Nation, 1960–73

TWO

"It Is a Difficult System to Beat"

As colonial rule came to an end in the early 1960s, the legal restrictions on the movement of Africans in the city were removed.[1] As a result, a great many more Africans moved from the rural areas to Nairobi, and the city grew much faster than it had in previous decades—so fast that it ceased to look like an improvised, back-lot copy of a European city and became more like the booming, chaotic capital of a developing country.[2] Although the central business district of Nairobi continued to look quaintly European, the outskirts of the city were expanding and changing at an unprecedented pace, and as Africans and Asians began moving to the city's margins they inevitably began placing new demands upon its civic resources, especially on the means of affordable transportation. But those means were scarce. There was nothing even remotely able to accommodate the swelling crowds of commuters to and from the city center. And yet, as if according to script, a few rickety matatus began trundling down the uneven streets, stopping like roadside Samaritans to offer Africans from the city's outskirts a crowded, bumpy ride to the city center. The vehicles were hardly luxurious, or even comfortable, but they were reliable and cheap—only three cents (*magoro matatu* in Kikuyu). And they offered the city and its new inhabitants more than just a wobbly ride to downtown businesses: the matatus' appearance marked the beginnings of one of the most—if not the most—independent and successful forms of Kenyan

FIGURE 3   Matatu, 1964. Courtesy of the Standard Group, Nairobi

entrepreneurship. Even more importantly, the owners and operators of matatus had created a business that was indigenous. In other words, these enterprising Kenyans were determining for themselves how they could gather and employ local resources to meet local needs—without the oversight or intervention of foreign or governmental authorities. The consequences of the matatus' sudden manifestation were both immediate and far-reaching; in every way, Nairobi was about to become less restrictive, less quiet, more vibrant, and profoundly more African. In many ways these changes were introduced and defined by matatus, and they soon became a symbol of the city's new identity.

The early matatus, however, were not much to look at. Almost any kind of vehicle that could be made to run and was large enough to carry passengers was turned into a matatu—dilapidated Ford Transit vans, unsteady Austins and Peugeots, wonky Volkswagen Kombis, and converted old pickup trucks. What mattered was size and mobility; if it could make it down the street carrying a few commuters, it could become a matatu. A report from the mid-1960s, for instance, describes how an aging "1952 Bedford microbus rattles down Racecourse Road, Nairobi, brimming with passengers and a conductor shouting 'Kariobangi,' 'Majengo,' or 'Makadara,' depending on its destination." The same journalist mentions "a wobbly Morris said ironically to have carried Adam and Eve to church on their wedding day," and he is careful to note that "on the windscreens of these buses are road licenses that expired as far back as 1960, but the vehicles keep running as long as there is a tiger in their tanks."[3] No matter their condition, around one hundred or so such vehicles crisscrossed the roads of Nairobi in the early 1960s. Outfitted with benches and hand straps, many of these fledgling matatus were capable of carrying up to twenty people, so long as the passengers were willing to forego all comfort and pack themselves tightly together like vegetables carted to market. However, the government considered these vehicles illegal because they lacked the proper government licenses. And yet these so-called pirate taxis soldiered on illicitly, careering through the streets, evading potholes and pedestrians, to provide a necessary service to the many Kenyans who had moved to Nairobi from the rural areas after independence.[4]

To the surprise of many—particularly the new government officials —commuters in Nairobi found these crude and uncomfortable vehicles a more attractive means of travel than the licensed buses of the Kenya Bus Service (KBS). It soon became clear to the government that matatus were competing with the supposedly more up-to-date and financially well-off KBS, despite the fact that the matatus themselves were hastily improvised contraptions that seemed more like mobile atrocities than a means of public conveyance. Their success baffled city officials, who complained continually about their presence on the streets and about the customers' inexplicable preference for them. Even more disturbing to the officials was the fact that the government could not find an effective means of regulating the matatus, let alone ridding the city of them.

For quite some time the KBS had been the only major legal form of public transportation in Nairobi, and this was still the case in the early 1960s. The bus service had been introduced to Nairobi in 1934 when the London-based Overseas Transport Company (OTC) put two buses on the road to serve the needs of the white colonialists. Three decades later, in 1966, the OTC merged with the Nairobi City Council (NCC), and the United Trading Company (UTC), a British firm operating and managing several other such companies all over the world. The merger was meant to help consolidate and control public transportation and, in return for a 25 percent shareholding, to give the UTC a monopoly on transportation in Nairobi.[5] The NCC, for its part, was to provide and

FIGURE 4   KBS buses, 1968. Courtesy of the Standard Group, Nairobi

maintain the infrastructure, and also to determine the fares. Ideally, the agreement would ensure affordable and regular transport on the major city routes.[6]

The plan seemed to be working well. UTC shares grew steadily, and by the late 1960s the company had acquired a total of about 130 to 146 buses.[7] The buses were bought from a variety of sources—from Leyland, Guy, Victory, to ERF Trailblazer—and were assembled locally by Labh and Harnam Singh Company.[8] The bus company had amassed a reasonable amount of capital—about £20,000 at the time of the merger—to keep the buses in good, operable condition. Normally each bus, whether it had mechanical problems or not, was taken in for maintenance every ten days at the company's depot in Eastleigh, east of the city, which had a fully staffed engineering department of nearly one hundred workers.[9] The depot was originally a semipermanent structure, though in 1967 the company spent £39,000 to build a larger, more elegant center on Temple Road, also in Eastleigh. The outlook was optimistic. "The new building has something of a beauty in its clean lines and neat layout," noted Charles Rubia, then mayor of Nairobi, who was the guest of honor at the center's opening ceremony. In his address, the mayor claimed that the new bus station would "lead to greater efficiency in the operation of the bus fleet." And he trumpeted the notion that "as mayor," he was "not only conscious of the new improvements, but also proud of the fact that the city council is now a partner in the activities of running public transportation services."[10]

Arthur Kent, the company's director, also at the launching party, spoke about the importance of the bus company to the citizens of Nairobi. He regaled the guests with statistics, boasting that in the previous year 112 buses had carried more than twenty million passengers (more than two times the population of the whole of Kenya), and that the KBS had also expanded its operations in Mombasa as well as across several rural routes. Kent proudly informed the guests of the company's intention to purchase twenty-five more buses at a total cost of nearly £150,000 during the following year, and he revealed that the KBS planned to spend much more time training its African staff, for which purpose the company had set aside space in the new building for three classrooms: one designed for trainee drivers, one mainly for the current group of management, and the third equipped for lectures in wildlife, geography, history, and other subjects.[11] The opening ceremony provided an attractive public relations moment for KBS—it was covered extensively by the daily papers, and government departments (for instance, the Ministry of Labor) and several private businesses added to the publicity by commissioning huge display ads in the newspapers congratulating the KBS for its new depot. One of them, the Firestone Tire Company, thanked the KBS "for the confidence shown in fitting locally made Firestone tyres to their fleet."[12] All was well and the future looked bright, or so the KBS officials had convinced themselves. The reigning mantra at the city council was, "Anything a matatu does, the KBS can do better."[13]

Given its stake in the success of the KBS, the Nairobi City Council naturally favored the KBS with its policies and its expenditures. For example, it provided the buses with their own designated bus stations in the central business district and in the city's outskirts. And for a long time, especially in the late 1960s, the NCC continued to emphasize the plans for the development of buses—even boasting that someday they would be providing for everyone a complete and effective mass transit system that would operate on new, unobstructed highways. In their annual reports to the Ministry of Transportation and Communications, KBS officials crowed about the robust condition of their business: in 1968 KBS buses had carried about 105,000 passengers each day, and they had also become a munificent source of employment for Nairobi's *wanainchi* (citizens).[14] This was all very impressive. But the reports never mentioned that the one hundred or so illegal matatus careering through the city's streets were actually carrying twice as many passengers each day, despite the fact that they received no funding and were continuously subjected to police harassment and government scorn.

———

It soon became clear to those willing to look that the KBS could not keep up with the hectic growth of the former white settler city. During the 1960s the population of Nairobi increased by 10 percent each year; by 1965 there were about 400,000 Africans in the Nairobi area—all of whom needed a place to live and a way to get to work.[15] Predictably, the new residents created a housing shortage. The fortunate few who obtained decent housing were those who had secured jobs as clerks and other middle management–level positions in the public or private sector.[16] They managed to find places in the one- or two-room council flats that had been constructed by the Nairobi City Council in the late 1950s and early 1960s in the eastern part of the city—in Ngara, Ofafa Maringo, Embakasi, Kariobangi, Jerusalem, Jericho, and Mariakani. But only about 1 percent of the population was able to rent these one- or two-room flats. Another 0.5 percent managed to rent similar flats built by the parastatal National Housing Corporation in Umoja, Lumumba, and Dandora, also in the Eastlands.[17] These neighborhoods were crowded and chaotic since small businesses quickly began to appear in street-side kiosks or tents, and shanties were hastily erected in areas surrounding the council flats. Even so, the flats were expensive and residents were often obliged to sublet space to other workers—which of course made for even more crowding.

In contrast to the relative comfort of the council flats, the vast majority of urban immigrants found themselves squeezed into the nearby slums of Kibera, Pumwani, Kaburini, Mathare, Kangemi, and Kawangware. Life in these makeshift shantytowns was harsh and merciless, and yet many still preferred to endure life in the city slums to—what they considered—the obstinate inertia that haunted the rural areas. The city offered a new life. In Nairobi discontented villagers could transform themselves into *watu wa kisasa*, that is "modern city people"—though the transformation was never easy or absolute; often connections to the villages remained. As one of my interviewees, Peter Mwelesa, recalled, "It was nice[r] to live in Nairobi, and even be poor in Nairobi, than in the rural areas; see, you had to do your best and try and earn some wages. Wages is what people needed, and if you made some money then you could send some of it back to the family in the rural areas."[18] Nevertheless, Mwelesa, who had moved to Kawangare in the early 1960s, still emphasized the city's vibrancy, and the fact that it offered opportunity: "I think people then moved to the urban areas because they wanted to experience new things, see new things, and learn new things. That is how you progressed in the world then. And staying in the village was not good for that kind of thing."[19] Most of the new immigrants lived as squatters on NCC lands, constructing tin-roofed houses out of mud and wattle, though some of the houses were even more rudimentary, fabricated out of cardboard or rags. A few of the shacks even sported grass-thatched roofs as if built in a village.[20] The houses typically lacked plumbing, electricity, and most other basic physical and social amenities—so cooking was done on open fires, water was hauled wherever needed, the only latrines were public, and waste often trickled down rivulets in the narrow alleyways.[21] Undeterred, many of these newcomers were industrious and managed to open and operate businesses selling food, making furniture, or setting up repair shops for bicycles, radios, pots and pans, and so on. Interestingly, officials displayed far more lenience with these small businesses than they did with matatus, most likely because they posed no threat to the government's vested interests and were deemed necessary services. In fact, the government actually provided some of these migrants with hawkers' licenses so they could carry on their businesses legally.[22]

The general air of enterprise made the shantytowns tumultuous places. The jangle of shouting vendors was usually accompanied by radios blaring Zairian music, lin'gala beat, or Elvis Presley's "Jailhouse Rock" and Sam Cooke's "Twisting the Night Away."[23] Also popular were local songs that focused on the social and economic hardships—and the survival—of the rural migrants to the urban slums of eastern Africa.[24] In stark contrast to the topical music were the frequent broadcasts of speeches by new African leaders, like President Jomo Kenyatta, who urged people not to migrate to the urban areas and to focus, instead, on developing land in the rural areas. Kenyatta's favorite mantra was, "Land Is the Heart of Our Nation," and he referred to Kenyans who left the rural areas as "traitors of the new Nation." We can of course only imagine how listeners responded to these reproaches when they themselves had eagerly abandoned the rural areas so they could try to eke out an existence in their adopted city.[25]

———

Despite the city's vibrancy, many of the new urban migrants sought to do more than simply get by. Some enterprising newcomers pursued clever and innovative ways of providing cheap transportation for the swelling numbers of Africans in Nairobi. Enter the matatu. Entrepreneurs invested what little capital they could collect, and, working with African mechanics in garages on River Road, they managed to rehabilitate cheap, old vehicles into serviceable minibuses.[26] These novel businesses were more or less homegrown. The initial start-up funds were mostly from private sources—money borrowed from family members or friends—since the few available banks, mostly foreign banks such as Barclays and Standard Chartered, offered loans only to elite Africans. It was an uncertain investment, and often a risky one. The businesses were not recognized by the government, and only a few of the mechanics had been trained by the colonials—a majority of them were self-taught, having simply spent many hours hanging out in the garages, watching car repairs, and practicing until they had accumulated enough knowledge to fix, or even build, vehicles of their own.[27] Given the simplicity of most post–World War II engine designs, it was not unusual for the mechanics to dismantle the engines, gearboxes, brakes, and suspensions of old cars and reassemble them into running wrecks still able to carry people around the city.[28] Some of the crude contrivances that resulted were indeed outrageous.[29] "Sometimes the matatus had no batteries and the passengers had to push the vehicle to get it going," recalled Joseph Nderi, one of the first people to own a matatu in Nairobi. Nderi remembered that the vehicles were in terrible condition and they broke down all the time. *"Ilikua shida shida tu"* ("We were just struggling then"), he told me. "Sometimes we would employ *totos* [little boys] as engine crankers and then if they worked well we would promote them to 'turnboys.'"[30] The job of the totos, according to Nderi, was to top up the radiator with water, turn the engine, collect fares, remove the stones from behind the wheels once it was time to get under way, and to keep watch for the police. "Sometimes we filled the fuel tanks with ordinary lamp kerosene," Nderi told me, chuckling. Usually, he said, the driver held a piece of petrol-saturated cloth over a carburetor while the "turnboy" turned the engine, until, "after some time, the engine started and there was great noise and the totos removed the stones that kept the wheels in place so the car could move."[31]

In spite of the decrepit condition of these early matatus, it is important to acknowledge the confidence, skill, and creativity of those who created these vehicles out of nearly nothing.[32] Again and again, matatu owners overcame supposed limitations with mechanical innovations that produced useful machines. By repurposing old and foreign objects, and investing them with local meanings, these early matatu operators were creating an altogether new and unforeseen line of work.[33]

In serving the immediate needs of the city, and trying to make some money, they were also creating a new economy. One could argue, in fact, that the resourcefulness and adaptability of matatu owners, and their refusal to accept their adverse conditions, represented a kind of "social bricolage"—that is, under conditions of adversity they actively adapted norms, values, and arrangements to suit new purposes.[34] Or, as the Kenyans would say, it was about *kufanya fanya tu*, making do with what one has.

This kind of audacious creativity still goes on today. In June 2010, I visited a car garage on Grogan Road, not far from River Road where the first matatus were assembled, to find out what the situation looked like in the early part of the twenty-first century. One of my interviewees, John Kihara, had brought his matatu to the garage to be fitted with new shock absorbers. There was no electricity or running water at the garage, and most of the tools were quite rudimentary. There were, of course, no hydraulic lifts, and so I watched in awe as seven men physically lifted the car up and then put large stones under each corner of the vehicle so that they could lie underneath the car and begin fixing it. Altogether, it took about six hours to get the old shocks out and the new ones fitted in. The work was hard, and the mechanics' overalls were filthy with grease and grime, their faces drenched with sweat.

Still, as physically exhausting as the process of repairing the matatu may have been, it was clear that Kihara was not simply looking for a more comfortable ride: the repairs would permit him to obtain his license and operate his business legally. This was not the case in the 1960s, when the vehicles were even more primitive and their owners were forced to operate stealthily outside the law. However, the illegal status of the early matatus did not deter the would-be matatu owners from pursuing their business. They were generally willing to employ whatever means necessary, and those who could afford it offered bribes to the clerks at the Trade and Licensing Board (TLB) in order to receive the required licenses to document the roadworthiness of their vehicles.[35] Other owners resorted to outright forgery.[36] One of the more common practices, according to Nderi, was to make a simple alteration to the vehicle licenses. Matatu licenses were numbered according to the month, and when a matatu's six-month license expired, "it was turned upside down and so it became a '9' and thus remained valid until the end of the ninth month.[37] Sometimes, we even made a 7 look like a 2 and a 2 look like a 7, in order to make licenses last for a whole year." The recollection of this easy trick caused him to laugh so hard his eyes watered with tears. Then again, many of the matatu owners did not bother with such clever improvisations: they simply drove un-licensed vehicles and risked arrest and a court appearance, and thus the likelihood of having to distribute even more bribes. Yet the busi-ness was lucrative enough that many of the owners felt it was worth the cost of the bribes to keep operating; bribes were simply written off as an unavoidable business expense.[38]

As for the vehicles themselves, there was room for improvement. By the mid- to late 1960s the matatus in Nairobi were starting to look a little less battered and improvised. Vehicles were starting to receive up-grades, and customers began to expect a little more than rough wooden benches bolted to the beds of pickup trucks. A number of the pioneer-ing matatu owners had begun to make enough money to invest in rela-tively newer, more commercially recognizable vehicles, such as Volks-wagen Kombis, Ford Transit vans, and converted pickup trucks. Even in the early days, Nderi told me, matatus had proved profitable enough to allow him to buy a more efficient and attractive vehicle. "But spare parts were expensive," he said, adding that occasionally he still had to borrow money from family members or friends "just to keep up." James Kamau, another pioneer in the matatu industry, recalled that he made enough money each year to allow him to upgrade his vehicle every two or three years: "Matatus have always made money . . . even back then."[39]

———

As all of these vehicles laid siege to the streets of Nairobi and other ur-ban areas of Kenya, it became clear that matatus were becoming a per-manent part of the landscape. Whether the vehicles were old or new, banged-up or updated, their success was mostly due to the flexibility of the services they offered their passengers.[40] To put it simply, matatu drivers went where the passengers wanted to go.[41] Drivers were adapt-able; they were able to adjust their routes to the haphazard changes in which Nairobi's neighborhoods were developing, and to accommo-date its lack of clearly defined streets or roads. If it was raining, they dropped passengers at their doorstep; if the passengers were running late, they waited for them. If their regular customers were absent, the drivers would take the initiative and honk their horns to announce their arrival, or start roaming the neighborhoods like anxious shep-herds to seek them out. "This was good service. The drivers knew you and they also knew that you counted on them. It was about living nicely in a community," said Melissa Vurigwa, a resident of Pangani, Nairobi. "The fares were low [matatus charged a mere 30 cents for a trip

FIGURE 5 Matatus driving in alleys. Courtesy of the NMG, Nairobi

from Eastlands to the town, while the KBS charged 50 cents], and if you did not have the money the drivers would give you a ride on credit." Since many of the matatu owners were men from the African neighborhoods and their customers were regulars, very few people tried to avoid paying the debts. Barter was also acceptable: "those without fares could exchange goods for fare or were given credit," Vurigwa told me.[42] This flexibility clearly resulted in an increase in the matatu owners' social capital as well as the passengers' loyalty toward them. It also created networks of mutual obligation, of reciprocity and trust, networks that also contributed significantly to the matatus' success.[43]

These personal relations also came in handy when dealing with the police.[44] Because of the trust and mutual dependency between matatu owners and their passengers, the passengers became adept at shielding the matatu operators from the oversight of the police. For instance, passengers often made it difficult for the police to prove that a certain vehicle was being used illegally for public transportation. Typically, when a matatu driver spotted a police van, he would speed away in the hopes of avoiding detection, but if the driver realized that he was about to be detained, he would hurriedly stop and ask all the passengers to alight before the police arrived. Once the passengers had scattered, the driver could claim innocence by pointing to the empty van, or, if the passengers could not get out in time they would gladly collaborate with the driver and pretend they were merely friends, not paying passengers.[45] "You would defend the matatu owners because you knew them. These guys were your friends, and you wanted to help them out because you knew they would help you out too when you got stuck," said Peter Kariuki, who lived in Pumwani in the 1960s.[46] He recalled that he was particularly dependent on two matatus that he rode every day. He had gotten to know the owners very well—"we became friends," he told me, "so how can you betray your friends?"[47] Alliances like this were hardly unusual, and the sense of mutual benefit no doubt led the passengers and the matatu owners and drivers to protect each other from the meddling of the authorities.[48] And such collusion—if it can be called that—certainly contributed to the success of matatus during the 1960s.[49] By helping keep the authorities at bay, the passengers themselves helped play a part in establishing matatus as an inescapable part of the city.

Given the conspiratorial attitudes of owners and passengers, it had become pretty much impossible for officials to rid the city of the pirate vehicles. But this did not mean they stopped trying. The police were determined to find a new solution, and, initially, they came up with the rather predictable idea of enlarging the definition of what actually constituted a matatu, and increasing surveillance. In 1967, S. K. Raval, the senior police superintendent, added an amendment to the section of the traffic law that dealt with plying for "hire and reward": according to the new law, private vehicles seen running regularly with passengers in the vicinity of a bus stop, or along the same route, more than three times in any single day would be presumed to be pirate taxis. If apprehended, the driver would have to prove otherwise. Basically, the policy presumed that all drivers stopped were guilty until proven innocent.[50]

The law's essential unfairness was a clear indication of the authorities' desperation, though, unfortunately for the police department, the new law failed to have its desired effect because—as mentioned—the passengers simply continued to deny that they were paying customers and claimed instead they were friends of the matatu drivers. And in many cases they were telling the truth: they *were* friends. Passengers and drivers often came from the same neighborhoods and had formed a social and economic reliance upon one another that encouraged them to evade the officials' regulatory zeal. This solidarity between drivers and passengers was not something the police could understand or appreciate—let alone regulate or destroy. So, eventually, the police resorted to other means: they changed their focus from the drivers to the vehicles themselves. Since the drivers turned out to be too popular to control, they decided they would simply stop their vehicles instead. If the police could not prove whether or not the vehicles were being used in the business of carrying paying passengers, they would try to prove that the vehicle either lacked the proper license, or was not roadworthy.[51] Surprise inspections were set up throughout the city, and if the vehicle failed the inspection—and many were likely to fail— the owner was either forced to appear in court or to offer the police a bribe. Many matatu drivers chose the latter option; they bribed the police and then drove off and continued business as usual. Although the policy did not prove particularly effective in keeping matatus off the streets, it did turn out to be a clever one in another regard—it allowed matatu owners to make "friends" with the police, and the police managed to supplement their incomes. Both parties benefited, and so, to the degree that the police were willing to accept bribes, they became just as complicit as the passengers in keeping the matatus on the road. And with the police—or at least the more pliable members of the police—now within their sphere of influence, the so-called pirate taxis could continue to carry passengers, make money, and multiply.

Eventually the police were forced to acknowledge the inevitable: matatus were there to stay. Even if it had proven impossible to eliminate them, the police still hoped to at least exercise some control over the anarchy they associated with the pirate taxis. The head of the police department responded to their defiance by offering several conciliatory measures, most of which allowed the matatus to fill in the gaps in service that the KBS had neglected to provide. The police began by allowing a significant number of matatus to operate all day within locations where the buses did not run; they allowed matatus to ferry the passengers to and from the bus routes; and they also started letting matatus run from the outlying locations to the city center and back from 6:00 p.m. to midnight and from 4:00 a.m. to 7:00 a.m. before the bus service began running its routes. And, of course, licenses would only be issued to roadworthy vehicles. All of these measures, they reasoned, would have the added benefit of giving the bus company a bigger slice of the business than it had before, and it was hoped that these compromises would relieve the already overworked traffic division from playing "cat and mouse" on the streets of Nairobi, a ridiculous game in which both sides knew that neither could really win.[52]

The police managed to carry it off for a few weeks, but it quickly became apparent that there were not enough police to keep track of the schedules. Even more detrimental was the fact that many of the available policemen simply preferred receiving bribes to convicting the drivers. Truth be told, many of the policemen were altogether too familiar with the matatu owners to subject them suddenly to harsher restrictions, and since the police, just like the drivers, were eager to earn a better living, it was much easier to accept a small payoff and let the matatu owners get on with their business. The collusion soon became systemic because it allowed the drivers, the passengers, and the police—everyone except the government—to get what they wanted. So, after only a few weeks, the matatus were again running their old routes during the peak hours, crammed with paying passengers—*biashara kama kawaida*, business as usual, the daily papers observed.[53]

Not to be deterred, however, the police superintendent made one last effort to rein in the unheeding matatus. Reasoning that customers who knowingly used an unlicensed matatu were as guilty as the owners, he thought it might be possible to force the matatus off the roads by arresting the passengers. Perhaps, just perhaps, legal action could be brought against passengers for "aiding and abetting the commitment of an offence against the by-laws."[54] Of course, this presumed that passengers could be easily identified and arrested. But this was hardly the case. Unlike the passengers in licensed private taxis, which could easily be recognized by their yellow band, or as was often the case, by their Asian drivers, anyone caught in an unmarked vehicle driven by an African could be presumed guilty. But this, too, proved an impossible policy to enforce because the matatu drivers could plead innocence by denying that their passengers had paid, and the passengers were not about to object since it would mean getting arrested themselves. As before, the policy was doomed to fail—this time because it criminalized everyone involved and thereby increased the levels of deceit and strengthened the collaborative ties between the drivers and their passengers. And sure enough, the superintendent soon decided to throw up his hands and "leave the matter to Nairobi City Council."[55] The matatus had defeated him.

But the Nairobi City Council did not want to deal with the problem either, and for quite a while a debate raged between the two groups— the police and the city council—as each blamed the other for the problems of "pirates" in the city. Reading through these exchanges in the files of the Nairobi City Council reports at the Kenya National Archives is like witnessing a playground argument. For instance, the NCC would claim that law enforcement was not its business, and the police department would quickly respond that traffic was not their only concern and that they had other, more serious crimes to tackle in the expanding city.[56] They continued to talk past each other every time there happened to be a major crisis in the city with regard to matatus; no one wanted to accept responsibility. Every now and then, the officials at NCC might ask a politician to use the forum of a public speech to appeal to the public's conscience by asking citizens to avoid using matatus, or to point out the dangers of riding the matatus and remind the public that matatu owners were evil because they evaded taxes and thus failed to contribute to the development of the *inchi ya Kenya*—the newly independent nation of Kenya.[57] But, as is so often the case, patriotic rhetoric had a limited effect, especially when it clashed with their price or the owners' profits.

Besides, there was a simple, practical reason for the success of matatus, one that had to do with the routes they served. They succeeded because they went where they were needed, rather than following some abstract plan mapped out by city officials. Unlike the buses, the matatus typically traveled a circuit from the Central Business District (CBD) to the areas of high population density, such as Eastlands, Parklands, Westlands, Southlands, and Industrial Area. These areas bordered the Central Business District and were therefore close enough to allow the matatus to make frequent back-and-forth trips, and to penetrate into areas off the main thoroughfares. The KBS routes, on the other hand, were generally limited to the main roads, and people who lived or worked any distance from these roads had to walk, sometimes several miles, to reach the closest bus stop.[58] Also, the KBS buses operated along routes passing through the CBD to the less densely populated areas of Kikuyu, Thika, Limuru, Ngong, Ongata Rongai, and Athi River, which meant that they made fewer stops in the areas where they were most needed. As is so often the case, new and poorer residents were neglected while the better off were taken care of. Matatus, on the other hand, sought out passengers who needed them, and they made more frequent trips—both of which increased their profits. It was surely a win-win situation for passengers and matatu owners.[59]

The owners also fared better than the KBS because they had far fewer overhead costs. There was no scheduled maintenance, no well-staffed team of mechanics to pay, and certainly no clean, well-lighted garages where they could take their broken vehicles for repair. Instead, they employed cheap laborers, mostly family or friends, and made necessary repairs only if their vehicles were completely immobilized. As long as the vehicles were able to move, it was a matter of indifference that windshield wipers did not work, or windows were broken, or mufflers were loose, or even that the brakes did not function. Utility trumped safety, and besides, "the money that was supposed to be used for repairs went toward fines and bribes to police" (as one matatu owner from the 1960s, Martin Lukova, remembered).[60] This remained the case throughout the 1960s. At every turn, what mattered was the ability to get people where they needed to go by whatever means, no matter where they lived, and no matter how much they might be handicapped by dubious vehicles or government interference.

In spite of these drawbacks, very few of the people I interviewed seemed much inclined to complain about their experience riding in those early matatus. "It is not like now when there are so many matatus," Joseph Kamau told me. "In those days all that mattered was that you got to the place of work on time. We did not talk about being squeezed in like people do now-days."[61] The rides then were more adventurous because the vehicles tended to take people all the way into the shantytowns where there were no paved roads and passengers were indelicately toppled onto one another. Kamau remembered with amusement that sometimes when the matatu hit a pothole, "people banged into each other, and the benches fell on the floor." But when people alighted they "simply straightened their clothes, wiped the sweat, and went off. Those matatus—ehhhh!—were something else. But that is all we had. It was not a matter of comfort or luxury; we just wanted to get home or to work."[62]

Mary Njuguna, another resident of Nairobi in the 1960s, echoed many of Kamau's feelings about matatus: "Then people were just making do and did not have much choice of matatus like we have today. We all got squeezed in, but it was okay because we knew some of these people we were squeezing next to."[63] Although in no way was Njuguna suggesting the commute was either pleasant or adequate—"see," she continued, "we did not pay much money for transportation then, so we were okay with being squeezed in as long as we got to our destinations safely." But early on the attitudes toward matatus were more tolerant; the reality of the vehicles' discomfort and danger could be excused out of necessity. And most passengers did arrive safely, even if they were forced to ride crammed in a vehicle that was little more than a roving wreck. And, hard as it may be to fathom, matatus were somewhat safer than the KBS buses; the early matatus simply did not have the engine capacity to travel at very high speeds, and so when accidents did occur they were rarely fatal—unless, of course, a faster vehicle managed to hit a slow-moving matatu. The main complaint concerned breakdowns rather than safety. Passengers were far more likely to be left stranded on the side of the road due to mechanical failures than to accidents.[64]

Meanwhile, the KBS struggled to meet the growing transportation needs of Nairobians, despite their relatively generous budget of £2 million.[65] There simply were not enough buses to keep up with the increasing population, a problem that proved particularly acute during rush hours. The public image of the KBS did not help. They had, after all, publicly promised to provide cheap, reliable, and convenient transportation for Kenyan citizens, though the fact that they were failing miserably was apparent to nearly everyone. Fair or not, they received the blame for nearly all the commuters' problems since, at least in theory, the KBS exercised a monopoly over transportation in the city. Throughout the 1960s, for instance, irate commuters wrote letters to the editors of the daily newspapers to complain, demanding that KBS increase the number of buses serving their neighborhoods. Such complaints typically came from people living in areas that matatus could not reach because they were too far from the city center, and matatus were not in sound enough mechanical condition to travel the long distances. Moreover, the bus schedules in the far-flung outskirts were irregular, especially during rush hours. Commuters from the Kabete and Ngong areas, for example, wrote to the daily newspapers about how they had to wait for a bus for more than two hours, even as they watched "two or three buses pass by without stopping because they are full."[66] Even if one was lucky and the bus stopped, it was still necessary to "push and shove" one's way into it.[67] For many, the experience of riding the buses was no better than the matatus, and far less convenient.

The excuse the KBS provided was interesting. As far as the regularized schedules were concerned, a white KBS official noted that the problem had emerged because of the process of Kenyanization, which in his opinion had been forced upon the company. Because of this unwelcome policy (for the whites), the company had actually been forced to hire black Kenyans, who, in the official's opinion, did not know how to keep time, or for that matter, did not even care about being punctual. The argument was not well received.[68] Africans were having none of it—"this is nonsensical," a fellow by the name of James Rukia wrote to the *Nation* in response, "there is no question of Africans' capability in handling such services."[69]

It was not going to do, simply to blame the Africans for the structural problems of the KBS. The personnel were not responsible for their failures. The cause was, rather, the recurrent breakdowns the buses suffered, and the fact that they were wearing out at a much faster rate than anticipated. Although KBS claimed to have more than 150 buses in Nairobi, the poor condition of the roads in Nairobi made it difficult for the bus company to keep the buses in operating order, and inevitably there were fewer buses on the road every day—and fewer still that could make it out to the distant suburbs. It was not surprising then to read of an infuriated man from Embakasi on his way to work waiting for the KBS, or of complaints that "the KBS does not give our area enough buses. Many people from here are late for work because there are few buses that serve this route." And even when the buses did appear they could incite a free-for-all: "When the KBS does arrive," recalled a commuter form Kagemi, "it is only the strong ones who get into the bus; the others are left standing."[70] Others simply griped that the KBS buses were "ugly old monsters."[71]

This latter complaint was not altogether unfounded. Passengers often criticized the "filthy conditions" on the buses, and that their journeys were jarring and "jerky"; some passengers alleged that not all the buses had doors and that people had fallen out of them.[72] These discomforts were no doubt exacerbated by the constant overcrowding, by the enormous packages that passengers lugged onto the bus, and by the livestock and chickens they invited on as their guests. As a result the buses became so overcrowded, and so heavy, that they "crawled" through the town at a snail's pace, which of course meant that it took passengers longer to arrive at their destinations than had they simply walked.[73] Everyone and everything became overheated—the noise, the overcrowding, the miserably slow progress ignited the tempers of passengers, conductors, and drivers, so much so that, as one commuter

FIGURE 6   KBS bus, 1968. Courtesy of the NMG, Nairobi

mildly put it, "unprintable and abusive words" often rang out over the clucking of hens and the chatter of passengers.[74]

The noise and congestion naturally had a toxic effect on the bus workers, and they eventually acquired a reputation for rudeness and aggressiveness. For instance, one of the Kenyan newspapers reported the unfortunate story of a pregnant woman on her way to the hospital. The conductor did not want her on the bus so he attempted to force her off, even to the point of physically dragging her off, all the while shouting foul language at her and asking why she thought she needed to be treated exceptionally—"Are you carrying a Kenyatta in your womb or is it a [Cabinet] minister's womb you are carrying?" After ordering the driver to stop the bus, the conductor grabbed the woman by the neck, and "pushed [her] to the ground," despite protests by other passengers. As a result, the woman sustained "injuries on the leg and [her] cheeks were swollen and red."[75]

The same kinds of criticism were not leveled against the pirates driving these illegal taxis, though it is doubtful that the typical matatu was much more comfortable. Matatus were just as crowded as the buses, just as filthy, and in the same disgraceful condition of disrepair. However, commuters apparently had different standards for matatus, or, perhaps

45

the KBS had set itself up for failure by promising too much to its passengers, by boasting of its endowment and the magnitude of its plan to provide "a mass transit system" for the growing metropolis. Inevitably, passengers began to demand that the KBS live up to its promises, and when it failed they turned on it. Still, it was probably next to impossible to fulfill its mission. Not only did KBS have to deal with the problem of its limited routes and the high overhead costs of bus repairs and spare parts, but the company also had to deal with the demands of its employees. The KBS workers were strongly unionized under the Kenya Transport and Allied Workers Union, unlike the relatively ad hoc nature of the matatu business, with its private owners and unorganized labor force.[76] This put them at a disadvantage. The union made persistent demands that the KBS improve its workers' pay and their working conditions, and if they did not consent the five hundred or so employees would go on strike. The union presented ultimatums like this fairly frequently during the 1960s, which often ended in a predictable impasse. In April 1968, for example, the KBS employees refused to go to work, saying that they were entitled to "public holidays like everyone else." Although the demand was probably reasonable, the resulting strike left thousands of families stranded on the Easter bank holiday—hardly an act that would commend KBS to the public.[77] A few years earlier, in March 1966, the workers staged a four-day strike demanding increased Africanization, a twenty-four-day annual leave, a Christmas bonus, a housing provision or adequate housing allowances, and a daily 6 shillings safari allowance.[78] Again, none of this was particularly unreasonable, but the ensuing strike inconvenienced thousands of commuters— once again during the important Easter holiday. The shutdown dragged on until Tom Mboya, then minister of labor, was forced to intervene.[79]

Similar strikes by the KBS workers were reported in Mombasa in the late 1960s, and these, too, took a toll on the bus company and its reputation. In June 1966, the Mombasa workers went on strike demanding the payment of overtime, the reinstatement of demoted inspectors, and the elevation of three employees to the rank of "management; they also wanted bus passes for employees to be made valid throughout east Africa."[80] A few years earlier, in June 1964, the KBS workers in both Nairobi and Mombasa went on strike because "a European staff member had allegedly insulted President Kenyatta." The staff member, it was reported, had responded to a laid-off employee who asked for his remaining wages by saying, "even if you went and saw President Kenyatta at Gatundu, I will not give you the wages."[81] This was an insult to the employee, but even more importantly, to the new president, at a time when nationalism in Kenya was at its height and many *wanainchi* (citizens) cherished their new black president, *Mzee*—the old wise man who had fought so fiercely for Kenyan independence. And it was doubly insulting—even criminal—for such words to be uttered by a white business owner. This particular strike brought everything to a standstill in all the main cities of Kenya. Whether or not the strike was justified, the matatus responded opportunistically—as usual—by stepping in to exploit the situation and take advantage of the buses' absence. "Pirate taxis," one of the newspapers reported, "swarmed in to do killer business."[82]

Gradually, as the number of matatus increased, and as they suffered no serious consequences on account of their illegality, the owners began to sense their political and economic power. Even those taxi owners who had previously sought licenses—whether through legal means or otherwise—now refused to get licenses because there was simply no point in obeying the law; there were no consequences to being unlicensed.[83] For the time being, at least, circumstances had liberated them from government control. They seized the opportunity. By exploiting the convenience they were able to offer, along with the complicity and corruption of police, and especially the passengers' loyalty toward the owners and drivers, matatus managed to conquer the streets of Nairobi. As one reporter from *Drum* (a leading African magazine) observed, the mutual benefits of matatu owners and passengers had turned the matatu business into "a difficult system to beat."[84] So unbeatable, in fact, that matatus began to proliferate outside of Nairobi—in the country's other urban areas, and even throughout the Kenyan countryside. The now indispensable matatu was helping to knit the new nation together.

THREE

"We Are Making a Living by Constitutional Means"

Although much of the matatus' success depended upon their affordability and flexibility, a significant part was owed to the strategic ways in which owners tapped into the "Kenyanization" rhetoric of the 1960s—sometimes out of patriotic fervor, but just as often to facilitate their own interests. Nationalism was good for business, and the owners were quick to seize on its potential to foster dedicated customers. It was, after all, their patriotic responsibility. Since Kenya had achieved independence its leaders had been speaking earnestly about incorporating more Kenyans into the economic development of the new nation.[1] Of particular importance in the discussions was how black Kenyans were going to take part in the running of small businesses that had up to now been dominated by south Asians—particularly retail and transportation.[2] The new leaders also spoke at length about the necessity that black Kenyans, many of whom had been relegated to menial jobs during colonial rule, begin to find more productive and gainful employment so that they might better support their families. Much of the rhetoric reflected President Kenyatta's popular concept of *Harambee*, the idea that self-help and unity (especially through voluntary group efforts) could help develop the newly independent country.[3]

Most matatu owners fell right in with the hype of *Harambee*. They felt, at least initially, that the government was describing them, that they themselves were a living example of *Harambee*'s ideals. They had, after all, identified an important need in their communities—the lack of transportation—and responded directly and independently; they had, after all, risked their own livelihoods by investing in matatus and thus helped fulfill one of the nation's pressing needs. That they were making enough profit to provide a decent basic living wage for themselves and their families was only right. Earning an honest living through hard work made them ideal citizens; they were serving the nation by "making a living by constitutional means."[4] None of the owners could imagine any plausible reason why the government would declare them illegal and try to deprive them of their livelihoods, and by doing so cut off the city's most important means of transportation. It was obvious to the owners that without their efforts the city would be crippled. How could *Harambee* prosper if the government itself was—quite literally—making it more difficult for citizens to unite and help themselves? Moreover, by making matatus illegal, the government had inadvertently contributed to the problem of corruption. In order to operate, matatu owners were more or less forced to evade the new laws and bribe the police. The owners were presented, then, with the unfortunate irony that their successful and patriotic businesses were predicated upon corruption.

It is no wonder that matatu owners wanted to be legal and licensed, and that they wanted to conduct their businesses openly and legitimately, as befits *mwanainchi*, or a "true citizen," of the new nation. They were not immigrants, after all, as were the south Asians or the whites, and so they too should have the same opportunities to make money and move up the economic ladder. The leaders' policies should live up to their rhetoric. And, as aspiring *watu wa kisasa*, as modern and upwardly mobile entrepreneurs, the matatu owners should be allowed to enjoy their status as successful businessmen in a city they had long desired to make their own.[5]

———

All those riding on the matatus could, in some sense, make the same argument. Although they were more or less colluding with the enterprising matatu owners and drivers to avoid the wrath of the police, the passengers were—at least conceivably—working in the spirit of *Harambee*. They were supporting the businesses of their Kenyan compatriots. Of course almost anyone could in some way claim they were promoting the values of unity and self-help so long as they went about their business with the right attitude. It was a wonderfully convenient argument when it served one's own interests, and the motives of those invoking all the benefits of *Harambee* could be decidedly mixed. Much of this supposed patriotism merely served to sustain the status quo. The fact was that many of the owners actually preferred to bribe the police when caught (rather than meet licensing requirements), which meant that the police were rarely able to attain any convictions of the pirate taxi owners.

This was not lost on the officials at the KBS. Because so few offenders were brought forward, the officials publicly alleged, over and over again, that there were not actually any significant legal repercussions for those engaged in pirating. In fact, they openly suspected that the officials at the Nairobi City Council (NCC) had intentionally disregarded the agreement they had signed years back (the agreement that gave the KBS a monopoly on the transportation business in Nairobi). With a growing sense of frustration, the KBS officials made repeated visits to the mayor of Nairobi or the police superintendent to request that they do more to control the pirates. Eventually, impatience got the better of them and they started to advocate that more decisive measures be taken: "A real war needs to be declared on pirates," argued Arthur Kent, the KBS director, in a conversation with the mayor of Nairobi, Seth Lugonzo, in January 1968. "Pirates are a menace to the KBS and to *wanainchi*; they should be eliminated," he insisted. The mayor would agree, and would equally assure Kent that in the future he would try to impose stricter measures upon the dreadfully unmanageable matatu business.[6] But always to no avail.

The KBS officials were, however, not the only ones who felt that the government's efforts to regulate the pirate taxis had proven lukewarm at best. Owners of legally licensed taxis, such as KENATCO, which was white owned, also complained repeatedly to government officials about the threat of matatus to their businesses.[7] A number of south Asians, who also kept a fleet of small sedans for hire by individuals or groups, also put up strong resistance—even though they were a conventional taxi service, which meant that they were not in direct competition with matatus. Moreover, most of the people who used matatus did not have the financial means to hire licensed taxis; it was usually tourists and other foreign visitors who hired the taxis, not the local commuters in Nairobi. Nevertheless, the owners of the legally licensed taxis appreciated the rare business they got from locals, and they were not willing to let it go, and were just as outspoken as the KBS, though they had no more luck than the KBS at getting the government to regulate matatus. In July 1968, for instance, some of the taxi owners approached the minister of power, works, and communications and pleaded with him to take more drastic measures against the illegal operators: "It is time

FIGURE 7 White-owned KENATCO taxis. Courtesy of the Standard Group, Nairobi

the public realized that pirate taxis [the matatus] have now become a very great problem. They pay no taxes to the government and are a great menace and a threat to livelihood of authorized taxi drivers. . . . The vehicles are also dangerous because they are in a state of utter disrepair."[8]

From their point of view the complaints were justified. And yet it seemed the more complaints the licensed taxi owners made the more matatus appeared—so many that they were able to expand their operations into the rural areas. This naturally incited the anger of the owners of the sanctioned rural buses, and so they, too, joined in with the others in the loud and angry chorus opposing pirate taxis. However, unlike the KBS buses and the majority of licensed taxis, the country buses were typically owned by Africans. Moreover, the rural bus companies—which included Mawingo, Tom Mboya (commonly known as OTC), Jogoo Kimakia, Kenya Taifa Bus, and Roadways—were fully licensed, and some of the owners of the buses even benefited from political relations of one sort or another with important government officials.[9] But neither their licenses nor their connections prevented them from feeling threatened by the encroachment of the matatus. At one point they even felt compelled to visit President Kenyatta at his home in Gatundu, to demand that he issue a total ban on the matatus. The story goes that Kenyatta listened to the woes of the bus owners, and then asked their leader, Dedan Nduati, owner of the Jogoo Kimakia Bus Service, how many matatus he would buy were he to sell one of his buses. "Several," replied the unsuspecting Nduati. Kenyatta is then rumored to have remarked: "Go and sell your buses and buy matatus."[10] There was nowhere else to make an appeal; Kenyatta was the last resort, and the leader of the country buses was left to nurse his grievances over the "utter nuisance" posed by matatu pirates. We can only imagine Nduati's frustration at Kenyatta's rather cavalier response.

In spite of the government's seeming indifference toward the owners of the legal transport carriers (and it is not clear whether or not Kenyatta was joking), on a few occasions the relevant officials did take the complaints seriously. When they consented to listen to the complaints, officials would usually respond by making an extra effort to increase the number of prosecutions of the pirate owners. At least in Nairobi, several high-level police inspectors would dutifully be asked to patrol the streets and to check on the work of their subordinates. For a short period, then, the police would become more conscientious and upstanding; they would forego their habitual acceptance of substantial bribes and produce some discernible convictions; and more matatu owners would be prosecuted because their vehicles lacked licenses or visibly revealed some major mechanical problem.[11] It was easy to punish these relatively insignificant misdemeanors during these intervals of heightened scrutiny—the matatus provided fairly easy targets. And during these periods owners would typically let the charges go uncontested, and no bribes would be offered or accepted (interestingly, the much more serious crime of operating as pirate taxis carrying paying passengers would go unnoticed—the passengers somehow remained invisible to the police). Knowing when not to accept bribes from the matatu drivers was a skill that the police and the owners had mastered; the police knew when to produce enough convictions to appear credible in the eyes of their superiors, and to the general public for that matter, and the owners seemed to accept the occasional exacting of fines as operating expenses. By and large, if enough convictions were made, the tempers of the KBS management could at least be temporarily calmed. Nevertheless, the police would never go so far as to alienate the passengers or the owners, or to lose for the long term the reliable source of income they collected from bribes.[12] It was a delicate balancing act.

To help smooth things over with the police department, the Nairobi City Council also made sure that the court trials and the convictions of the pirate taxi owners were widely published in the newspapers as evidence of the seriousness of their efforts—"It Is War on Pirate Taxis," proclaimed a newspaper headline, or "Pirate Taxi Man Fined 800 Shillings," and, "Pirate Taxi Man Fined 300 Shillings."[13] Not so subtle public reassurances of this kind were common throughout the 1960s. And, for instance, whenever there happened to be a police chase in the city the NCC made sure that it was vividly described in the papers. Breathless descriptions of determined policemen clad in khaki shirts and shorts running down fugitive matatus were frequently offered to readers— for instance, a report in *Drum* magazine in May 1966 portrayed one such scene: "Often," it began, "one finds the dark blue patrol car and two motorcycle police cruising slowly down Nairobi's Pumwani Road with their eyes on the street ahead. 'Here he comes,' a police inspector would whisper, 'Look out. He's seen us. There he goes. After him!' The patrol car would shoot forward as the vehicle in the front turned sharply across and scurried off down Nandi Street. The police car and motorcyclists would speed in pursuit."[14] In this instance the chase was short and dispirited. The driver of the hunted vehicle, having no heart for it, pulled over as a police inspector rushed forward toward the door, cutting off any hope of escape. The driver climbed out, shrugged, and the gathered crowd took a look and concluded that nothing interesting was going on. No bank robber, no stolen vehicle, and no thief: "Just another *matata ya matatu* [problem with a matatu], another pirate taxi on the yardarm of the law."[15]

Despite the almost Keystone Cops quality of the descriptions, the papers and magazines would report on about twenty or so cases of this kind every year in the 1960s, enough at least to allow the pretense that the police were making a serious effort at enforcing the law concerning illegal carriers.[16] But it was plainly clear to anyone on the streets that the police were not going to curtail matatus. Vivid stories of matatu arrests might calm the tempers of opponents or encourage the police department, but they did little else. Matatus were still everywhere, regardless of the examples the press provided. Most of the drivers caught by police were sentenced according to a 1963 Taxi Cab By-Law that stated: "any person who drives an unlicensed or un-roadworthy vehicle shall be fined up to 50 shillings or sent to prison for up to one month or both."[17] Many of those caught, usually repeat offenders, appeared in court, were fined, and had their cases publicly reported in the Kenyan daily newspapers—and they casually returned to their matatus and resumed their labors. Joseph Nderi, one of my main interviewees, was one such offender. In June 2004, I spent some time with Nderi at his house in Eastleigh, where he informed me at length about the history of Nairobi in the 1960s. He was one of the early entrepreneurs who had profited from the burgeoning business of matatus, from the 1960s through 1980s; he was also founder and chairman of the Matatu Vehicle Owners Association (MVOA), an organization he created to allow matatu owners to air their grievances to the authorities.[18]

One Sunday morning in June 2004, I paid him a visit at his office. I had brought along all the media clippings I had gathered about him—and there were many, a full folder of them. Nderi was delighted to see the clippings and grinned happily as he flipped through them, thanking me for taking him back to "the days." I stopped him as he came upon a clipping I had marked and asked him to read it. "Two men operating pirates were fined 185 shillings by a Nairobi magistrate," began the clipping. "Both men pleaded guilty to plying their motor vehicles for hire without licenses. Joseph Mwaura Nderi of Nairobi was fined a total of 100 shillings on 8 counts and John Rubia Kairo of Kiambu was fined 25 shillings."

"I can't believe this," Nderi stopped, looked up at me, clapped his hands and chuckled. "Nderi," he then read, "admitted 16 previous convictions for traffic offences. The magistrate noted that if his powers were not limited he would have imposed imprisonment."[19] When he finished he turned to me with tears of laughter in his eyes, patted my arm, and said, "I was really tough then; I was strong too, aaaaihhh!!" He then reminisced how he often had to flee police pursuit—"Those policemen were bad news," he shrugged; "I was bad news too because I had to make a living."[20] I believed him. Despite his broad smile and gleaming teeth, Nderi had penetrating eyes and a rather edgy presence, so that I was relieved and amused when he let loose, threw back his head and chortled with hilarity. He seemed a man who could still make things happen in the world of matatus.[21]

But Nderi was hardly the only person who was repeatedly caught and forced to pay fines. As I have suggested, repeat offenders were common. On March 1, 1967, for example, it was reported that Thuo Mariga was fined 100 shillings for driving a motor vehicle from Makadara to central Nairobi while illegally carrying passengers for hire and reward. The inspector said that Mariga had stopped his vehicle at the Makadara bus stop and asked two plainclothes police constables if they wanted a lift to central Nairobi, and when they reached the center of Nairobi Mariga asked them to pay their 30 cents' fare. Mariga was quickly taken into custody; it was not his first offense.[22] Another pirate taxi driver was fined 68 shillings for operating without a license, and for driving a defective vehicle; he admitted to two previous convictions for similar offenses.[23] And yet another driver was fined 50 shillings or three months in jail in a Nairobi traffic court on February 20, 1968, for apparently overloading his van—by the astounding total of 1,584 pounds.[24] Offenses like these eventually led the city traffic police to conduct an all-out campaign, in May 1969, to eradicate accident-prone matatus from Nairobi roads. They arrested a total of thirty-five vehicle operators in one week.[25]

––––––

The newspaper accounts of the arrested matatu owners typically generated a fair amount of resentment among the owners. Many of them wondered—somewhat disingenuously—exactly what the point of independence was if they did not have the freedom to pursue their business and make a decent living, and sooner or later they would begin to question whether or not they were really living in a free country.[26] Despite their rather blinkered self-concern, some of their complaints were actually valid. The owners were not simply complaining that they were not allowed to operate freely in a system without legal constraint, they were complaining about a system that played favorites. Why, they wondered, were mostly Asian and European companies, companies such as the KBS, granted legal rights to monopolize the transport business in Nairobi while they were being harassed? Why were they, as Kenyan citizens, as *wanainchi*, being excluded from reaping some of the fruits of independence? For the matatu owners the issue was not just economic, it was political; it was also raising serious questions concerning racialist policy and national identity.

The question as to who was or was not legitimately Kenyan was complicated and inevitably involved issues of race. Many of the Asian and European businessmen were Kenyan citizens, though in the eyes of many black Kenyans the Asians and Europeans were considered *immigrant citizens*, not *real* or *true* citizens as they were. Such labeling was important, especially in terms of the kinds of economic and political claims one was allowed to make.[27] In fact, the immediate postindependence period was a time of significant racial anxiety for the immigrant citizens. Since Asians and Europeans had occupied the top rungs of the economic and political ladder during colonial rule, many black Kenyans felt strongly that these immigrant citizens had no business claiming a piece of the independent Kenyan pie. They had had their time to eat, so to speak.[28] But, remarkably, it was the South Asians rather than the Europeans who received the brunt of African anger. This was due in part, perhaps, to the fact that they had lived in close proximity to each other. Africans had frequently interacted with Asians while serving as their employees and were now becoming resentful of their employers' authority (as well as the racism they endured from the Asians). Perhaps even more importantly, many of the Asians were traders who had opened *dukas* in Kenya, in the major cities and remote rural areas, and as storeowners they were, relatively speaking, better off than a great many Africans.[29] Africans were naturally envious, and now, given that this was their country, they felt they had the right to make money just as the Asians had been doing. More often than not, all the talk among Africans about developing the new nation often meant being given a chance to become retail traders and enjoying the same or better opportunities as those enjoyed by the Asians in their *dukas*.[30] It was now the Africans' turn.

As a result of this antipathy Asians faced significant social, economic, and political pressure. Indeed, much of Kenyan economic planning immediately following independence was focused on the issue of retail trade, and one of the main concerns was how to Africanize this section of the economy.[31] Europeans, too, experienced their share of patriotic resentment, but mostly with regard to the huge tracts of land they amassed during colonial rule. The questions they faced concerned the redistribution of those lands back to the Africans after independence. When it came to the larger businesses, however, particularly the larger industrial companies, Europeans tended to occupy high-level management positions, and the thinking among certain African political elites was that Kenyanization at this level should take place gradually. Since few Kenyans had the necessary training to work at the executive level they supposedly needed time to catch up. The Europeans who remained in these positions were for the time being deemed beneficial to the new nation, and they would be allowed to stay a little longer.[32]

To put it another way, Europeans tended to be regarded as *expatriates*, which implied that they had come to Kenya with sophisticated knowledge and skills that were important to the development of the new nation. Asians, on the other hand, were considered *immigrant citizens*, a highly derogatory and racist phrase that suggested that they were not needed in the new nation, despite the fact that most of the Asians were determined to stay in Kenya (many of them had been born or raised in Kenya and knew no other place).[33] It is no surprise that Asians felt more vulnerable than whites in independent Kenya, and for the most part their alarm was justified. They needed only to listen to the negative, if not outright racist, references by Africans toward the Asians. Their vulnerability was exacerbated by the fact that a high percentage of Europeans had left the country after independence.[34] But even before independence the anti-Asian racism had been well ingrained—and, in many ways, it had been perpetuated by Europeans. In order to divide and conquer the nonwhite population, many colonialists had become cynically adept at pitting Africans against Asians.[35] Racial stereotypes, always ready to hand, were useful to those in power and had proven an expedient means of control for colonial officials: as long as Asians considered the Africans lazy and childish, and the Africans considered Asians treacherous and surly, they were unlikely to fight for each other's interests. The Europeans, on the other hand, did not at all mind being thought of as smug and snobbish and privileged, so long as the status quo could be conveniently sustained to their benefit.[36]

The same message was coming from important African leaders, from President Kenyatta to the mayors of Kenya's major cities, who showed only disdain for the Asians and their claims to be Kenyan.[37] For example, Kenyatta spoke out against Asian shopkeepers in a speech in 1967 to all Kenyans on Madaraka Day (Independence Day). The Asians, he said, were ostensibly betraying the ideals of *Harambee*: "because of their wealth [they] showed no respect to the ordinary African"; he also alleged that for the Asians, "*Uhuru* [independence] was nothing," and that "some of these people have not even realized that there is now an about-turn." He ended by suggesting that if they wanted to stay they had better become adequately Kenyan—"one leg should not be in Kenya and the other in India."[38] On another occasion Kenyatta addressed a group of Africans and exulted that Indians, "should know that you [Africans] are the *bwana mkubwa* [the powerful men of this country]."[39] For all these reasons Asians became more and more excluded and were considered more and more alien, while Africans were becoming more empowered. Understandably, they felt anxious about their social and economic future in Kenya, and they began to fear that reprisals were in the offing.[40]

Taking their cue from Kenyatta, various MPs (Members of Parliament) in the Kenyan National Assembly voiced similar complaints about the Asians' pervasive presence in retail trade. One minister wondered why citizens of India and Pakistan were being licensed to trade in Kenya while, at the same time, "there were no African traders in Bombay, Delhi or Karachi."[41] Nor did it seem that the Asians were willing to act the part of committed Kenyans. David Ogina, the secretary of the Mombasa KANU (Kenya African National Union) branch, remarked dismissively that the Asian community was not inclined to come out in the open and join the Africans in welcoming presidential processions. Instead they watched the ceremonies through the windows of their flats or from the roofs of their buildings and refused to join Africans. "The spirit of *Harambee* has not permeated through to this type of people," he said ominously, and he admonished the Asians to change with the times, "as Kenya is now an independent state run by Africans."[42]

It was not just the African people and politicians who were expressing their aversion. The major newspapers got into the act as well, avidly publishing letters to the editor denouncing Asians for one thing or another—for their culture, for their practice of cremation, even for being bad drivers. One such letter grumbled that Asians acted "as if to show every motorist that they are better drivers," and that they had no respect for driving regulations. "It is not surprising to see many an Asian driving into a roundabout—doing 50 mph—irrespective of whether other vehicles are approaching on his right side. . . . I think that public feeling should be roused in order to curb these reckless and devil-may-care drivers."[43] But surely there was little evidence that African drivers—and matatu drivers in particular—were any better.

On the whole it seemed that in the immediate postindependent years one almost had to be anti-Asian to be a good Kenyan citizen.[44] Without the colonial officials to blame, a new scapegoat was wanted, and in the eyes of much of the public the Asians quite capably filled the need. This was of course deeply unfair. Quite a few Asians had played an important role in resisting colonial rule, though few Africans were willing to recognize their contributions.[45] The failure to give credit may very well have been a result of willful blindness, but the unanimity of the neglect often made it seem calculated. In fact, the Asians' contributions to the independence struggle were not only routinely disregarded but also turned against them. Any African who managed to associate their personal plight with Asian oppression and economic dominance was often more likely to receive sympathy from African leaders. Similarly, if an argument could be made that a certain policy trumped Asian interests it stood a much better chance of success. If Asians' contributions remained invisible, their successes were altogether too visible and had to be resisted.

––––––

Matatu owners offered no exception to this anti-Asian bias. Time and again they were among the first to exploit it as a strategy to earn favor from government officials. Sometimes the prejudice was merely implied—for instance, when confronted by the police matatu owners often argued that they were being "deprived of a livelihood in our own country, as the *true* citizens of the new nation."[46] If their insinuations did not prove sufficient, they would not hesitate to become more explicit and demand that the police harass the Asians. In 1965, the secretary of the Kenya Transport and Allied Workers Union (a union representing African transport workers) proclaimed that the union would not tolerate police oppression and demanded that the TLB give licenses to African vehicles and entirely stop the Asians and their system of car hire. In addition, matatus had to be made legal—like the Asian taxis—so that the police could be prevented from interfering with Kenyan "pirate" taxis. "These pirate taxi men," proclaimed the secretary, "had decided to earn a living by constitutional means; they were simply poor *wanainchi* [citizens] trying to make ends meet."[47] The not-so-subtle implication was that Asian operators needed to be cleared out of the way.

By righteously comparing themselves with the legal taxi companies owned by Asians, and then demanding that their rights as Kenyan citizens be recognized, the owners were all too obviously basing their appeal upon race.[48] The Asian taxis for hire posed no threat to the matatu business—but bias against them could be leveraged to gain other benefits. The real enemy of the matatu was the KBS and its ties to the Nairobi City Council. Since the NCC had bought a large percentage of shares of this British company, it had become difficult for them to revoke their agreement with the KBS since this would mean losing their investment. The matatu owners no doubt knew this, and yet they still wanted something done. So, knowing there was little they could do to undermine the NCC's economic ties to the KBS, they promptly deflected their frustrations upon the Asian taxis (an easy target since the Asian taxis were legal and matatus were not).

This infuriating fact presented matatu owners with an opening, and once again the Asians provided an easy scapegoat. Whenever the matatu owners brought up the Asian taxis the government officials were forced by their own rhetoric of *Harambee* to listen and respond, or be deemed "un-Kenyan." In January 1966, for example, about two hundred people summoned for traffic offenses staged a strike outside the Nairobi Magistrate Court; they refused to go into court because, they argued, Africans were being fined more than Asians. The magistrate denied this and countered with the fact that many Africans were actually being fined only 50 shillings, the minimum fine, while convicted Asians often had to pay more. But the facts were not persuasive, and the magistrate ended up backing down and reducing the fines for the two hundred matatu owners by half. As justification for the concession he volunteered the argument that many of the pirate owners "were having a hard time as some of them were still paying for the purchase of the cars."[49] The leniency was no doubt appreciated by the owners, but it raised a legitimate question as to whether or not the matatu owners had received preferential treatment by invoking prejudice against Asian taxi operators. The economic difficulties of the Africans were certainly real, but it is also true that as soon as they couched their appeals with Kenyan solidarity and anti-Asian bias they seemed to have gotten what they wanted. It certainly appears as if the covert call for racial solidarity helped drive home the urgency of their cause—and get results.

These kinds of disputes were not just limited to Nairobi. Mombasa had also experienced major tensions between matatu owners and government officials, and there, too, the owners repeatedly declared that they resented the fact that matatus were illegal while the Asian taxis were considered legal. Like their compatriots in Nairobi they tried to change the policy in very much the same manner. In February 1968, Mombasa pirate taxi drivers sent a delegation, led by their spokesman, Peter Gitau, to the local branch of the KANU branch. Gitau, speaking to the KANU chairman, contended that "we as pirate taxi drivers are jobless and we think we can only earn our living by operating such jobs without any interference in other peoples' jobs. We do not like it that Asians are given preference over us."[50] Although some of these owners he represented could have gotten licenses from the TLB had they sought them, many of them chose not to because they knew their vehicles were unlikely to pass the inspection test. They claimed— insincerely—that they simply wanted the police to leave them alone so that they could "make an honest living as the *wanainchi* of independent Kenya."[51] Evidently they hoped that a concern for politics—and by implication, racial politics—would trump the government's concern for safety. And once again, a not-so-subtle appeal to racial unity might just help them make an end run around the law and allow them to get their vehicles legalized.

Joseph Nderi also participated in perpetuating the Kenyanization rhetoric on behalf of the matatu owners. When, in June 1968, he helped found the Matatu Vehicle Owners Association, he understood exactly the kind of political influence the organization would have— even though the organization was not officially recognized by anyone in the government. It would foster the claims of the African matatu owners. In a letter to the director of the licensing board, he noted: "We as pirate taxi drivers are jobless and we think that we can only earn our living by operating such jobs without any interference in other jobs.

Matatus should be asked to apply for licenses, made legal."[52] He also made the familiar complaint, saying, "the government has not issued us with licenses so as to recognize our existence as true *wanainchi*. We are helping ease the transport problems and that of unemployment as well." As so often, the apparently good-faith appeals for the advancement of "true citizens" also conveyed a veiled appeal for racial solidarity. It was certainly conceivable in this instance. When I asked Nderi if this were the case, he deflected my question and instead launched into a discussion of the need for licensing: "We were just poor people then. If matatus became legal, they would not pose any danger. And that is all we were asking for."[53]

But as Nderi knew, even as they were crying out to be licensed, many of the owners' vehicles would not have passed inspection.

"So why were you insisting on being licensed?" I asked.

"It was just talk, *ilikua siasa tu*, it was just politics, you see," he replied. "We were just making noise in order to be heard. See that is how we *wanainchi* talked then. We had to say we were true *wanainchi* in order to be heard; it was a good language to have then."[54]

I pressed him a little: "So what exactly were you asking the government to do for you?"

"We just wanted to be set free to do our business because the business was working and we were getting passengers in our cars which meant that there was nothing wrong with our business. See, we were making money in the best way possible. We were not criminals; we were making a living by legitimate means. We were helping develop the nation—not like the Indians who sent their money to India. We earned our money by honest means and used it here in Kenya."[55]

It may be questionable whether or not the owners should have been completely "free to do their business" simply because their "business was working," but the important point is that the matatu owners did not think of themselves as criminals, and at the very least they should be considered as legitimate as the Asians in the taxi service. Regardless of the number of fines imposed upon pirate owners like Nderi, the owners and drivers of matatus did not believe they were committing crimes; rather, they were providing a much-needed service, and certainly not robbing others like actual outlaws. And they were helping to build the country by building successful businesses. They believed, in fact, that the matatu industry was one of the only feasible pathways to success, and that anyone with enough enterprise and a small amount of capital could fix up a car and try to make a go of it. This was not typically the case when it came to small retail ventures. Start-up costs were much higher, and most Africans felt excluded from opening small shops by the monopolistic tendencies of the Indians, and, indeed, there were frequent complaints that the monopolistic ways in which Indians carried out their businesses in the *dukas* was in fact criminal.[56] But the matatu industry, the argument went, was a good Kenyan industry, an industry by Kenyans and for Kenyans.[57] Operating a pirate taxi business, then, could not possibly be a crime.

Look, for instance, at an interview with Bwana M., a pirate taxi owner from Nairobi. Bwana M. was in his late thirties when he was interviewed by *Drum* magazine. "He smiles a lot and has an honest face, two wives and seven children," the interviewer noted. At the time when he was interviewed he owned only one matatu, but he had at one time operated five: "There is a lot of money in it for us," he said, but then immediately began complaining about the fines: "We are lucky if we break even or make a little profit to feed our families. The police know me, for I have a large number of convictions (the police say 33) for traffic offences, and I have paid more than 1,000 shillings in fines. I suppose you could call my fines my income tax."[58] Nevertheless, Bwana M. did not consider himself a criminal despite the fact that operating a taxi was officially illegal. Although he knowingly broke the law and was aware of the consequences, he still considered himself blameless— after all, he voluntarily paid his poll tax of 96 shillings a year, and when he was caught in a police raid he always paid his fines without a fuss. Nevertheless, according to the government he was breaking the law and had to be punished. He certainly wanted to operate legally, but the police policies had gotten the matatus "upside down," and, he insisted, "none of the boys in the network likes working outside the law, since it embarrasses the KANU government and President Kenyatta."[59]

When asked about the competition the matatus were giving to the KBS, Bwana M. answered with an outward show of innocence, and an apparent warning: "We are not out to ruin the bus company. We just want to make a living and would very much like to get legitimate licenses, but the city council have been a long time considering the proposal our deputation put to them that they allow matatus to become legal. And things are getting worse. If something isn't done soon the police will have us out of business and then some of the boys will turn to stealing or robbery as the only way of living." He prefers continuing his business and paying a fine when caught rather than quitting altogether and potentially becoming an out-and-out crook. Better to own a matatu since they are "profitable," and operating them "is better than going into crime."[60]

The occasional editorials in the Kenyan newspapers and magazines also presumed the guiltless goodwill of the matatu owners. For example, an editorial in the *East African Standard* acknowledged that "the matatus' untiring efforts to ferry *mwanainchi* with his or her luggage to even the remotest area of the republic cannot be disputed."[61] A letter to the editor in the same newspaper proclaimed that "Matatus are the saviour of *wanainchi*."[62] The more such pieces appeared, the more it was evident that the matatu owners were onto something: as long as they could appeal to the new sense of Kenyan solidarity, they would be perceived as good citizens, citizens who, like most people in Nairobi and elsewhere in Kenya, were simply struggling to make ends meet by means they judged legitimate. Surely they were not criminals, they were simply hustling to make it; they were "making a living by constitutional means," as was the right of any true Kenyan.[63]

———

Or, to put it another way, they simply sought respect. As a means of motivation this cannot be overstated. As good, striving citizens of the newly independent country, matatu owners wanted to enjoy their lives in the city in ways they had not been able to during the colonial period. But it was not just a matter of making a living and enjoying their success. Of particular interest to them was their public image. It had become a point of pride. The typical matatu owner wanted to convey an image of himself as socially up to date, as a rising entrepreneur whose business was vital to the city's development—and not just as an illegitimate hustler conducting a renegade taxi service. To this end, some of the matatu owners spent the profits from their businesses to better the public's perception of them by upgrading their living conditions and moving to better housing in the eastern part of Nairobi (to estates [suburbs] like Bahati, Gorofani, Ofafa Maringo, Jerusalem, Jericho, and Mbotela), where the Nairobi City Council had recently constructed over 2,000 housing units with indoor plumbing and electricity.[64]

Henry Makau was one such matatu owner. Born and raised in a small village in Machakos district in the 1940s, he was one of thirteen children. One of the older sons, Henry left home "to learn mechanics" when he turned sixteen and moved to Nairobi where he lived in a one-room mud hut in Kibera with his "mechanic" uncle who had been working for the past few years as a casual laborer with the railway company.[65] Henry became interested in car repair through this family connection, and since there was no steady work for him at the railways, he usually ended up hanging out with friends and watching them do repairs. He was encouraged by his uncle to try his hand at mechanical work, and he picked it up quickly: "my uncle would say to me come let us go so you can learn how to fix cars." Eventually he learned to negotiate his way around the city and was able to find temporary jobs in the industrial area, mostly menial work hauling goods or cleaning. But the work was tedious and unrewarding, and besides, his "heart was in mechanics." Henry managed, however, to save enough money to purchase a bicycle, which he cleverly transformed into a vehicle capable of transporting people and goods—and he began making a little money.

Freed from menial labor, and now with a little free time, he again started haunting the open-air garages, and in good time bought his own car, a "very old car" with "no engine, brakes or windscreen."[66] But he repaired it, gave up his bike, and once again started transporting people short distances around town. It proved lucrative, and before long he was able to rent a cubicle in Makadara estate in Eastlands and upgrade his car to a converted dodge pickup and also buy an old beat-up VW Beetle—all this while supporting his wife and three children back in the village. But more than that, he was now a proper *paterfamilias* who could buy a sofa set and a gas cooker, and he had managed to bring his older son to live with him so he could send him to a good primary school in Eastlands (Henry's son did so well that he was accepted at Alliance High School, the most prestigious high school in Kenya). In the late 1960s his wife was able to move to Nairobi and start her own business selling goods in a makeshift kiosk near the matatu station. It is abundantly clear, then, that for Henry and his family, and many others just like him, owning a matatu meant mobility; it meant being able to move from the village and into Nairobi's middle class, and to enjoy a more comfortable and respected life. The matatu gave them class mobility, so to speak; they were now aspiring *watu wa kisasa,* modern people.

Other matatu owners who, like Henry Makau, had started out with few resources ended up investing their profits in real estate. For instance, Joseph Nderi used the profits he made transporting people in his matatu to purchase a two-bedroom house, which he then rented to earn additional income. "When you earned a bit of profit," he advised, "you reinvested it quickly . . . because you did not want the money just to sit there. You had to turn your money into something concrete in order to feel good about your profit."[67] For Nderi, real estate was a reliable investment because, "anything could go wrong with the matatu . . . you could get into an accident and then your business is finished. So you see, real estate was stable." Nevertheless, he insisted the matatu business is where the real money was: "You could make good money in the matatu business."[68] For quite a while, in the 1960s, Nderi did very well. He was able to buy a house for himself in more fashionable Eastleigh and have his wife join him; she too started a small business—she opened up a kiosk that sold convenience items. "It was a very smart house" in one of the neighborhoods located near a brightly lit beer garden where he and his peers could enjoy a "sundowner" outdoors. Nearby was a community center where motivated citizens could learn English, yet another sign of upward mobility.[69] And once they began learning English and living in an immaculate new housing development, matatu owners could at last feel that they were members, or at least potential members, of the new urban society of Nairobi.[70] As Henry Makau proudly boasted, *"Tulikuwa watu wakisasa kabisa* [We were fully modern people]."

This was a significant step up for upwardly mobile matatu owners like Nderi and Henry. It was a recognized prestige to live among Africans who worked as clerks or in middle-management positions for companies making footwear, textiles, and alcohol in the nearby industrial area. Some of these managers earned the giddy salary of 1,000 shillings ($150) per month, and were able to purchase such luxuries as a Columbia gramophone.[71] The earnest members of this rising middle class usually made a conscious effort to distinguish themselves from the working classes by, among other things, dressing properly in a necktie and long trousers.[72] Some were even able to buy Raleigh, Humber, or BSA bicycles, and a lucky few owned Vespas—"the sure lady-killer bachelor mode of transportation along Doonholm Road [later Jogoo Road]."[73] But no matter how well off they became, the majority of these new middle-class residents of the city depended on matatus as their primary means of transportation.

As matatu owners began living and working among the middle classes, as they started bringing their families to live in Nairobi with them and sending their children to the same city schools, they adopted other conventions of middle-class life.[74] Determined to convey an image of probity and respectability to the other members of their communities, wives of the matatu owners became involved in community activities—for example, Rachel Munene, who left her rural village in Kitui in 1966 to join her husband, who owned two matatus and had recently moved into a two-bedroom flat in Mbotela. "It was a good time to be in Nairobi," she recalled, and she described how she and other wives would travel—in matatus, of course—to Kaloleni and Pumwani, where they met with *Maendeleo ya Wanawake* (women's progress organizations) in a town hall, so that they could begin training in home economics, weaving and spinning, and health and hygiene.[75] The halls were also used as classrooms where the women could, like their husbands, receive lessons in the English language. Exhibitions, tea parties, and sports events were also frequently organized; in 1965 alone 101 dances and 300 meetings took place in the Pumwani Community Hall.[76] Incidentally, Pumwani had been the vanguard of colonial social welfare activities aimed at encouraging "respectable" urban African life in the 1950s, and continued to be so in the 1960s.[77]

One woman who lived in Pumwani in the mid-1960s remembered it as a "smart place." The neighborhood had "proper City Council flats. The houses were arranged in good long rows, the Muslims were sitting on their verandas, nicely; you admired everything. The Kikuyus were doing their business in a sober way. I remember the hotels, which were open, all night with music going on."[78]

It was also in Pumwani, in the community hall, that Kenya's first jukebox was installed in 1958. Here, Kenya's emerging working and middle classes, matatu owners among them, came to listen to songs by popular Kenyan musicians like Daudi Kabaka, David Amuga, and John Mwale. Most of the music studios consisted of nothing more than a tiny room in the back of a store where musicians hung out, composing songs that reflected the dusty realities and desires of the people in the streets outside. Since they were playing exclusively for dancers in the clubs, these Kenyan musicians could afford to work local, topical issues into their Congolese-influenced songs. Since Nairobi did not have its own unique music style, and it lacked the glamour of Ghanaian highlife or the sophistication of Zairian musicians, the music achieved significance in another way: it directly addressed urgent topical issues.[79] The lyrics of the songs spoke candidly about urban issues in Nairobi, or about Kenyan politics, in ways that could not be heard over the airwaves and from politicians, they expressed the complexities of urban class distinctions, the seduction of "modernity" and emerging individualism, the fickleness and foibles of modern love, of gender and marriage.[80] For the majority of Kenyans, the songs revealed the struggles of daily life with a simple exuberance that reflected their audience. And the musicians could speak to these issues with authority. Too poor to afford their own instruments, even the best-known musicians had to hold down other jobs, some of them as workers in the matatu industry.

Boxing and billiards were also popular activities in the community halls in the 1960s, and in these places young men and women in Nairobi could read magazines like *Drum* to follow sports, entertainment, and politics in other parts of Africa as well as news concerning African Americans. *Drum* carried advertisements of all varieties, seducing consumers to buy the new necessities required for modern urban living— skin-lightening lotions, radios, weight-gaining tablets, and medicines for pimples, malaria, and stomachache. The magazine also contained an advice column for the lovelorn and another column to prescribe treatments for the sick written by a so-called Dr. Drum.[81] Won over by the promise of all these products, and now busy with reading, music, dancing, sports, and homemaking, all their recently acquired pursuits, this new generation of African men and women had arrived; they considered themselves as members of the modern urban culture of East Africa, *watu wa kisasa*.

––––––––

There is no question that matatus played an important part in making this culture possible. They transformed the city and the country. Modern, independent Africans relied on the matatu for their mobility—in every sense of the word; without matatus to move them into the city and through its streets, there would have been none of the upward mobility that the new Kenyans so prided themselves on. To be able to move up, they had to be able to move around, and the matatu made both possible. The matatu owners and the workers rightly saw themselves as playing a pivotal role in helping build the economy of the new nation by transporting workers to their places of work and enabling them to earn the wages they would use to move them up the economic ladder. This is in part why they were so concerned that the government officially recognize their businesses and make them legal. Without them, much of what this new generation of Kenyans valued and desired could never have been attained. And they were also, in a sense, leading by example; their businesses were helping to build Kenya's modern working and middle class by showing the way, and by making it possible for the Africans to exploit opportunities that had largely been monopolized by the immigrant citizens—South Asians and whites—during colonial rule.

It is no surprise, then, that they wanted some of the credit for making these new lives possible. It is perhaps understandable, too, that matatu owners sometimes deployed the racially charged language in which they saw themselves as *true* or *real* citizens, as opposed to *immigrant* citizens. They felt it only fair that as *wanainchi*, they be granted official status and be made legal, and thus be given the same legitimacy offered to Asian and European business owners. And, at least during the 1960s, the public's perception of the industry was still fundamentally positive, and many Africans in the working and middle classes recognized the matatu industry as the only major business that had actually been started by people like themselves. It was considered a uniquely Kenyan industry, made by and for Kenyans. At this decisive period in the nation's history the matatu itself came to be seen—and rightly so—as a proud part of Kenya's project of nation building, and a symbol of Africans' ability to make it on their own and earn a living by "constitutional means."[82]

PART THREE

Deregulation, 1973–84

FOUR

Kenyatta's Decree, 1973

In Gatundu, about 50 kilometers north of Nairobi, there stands a well-tended mango tree with deep green leaves that bears fruit twice a year. Next to the tree is an equally well-cared-for palatial house in which President Jomo Kenyatta had spent most of his nights since the early 1970s because he believed ghosts haunted the State House in Nairobi, the official residence of Kenya's president. Kenyatta was born and raised in Gatundu and, as is often the tradition, he built a country house in his hometown. Weather permitting he liked to entertain those who came to pay homage and to carry out state business, *baraza* style, under the mango tree.[1] The popular belief was that if Kenyatta promised you something while you sat with him under the tree, he was much more likely to keep his promise.[2]

It is under this celebrated tree that Joseph Mwaura Nderi, along with four other matatu owners (all men), sat with Jomo Kenyatta in January 1971 to discuss the problems facing matatu owners and, more specifically, to ask that the government license matatu businesses.[3] "We arrived at Mzee's house at 10:00 a.m. sharp, dressed in suits; we looked very smart," recalled Nderi when I questioned him about his visit to Gatundu. "We were a bit nervous but felt very privileged that Mzee had agreed to receive us; that was a special thing in those days, you know, for Mzee to invite you to Gatundu. We talked for some time and Mzee praised us for our work in transporting people in the city and we were very pleased."[4]

Nderi was naturally gratified when, five months later on June 1, 1973, during the celebrations of Kenya's tenth anniversary for independence, Kenyatta stood up at the stadium to give the presidential speech and announced, "with immediate effect *no* vehicles under three tons would be required to pay for road licenses." He believed that Kenyatta had listened to him and his delegation, the "Gatundu delegation," as he called it.[5] "I think he heard us, matatu people," Nderi told me when I spoke with him in June 2004, a little over thirty years after the announcement.[6]

But it was not only the Gatundu delegation that was exuberant at Kenyatta's announcement. The huge audience in the stadium where Kenyatta spoke was equally delighted; when the president announced that matatus would be freed from any form of licensing requirement, he received a standing ovation, accompanied by several minutes of cheering and ululating.[7] The declaration was momentous for anyone who traveled Kenya's roads: matatus constituted nearly 65 percent of the total vehicles, and they were now the largest category of vehicles exempted from licensing. For the owners this meant, significantly, that they would no longer be subject to assessments by the Trade and Licensing Board (TLB), which had stubbornly sought to ensure that vehicles met basic mechanical standards. Kenyatta apparently understood the potential dangers that accompanied this decision, and he warned matatu operators to "drive their vehicles carefully and avoid endangering the lives of people."[8] But no matter the possible danger, Kenyatta had made it clear to the crowd that any kind of contraption that could transport passengers would now be legal. To quell any doubts, he assured the audience that the matatu operators were doing a terrific job of contributing to the development of the new nation, and he insisted that they, too, deserved their freedom since their efforts had helped Kenya emerge from the shambles of colonial rule.

Of course, Kenyatta's words could not be directly contested by those who were skeptical of the proclamation; there was nothing anyone could do to oppose the decree of His Excellency, the father of the independent Kenya and the head of the ruling party, KANU.[9] The Mzee was a powerful man. He had exercised a personalized, authoritarian form of government since taking power, and in the early 1970s he continued to use this power to issue decree after decree, often as a favor to those who paid homage to him at his palatial estate in Gatundu. It also helped if such a person or group was Kikuyu, since Kenyatta's politics were largely based on ethnicity; he tended to help his own Kikuyu people while ignoring or even undermining the interests of other ethnic groups.[10] His ability to listen was often selective, and since most of the matatu owners happened to be Kikuyu, the matatu decree can reasonably be considered as another of Kenyatta's rewarding gestures to his fellow tribesmen. It is certainly possible, given the president's bias, that the matatus were freed from licensing requirements because he was doling out favors, not because the "Gatundu delegation" had been so convincing. He may have listened to the "matatu people," as Nderi concluded, largely because they were Kikuyu people.

Regardless of Kenyatta's motives, and despite all clapping and singing that had initially followed the president's decree (as was always the case when Kenyatta proclaimed anything at Madaraka Day celebrations), his decision to free matatus from licensing requirements ended up receiving a decidedly mixed reaction in some circles. It was particularly suspect to owners of public transportation vehicles not included in the decree.[11] When newspaper reporters interviewed Peter Brice, general manager of the Kenya Bus Service (KBS), he was cautious and evasive, and would "not comment" on the decree until he had met with the head of the Nairobi City Council (NCC), who were part owners of KBS.[12] The spokesman representing the Rift Valley Peugeot Service (which owned a fleet of cars operating from Nairobi to Nakuru) was also unhappy with the decision, though he chose not to remain cautiously silent; he chose, instead, to be judiciously vague. He worried that the decree would eliminate competition and that this would be bad for the transportation business: "any commercial business," the spokesman claimed, "is never business unless there is competition."[13] The comment is remarkably banal (and it sounds as if he is frightened it will be the loss of his own company that destroys the necessary competition). What is clear, however, is that the spokesman does not dare speak freely; he has to couch his skepticism in stuffy platitudes about the nature of the business world. The matatu owners, on the other hand, were effusive. One owner of multiple matatus declared with satisfied delight that the decree "is a great relief to us, as it shows the great concern our Mzee has over the interests and wishes of the people."[14]

It took some time, however, for Kenyans to understand the implications of the decree. For over a decade matatu owners had been asking the government to make their businesses legal by providing them with vehicle licenses, and now it seemed they had suddenly been declared legal. And yet their status was still uncertain; the Mzee's decree did not make it clear if the matatus were now legal, or still illegal and simply absolved from the need to acquire licenses. In some respects, it seemed the roadways had simply been declared open to anarchy.

———

Already for years, efforts had been made to mitigate the existing anarchy, mostly by finding some way to regulate matatus to make them safer. Although the initial effort to get the government to grant them licenses had come from the matatus' owners, parliamentary discussions on the topic had been going on since the late 1960s, and ordinary citizens had been petitioning for some kind of regulation since matatus had begun to appear on the streets. Most of those concerned—which meant most everyone living in the city—believed that licensing would force the matatu owners to observe the laws, and that in return they would be rewarded with legal status. This seemed the clear way forward.

The necessity of some kind of regulation was becoming more and more urgent since the number of road accidents in the city involving matatus had sharply increased. The government could no longer stand idly by. The sharp increase in the number of accidents had reached a critical point by the late 1960s, partly due to the fact that Nairobi's population had increased so extremely—it had more than doubled over the previous decade to nearly a million people.[15] Moreover, the number of matatus had also doubled, though the roads had not been expanded, widened, or repaired during the previous decade. All manner of obstacles—traffic, mud, potholes, even garbage—contributed to the decay of the roadways and an increase in accidents, and there were of course more pedestrians in the city than ever before. Now, on average, around 1,000 people were killed in road accidents every year, a 33 percent increase from the mid-1960s, and, because of their sheer numbers, a great many of those involved matatus.[16] Since nearly everyone on the streets of Nairobi had a stake in them—from poor pedestrians to limousined officials—the perils they presented had become a pervasive topic at street *barazas*, in newspapers and magazine editorials, and in cabinet meetings.[17] Up until Kenyatta's decree the discussions had always centered on how to authorize and regulate the matatus to make them safer, not how to free them from any regulatory requirements. Kenyatta's sudden decree had abruptly disregarded years of debate on the issue.

An important moment in the debate had come a few years before his decree: in December 1970, just as the parliamentary session was coming to a close, Ronald Ngala, minister of transport and communications, introduced a new Traffic Amendment Bill with the hope that the MPs might be ready to begin discussing the matter at the start of the next session. The bill sought, among other things, to "tighten measures to curb road accidents through careless driving and the use of unroadworthy vehicles on Kenyan roads."[18] Minister Ngala's bill had, in many ways, been designed to achieve a decisive solution to the matatu problem by requiring licenses. The minister understood that matatus were indispensable as they provided services that the KBS did not offer, and he argued that they needed some way of assuring their safe operation: "vehicles in good condition should be licensed and allowed to operate but be subjected to frequent police checks."[19] In a similar vein, Jeremiah Nyagah, the minister for agriculture, pointed out that even though matatus remained unlicensed, they nevertheless risked prosecution for other infractions. They would be penalized if their owners carried too many passengers or drove dangerously fast to increase their profits—which they needed so they could pay their fines when caught by the police.[20] Ironically, the policing of matatus had created a vicious cycle: the more recklessly they operated, the more fines they paid, and the more fines they paid the more recklessly they operated. This impasse might be broken, Nyagah reasoned, once matatu owners were obliged to get licenses. Since licensing would most likely reduce the number of illegal vehicles on the road, drivers would not need to drive so recklessly or carry so many passengers, and consequently the number of accidents would decline. The police would be expected to keep "an attentive eye on pirate taxis" in order to make sure that vehicles were licensed, carried the correct number of passengers, and did not travel at dangerous speeds. But, he also concluded that if the police could not regulate the matatus, the matatus "should be eliminated altogether."[21] Apparently, for Nyagah, there could be no compromise.

Attorney General Charles Njonjo joined the discussion by indicating his support for licenses, and he agreed that there was an obvious demand for matatus to serve the increased number of passengers in the city: "The fact that the 'pirate taxis' charge more or less the same fares as licensed buses and still manage to get customers in spite of their well-known faults is a clear indication of the great need to supply adequate, safe, and cheap transportation throughout the city." But, like Nyagah, the attorney general concluded by expressing his unreserved criticism of the pirate taxis: "Matatus are dangerous and people should not use them."[22]

The officials' disparagement of matatus was not very helpful since it ignored the fact that Nairobi residents really had no other options. Year after year, the KBS services had again and again proven inadequate. Furthermore, it was naive to assume that the police could successfully regulate matatus. Nyagah was conveniently ignoring the fact that the police often worked in cahoots with owners of defective vehicles by accepting bribes and overlooking misconduct. Other ideas tossed around by members of Parliament were just as ineffective—for example, asking passengers' bosses to stagger working hours, or requiring housewives to go shopping outside of rush hours. Of course, no one had any idea how such laws could be enforced, and it was plainly unfair to place the responsibility for reforming the matatus' delinquency upon anyone other than the owners themselves.[23]

When the minister of transport realized that the issue was going to require a more sustained discussion, he arbitrarily decided to postpone the debate. As Christmas was nearing, and most of the MPs departed for their comfortable country homes (in their private cars), they left the city's transportation problems behind. Even after the holiday break, during the next parliamentary session, the politicians continued to avoid—or kicked to the curb—the pressing problems of the city's transportation.

However, a few months later, in March 1971, Ngala reintroduced the issue to the Parliament by summarily informing the members that there were enough buses now operating in the city, and therefore he saw no need to bother licensing matatus. Whether he had had a change of heart or was reacting to pressure from above is unclear. In either case, it was a complete about-face—suddenly, somehow the bus service was deemed adequate and matatus had become expendable. The minister's new solution was to eliminate matatus and free up the roads for the KBS buses, rather than, as before, to provide the matatu owners with licenses: "If we give licenses to matatus," he now argued, the "KBS will not be able to run at a profit, for matatus operate only at peak hours while the buses have to provide a full service even on unprofitable roads and at less lucrative times of the day."[24] The buses clearly suffered economic disadvantage that had to be remedied, and besides, Ngala claimed, it was after all traffic congestion rather than a lack of buses that produced the delays and inconvenience, not the number of commuters. He subsequently announced that the KBS planned to increase the number of buses on city roads by 30 percent (though he did not explain why this was necessary if there were already enough buses). In his mind, the proposed increase in bus service would no doubt solve the problems, so he saw no reason to bother giving matatu owners any kind of license or legitimacy.[25] During the holidays Ngala had apparently received the gift of enlightenment, and it was revealed to him that there was no need to bother with matatus any longer.

Several MPs were predictably dismayed by Ngala's abrupt change of position and could not account for the minister's altered approach. They pushed back: "matatus would not be successful if there was no demand for them," protested Grace Onyango, the MP of Kisumu (and the only woman in the Kenyan Parliament at the time).[26] "The people want reliable transportation at a cheap price. If given some guidance, the matatu would operate an excellent transport business and would provide some competition to the KBS. We must look at things objectively," she argued, "because it is not just matatus that get involved in accidents, people are killed in brand-new cars." Her argument may have been slightly disingenuous, but Onyango did manage to revive the argument about licensing matatus; besides, it was incredibly naive and unrealistic to assume that they would simply go away—despite any improvement in the bus service or increase in police surveillance. She also contended that intensified surveillance by the police would only serve to compound the dangers: "I am given to understand matatus are still running and are now charging 50 cents; they are fully packed with passengers and will in the event of trying to dodge the police cause accidents."[27]

As the member for Kisumu, the third-largest city in the country, Onyango knew exactly the kinds of transportation difficulties people in urban areas were experiencing. She was also aware of her constituents' many other socioeconomic problems and argued strongly in support of Kenyans struggling with their own business ventures, and for the importance of "Africanizing" the Kenyan economy. "A situation is arising," she noted, "where Africans are being squeezed out of the transportation business in Nairobi by some big companies who own large fleets of taxis." In accordance with her nationalistic arguments, she opposed allowing the taxi companies to take over local business and reiterated the case for granting licenses to matatus so that they could operate legitimately. After all, they were owned by Kenyans and provided employment to Kenyans.

Her message resonated, perhaps because it was far more objective than Ngala's—she at least acknowledged the inescapable presence of matatus, and soon she began to garner support in all parts the country. For instance, an MP from the rural district of Kitui agreed, noting that the rural areas were hit hardest by the lack of transport: "matatus should be legalized to provide *wanainchi* [citizens] with transportation."[28] In addition to this now familiar appeal he added other popular recommendations: the fines imposed on matatus were unreasonably high and should be reduced, and made payable in installments; he argued that "convicted drivers should be subjected to refresher courses"; and finally, he pointed out that roads should be repaired because their poor conditions caused accidents, especially in rural areas where many "had not been graded since the colonial days."[29] This last recommendation was particularly important as it recognized that it was not just the matatu drivers who were the problem.

The Member for Mombasa immediately agreed that poor roads and increasing vehicle numbers also contributed to accidents in his city. But in this coastal city "tankers driven by drunk drivers" were causing most of the accidents, not matatus. Yet this, too, served as an argument for licensing matatus. If tankers could be forced to drive only at night, as Mombasa's MP suggested, the streets would be safer and matatu traffic could be better regulated—through licensing, naturally.[30]

But it was Martin Shikuku from western Kenya who seemed to best understand the problem. An outspoken politician, and a fiery spokesman for the rights of ordinary Kenyans, he had earned the nickname of "people's watchman."[31] Happily, fate had rendered him a compact, voluble man, determined to be heard regardless of the opposition, just the kind of presence that demanded more than its share of space on the Parliament floor. Shikuku began by speaking knowledgably about the social networks between passengers and matatu owners, acknowledging that passengers fully supported the matatu owners and could not be expected to testify against them. "The passengers and owners have their own rules," he said, and gave an example of a matatu that "fetches the poor person from his house [not from a KBS stop] and carries him to his office even on a rainy day."[32] And he shrewdly connected the matatu problem to Kenya's larger socioeconomic problems, insisting that the government become more attuned to the daily difficulties of ordinary people. "Why," he began, "does the government spend most of its time harassing *malaya* [prostitutes] and matatu owners when it is unable to feed the citizens of Kenya. The policy of this country . . . is to let a few people become richer. We should remember that one day the hungry people of this country are going to rise against the government. Why should the government wait until such a time? Who does not know that a hungry man does not understand the law?"[33] As far as matatus were concerned, he asked rhetorically: "What will happen to this government if they licensed a few of the matatus. Would this government collapse?" Shikuku thundered on, listing the major problems facing Kenya, from the poor roads, to health, education, housing, and land shortages, to the high costs of living, and to the huge inequalities between rich and poor. Transport undoubtedly deserved its place among all these obstinate problems.[34] Usually members could be counted on to dispute Shikuku's radical opinions, but for once they listened to him, nodding their heads quietly in assent.[35]

After Shikuku had spoken the minister of transport stood up to conclude the session by assuring the Parliament that his ministry would consider the matter seriously, and he assured the MPs that, should the KBS fail to meet the needs of Nairobi residents, they would then consider licensing matatus.[36] In the meantime, he appealed to his fellow MPs not to be tempted to purchase their own matatus to augment their financial position.[37] Unsurprisingly, the session ended without an answer to the main question: whether or not to license matatus. No one had anticipated President Kenyatta's decision to simply free the matatus from licensing altogether, and no one knew how to respond.

———

While Ngala and the other MPs may have appeared indecisive, the general public seemed to favor licensing matatus—at least according to letters to the major Kenyan daily newspapers. For instance, a typical letter to the editor of the *Nation*, from Peter Muchira, a Nairobi commuter, began: "I live about four miles from Ngong town and I work in Nairobi. I have either got to wait for the only bus on this route at 7 am or worse still walk. This one bus is very unreliable. . . . Now this only bus on the route broke down early last month and I have had to walk and so does everybody else. Walking against time is by no means a very pleasant task. Everyone living along this route, I am sure, is experiencing the same problems. So can somebody allow matatus to run?"[38] Areas primarily served by the KBS buses generated quite a few letters like this, often with pleading, melodramatic titles: "Matatus must be licensed," "We need Help," "Please Hear our Cries." Routinely, at some point in the midst of their catalog of woes, the writers would beseech the government to license matatus.

Editorials in the Kenyan dailies also favored licensing matatus. One particular editorial argued convincingly that "the matatus have taken up the challenge that nobody else is prepared to face," and argued that, "the pirates have not come forward to seek licenses for fear of being subjected to severe vehicle tests. Yet we know that in cases where some have applied for licenses, established transport companies or licensed taxi owners have always objected. The same old argument has been advanced: that more licenses would throw the KBS out of business."[39]

Matatus, the writer continued, were going to "mushroom illegally," regardless of all the objections, so it was time to regulate them—besides, the government was losing revenue by not issuing licenses. The solution seemed simple: "It would make sense to license more taxis, check them regularly for roadworthiness and thus reduce the risk of accidents resulting from defective vehicles. . . . More competition with *bona fide* transport services would reduce fares to reasonable rates. The chances of travelling by pirate would be diminished." And quite cleverly, the editorial linked housing and transport, reasoning that "a good deal of the city's house planning would be self-defeating without transport. A worker who lives nine or ten miles from his place of work and has no independent means of travel is not an asset to the city's or nation's economy."[40] Among the general public there seemed to be a consensus growing, a consensus that the Members of Parliament could not ignore.

The MPs were to come under even more pressure when the charismatic Joseph Nderi, the head of the semiphantom Matatu Vehicle Owners Association (MVOA) spoke up on behalf of matatu owners in a manner that was sure to provoke a confrontation. Writing to Ngala, he claimed that members of MVOA had pooled together enough money to purchase their own new buses to serve *wanainchi*, in accordance with the law, and that the association wanted the government to issue them licenses. The request was a not very subtle challenge to the competence and authority of the KBS and its supporters. Nderi contended that "an additional bus company should be licensed to operate in Nairobi which will assist in eliminating matatus and reduce accidents which are caused mainly by unlicensed public service vehicles."[41] For the KBS, the implications were clear: Nderi was claiming outright that the matatu owners could do better. "We have a working force of 240 people and if government grants us PSV [public service vehicle] licenses to operate in the city, we can buy more vehicles and increase our employees to 800," Nderi said, adding that the move could also help solve the perennial problem of unemployment.[42] It was, however, doubtful that the MVOA actually had the money to buy buses, and it was not interested in the larger buses anyway; they were simply making the threat because they wanted their matatu minibuses licensed for legal operation. Unsurprisingly, Minister Ngala denied the MVOA request, arguing that he did not want to encroach on the rights of the existing KBS franchise.[43] The letter, as was probably intended, forced Ngala to reveal that his true allegiance was to the KBS, not to the well-being of the city and its striving *wanainchi*.

Nderi's reaction was sudden and vehement: he publicly denounced Ngala in an article in the *Nation* as a liar for stating in Parliament that matatu operators "did not come forward and ask for registration." Matatu owners, he argued, had complied with the TLB regulations and were even ready to buy new, safer vehicles, despite the fact that some matatus were newer than buses operated by KBS; the article also stressed that "matatus were rendering useful services to *wanainchi*."[44] Nderi claimed to be especially upset that the minister seemed to be favoring foreigners over citizens, despite the fact that the "Mzee had said that transport businesses should be Africanized."[45] Again, the rhetoric of nationalism had become part of the argument. With some cunning, Nderi revealed that he had visited the Mzee at Gatundu to lobby on behalf of matatu owners and had politely solicited for their licensing, and he came away believing that Kenyatta wanted the government to consider transportation issues to be as crucial as health, education, and housing.[46] Nderi was clearly trying to claim the high ground—and playing savvy politics to get there, and, at this point, he still apparently believed that Kenyatta had been receptive. So long as matatus could be associated with education, health, and housing—and what better authority than Kenyatta's—it would be dangerous to question the legitimacy or their importance to the country.[47]

The leader of the Transport and Allied Workers Union also wrote to condemn Ngala's position: "We fully support the whole idea of licensing matatus. It must be acknowledged that they are rendering an important social service . . . hundreds of Nairobians would be greatly inconvenienced if the matatus were put off the roads abruptly." The letter concluded that "the services rendered by the KBS are inadequate."[48] Nevertheless, as the controversy over licensing matatus increased in the early 1970s, the KBS officials continued to defend their business and attack the matatus. The arguments were fairly predictable and had certainly been heard before. "To license pirate taxis," insisted A. R. Walters, chief executive of KBS, "would be a clear breach of franchise; it would be illegal."[49] He also adamantly argued that if the government licensed matatus the KBS would be put out of business. The irony of his argument seemed to escape him. He was, of course, tacitly revealing that the KBS could not survive competition with the matatus, and that the existence of the KBS depended upon the continued illegality of matatus. He might have more constructively argued that matatus actually complemented the KBS services, and then worked to avoid direct competition by securing a clear division of schedules and routes between the competing businesses. After all, Walters argued, the KBS was not just an employment service; it too provided services to its passengers and had its place in the city's transport system. In

May 1971, the company had increased the number of buses by fifty and had recently improved the benefits and working conditions of its eight hundred employees. The KBS was also serving the nation and its *wanainchi* as well as could be expected given its resources, and it might have constructively made the case that it, too, was part of the national development project.[50]

But Walters was more or less blind to the role of matatus in the city's economy and could see no reason to compromise. He was, however, eager to show the KBS's strong connections to Kenya, and he insisted on providing the history of KBS, listing the trials and tribulations the company had gone through since the early 1930s in its mission "to serve the masses come rain or shine." Some people will remember, he joked, that when the KBS was first introduced "rumor had it women who rode in the buses would render themselves barren."[51] But it had survived superstition, and it was clear Kenya and the KBS had come a long way, they had grown up together, and its officials were confident that they were doing their best to serve the citizens of Nairobi. Obviously, there was no need to license a bunch of renegade matatus poaching the bus line's passengers and imperiling the city's commuters. Matatus had no historical precedent.

———

Peter Brice, the general manager of the KBS, was as shocked as anyone when Kenyatta announced that he had released matatus from any licensing requirement. It was not clear what this meant for his company, or for the (part-ownership) agreement it had with the Nairobi City Council. Now that matatus were apparently legal, they were not only free from government control but also free to encroach upon the operation of the KBS buses. At least if matatu owners had been forced to obtain licenses they might have been held accountable to something other than market dictates, and they would have been subject to some authority that might curb their more dangerous and disruptive conduct. They might also have been required to invest time and money in their vehicles. None of this was likely now.

But to oppose the Mzee was to commit sedition, a crime punishable by years in prison, and even the possibility of torture.[52] So Brice remained mute, voicing only the most circumspect of criticism in response to questioning by journalists, though it is not hard to guess what he might have said in private to his colleagues at the KBS, or to the head of the Nairobi City Council (NCC). But even if all the optimistic claims made on behalf of the KBS were true, it was still clear that it had never been able to meet the needs of Nairobi's rapidly growing population, and it was unlikely ever to do so. Whether matatus were a suitable solution to the city's transportation needs was certainly debatable, but these illegal private taxis were the only available alternative, and that they were far more convenient was beyond question.

In addition to the inability to compete, there were other factors that contributed to the KBS's difficulties. It was ailing financially. The oil crisis of the early 1970s had hit the KBS hard, especially because the KBS fares were still controlled by the NCC, which was unwilling to increase them from 1966 levels despite the higher oil prices. Moreover, without increased fares the bus company could not expand its services to meet growing needs; in addition, the bus company was forced to pay tariffs and other taxes to the NCC and the government.[53] The freelance matatus had none of these overhead costs. It is also true that the economic stress on the KBS was a reflection of the inefficient and mismanaged services they offered. Too often service was subject to the whims of its drivers. For instance, KBS drivers were widely known to decide en route to stop proceeding if they had no passengers; sometimes, for whatever reason, the driver could just decide to call it quits even if he still had passengers on board. One passenger reported just such an experience with a KBS bus:

A bus with the name Duke Street on it pulls up and we eager *wanainchi* jump in and pay the correct amount. After a short drive, the driver pulls on the side and the conductor shouts, "*Mwisho mwisho, shuka hapa hapa ndio mwisho*" [here, here is the end of the journey, get off]. The money is not refunded, so we foot the rest of the safari. The KBS authorities ought to instruct their drivers fully or else we shall boycott the buses and go to matatus. We already have enough problems in our lives and KBS should not add to them.[54]

Despite all these weaknesses in the bus service, whether self-imposed or not, it still seemed unreasonable to the KBS that Kenyatta had exempted matatus from any form of licensing; it was not something the KBS could tolerate—or compete with. And it seemed especially odd because the matatu owners themselves had asked for licenses. On the other hand, while matatus now officially had permission to operate without regulation, Kenyatta's decree was just as inexplicable to the matatu owners, who were now compelled to operate without any kind of official recognition or legitimacy—except, of course, the Mzee's say-so. Although in some ways they may have enjoyed some advantages in working outside of government control, matatus would still be subject to suspicion and harassment, and they would have no recourse, no authority to which they could make an appeal should they find it necessary. Kenyatta's decision appeared to please no one, but for all practical purposes, he seemed indifferent to the dilemma.

An argument could be made that Kenyatta was concerned that granting licenses to matatus would end up giving the matatus too much power. If owners received licenses for their matatus they would at least implicitly be endowed with important rights that would be difficult or costly for the government to later retract.[55] A similar dynamic has played out in Africa and elsewhere with land registration, whereby a government allows people to become squatters rather than land owners: as long as residents are considered squatters, the government has the option either to grant them squatter rights or root them out; what is important is that the choice remain open.[56] Understandably, governments are reluctant to grant squatters more rights than absolutely necessary, even if they have had access to the land for many years. If, however, squatters are granted some form of title to the land it could prove costly for the government later on, especially if they need access to the land to build roads, for instance, or to give valuable land to their favorites, or to demolish the slums that were sometimes erected on the sites. In a similar way, granting licenses to matatus, Kenyatta may have believed, would make the government vulnerable to future obligations.

But this is perhaps giving Kenyatta too much credit for political foresight. It is just as likely that he simply preferred not to deal with the matter of matatus, just one of many pressing problems facing Nairobi and Kenya as a whole.[57] In the early 1970s, for instance, the Nairobi City Council (NCC) had to deal with all manner of critical issues concerning basic amenities—housing, schools, roads, transport, and sanitation—for a population that had increased dramatically during the previous decade. It was, for instance, estimated that more than 20 percent of the population of Nairobi lived as squatters in shantytowns scattered all over the city, in places like Kibera, Mathare, and Kwangware.[58] The makeshift dwellings of the new Nairobians were usually cobbled together from little more than canvas, cardboard, sticks, and paper, and of course the densely populated slums had no water, electricity, or sanitation. Conditions were so bad that the mayor of Nairobi complained that the city's rat population had reached record numbers and warned of the dangers of plague or typhoid. To discourage these ad hoc shantytowns from cropping up—really, to discourage people from moving into the city from rural areas—the Nairobi City Council would callously raze homes in the shantytowns with no concern for the welfare of the residents. (In this regard, there was very little to distinguish their actions from those of the colonial government.)[59] Every few months, smoke and flames would billow from the slums, surrounded by clusters of distressed urban refugees who sadly watched as what little they had disappeared. Still, the dispossessed could count on the city's neglect, and soon after their homes were demolished they would rebuild in the charred, debris-strewn areas left vacant by the fires, or seek new areas adjacent to the recently obliterated slums. Kenyatta and the new leaders would make public speeches to discourage more people from moving to the cities, calling them "enemies of the nation," yet people refused to listen and kept moving to the city for better opportunities.[60]

The conditions of the slums so many moved into are vividly portrayed in Meja Mwangi's novels.[61] If there is such a thing as "the greatest hits of poverty in Nairobi in the 1970s," his novels certainly top the list.[62] From *Kill Me Quick*, on the plight of young educated men unable to find honest employment, and *Going Down River Road*, which chronicles the rough-and-tumble life of Nairobi's construction workers, to *The Cockroach Dance*'s picaresque adventures of a meter reader in the squalor and violence of the slums, Mwangi shows the sad, dog-eat-dog lives of the masses in the Nairobi back streets, a landscape of unrelenting poverty and heartbreak.[63]

The Cockroach Dance can be read as an allegory of the poverty in the city. Dusman Gonzaga lives in a squalid old apartment building, the Dacca House, overrun by cockroaches so comfortable in their surroundings that they are unafraid of light. The garbage is not collected by the city council, and the single public toilet smells so bad that men and women use the building's only shower to relieve themselves. Dacca House is owned by callous slumlord Tumbo Kubwa ("fat stomach"), and occupied by an eccentric mix of garbage collectors, hawkers, conmen, witch doctors, and other marginal figures. Dusman tries to force the landlord to listen to their woes by organizing the tenants to stop paying rent, but nothing succeeds, and the scamming, corruption, prostitution, and greed persists. As does the unemployment. For many, the miserable old apartment building was a metaphor for Nairobi, a place of gnawing grievances and festering envy. Any attempt to change it was like trying to write your name on water.

Yet homelessness and unemployment were not the only problems that assailed Nairobi and the nation in the early 1970s. The OPEC oil embargo of 1973 resulted in unprecedented inflation and drastically increased the cost of living, making lives just that much more difficult for the already afflicted poor. Indeed, on the same day Kenyatta issued the matatu decree, he also pronounced another decree ending the required payment of the Graduated Personal Tax (or personal income tax) to relieve some of the pressures of the high prices.[64] These were tough economic times.[65]

Still, in order to understand why Kenyatta exempted matatus from licensing we need consider more than the nation's economic problems. Another crucial factor was Kenyatta's personalized rule, his "patron-client" form of government. Kenyatta enjoyed being sought after so that he could dispense personal wisdom. And, as previously noted, he relished the bestowing of favors upon friends, especially those from his own Kikuyu tribe, and he often did so without considering the consequences of his actions on the larger population. Over the years he had come to rely on personally handing out cash or other favors to maintain civic order or solve whatever problems presented themselves.[66] It was his way of avoiding the unavoidable. Or at least give the appearance of doing so. It was really a system of patronage through which he could buy political influence and loyalty in exchange for material benefits. And it allowed him to disregard the aftereffects—since they could be bought off too. Regrettably, the personal loyalty he procured with patronage often triggered a multitude of public problems, and his practice of personalized rule contradicted the rhetoric of Kenyanization he so avidly espoused in his speeches.

For the matatu owners, however, Kenyatta's style of personal rule had resulted in the conferring of immediate benefits. As Nderi revealed, once he and others in the Gatundu delegation had lobbied Kenyatta to legalize their business—invoking the ideals of *Harambee* and entreating the Mzee for help—Kenyatta had little choice but to offer them something.[67] Once he had decided to give a sympathetic hearing to his petitioners he could not help but act out the role of the nation's beneficent father. How could he deny those he had received favorably and who had invoked the ideals of cooperation and self-help? And once he had granted the favor, how could he not fulfill the promises he had made to the Gatundu delegation under the sacred mango tree on that lovely January morning in 1971?

Another factor that might have played a part in Kenyatta's decision was his failing health. In May 1968 the president had suffered a serious stroke while on holiday in his house in Bamburi, Mombasa, and he was weakened for many months afterward. It is possible that he might have made his surprise declaration to free matatus from regulations to deflect attention from the declining condition of his health and demonstrate his continued control. Kenyatta had always been overly concerned with an "ideology of order," which too often meant covering up problems instead of addressing them head on and working out solutions.[68] He had always insisted on compliance and obedience so that order could be maintained, and his single-party regime promoted a vision of the country in which national unity and national security were seen as inviolate. This worked for a time because he had cultivated the aura of the respected male elder, the Mzee, and people were happy to follow him.[69] Yet this aura would only work so long as people were willing to wrap themselves in its consolations. Unfortunately, the nation's persistent problems could not be willed away by a benevolent leader, whose desire for political order took precedence over justice or pragmatism, and whose decisions addressed appearances rather than the problems themselves.

A combination of all these factors—the ambition for order and his style of personal rule, the serious economic problems, the obligations surrounding the visit by the Gatundu delegation, perhaps even his health—may have affected Kenyatta's decision to allow matatus to work the city's streets without licenses. Perhaps he was simply throwing up his hands at the impossibility of a solution. As Nairobi was growing so fast, and matatus were in such high demand, it would have been very difficult—and probably impossible—to regulate them anyway. Nor could the KBS in any way counter the rapid increase in demand for the matatus that had grown along with the city.[70] A sympathetic judge might conclude that Kenyatta had no real options available and simply did what he felt was needed at the moment; a less sympathetic judge might see it as rank favoritism, or an old man's indifference.

––––––

No matter one's perspective, the situation remained complicated, and all the parties had their own agenda. The matatu owners were, of course, eager to be recognized with legal status. On the other hand, government officials were eager to point out their achievements to *wanainchi* after the first full decade of Kenya's independence, and to demonstrate that they were addressing obstinate problems—which included matatus. By the same token, President Kenyatta was determined to appeal to the importance of *Harambee* and a united Kenya under one-party rule.

Of crucial importance to the government was the new five-year development plan with its "target of 6.7 percent growth rate" for "the first half of the decade."[71] Accomplishing this rate of growth would naturally depend upon the united efforts of politicians and businessmen, farmers and wage earners. "The challenge," Kenyatta emphasized, "is not to reach the moon [as Americans had recently done] but to keep our feet on the ground, to put first things first."[72] Kenya had very basic needs to address, and Kenyatta might just as well have said that everyone should stay in the rural areas and work—this was more or less recognized to be his real message. He still considered agriculture the key to building the nation, and he encouraged people—especially high school graduates—not to move to overcrowded cities but to stay in the rural areas instead and find their livelihoods on the land. He warned Kenyans of an "uncontrolled rise in population" that, if it continued, would undermine "many of the benefits of economic expansion." Over the next decade, he proposed that Kenya become "a united nation under a resolute Government which knows what it wants and where it is going."[73]

Whether the government knew what it wanted or where it was going is debatable. Kenyatta could speak with great fervor and certainty, though his enthusiasm could sometimes appear exaggerated or misplaced, and at times he revealed a strange combination of breezy self-confidence and nervous insecurity. Although his magisterial decision to exempt matatus from licensing may have initially seemed to provide a definitive solution—at least for some—in reality it only complicated matters. It ignored the serious problems that affected the KBS, the passengers, and especially matatu owners, who would have to deal with the consequences of their new freedom for many years to come.

FIVE

"Jump In, Squeeze, Jump Out—Quickly!"

It took only about three months for the city of Nairobi, indeed for the whole country, to feel the impact of the Mzee's decree. Its effect was dramatic. In the few months after Kenyatta's pronouncement the number of matatus more than doubled, resulting in even greater congestion on Kenya's narrow, potholed roads. Now that matatus would be (presumably) legal and unregulated, nearly anyone who could put together the cash attempted to enter the business, with little regard for the meagerness of their resources or the dilapidated state of their vehicles. Once on the crowded, competitive streets they were obliged to vie for customers with existing matatus by driving wherever they could find space—in alleyways, on pedestrian paths, or through markets. Many of the new matatus had unusual, even questionable, origins. "Some of the matatus were once delivery vehicles. . . . When they are bought some are not even repainted," noted the *Standard* newspaper in an article describing the eagerness to capitalize on the opportunities made possible by the decree. "There is a matatu that used to be a Kenyan prison van, still bearing its green color," the newspaper reported, and "a Hare Krishna sect van and a post office mail van which transports people between Nairobi and Kangemi."[1]

In the months and years to come, a motley variety of vans, cars, buses, and trucks would be transformed into matatus—from decrepit Model T Fords dating from the 1930s to late-model Chevy and Dodge pickups. Some ran

89

FIGURE 8 Former police car turned into a matatu. Courtesy of the NMG, Nairobi

tolerably well, but many of them were dodgy and even dangerous. It did not seem to matter—as we can see in Ngũgĩ wa Thiong'o's *Devil on the Cross*, where the celebrated Kenyan writer depicts the matatu as if it were some wheezing, dyspeptic old man. In the novel, the owner of the vehicle has tried to disguise its age by painting it with eye-catching slogans: "IF YOU WANT GOSSIP OR RUMOURS, RIDE MWAURA'S MATATU MATAMU. YOUR WAYS ARE MY WAYS. TOO MUCH HASTE SPLITS THE YAM. CRAWL BUT ARRIVE SAFELY." But the matatu's ancient origins cannot be disguised; it is a Model T Ford, undoubtedly the "very first vehicle to have been made on Earth; its engine moaned and screamed like several hundred dented axles being ground simultaneously. The car's body shook like a reed in the wind. The whole vehicle waddled along the road like a duck up a mountain . . . The matatu gave spectators a wonderful treat. The engine would growl, then cough as if a piece of metal were stuck in its throat, then it rasped as if it had asthma." When the auto's illness eventually got the better of it, the conductor, who also served as the matatu's "public relations officer," would "open the bonnet dramatically, poke here and there, touch this wire and that, then shut the bonnet equally dramatically before returning to the steering wheel. He would gently press the accelerator with his right foot, and the engine would start groaning as if its belly were being massaged."[2]

It is clear that the matatu's fictional riders enjoyed this pantomime just as much as the novel's readers. They joked with Mwaura, the owner, asking if his matatu came from "the days of Noah"; he answered with a shake of his head, a smirk, and then he leaned back against the car and began deflecting the passengers' misgivings with a salesman's account of the car's excellent qualities:

"I tell you, honestly, there is no modern car that can match the Model T Ford construction-wise. Don't simply contrast the gleam of the bodywork. Beauty is not food. The metal from which modern cars are made—models like Peugeots, Toyotas, Canters, even Volvos and Mercedes-Benzes—fall to pieces as easily as paper soaked in rain. But not the Model T Ford, oh no! Its metal is the kind that is said to be able to drill holes in other cars. I'd rather keep this model. A stone hardened by age is never washed away by the rains . . ." People were beside themselves with laughter and whistled loudly.[3]

Antics like this were not merely the stuff of fiction. All kinds of people—not just the middle-income entrepreneurs that Kenyatta expected—were becoming matatu owners. In addition to these eager pitchmen driving old jalopies and cajoling their customers were government ministers, prominent businessmen, and other well-heeled Kenyans eager to take advantage of the new liberties granted matatu owners.[4] Even investors from the neighboring countries of Ethiopia and Somalia flocked to cities like Nairobi and Mombasa to set up matatu businesses.[5] Some were rumored to have made their money looting banks during the Ethiopian crisis of 1974.[6] With little regard for the would-be moguls in their Model Ts, the wealthier investors purchased better vehicles and bullied their way into the matatu industry. Evidently, these prosperous speculators found it too hard to forego the prospect of running a profitable business without government oversight.

One such affluent investor was John Kipkurgat, the Kenyan runner and gold medalist in the 1974 Commonwealth Games in New Zealand. In a lengthy feature article in the *Standard* newspaper he is pictured standing next to a new Chevy pickup. Strong, lean, and bright-eyed, Kipkurgat smiles proudly as he tells the reporter that he is planning to turn his vehicle into a matatu: "There is money in the industry," he claims.[7] His optimism was warranted. The shiny new vehicle he stands next to is a tangible and powerful symbol of his success, much more so than his symbolic gold medal. Kipkurgat was in many ways the ideal new matatu owner, the perfect *mwanainchi*; he was a popular figure who had achieved his success legitimately, with his own sweat, and who was working hard to start up his own enterprise, in contrast to the affluent investors who had elbowed their way into the industry to make themselves even richer.

Still, others followed the same path as Kipkurgat. Despite the competition from the moneyed ministers and businessmen, owning a matatu was possible for more than the prosperous urban investor. In the rural areas the local farmers were also turning their pickup vans into matatus to earn a few shillings conveying passengers from village to village or into the city—though it was not unusual to end up sharing the cabin with livestock or fowl. Jane Njeri, who lived in Kiambu, a rural area not far from Nairobi, remembered her commute from the countryside with a sense of lingering exasperation: "You would be traveling in a vehicle and when it stopped, the farmer entered with his goats or chickens or animal feed," and yet, "everybody in the car moved around and squeezed in to create space for the animals. Traveling in a matatu was not always an enjoyable experience."[8] Another countryside resident, Mathew Ogoma, recalled the discomforts of matatu travel, though he was a little less inclined to understatement: "passengers were squeezed together all the time," and the conductors would rudely

FIGURE 9 A matatu in the rural areas, 1974. Courtesy of the NMG, Nairobi

"tell passenger[s] to sit on someone else's knee for a distance until another passenger got off. Can you imagine?" He shook his head, stupefied at the memory. Even worse than the crowding was the heat and lack of air—"The vehicles had few windows so passengers ended up not having enough air. They suffocated and sometimes even vomited."[9]

———

All the discomfort aside, the matatu business was "booming," according to newspaper accounts, and the changes taking place were mostly beneficial—more matatus on the roads meant more access to transportation and more opportunity for Nairobi's new citizens.[10] Unfortunately, many of these benefits were somewhat intangible and were obscured by the more obvious realities of the increased traffic and the competition. As the number of matatus multiplied, their drivers became more reckless and irresponsible as they responded to the pressures of the marketplace—"they would drive anywhere, to backyards, back roads, and even drive on the grass, anywhere they can possibly find passengers to carry."[11]

The competitive pressure also meant that their jobs were less than secure since wealthy owners did not hesitate to dismiss drivers who had failed to collect a sufficient daily profit. Quotas had to be met, or else. Nor were the drivers themselves particularly reputable since they would often, out of necessity, opt to hire conductors who were willing to do just about anything to solicit—such as acting like sideshow promoters to solicit fares, or like strong-armed thugs when called upon to protect against thieves or pickpockets.[12] In the parking lots they occasionally resorted to puncturing the tires of rival matatus.[13] On the streets the behavior of the drivers and touts could border on the anarchic. Drivers frequently pulled away from the roadside while passengers were still boarding so that they could race ahead of competing matatus to get first crack at the riders at the next stop.[14] Conductors would also overload already full vehicles by cramming passengers in until they could barely breathe, insisting that they *kaa kibiashara* (squeeze in more tightly) so that more profit could be made, and the passengers who wanted to exit would be practically tossed out of the moving matatu, with no regard for safety, because drivers refused to come to a full stop—the crews even had the temerity to shout at the passengers, *"Ruka kama sitima!"* (jump out at the speed of electricity).[15] Nevertheless, most of the passengers put up with this heedless behavior because they had no choice; they needed the service, and in all likelihood they shared with the owners a sense that the pursuit of profit was necessary and difficult. They were aware that drivers' and conductors' working conditions—the eighteen-hour days, the seven-day weeks, and for those with families, the scant amount of time spent at home. And many working on the matatus were, in effect, driving under the influence since they habitually chewed *khat* or *miraa*, an addictive tobacco-like leaf with an amphetamine effect. It was the only way they could stay alert during their overlong shifts.[16]

Much of the recklessness of matatu drivers was a result of the unfavorable pay arrangements between the matatu owners and the drivers and conductors they hired. The owner's demands that their driver and conductor deliver a fixed amount of money from the daily proceeds typically left drivers and conductors with little to divide between themselves once their obligations were met. Many could barely make enough to support themselves. In the mid-1970s, for instance, an owner of a small pickup usually demanded about 120 shillings per day; the driver would be left with about 15 shillings to take home, and the conductor with about 5 to 10 shillings. This income was just enough to feed a family of four for a day, though to earn this meager living the drivers and conductors found it necessary to put in long hours and behave unscrupulously, heedless of their safety or that of the passengers.[17]

Shiva Naipaul captures some of these experiences in his book *North of South: An African Journey*. Following in the footsteps of his famous brother, the writer V. S. Naipaul, Shiva took a long trip through East Africa in the mid-1970s.[18] Apparently determined to "rough it" in a rural area not far from Nairobi, he traveled by matatu—"an ancient Peugeot station wagon" with the words "LOVE YOU BABY" splashed across its rear window in "garish lettering." He recounts the ride he made with his fourteen fellow passengers:

We lurched out of the bus station, horn blaring, pedestrians scattering. I was on my way to the Highlands.

We plunged into the maze of dirt alleys dissecting the shanty colony that fringed the town. I say "alleys"—but that is an exaggeration: there was nothing to indicate that they were anything of the sort. Much of our course took us through what looked like people's backyards—and, were, I suspect, exactly that. Startled goats, chickens, and children fled before us. We splashed through pools of muddy water, inches away from doorways. The driver hunched vengefully over the steering wheel, sounding his horn without cessation. This was not meant as warning to the unwary: it was a joyous proclamation of his daredevilry. More than once the car, in negotiating the deeper pools of water, threatened to become bogged down in mire. No one, however, seemed in the least worried. On the contrary. They were enjoying themselves, laughing and waving at the astonished people who watched from their hovels. I tried not to think of the small item in that morning's paper, which had quietly reported the matatu crash in which fifteen people had been seriously injured.

We arrived, finally, on the tarmac road. This, if anything, made matters worse. The Peugeot lurched and shuddered as the driver put his foot down on the accelerator. Each car we passed raised a cheer from my fellow passengers. I closed my eyes as, tires screeching, we took a blind corner, swerving across into the right-hand lane. This too raised a cheer. Did death mean nothing to them? They had slipped beyond my imaginative reach.[19]

Naipaul's account might be dismissed by a skeptic as a sensationalized account of a frightened tourist, unaccustomed to traveling in a developing country and bent upon dramatizing his exotic experience. But my conversations with people who had been passengers in the years after deregulation indicate that matatus were truly out of control.[20] Naipaul's report was no exaggeration. Reckless driving was the norm in the 1970s and early 1980s—speeding in particular, but also driving on sidewalks or on the wrong side of the road, overtaking on blind corners, and overlapping, and it was often cheered on by the passengers, who acted as though they were on an amusement park ride. Of course, none of this behavior lent itself to the safety of anyone on board or in the way, and by the late 1970s accidents with injuries involving matatus had increased by 30 percent.[21] But who was to stop it? There was not a sufficient police force, and no one else had the authority to administer or regulate the fledging industry. Whether or not Kenyatta had intended it, his decree had absolved the government of responsibility, allowing the new owners to make as much profit as possible, and abandoning the matatu workers to eke out their scant livings in dangerous and endangering jobs.

"This time in the 1970s was the birth of bad behavior," John Njenga told me when I asked him about the effects of Kenyatta's decree.[22]

"So were matatus different before Kenyatta's decree?"

"Yes, the owners were more real, for you knew them well; they were nice people and you worked with them. But at that time in the 1970s, matatu owners came from all over the place and all they wanted was to make money and they acted like thugs," Njenga replied, "and that reputation still stays with matatu people up to now."[23]

This reputation for shameless behavior still prevails among those who remember the matatu industry of the 1970s, and most believe it originated when Kenyatta passed the decree to deregulate matatus.[24] Deregulation had no doubt opened up the industry to new, less principled investors and led to its unprecedented growth, but as the industry expanded—and with nothing to check it—everyone involved was pressured to become less scrupulous. As owners began demanding more profits, drivers and conductors were forced into ever more extreme measures to attract and transport passengers. And everyone noticed— matatus parked anywhere they pleased, even in the middle of the road; they took over public parking lots; routinely entered through exits and exited through the entrances; and they imperiled everyone on the streets along with the passengers inside. In one dramatic instance, a matatu parked in the middle of the road in the city center caused a private car to swerve and crash into a deserted office (the matatu then allegedly left the scene of the accident).[25]

Negligence like this elicited an inexhaustible flow of complaints about matatus during the 1970s and early 1980s, all of which advocated for the tightening of matatu laws.[26] I read Njenga a letter I had clipped from a newspaper from 1974, complaining about matatus refusing to line up on a first-come, first-served basis. "On Sunday," the letter began, "I was escorting a guest, and as we approached the parking lot, two *manambas* [touts] snatched from us the boxes we were carrying, arguing that they knew where we were going. One even went to the extent of finalizing our destination and concluding that we were his customers. A policeman was watching and said to us, 'This is life in Nairobi.'"[27] Frustrated by this kind of aggressive practice, the letter writer suggested that matatu operators "contribute a little" and establish a booking office rather than use touts.[28] As reasonable as the suggestion might have seemed, it was unlikely to happen: increased competition meant that conductors needed the touts to round up passengers at the major bus stops. Without the touts fishing for passengers many of the drivers and conductors would not have been able to make their payments to the owners; and since they were paid on commission, the touts were forced to scramble desperately for as many passengers as they could round up. The result was often chaos. The touts, who always seemed underfed and frantic, haunted the lots "dressed in oversized, dirty clothes" while "calling on passengers and harassing them." If they were loud and lucky enough, they might be able to coerce enough victims onto their matatu, for which they would usually receive a shilling. If you complained about their conduct, the touts would snidely suggest that you "buy your own car or use KBS buses"; they knew matatus had a monopoly on the market.[29]

Although it was clear that touts were more or less allowed to stalk potential passengers—and abuse them—without suffering any reprisals, there still remained questions about the passengers' role in shaping the matatu workers' behavior. Why would anyone voluntarily squeeze into an overcrowded matatu and put their life at risk when the next available matatu was bound to arrive within a few minutes?[30] Surely, if the competition for passengers was so frenzied, they should have been able to ask for and get better behavior from the drivers and touts. Yet when I questioned my interviewees about this they looked surprised. For them the answer seemed obvious:

"In those days," Mary Njuguna told me, "one usually received a hearty welcome from a *manamba* [tout], who would yell out something like, '*Kazeenjootwende, garitwazi!*' [Hey, man, come on; let's go; the vehicle is empty]. A passenger would enter the vehicle, and as soon as he or she was inside the car, the tout would stand right behind them preventing their escape. The tout would start telling the fellow next to the newly arrived passenger to '*Kaa square, songa, gari badoo jaa!*' [Squeeze in man, the car is not yet full]. More people would enter the vehicle, and the tout would still be shouting for more. Once he felt that no more passengers were willing to enter his matatu, he would bang loudly on the side of the matatu and yell, '*Fire!*' [let's go], and off they'd go! And that is how the matatu people treated us; they treated us just like we were children."[31]

I asked if passengers were so routinely caught off guard and tricked into believing there was enough space in the matatu. Njuguna nodded affirmatively.

I was also curious about the experience of riding in the speeding vehicles. Angry at being squeezed into already full vehicles, passengers then had to anxiously endure the excessive speeds. Compacted inside a matatu, barely able to see or breathe, the passengers could still sense the speed as the matatu pitched one way and another when it rounded corners or bounced over potholes. Everything amplified their vulnerability.

"You quietly said a prayer," one passenger told me.[32]

"You asked God to bless you," another answered.[33]

"You prayed to God," said another.[34]

Of course, most of their matatu trips ended successfully, though it seems as though few atheists were allowed aboard. While God may have helped deliver them to their destinations, for many the matatu ride was inevitably considered a sort of prolonged purgatory. Nearly everyone I spoke with revealed that they were more likely than not to have endured some kind of distressing incident as they fretted over the possibility of an accident—a disagreement over the fares or seating arrangements, a dispute among the passengers themselves, a theft, or even on occasion a knife attack.[35]

The likelihood of some kind of crime or disagreement triggered strong reactions among the passengers. "Anger boiled in my stomach," complained one female passenger.[36]

"I felt it in my gut," said another who had been involved in a minor matatu accident.[37]

Memories of their sense of trepidation, or even the anger, aboard a matatu could still be visceral. The noise of the engine and the yelling of touts, the heat, the pungent smell of a crowded cabin, the lurching and shaking, the sudden turns, the rapid glimpses of the city speeding by, and thoughts of the lurid accounts of past accidents, all tended to provoke unease among the passengers. The stimulations aboard a moving matatu could generate feelings of anxiety, or bodily distress, particularly vestibular disorders—sensations of vertigo and dizziness, or imbalance and spatial disorientation. Unfortunately, in a speeding matatu, the flight response usually prompted by heightened levels of adrenaline was inevitably thwarted.[38] There was no escape; once you had submitted to a matatu trip, you were more or less helpless.

Nevertheless, when I asked those who had been passengers at the time whether they remembered being in constant fear whenever they entered a matatu, they recalled their experiences with the pride of survivors. They were not reluctant to acknowledge their anxieties, but they were also adamant that their anxiety had forced them to become more vigilant. They had learned to avoid dangerous situations—particularly matatus they perceived to be dangerous.[39] All the qualms they suffered had, paradoxically, ended up making them more self-assured and self-reliant. Experience had made them streetwise, and they were quick to assure me that riding matatus had provided them with the confidence necessary to move freely about the city. In many ways, then, the near constant apprehension of riding in a matatu rewarded passengers with a practical knowledge that helped them appreciate the collective social, cultural, and political space of Nairobi. Matatus were, in many ways, a rite of passage, and riding them taught one how to live in the city, to become more vigilant, attentive citizens adapted to the exigencies of the new urban environment.[40]

────────

While passengers may have been doing their best to adjust to the precipitous increase in the number of matatus, as well as the rowdy workers and dangerous travel conditions, the owners were not doing nearly as well. Many of the owners had become so unprincipled and antagonistic that they had managed to jeopardize their own chances of survival. The current state of affairs was unsustainable, and it was becoming clear that some sort of backlash was looming, from the government if not from the passengers themselves. The more thoughtful owners were even reconsidering the need for government regulation in the industry. It made sense, given the explosion in the numbers of matatus and the unregulated competition, along with the antisocial behavior of their own workers.[41] "Lack of regulation was not a good thing for business," recalled Innocent Kamau, a matatu owner in the 1970s. "See, not all the people in the industry were good people and sometimes tried to cheat you, so you needed the government to help out, but they were not doing so; they left us just like that," and he waved his fingers sideways, shook his head, and pressed his lips together in disgust.[42]

Kamau was not alone. Many of the people who had bought matatus in the 1970s felt that the industry needed to be controlled—though, it must be granted that they were saying so in hindsight. By and large, matatu owners who had vehicles in good mechanical condition wanted defective vehicles off the roads (no doubt for safety reasons; not because they wanted to expand their business and profits). They also wanted some controls placed upon the touts' aggressive and rude conduct, and death-defying stunts of their drivers, so that passengers might become more trusting and less combative. It was gradually becoming apparent to the more responsible owners that good vehicles and good behavior were better for business.

An even more pressing issue for owners was the requirement that all matatu owners be made to purchase insurance for their vehicles, to cover damage to third-party vehicles or injury to passengers.[43] Too often insurance requirements were simply ignored by owners, and, so long as the industry remained unregulated, it was nearly impossible to determine adequately who did and did not carry the necessary insurance. What is more, the increased number of vehicles on the streets meant more accidents, and this, along with the poor mechanical condition of many vehicles and the treacherous state of Kenyan roads, had forced insurance companies to increase premiums sharply. The situation was so bad that by the mid-1970s only 30 percent of matatu owners could afford insurance, a number that was not likely to improve since the increasing number of uninsured vehicles made the costs of insuring a vehicle that much higher.[44] The state of affairs had simply become untenable for the more responsible owners.

The uninsured vehicles did not go completely unnoticed by the authorities. The police began setting up checkpoints to stop matatu drivers and check their insurance papers, but this unfortunately led to more widespread bribery and corruption. When I spoke with Peter Chege, one of the occasionally uninsured drivers in the 1970s, he told me that he and the other drivers "wasted all our money on the police." When the police stopped him, rightly suspecting that his car was not insured, he knew immediately he would be required to grease some palms. First, he told me, the police would run through a quick safety check—"'Switch off all lights, depress your brakes, put on your tail lights, dip your lights, full lights, side lights'—then they would pause and ask for my insurance card." When Chege admitted that he did not have the insurance, they would demand his driver's license. "You then handed him the license and put a ten bob note [ten shillings] in the middle of the license. He looked at it, took the money, and waved you off."[45] This was common practice, and Chege traced the increasing reliance on bribery by the police back to Kenyatta's decree—"We were just at the mercy of the decree," he said. Although it may have seemed a goodwill gesture from the president at the time, the consequences of the decree had left the matatu owners defenseless, especially in cases like Chege's where the police were corrupt. They were left with no recourse.

It was also during this period that MVOA gained ground, another sign that total deregulation was not working and that some authority needed to step up and help control the industry. The association had been in existence since the late 1960s, but the government had never recognized it as a legal body. Before the MVOA, matatu owners' organizations had consisted of small informal groups that managed terminals and scheduled daily routes for their members. As numbers increased, the group leaders decided to unite to form a stronger, more cohesive lobbying group to deal with the chaos arising from deregulation. Joseph Nderi became the unofficial chairman of the group. Under his leadership, the association gradually took over the role of organizing and representing matatus, although it remained an unregistered, quasi-legal entity that answered only to itself. MVOA branches were opened in the major cities, with the expectation that new matatu own-ers would have to apply to the MVOA to be assigned a route. Owners were also obliged to contribute a small fee every month for mainte-nance of the matatu parking stations and to pay the MVOA officials.

_____

Despite help from organizations like the MVOA, small-time owners like Chege were finding it difficult to stay in business. Soon after Kenyatta's death in August 1978, the wealthy matatu owners put pressure on Ken-yatta's successor, Daniel Moi, to streamline the industry and place re-strictions on who could and could not operate a matatu. With Kenyans still in mourning, he dared not nullify the decree immediately, but as soon as he deemed it prudent—about five months after Kenyatta's demise—he began chipping away at the founding father's decree. The readiest solution was to target the vehicles rather than the drivers, and so on January 24, 1979, Moi authorized police to identify vehicles in poor mechanical condition so that they could be marked as ineligible for a license from TLB. On the first day alone at least four hundred matatus in the Nairobi area were declared unroadworthy. The cited ve-hicles had to be repaired and obtain certificates from the inspection center before they could operate on the roads again.[46] In many cases the inspections were justified (some of the vehicles detained had no brakes, no horns or headlights, and still had been allowed to operate under Kenyatta's decree). The crackdown continued for about a week, giving rise to speculation that the government was determined to re-move matatus from the roads altogether, and some people began to think that the government had gone too far.[47] However, Moi parried these fears by proclaiming that "matatus are here to stay," and that "the swoop exercise is only aimed at ensuring public safety."[48]

He may well have meant it at the time, but a little over a month later, on February 8, 1979, Moi ordered a further round of matatu in-spections. This time the police impounded vehicles without insurance, along with those guilty of overloading. Again, many of the matatus detained proved unroadworthy, but this time owners began abandon-ing their malfunctioning matatus at roadsides rather than pay the sentenced fines.[49] The resulting decrease in the number of available matatus inevitably compounded the problem of transportation in Nai-robi, and as always, buses were scarce and could in no way handle the increased demand. Gradually the city streets descended into chaos. The morning rush hours in the working-class suburbs of Eastlands and Kibera resembled a battlefield as schoolchildren and workers crowded the bus stops and pushed their way onto the infrequent buses—in some cases, people lunged onto the buses before they had come to a stop.[50] Others, in an attempt to beat the crowds and secure their place, boarded a bus going in the direction opposite their destination, even if it meant paying again when the bus reached the end of the line and turned around.[51]

Predictably, the matatus still on the roads tried to cash in on the chaos by overcharging their passengers, and when passengers complained about being fleeced, the conductors simply answered that they must *"fata nyayo"* (follow the footsteps), a notoriously manipulative mantra used by Moi to compel citizens into following his wishes.[52] As frustrations began to mount, people started turning against matatus: "If this situation continues," one matatu passenger protested, "I may forego to buy a house I was planning to buy and buy a car instead."[53] Another commuter who was late arriving home to his family grumbled that he "was as sober as a nun, but not even my wife could believe why I was late. They all thought I had gone in for 'a cold one as usual.'"[54]

The changes that Moi had imposed upon matatus were, however, short-lived. Less than two months after the first crackdown the impounded matatus were back on the roads again, and newspapers were again reporting accidents involving matatus. Reluctantly, Moi acknowledged the failure (particularly the failure of the KBS) and ordered a detailed transport analysis by Nairobi City Council (NCC), putting an engineer from the council, Peter Mbau, in charge. He submitted his report on May 4, 1979; it found that KBS was far from adequate and that if the company could not increase the number of buses and improve services, the NCC should consider not renewing its contract, due to expire in 1985. With regard to matatus, the report acknowledged their indispensability but nevertheless called for urgent measures to improve their quality, roadworthiness, and safety standards. The report also welcomed an offer by the Automobile Association of Kenya to provide matatu vehicle inspection services and an advanced driving test for matatu drivers. It even suggested that the government might begin requiring matatu owners to get Public Service Vehicle (PSV) licenses for their matatus, a requirement that would directly overturn Kenyatta's 1973 decree. Finally, the report strongly advised that matatu owners form organizations to oversee members and to ensure appropriate self-regulation.[55]

Until the report came out, KBS officials had remained silent on Kenyatta's decree. But now that the new government was apparently willing to reconsider the decree, they decided it was time to speak out.

They were not pleased with the recognition given matatus: "What we say is that if this competition which is undoubtedly one-sided and in parts unfair is allowed to continue, the organized and formal transport that cities of stature like Nairobi and Mombasa must have and deserve will be eroded"—so wrote J. C. Clymo, chief executive for KBS, to the editor of the *Weekly Review*, then Nairobi's leading weekly paper.[56] "It cannot be sensible," he continued, "to allow unregulated competition from a form of transport which in many cases is operated without proper regards to the rights of other road users and often with danger to life and limb."[57] When Clymo was asked, in a later interview, if matatus flourished because the KBS was inadequate, he was carefully ambiguous: "This is a case of which comes first—the chicken or the egg."[58] Whether the KBS was the chicken or the egg was left for the reader to decide, though in either case he did not seem to appreciate the fact that without the chicken there would be no egg, and vice versa. What his statement did make clear, however, was that the conflict between the KBS and matatus would not be easily resolved.

Clymo had much more to say in the interview and eagerly took the opportunity to complain about almost everything to do with nation's roads and the traffic on them: he complained about the abysmal state of the city's streets and demanded that the government repair them; he objected to the glorifying of car racing in Kenyan culture (referring to the famous Kenya Safari Rally that occurs every Easter holiday); he asked why matatus were blamed for reckless driving when the whole "country glorifies motor racing as a manly sport"; and he even found fault with the behavior of commuters on his own buses—"Commuters," he said, "should take the nearest available seat after boarding the bus. If the seats are taken, they should move forward to make room for people behind. . . . You cannot expect the conductor to be in good humor if he has to constantly be saying, '*tafadhali songa mbele*' [please move forward and create space for others]."[59]

It was probably true that Clymo and the other KBS officials had tried in good faith to provide adequate transportation for Nairobians, and they had increased the number of buses operating in the suburban routes as the city grew and as more people settled in satellite towns. Despite their best efforts, however, matatus had come to dominate transportation in these areas outside the original spatial boundaries of the city because of their numbers, and also because they could avoid direct surveillance by the city police. And when challenged, the matatu owners were not afraid to assert their rights. For instance, they begrudged the fact the KBS buses were permitted to carry standing passengers and could therefore charge lower fares than the matatu. Even worse, when the KBS expanded its service into the suburbs, matatu owners came to view the expansion as a direct encroachment upon the matatus' territory, and their resentment was compounded by the fact that the KBS enjoyed an exclusive franchise to operate within the city. In strictly legal terms, the city was theirs, and matatu owners knew they operated freely only due to the lingering reverence granted to them by the former president. Unsurprisingly, the matatu owners felt that the NCC was favoring the KBS.

That matatus still operated in a legal limbo was underlined when the owners complained about the KBS to the Trade and Licensing Board (TLB). They were brusquely told that they had no right to present their grievances since matatus were neither licensed nor licensable because the TLB had no jurisdiction over them; after all, the TLB had no choice but to accept the ruling of the presidential decree.[60] It was clearer than ever that the decree had become a double-edged sword for the matatu owners—and not one that they were wielding. Perhaps now, thought the MVOA, it might be time to give in a little, and take comfort in the fact that the Nairobi City Council had acknowledged matatus as indispensable to the city. Now that the owners knew they would not be summarily removed from the streets and could continue operating, they could afford to surrender some of the freedoms they had enjoyed under Kenyatta's decree. It might ultimately be to their advantage.[61]

In response, the MVOA hired a lawyer to argue in court that it was not the fault of matatu owners that their vehicles were not licensed, and that many owners really wanted the TLB to legitimize their businesses; he also hoped they would finally be granted licenses so that they could demonstrate to the government, and to the public, that their vehicles actually were in sound mechanical condition, that they had made all the necessary repairs. In an added effort at persuasion, the MVOA lawyer tried to smear the KBS by claiming its officials were out to enrich themselves at the expense of poor *wanainchi* (citizens), and he alleged that the officials invested the money they had earned in Kenya in European businesses.[62] However, the lawyer's brazen invocation of nationalism failed this time, in part because KBS officials reminded the court that they had reduced bus fares in order to serve people better.[63] Neither side prevailed and the case was eventually dropped, and the existing—and unsatisfactory—transportation arrangements remained in place.

Likewise, the police crackdowns on matatus remained in place. For instance, on October 12, 1980, several matatu drivers were arrested for flagrant disregard of traffic rules. Not long after the arrest, a senior police spokesman told the press that he had ordered the suppression of matatus because of many recent deaths in accidents involving matatus.[64] The continued crackdowns did not go over well. Angry matatu operators in Nairobi and outlying areas threatened to take matters into their own hands by organizing protests and suspending services for a week. They refused to ignore—or allow others to ignore—their alleged "victimization" by traffic police: "We shall be calling for a mass withdrawal of all matatus from the roads sometime next week. It is clear wanainchi will be the sufferers," Joseph Nderi (spokesman for matatu owners) told the daily newspapers.[65] As tensions continued to mount, and with neither side willing to back down, Moi decided to step in. In a nationwide tour from Mombasa to Kisumu on October 15, 1980, he warned matatu drivers at every stop along the way that matatus would be taken off the roads if they continued driving carelessly and endangering lives. It was a significant trip, with stops at seven different towns and extensive coverage by the media, which meant that Moi's instructions to the police to watch matatus closely would not go unheeded. He also made it clear that the owners' artful appeal to wanainchi was not going to achieve its desired effect: "Greed for money," he warned them, "can not be made more important than human life."[66]

The not-so-veiled threats in Moi's speeches served their purpose. The matatu operators were alarmed. After Moi's national tour, Nderi hurriedly called a meeting of matatu owners to rally the troops. He reiterated the matatu owners' pledge of unity, and their determination to prevent police harassment and to provide better services for their customers, but he also made it clear that he wanted the government to recognize police corruption, including the taking of bribes and the unreasonable demands for often unaffordable vehicle repairs. Nderi also argued that, unlike the KBS, the matatus had no fixed parking stations and this was a major contribution to the chaos in the city.[67]

Still, despite the indomitable front they presented to themselves and the public, Nderi and the MVOA also made it clear that they were willing to make some concessions. He urged matatu operators "to ensure their vehicles' doors were closed when the matatu were moving," and for the sake of further safety, "they should not stop anywhere at any time or change lanes without giving signals." In fact, the MVOA offered to cooperate with the police and report irresponsible matatu drivers and owners to the appropriate authorities.[68] Nderi also stressed the need to insure vehicles and appealed to all matatu owners to join MVOA.[69] The association had also, in a more tangible action, rented a large space east of the city center where matatus could park and where they could pick up and drop off passengers. It was a practical measure and was intended, in part, to make the matatu industry a more "streamlined and effective transport system to supplement the bus service," but it also was intended as a sincere demonstration of their willingness to reform. Finally, and perhaps most significantly, Nderi urged President Moi to register MVOA as a legal organization so that it could help regulate matatus. All the MVOA's proposed changes—and it should be noted they had more to do with self-regulation than government regulation—were intended as gestures of respect for President Kenyatta's decree.

Moi eventually relented and on July 7, 1982, he authorized the MVOA as a legal organization, proclaiming that the association should serve as a self-regulatory body and would help establish "peace and discipline to the often chaotic public transport sector by educating and advising all the matatu community and general public."[70] Nderi was elected as the legal national chairman, and the association, based in Nairobi, quickly made an impact on the national scene. About a year after its authorization, the MVOA began publishing *Matatu: The Official Journal of MVOA*, printed by the Kenya Times Limited (the first issue appeared in June 1983). *Matatu* was circulated nationwide, and the first issue coincided with the twentieth anniversary of Kenya's independence. Its editor, Muiru Mugo, pronounced excitedly "that the *Matatu* journal will act as a forum of communication; a meeting place and a place to exchange views and ideas." He also hoped that the journal would change the matatus' "tarnished" reputation. "Matatu men," Mugo wrote optimistically, "have been the subject of scourge, but have survived persecution and have been working with traffic police and relevant authorities to improve their tarnished image."[71]

The journal did fairly well at first, presenting reports from the various branches and articles about driving courses, or advice on car insurance and first aid instruction; it also provided a matatu chart of bus stops that proved a useful source of information for both matatu owners and passengers. Unfortunately, the association soon ran out of funds for the journal and stopped putting it out. Still, the MVOA carried on, acting—or at least trying to act—as a responsible parent guiding its children. It tried to urge its members to behave responsibly and discipline them when they failed, and the MVOA also hoped to become a safe haven for its members, protecting them from exploitation by insurance companies and defending them from extortion by traffic police.[72]

Although its efforts were admirable it soon became evident that the industry had become too large and unruly for the MVOA to handle alone. And it could do nothing to control the police. It was not long before the police resumed impounding vehicles and demanding bribes.[73] This of course evoked a reaction on the part of the matatu operators; their efforts at reform having been so manifestly scorned, they soon became even more unmanageable than they had been before the MVOA had been authorized.[74] Many of the owners rebelled by reverting to their former crimes—they failed to pay for insurance, continued to overload their vehicles and verbally abuse passengers, and they kept on exacting higher fares from passengers when it rained. If anyone complained they were rudely shouted down.[75] Inevitably grievances began mounting once again, as did the number of serious traffic accidents: "Matatu crashes into a bedroom, killing two children," "Six killed in a matatu crash," "13 killed in a horror matatu crash," and so on.[76] The police response was to intensify their crackdown by setting up more checkpoints to inspect vehicles and issue fines (or collect bribes). So the cycle was again in place—the police clamped down on noncompliant vehicles and defiant drivers, and the drivers and touts, made more desperate than ever, began cutting even more corners. Chaos had arisen again—so much so that, eventually, the exasperated owners felt the only exploit capable of ending this vicious cycle of defiance and reprisal was to bring everything to a halt. And this is exactly what the operators did: they organized a strike and brought the economy of the city to a standstill.

None of the parties involved had wanted or anticipated this kind of impasse, neither the owners nor the government, and least of all the city's commuters. The disillusionment was palpable. Back in 1973 almost everyone had expressed confidence in the supposed virtues of Kenyatta's decree—or at least pretended to. The editor of the *Standard*, for instance, had written with enthusiasm about the recognition of matatus and their exemption from licensing, but now, in retrospect, his naïveté is more striking than his forthright optimism. Now that the Mzee's decree is in effect, he writes, "The one source of corruption and ill will between police and members of the public will disappear overnight. . . . The decree is a realistic appraisal of the transport problems in the country. . . . Moreover, the burden of checking the pirate taxis was distracting the police from more important duties. And everybody will be happier all around."[77] It is hard to look back on these predictions without a sense of pathos, particularly the prediction about the elimination of bribery. Not only had it failed to disappear, it had become an even more pervasive problem in the decade following Kenyatta's decree—as had the ill will. No one was happier. But the editor was right about one thing. For better or worse, a lot more people were now involved in the matatu business: "The decree will also inject an element of competition in the transport business. Without the TLB restrictions there will be an increase in the number of vehicles available to the public. . . . It can also be expected that many enterprising individuals will use the new freedom to start their own transport business and this will be important on many rural routes that do not have adequate transport."[78] This prediction turned out to be entirely accurate. Many more operators had entered the business, and the countryside was better served, even if it had become plainly evident that more matatus meant more problems. But perhaps most important in his easy forecast of the industry's growth was one brief, instructive remark that was destined to be proven true—and sadly so. Buried in the editor's piece was the succinct, incisive statement that "laws if not enforced will discredit the system."[79] The editor's warning was astute, though it is hard not to find irony in the fact that there were really few, if any, laws to be enforced; Kenyatta's decree had ensured this. But whether because of the lack of laws, or the lack of enforcement, by the early 1980s the system *had* become discredited. Kenyatta's "goodwill gesture" had created havoc, and the deregulation he initiated had ended up pitting the matatus against the KBS, the passengers against operators, the established operators against poor upstarts, and all of them against the police. Overseeing the mayhem was a paralyzed government that seemed able to do nothing. But perhaps there was not much that could be done: a favor was a favor, especially when granted by the Mzee.[80] And yet, by the early 1980s, it seemed that the whole city had been punished by the unintended consequences of Kenyatta's good deed.

PART FOUR

Government Regulation, 1984–88

SIX

The Matatu Bill of 1984

Information surrounding the circumstances of the Matatu Bill's passage—how it was discussed in Parliament, who said what and why, and the public's initial reaction to it—simply does not exist, despite the fact that it decisively overturned Kenyatta's deregulation decree of 1973. There are reasons for this obscurity. First and foremost, President Moi wanted the bill passed, so it crept through Parliament without receiving any formal debate and without the public's awareness. Members of the press had never been officially informed of its existence so they had little idea what was happening, and even if they did, they would not have been permitted to write about it openly. The few who dared to address the bill in print had to proceed with caution so as not to offend Moi, so most journalists simply chose not to report on its passage. Hence reaction to the bill was oddly muted.[1] The Parliament voted unanimously to pass the bill without any real debate, without any input from the public, and without having to address any objections that adverse press might have provoked—and the bill slipped quietly into law without much fanfare, or much explanation. It went into effect only a month after passage, in September 1984.[2]

The contents of the Matatu Bill were straightforward. It ordered the matatu industry to comply with fundamental safeguards: drivers had to be over twenty-four years of age and have held a driver's license for at least four years; they also had to obtain a Public Service Vehicle (PSV) license, purchase third-party insurance, and make sure their vehicles could pass an annual inspection. The bill also limited the number of passengers allowed in each vehicle.[3] Although these seemed to be reasonable measures, and were more than likely to reduce the number of matatu accidents, several questions remained as to the nature of the bill's passage: why had there been no open discussion? Why had the bill been passed in such secrecy? And why had the public been kept in the dark concerning a bill that addressed the industry's acknowledged problems?

To answer these questions, we need to understand the uncertain state of affairs in Moi's regime in the early 1980s. To begin with, the government had become acutely anxious and insecure after having survived an attempted coup in 1982. The coup attempt had nearly toppled Moi, and in the succeeding years he tried to paper over the cracks revealed in his government by exerting his power over Parliament, the army, and the police. To compensate for the government's perceived weakness, and to demonstrate that Moi was securely in control of the country, the regime moved swiftly to centralize—and personalize—his power by amending the constitution in a way that effectively transformed the country into a single-party state. Of course his party, KANU, was given sole legitimacy.[4] In another move to consolidate power, he rescinded the MPs' constitutional right to information from the office of the president, thus denying MPs and their constituents the ability to scrutinize the president's actions, and effectively making the MPs subordinate to the president and the ruling KANU party.[5] Finally, he reintroduced a policy that allowed the detention of prisoners without trial, a policy that had been suspended by Kenyatta as recently as 1978. The message was clear, and it did not take long for people to realize that the failed coup had only served to tighten Moi's grip on the government and consolidate his power.

Even so, Moi and his government still relied upon maintaining the appearance of legitimacy; they still needed the public's approval, even as they presented themselves as safe and unassailable. Hence the regime's reliance on patronage.[6] In some ways, Moi's patronage could be considered a necessary evil meant to be deployed strategically, and only in order to secure the regime's survival; in other words, it allowed Moi to smooth over resentments and suppress the ambitions of those who might oppose him, while still allowing him to pull all the strings. But it was not always used this way, or at least it did not seem so to the public. To those who did not directly benefit from his largesse, the president's practice of patronage seemed to provide nothing more than off-the-cuff answers to the country's crisis of the moment. There seemed to be no plan, no ascertainable purpose other than the need to act. And Moi's makeshift policies inevitably smacked of favoritism. The matatu industry was a case in point. The Moi regime had to be mindful of the feelings of the different groups affected by the industry—the matatu owners and operators, their passengers, the traffic police, and the general public. And yet it was impossible for Moi to accommodate all these groups without appearing to weaken his position. Although it had become clear that the matatu business needed to be regulated and streamlined, and that vehicle drivers needed to be licensed, simply ordering these requirements by fiat could lead to a strike that would paralyze the city and its economy. This, in turn, would likely generate criticism of Moi and his compliant MPs, and the resulting discontent could weaken his control. Then again, a successful confrontation with the unmanageable matatu industry could conceivably establish Moi as a strong leader willing to enact necessary reforms. He was attempting a high-wire act. The question was how to force reforms onto the matatu industry without upsetting matatu operators, and without provoking an adverse reaction that might cause his fall from power.

Moi's strategy was not immediately clear, and his habit of simply dealing with problems by responding positively to others' expectations—no matter how contradictory—meant that he often appeared duplicitous. All these factors made it difficult for journalists to write about his policies with any accuracy; and the threat of reprisal was always present (which usually meant detention without trial) if Moi disliked a journalist's story.[7] Jasphat Okwaro, a leading journalist in Nairobi in the 1980s, recalled how impossible it was to write about the Matatu Bill, "it was not really clear what it was; and [it] was also passed on that sacred second anniversary of the coup. It made sense for Moi to pass a controversial bill on that day because he knew that that was a day people would be scared of criticizing him. You could not criticize Moi on that day; if you did you would be put in detention." The timing of the bill was decisive, and Okwaro could not help but underscore that fact: "it was also no coincidence that Moi passed the bill on August 1, for that is a day that Moi always wanted Kenyans to remember that he was a tough president and he cared for regular people."[8]

Eventually, as the anniversary of the attempted coup retreated into the past, journalists began to write a little more freely about the bill, offering cagey criticism of the repressive tactics Moi had used to secure his power after the coup attempt. Also under scrutiny was his habit of making policy on the run, policy that by its very nature was rarely thought through clearly or adequately explained to the Parliament or the public. However, the aim of his policies was not usually long term; they were policies meant merely to appease particular groups and offer simple, short-term solutions to complicated problems. And of course, they were policies intended to maintain the ever-important appearance of power and stability.[9]

It was under these circumstances that the Matatu Bill of 1984 was conceived and implemented. Needless to say, it took matatu operators by surprise. Most of them were indignant; they had received no notice of the bill's appearance or been advised of its contents, and at no point had their input had been sought.[10] What is more, the new regulations were to be enforced immediately. Owners were granted no warning, no grace period, and no assistance in meeting the new conditions, many of which—getting licenses and inspections, making repairs, and finding insurance—were likely to take weeks, if not months. In many cases, fulfilling the new rules was impossible since insurance was not easily available, and the government was not at all prepared to provide licenses and inspections.

From the start, officials of the Matatu Vehicle Owners Association (MVOA) expressed their vehement resistance to the new rules. Once again, Joseph Nderi became the MVOA's main spokesperson. He was a particularly vocal opponent of the new financial hardships that would face matatu owners: "The average matatu operator," he insisted, "is a man of comfortable but not excessive means who services and repairs his vehicle in open shade garages," and, he added, "a matatu operated purely on consideration for passenger comfort rather than for economic factors" is "utterly uneconomic."[11] To bolster his case, Nderi speculated that only about 50 out of 3,000 matatus would be able to operate on the roads in Nairobi under the new regulations, and everyone else would be forced off the roads because they feared the police would impound their vehicles. His estimates were exaggerated, but by offering dire predictions of impending losses and economic hardship he managed to inform the public that owner income (usually between 5,000 and 6,000 shillings a month) was not nearly enough to make an owner rich. They had to keep up the repairs on vehicles, and licensing and insurance costs were also high; if these were not kept to a minimum the industry would not remain "viable," and it would not be able to play its "indispensable role" in meeting Nairobi's growing

FIGURE 10   Joseph Mwaura Nderi, September 1984. Courtesy of the Standard Group, Nairobi

transport and employment needs.[12] Matatus, he warned, were fundamental to the economy's health, and if the new rules went into effect immediately, they would drive 90 percent of matatus in the country out of business. Unable to meet expenses, or repay the funds they had originally borrowed to purchase the vehicles, most owners would be forced to shut down.[13]

Nderi complained as loudly as he dared throughout August and September of 1984, but the government neither listened nor relented; its officials insisted that matatu owners immediately comply with the requirements of the bill. Peter Okondo, then minister of transport and communication, had little patience for grievances like Nderi's and responded to them with scornful indifference: "When the late President Kenyatta gave a go-ahead for matatus to operate, he did not say they should go without brakes."[14]

Having been so blatantly snubbed by the minister, Nderi pressed on and tried to speak with President Moi himself, to plead that the government give matatu owners more time to meet the new requirements.[15] But Moi was unsympathetic, and he continued to be dismissive in his criticisms of matatu operators. In a speech given to Kenyan supporters at the airport (after a state visit to Ethiopia) on September 13, 1984,

Moi taunted, "Matatu people are getting on my nerves," and he justified his disdain by asserting that "when Parliament passes any law
against them [the matatu owners], they ask the President to waive the
law instead of . . . respecting the Parliament's decision."[16] The crowd
responded with enthusiasm. But Moi's remarks were clearly deceitful
since the Parliament had only followed his own wishes in passing the
bill; moreover, his contemptuous branding of matatu workers as unprincipled ingrates appears to have been a tactical move designed to
appeal to the public's reliable resentment of matatu owners. Many in
the audience were happy to share in his contempt, having either been
angered by disagreeable experiences or been made envious of the owners' relative wealth and power.

"Are they not the rich?" Moi asked mockingly. "Yes!" the crowd responded. "They have buses and countless matatus and they don't pay
income tax. Would you like the President to look at people dying because of the riches of such people?"[17]

No doubt Moi's incendiary comments can be considered as out and
out demagoguery, but in a way he had a point. Some matatu owners
had obviously benefited from Kenyatta's deregulation of the industry
back in 1973 and had been able to make a very good living; some of
those who had weathered the competition had even managed to buy
more than one matatu and become motivated entrepreneurs. They
were, in effect, fulfilling the Mzee's wishes and contributing to the
development of the young nation as productive middle-income Kenyans.[18] But many of these operators were not contributing to the welfare of the state as they should have been; only one in five matatu owners were prosperous enough to afford to pay the taxes, and even if they
could they rarely did so. Even more outrageous were the 1 to 2 percent
of wealthy owners who operated fleets of vehicles and paid no taxes at
all—even though it would have been fair to tax them at even higher
rates. This elite group, comprising mainly government ministers, as
well as a few Ethiopian and Somali businessmen, had taken advantage
of Kenyatta's decree to venture into a tax- and regulation-free business.
Many of these owners wanted their involvement in the matatu industry to remain confidential so they could shield themselves from potential tax liability, or possible legal liability. So long as they remained
comparatively invisible they could continue to run their businesses
without regard for the welfare of the nation, and still convince themselves they were reputable citizens.

And yet the large majority of matatu owners were small-time, struggling entrepreneurs who made a relatively meager living operating a single matatu. But the public did not acknowledge this. They assumed that anyone who owned a car in Kenya in the 1980s was necessarily well-to-do, no matter the vehicle's state of disrepair.[19] It was a matter of appearances; simply owning a prestigious object was enough to convince others of one's undeniable good fortune. "A car was a car," said Jane Ndoro, who worked as a shop assistant in the 1980s. "If you had a car you were doing well."[20] Her friend Petronella Mwisha agreed: "You could not say you are poor when you had a car," and she wagged her finger at me, to make sure I understood her point of view: "poor people don't own cars."[21]

Then again, most of the owners disagreed; they were still trying to pay for the vehicles that supposedly proved their wealth. Despite the common perception that they were prosperous, and notwithstanding their generally improved financial position (some owners did operate fleets of cars), most matatu owners did not consider their status as particularly exalted, or their financial outlook as secure. If confronted by people envious of their supposed wealth, they typically responded—sometimes quite shamelessly—by invoking nationalist rhetoric to protect their interests and garner public support. If that tired expedient did not work, they could count on the popular perception of the industry as coarse and unruly, and then humbly claim that matatu owners were actually poor, abused laborers trying to provide a vital service: no one as rude and undisciplined as a matatu worker could possibly be wealthy. Apparently, the owners thought, it was better to be resented for boorish behavior than envied for success. That they were perpetuating negative stereotypes did not seem to matter so long as they deflected accusations that they had become too wealthy. Whatever their rationale, the owners could not sit on the sidelines while Moi defended his actions by stoking up the popular prejudice against insolent matatu workers. Besides, they justifiably feared accusations that they had unfairly profited from the former president's favoritism, or that they did not share in the same harsh economy that challenged the majority of Kenyans.[22]

———

At first, it did not seem to matter who was winning the rhetorical battle. The matatu owners simply ignored the new rulings and carried on with their business. But eventually they were forced to contend with the reality of the Matatu Bill, especially once the police started setting up roadblocks to check for matatus that were potentially unfit for service. As the scrutiny gradually increased, Nderi and his group began to realize that there was no way around the new law, and that business could only continue if they managed to cooperate with the government. And, after all, the role of the MVOA was to keep matatus in business, and at least in one area—that of passenger safety—their interests coincided with those of the government. Everyone wanted better vehicles and better service. Nevertheless, the burden of the new rules rested primarily upon the matatu owners, who somehow had to find the money to repair or update their cars and vans, and then insure and license them.

Of course the wealthy owners had little problem meeting the costs of improvements, if their vehicles needed improvement at all. Less moneyed owners usually went into debt by borrowing money from family and friends to pay for the necessary repairs. In some cases, the MVOA was able to offer small loans to those who were utterly desperate, but they certainly could not meet everyone's needs.[23] And sometimes those needs were extensive. Soon after the legislation was passed there were reports of owners who had "found themselves having to buy wipers, give their vehicles a coat of paint, have them panel beaten, fix brakes, have an emergency door fitted and the engine overhauled and fit new tires before taking their vehicles for inspection."[24] What is more, the drivers and touts had to get new licenses as well, an obligation that made at least one driver feel "like a person who has just given birth to a child."[25]

His sentiment was not altogether an exaggeration since some owners actually had to start from the beginning if their vehicles could not be repaired well enough to comply with new standards. Philip Macharia recalled wistfully that the "Matatu Bill nearly killed us." He had owned a matatu in the 1980s but was forced out of business by the exacting strictures of the new law: "It was the first time I took my vehicle for inspection, and it didn't pass, so I had to get out of the business for about a year until I found money to buy a better car."[26] Shem Mungai had a similar experience, though in his case it was a sense of political pressure as well as the lack of funds that had forced him off the road—though he prudently recognized that "it was important to take the President's bill seriously. Back then you could not argue with the President because he was the President and you had to obey him." Nevertheless, Mungai managed "to do well," as he put it, and by the end of the 1980s he had recovered and was back on the road with two matatus.[27]

Although it might seem that the government and the matatu owners had a mutual interest in improving the vehicles, many of the matatu owners' reservations about the law were justified. Most of the owners agreed that it was important to regulate the industry to reduce accidents, but they were still concerned at the manner in which officials had implemented and enforced the regulations. What's more, the owners could not help but recall the furtiveness with which the Parliament passed the bill. As a result, many quietly began questioning the zeal with which the bill's provisions were being carried out, even to the point of questioning whether or not the bill had even been passed in the interest of public safety. Given the bill's timing and the need to fortify the government after the attempted coup of 1982, it certainly seemed possible that it was passed to serve Moi's self-interest rather than to improve safety on the streets. To make matters worse, the intransigence of the police toward matatus also contributed to the owners' doubts. Along with the suddenness of the bill's appearance, and the fact that it received so little consideration, the rashness of the police crackdown contributed to the notion that Moi was merely using the legislation to demonstrate his authority and prop up his government. Perhaps it was inevitable, then, that doubts about the bill's intent would eventually surface. In fact, the sense of skepticism seemed to infect nearly every aspect of the political atmosphere. In an interesting twist, many of the owners, especially Kikuyu owners, felt that Moi's overturning of Kenyatta's 1973 decree had not so much tarnished his reputation as it had Kenyatta's. They considered the act less an affront to the previous president than a sign of his weakness; after all, if Kenyatta's decrees could be so easily overruled, his undisputed standing as father of the nation could no longer be considered absolute.[28]

Another cause of skepticism came to light in the weeks and months after its initial enactment: the Members of Parliament who voted for the Matatu Bill had never considered the details of its implementation or the potential problems caused by its sudden ratification. Apparently no thought had been given to who would actually license the drivers, who would carry out inspections on the matatus (the police, or government-appointed garages?), or what penalties would be imposed for their failure to comply.[29] The lack of foresight had predictably led to all sorts of confusion—for instance, it might be weeks before an operator was issued a license, which meant his vehicle had to be kept off the road, and that the operators would be forced to suffer financial losses, or even be threatened with bankruptcy. Or, if a case eventually made it to court and the defendant was found guilty, the judge could simply levy any fines or impose any jail time he felt appropriate.

Yet another significant problem with the legislation was the failure to hold the Transport and Communication Department accountable for the regulation of insurance premiums. No one was in charge of monitoring what the insurance companies could charge for premiums, and so—predictably—soon after the new law passed, third-party insurance rates for matatus nearly doubled, increasing from 7,000 to 12,500 shillings per year.[30] When challenged, insurance companies justified the higher premiums by citing increased demand for matatu vehicle insurance, and consequently the potential for a higher number of insurance claims. According to Nderi, this increase was farcically unfair; it ignored the obvious fact that an increase in the number of claims would be offset by the increase in the number of policies. Nevertheless, the higher premiums forced about 20,000 matatus off the roads and rendered approximately 60,000 people jobless—the aftereffects were unavoidable. The lives of tens of thousands of commuters were disrupted, the profits of businesses suffered, and the overall economy declined. When Nderi asked government officials to intervene with the insurance companies and save the industry from possible collapse, they refused. Eventually, the MVOA officials were forced to hire a lawyer and sue the insurance companies.[31] The suit was ultimately unsuccessful, though the insurance companies did respond by making a few negligible reductions in the cost of premiums. But the table scraps were not enough, and Nderi, despite the loss in court, was not about to remain silent. He had no choice but to make an appeal to the public, regardless of the outcome. But at least he had logic on his side. In one of his many eloquent discussions with the press, Nderi posed the obvious question: why had these firms "increased the premiums at a time when matatus were well maintained with very little risk of getting into accidents?"[32] He received no answer.

There was, finally, one more reason to be skeptical of the bill's merit. In addition to being stonewalled by the insurance companies, the matatu owners also felt that they were being unfairly targeted in comparison to the Kenya Bus Service; the KBS was not affected by the new bill. Naturally the matatu owners felt this to be unfair, though yet again there was no recourse but to make a public appeal. Consequently, there appeared a number of letters to newspapers arguing that the bill's provisions should apply to the KBS as well as the matatus—especially since the KBS drivers drove just as irresponsibly as the drivers of matatus.

And just as dangerously. As one matatu owner complained, the KBS drivers would routinely "overtake at blind brows and corners, go over the speed limit, and hog and bully every vehicle smaller than their yellow monsters."[33] No one, except perhaps those in cahoots with the KBS, wanted the law to be applied selectively. If the roads were to be regulated, and the KBS drivers were just as heedless of the laws as the drivers of matatus, it was only fair to regulate everyone.

———

In spite of all these grievances, the matatu inspections continued as the momentous year of 1984 came to an end. Many of the poorer matatu owners were left out in the cold. About 20 percent of matatus failed inspection and were shut down because their owners could not afford the repairs needed to meet the required standards. On the other hand, those whose vehicles managed to pass inspection had become more valuable, and the owners of these matatus wanted to make a better return on their investment. With less competition on the streets their matatus were in even more demand, and they now had the opportunity to make more profit. But what the MVOA really wanted was acknowledgment from government officials. It was one thing to have passed inspection and increased profits, it was altogether another to achieve a measure of stability and security sufficient to operate without fear of another government crackdown. Again, the MVOA argued that some form of legal recognition might provide some stability and security to the business. They knew the Moi government could turn violent at the slightest provocation; it was, after all, a vulnerable regime that had to be continually placated, and that would not hesitate to reassert its power. If MVOA could somehow be recognized as a legitimate organization, it might then have a platform from which to advocate for the owners and operators—one that the government had to acknowledge.

To accomplish this the MVOA officials took advantage of what came to be known as the *Nyayo* philosophy. The idea of *Nyayo* ("footsteps") had become a significant part of Moi's rhetoric, and it was originally intended to persuade citizens to "follow in the footsteps of Kenyatta, the respected father of the nation." *Nyayo* had been the driving spirit behind *Harambee*, Kenyatta's idea of African socialism, where the communal effort to build and share resources was intended to enable individual productivity and creativity.[34] However, Moi tended to use *Nyayo* as a way of lending credence to his regime and to his self-proclaimed paternalism rather than to encourage an ideal community that fostered "love, peace, and unity."[35] When Moi invoked *Nyayo* it was usually with the intention of persuading people to adhere to his political agenda—especially after the attempted coup, when the term came to mean something entirely more imperious.[36] Now when Moi employed the phrase, "follow in *my* footsteps," he meant it much more literally.[37] Whereas *Nyayo* had once implied community and fidelity to fellow Kenyans, the connotations of this new, disingenuous usage pointed to the autocratic side of his rule and his covert efforts to dominate through patronage to his supporters.[38] Of course anyone who needed something from the government picked up on the term's new meaning. As Nderi once told me, "it was one of those words you had to use, even if you did not mean it, in order to get ahead."[39] Failure to obey the government, to follow *Nyayo* philosophy, was more or less tantamount to treason. So it was politically prudent for MVOA officials to appear to be following *Nyayo*, which in this instance meant publicly urging matatu owners and operators to maintain their vehicles in good condition and obey the new traffic laws. This was the path Moi had set for them.

For example, in a speech to matatu owners on January 12, 1985, Nderi urged them to "Fata Nyayo" (follow in the footsteps): "We all have a moral obligation toward one another and the suffering of one section of our society has an adverse effect on the rest of society just as a finger is necessary to the whole body, and when it is attacked by bacteria it gives fever to the whole body. Let us all cooperate in the spirit of Nyayo regulation, which demands that we be orderly, no touting, hooting unnecessarily, no hanging on a moving matatu, no speeding, no overloading, and above all be kind to the commuters."[40] To supplement their rhetoric MVOA officials organized several refresher courses for drivers, and Nderi arranged for motor vehicle inspectors and police officers to speak to drivers and owners about exercising good conduct and avoiding accidents. Nderi could often be seen in the parking lots dutifully reminding participants to act in the spirit of *Nyayo*, and to be "mindful of other people."[41]

To help promote good behavior among matatu operators, MVOA officials also employed "responsible" former matatu drivers in the matatu parking lots throughout Nairobi and in Kenya's other major towns. The intention was to ease the atmosphere of anarchy in the lots. The job of the officials was to ensure that the drivers lined up on a first-come, first-served basis, so that they might avoid the usual chaotic scramble for passengers; they also sought to lessen the clamor surrounding the vehicles by discouraging touts from "shouting, banging vehicles, sounding horns, and so on."[42] As a positive measure, MVOA officials encouraged matatu owners to hire drivers and conductors on a permanent basis, rather than the more typical ad hoc basis, so that employees would invest "a serious commitment to the vehicle" and its care.[43] This would also—presumably—compel drivers to avoid speeding, mounting curbs, and harassing passengers. The MVOA reasoned that the more matatu workers became professionalized, the more pride they would take in their work—all to the good of the industry's reputation.[44]

Taken all together, these changes made the beginning of 1985 a watershed moment, at least for those who had managed to stay in business (for those who had been forced out it was no doubt just as momentous). Muiru Mugo, a former editor of the *Matatu Journal*, proclaimed some months later that matatus "had for so long wandered lonely as a cloud," but now they could finally be considered legitimate. It is not quite clear how Wordsworth's metaphor applied to matatus (nothing could less resemble a wandering cloud than a noisy overloaded matatu), but at least his message was clear: the matatu community "constitutes a large part of our society," and "legalizing the matatu business [would bring it] within the laws of this land."[45] It at least seemed within the realm of possibility, and at least for the moment it seemed that the industry's future was less gloomy. The MVOA's cooperation with government officials appeared to have improved the matatus, the workers' behavior, and their reputation. Even more telling was that matatu operators began acting as if the new working conditions had been the norm all along.

———

But matatu owners wanted something in return. Because they could claim to have met the Matatu Bill's obligations, and to have bettered the working conditions and safety of their vehicles, they were not going to let their accomplishments go unrewarded. They wanted more rights from the government; in particular, they wanted more respect and an atmosphere more favorable to the operation of their businesses.[46] Although the demands were not very specific, they were real. Given that they had accommodated the government as best as they could, the owners felt they could rely on their improved standing and push back against the government.

They were soon given the opportunity when, on May 15, 1985, the police carried out the first nationwide crackdown.[47] Just eight months after the passing of the bill the police conducted surprise inspections, at dawn, along the main roads of Nairobi; the targets of the crackdown were vehicles that had failed—or refused—inspection, and those that were carrying too many passengers.[48] Every matatu was forced to

stop at the roadblocks during the morning rush hour, and the resulting bottlenecks instantly brought traffic to a standstill. The result was
chaos.[49] According to the newspapers several of the roadblocks were
overrun as soon as the vehicles were stopped because all the passengers illegally standing inside the matatus "took to their heels for fear
of being arrested." Before long the Jogoo, Juja, and Muranga Roads "became scenes of mass trek as workers poured into the city."[50] Not to be
deterred, the police, harried by drivers and touts, gathered around the
impounded vehicles and removed the license plates and confiscated
keys from drivers of vehicles they deemed unroadworthy. The police
considered the inspections a success. Despite the bedlam they caused
commuters, the head of the police department celebrated on the eve-
ning news broadcasts the great good the police had accomplished, and
he insisted that the police would continue to curb overloading and to
ensure that matatus were safe. He expressed little concern for the commuters forced to walk.

Even if the impromptu inspections increased safety, which is doubtful, the matatu owners considered the actions unfair, and even illegal. They did not hesitate to air their grievances, accusing the police
of harassment and illegally removing their license plates and taking
their ignition keys—even if the offense only required an appearance
in traffic court. They also complained that the police had started arresting matatu operators for picking up passengers at random locations—at zebra crossings or at traffic lights.[51] Nderi, always the most
outspoken advocate, argued that they had always done this, and that
matatus should not be penalized for picking up passengers wherever
necessary because police and Nairobi City Council officials had failed
to provide matatus with parking areas in the city center, and he went
on to suggest that the authorities consider establishing roadside stops
for matatus in the city center, like those set up for the KBS. A discouraged Nderi told the media, on May 16, 1985, that operators were "at sea
about what they should do" because even when they maintained their
vehicles as required and kept to the official number of passengers, "the
police kept detaining their vehicles sometimes for two days without
any reason." In the end he simply "appealed to the authorities to let
[matatu operators] conduct their business as long as they were within
the law."[52] Although Nderi left it unmentioned, the MVOA officials
were well aware that an increase in police powers meant an increase in
the demand for bribes.

Luckily for the matatu operators, Moi was visiting a Nairobi sub-
urb on the day of the crackdown, and he observed schoolchildren,

some of tender age, walking unconscionably long distances to school because the matatus they usually traveled in had been impounded.[53] Moi's sympathy for the children and other commuters compelled him to ask the police to respect "the Nyayo philosophy of being mindful of the welfare of others." Implying that the blockades were "brutal" and "anti-Nyayo," the president seemed to feel—at least for the moment— that the actions harming the comfort of *wanainchi* (citizens) should be guided by "commonsense and maturity." He even suggested that the "indiscriminate impounding of public transportation . . . reflected heartlessness on the part of the police."[54] Moi's support was totally unexpected. On the spur of the moment he had aligned himself with the MVOA's position and argued that drivers of vehicles with minor defects be issued a notice to attend court, and be permitted to continue their routes so that passengers could reach their destinations.

It seemed that, once again, Moi had changed his policy to win affection, though few considered his bout of compassion sincere given the background of suppression. After all, he had persistently called for more police control of matatus and had hastily passed his Matatu Bill without allowing discussion. Both moves were revealing. The bill's clandestine passage and the abrupt reversal of policy exposed his susceptibility to public approval; he feared matatu strikes might represent defiance of his government, and the anger at the ensuing chaos might be directed at him. Either way his image would be damaged. So he ended up sending mixed messages, to the police and to the public, messages that were so riddled with contradictions and inconsistencies they ended up helping no one but the matatu operators, who took advantage of the confusion by advancing their own agenda.[55]

The matatu owners' first real opportunity to turn Moi's apparent policy changes to their advantage came nearly a year later, during the transport dispute of April 14, 1986. Now prepared to test their standing with the government, the owners parked their vehicles at Nairobi area traffic headquarters to protest the "police harassment" and its "inconveniencing [of] commuters." The protest came in response to the police having impounded one hundred matatus and charged their drivers with various offenses. According to the police, the matatus had been seized for obstructing the KBS by parking at KBS bus stops, but MVOA was not satisfied with the reasons given for the arrests. Nderi contended that matatus should be able to use the KBS bus stops, and that it was a calculated act of discrimination against the industry to prohibit their use.

FIGURE 11   Matatu workers' strike, April 14, 1985. Courtesy of the *Nation* Media Group, Nairobi

The confrontation escalated until it became a public spectacle that the police could not ignore, and eventually the police inspector arrived to arrest Nderi. As he was taken away, the protesting drivers followed the arresting officers in their matatus, purposefully causing gridlock in the city during the lunch hour rush.[56]

Once again, Nderi had caused the police embarrassment, and, to make matters worse, he had effectively invoked the rhetoric of "commonsense and maturity" that Moi had used the previous year to admonish the police.[57] In truth, the police were outraged that Nderi would assume the higher ground and make a patriotic appeal simply to bolster the MVOA's position and attain the release of the impounded matatus; it was not, they believed, how President Moi's directive to avoid "indiscriminately harassing" matatus was meant to be followed—and they certainly had a point.[58] Yet somehow, to everyone's surprise, they managed to get Nderi to agree with them. After only an hour in custody, the MVOA president was released, and his views had mysteriously changed. He now seemed to be aligned with the police; as he left the police station Nderi admonished the matatu operators, directed them to resume work, and then vowed that he would no longer protect those caught violating traffic rules. He then concluded his address to protesters with a piece of expedient advice—"rules should be adhered to for matatu operators to be taken seriously by the public and government."[59] All of a sudden Nderi sounded like a police spokesman. He even, in a display of Moi-style politics, called for matatu operators to raise their hands and pledge loyalty to the government and cooperation with the police—as long as police treated them respectfully. This was not the assured and defiant leader they had come to know. In fact, his words and actions seemed utterly out of character, and his well-rehearsed script, which now seemed to lend public support for Moi, advocated positions he was known to have opposed since he had become MVOA president. It was such an abrupt shift in attitude that many suspected that Nderi had been bribed or threatened while in police custody.[60] It was certainly a possibility given the reputation of the police, and perhaps it should be said in his defense that this kind of performance was the only way Nderi could continue to survive as the leader of the matatu industry in the oppressive climate of the mid-1980s. In any case, it was becoming clear to everyone that the meaning of "commonsense and maturity" was relative and could mean different things at different times.

Off stage, however, it soon became apparent that little had changed for Nderi or for the matatu owners. They remained adamant about their expectation of police respect. Since they now operated under the auspices of the Matatu Bill and were legitimized by their licenses and business rights, they had acquired a sense of prerogative and were willing to exploit it (in a more just world, however, some of those prerogatives would have been eclipsed by their defiance of the bill's provisions). Now, confident of their privilege, Nderi and the matatu owners continued parking illegally and setting up blockades, even though they knew they were breaking the law. But they were not merely violating the law to make their own jobs easier or to belittle the police; their offenses were strategic. The matatu owners purposefully defied the laws, over and over again, because the more they could take advantage of the inconsistencies of Moi's policies, the more influence they could acquire. The more ambiguous the government's policies, the easier they were to exploit. So long as the president could not be pinned down, so long as he could be counted on to acquiesce to interest groups, the matatu owners could excuse or justify their behavior simply by invoking Moi's own rhetoric. The law was only as strong as the leader, as is usually the case in dictatorial regimes.[61] Because Moi feared the backlash of the MVOA and the outcry caused by their matatu strikes, he usually gave in to the operators' demands, and over time it became clear that matatu operators could ignore the Matatu Bill's provisions whenever it suited their interests.

———

The law they most often ignored was the prohibition against carrying standing passengers. Since the KBS was allowed to transport standing passengers, the matatu owners argued that it was just a matter of fairness that they be granted the same privilege. Even more to the point was the fact that matatu owners and drivers needed to overload their vehicles or increase fares to help pay off the debts they had incurred by fixing their vehicles—as was stipulated by the Matatu Bill. There was really no other way to meet these expenses. Because Nderi's complaints to government officials about repair costs had been rebuffed, matatu owners had to raise their fares and increase the number of passengers they squeezed into their vehicles. They had no choice but to do one or the other, regardless of the law against standing passengers. Of course their actions were not likely to go unchallenged, and soon passengers began to boycott the matatus, with the backing of the government.[62] An interview with a female passenger who participated in the boycott and chose to ride a KBS bus remarked that the matatus' fare increases had made it more difficult for her to support her family. The 50-cent fare increase was enough to buy her children their daily milk. And by traveling on the KBS she could also avoid "traveling so dangerously in vehicles which were usually overloaded."[63] Eventually the boycott forced matatu conductors to change their tactics—in fact, some of them "pitifully begged passengers to enter their vehicles" in order to compete with the KBS's lower fares.[64] Yet the boycott was not unanimous; some commuters felt that the matatu fare increase was not unreasonable—"I travel in a matatu daily" wrote one rider, "and I would rather pay an extra 50 cents to be in a mechanically sound matatu than to get a free ride to death." But he was clearly in the minority.[65]

Not everyone understood the constraints under which the matatus operated. Many poor and working-class Kenyans saw matatu owners as unjustly privileged—especially in the mid-1980s; they also considered the fare increases as merely another example of the owners' avarice. "Matatu people made more money than many of us; they were not poor, those people," Patrick Luganji told me. Another indignant passenger, James Mwashi, agreed; he insisted in a letter to the editor of one of the daily newspapers that "Matatus are a disgrace; they are voracious and profiteering is part of their human nature."[66] Another letter to the editor made the grandiose assertion that "the pursuit of wealth which leads to extremes of ill behavior among the matatu operators is symptomatic of the Kenyan society at large."[67] The letter's tone suggests that the writer was not trying to absolve matatu operators as mere symptoms of a corrupt society so much as he was condemning them by association. It did not matter; matatu operators were more or less forced to charge higher fares during rush hours, even though they knew that many commuters were desperate—and just desperate enough to pay. Nor did the conductors stop overloading their vehicles, or stop paying bribes to the police so they would overlook the excesses of passengers standing in the aisles.[68] The fact was that matatus were just too necessary to too many for a boycott to work.

And yet regardless of the boycott's success or failure, there was evidence of some slight improvement in the operation of matatus—part of which may be attributable to Moi's Matatu Bill. In February 1985, about five months after the Matatu Bill was instituted, one of the daily newspapers conducted a survey to ascertain whether the new laws had improved the matatu industry. Only 10 percent of those polled said that there had been an improvement, yet there were respondents who noticed that some matatus had been spruced up and made more mechanically sound, and also that there seemed to be a few newer-looking vehicles on the streets.[69] A few commuters noted that matatus were jumping the curb and driving on the sidewalk a little less than they had been; indeed, one commuter could not believe that drivers now had to "drag their vehicles through the traffic jams" like everybody else. Government officials were eager to take credit for any progress, such as it was. For instance, the head of the police department, contradicting the mostly inconclusive polls, enthused about the "overall improvement in the performance of matatus."[70]

But for many commuters it was a different, more complicated story. Mechanically sound vehicles did not necessarily mean safer vehicles. One commuter noted sarcastically that newer was not necessarily better, since the new matatus had stronger engines that enabled drivers "to speed even more and compete with the other matatus." She complained that "they still use the wrong lanes . . . and at round-abouts the conductor hangs by the door and warns the other motorists to keep clear, waving his hands and legs as if in a dance hall, and then tells the passenger, *Ingia!* [enter]. If they see a passenger they stop suddenly and without signal. If the passenger happens to hesitate because the vehicle is full, the conductor will say, *Nafasi iko kama stadium!* [come on, enter, let us go, there is as much space in here as in a stadium]."[71]

What most commuters failed to acknowledge was that they were helping matatu operators break the law by agreeing with the conductors' demands. They more or less knew what to expect, so when they chose to squeeze in to an already full vehicle they were in their own small way colluding with the operators' misconduct. This question of who was actually to blame for the overcrowding of matatus was one that had plagued the industry for some time.[72] Philip Ochieng', a prominent columnist, admitted the public's culpability in a rare instance of evenhandedness: "sadly, we ourselves have voluntarily and with enthusiasm squeezed our bodies into vehicles already full to overflowing." Discouraged by commuters' failure to protest against matatus in any kind of meaningful or lasting way, he admitted that commuters still demonstrated an "utter unconcern" when they chose a matatu that "hurtle[d] at the speed of light," and, more often than not, the passengers remained indifferent when "drivers bribed policemen following an accident of the matatus' own making." Ochieng' ruefully concluded that "it is we who have indulged the matatu industry."[73]

Others also noted the passengers' complicity with the daredevil behavior of matatu touts and drivers. William Mureithi Kimarau, the Nairobi area traffic manager, insisted that "the key to controlling passenger harassment by touts largely lies within the commuters themselves." He argued that commuters "have to become disciplined and openly protest against harassment and ultimately deny offering matatus their share of business." Kimarau also wondered "why people board a matatu that is already full, knowing very well that they will be packed in tightly. . . . Why not wait a few minutes for the next vehicle?"[74] Members of the traffic police concurred. In their view, the Matatu Bill had done little to ease the problem of reckless overloading and speeding, which was only controlled, as one policemen noted, when "the police mount road blocks." But even then, he added, "the matatus have their own way of passing word to others and so they then avoid using the road we are on or they come here with the exact number of passengers."

Indeed, drivers and conductors occasionally confessed that the new laws had not affected them much at all. A conductor who plied his trade on the Riruta Road admitted as much to a newspaper reporter: "I am still carrying as many people as I used to and when there is a road block on Ngong Road I use route number 46 which is a bit longer, but it gets me to town."[75] The conductor also confessed that he only carried the permitted number of passengers when he had no choice, and he justified himself by making the familiar argument that since most matatus were bought on loan, the owners had to make enough money to meet the monthly payments. The new passenger limit, he insisted, made it impossible to earn enough to make the payments, do the repairs, and pay the workers. And, after all, the number of accidents caused by matatus had decreased slightly, and "these days," he reminded the reporter, "you hear that the accidents are caused by KBS rather than matatus."[76]

In general, Nairobi motorists were not much impressed by the impact of the Matatu Bill. As one female motorist told the press, "when I am on the road, I am actually taking care of two vehicles, mine and a matatu. . . . If you do not watch out and know where the matatu driver is going," she said, "he will crash into you."[77] One of the most revealing comments made about the impact of the Matatu Bill came from the secretary of the MVOA, who was happy that the Matatu Bill had finally granted matatus legal status. "But," he argued, "it was interesting that in September 1984 . . . when *legal* [my emphasis] matatus began operating on the roads, that was when many Kenyans became stranded on the roads because there were not enough vehicles on the road, since many matatus could not meet requirements for PSV licenses."[78] Becoming legal did not necessarily mean becoming more efficient any more than it meant obeying the new laws. For this MVOA official, legality, with its prohibitive regulations and extra costs, had become a burden— which, God forbid, had caused passengers to suffer.

All of these attitudes—the government's, the owners', the passengers', even those of the police—tell us much about the meaning and implementation of law in Kenya, and often in Africa in general.[79] Of course, circumstances were complicated, and good intentions were often compromised for reasons that were beyond anyone's control, as is probably true everywhere. Still, the lack of discussion and input, the absence of planning, and the overall failure to exercise any foresight speaks directly to the haphazard manner in which the Parliament passed the law. It also speaks to Moi's tendency to rely upon the most expedient answers, or to grasp at the policy that presented him in the most flattering, authoritative light. It is no accident, for example, that Moi's government was more interested in passing this controversial law exactly on August 1, 1982, a day on which Moi was unlikely to receive criticism from Kenyans, than in examining the logistical consequences of the law. Surely government officials should have anticipated a shortage of transportation once the Matatu Bill was enforced and sought alternatives for the public—at least for the few months it would take matatu owners to update their vehicles. Yet Moi was determined to pass the Matatu Bill on this particular day, without considering its practical consequences. As a result, the bill became a political stunt rather than an effective legislative remedy.

What is more, the government's preoccupation with the political repercussions of the bill seemed to take precedence over its practical effects. It was opportunistic. By placing emphasis on the bill's politics, rather than its implementation, Moi and the Parliament could claim credit for its passage and then claim they had done their job. Or they could use the new laws to justify a crackdown and reassert their power. In either case, the bill offered them cover. Whenever it needed, the government could invoke the bill in order to conceal their incompetence or convince the public that the government was in control.[80] But by and large the bill's passing meant that nothing much would change. Moi and the government could claim they had passed a significant law, the owners could claim legitimacy for their business, and the police could still claim their bribes—but the safety issues, the congestion, the overcrowding, and the insolent behavior remained stubbornly unimproved. In this regard, the bill ironically ended up giving everyone what they wanted—except of course the passengers, who ended up paying more for more crowded accommodations. Perhaps the most significant thing the bill revealed was that the government could not maintain the upper hand. In fact, the matatu owners were frequently able to turn the Matatu Bill to their advantage, even though its passage had been intended to subject them to government control. For instance, owners exploited the licenses that had granted them legal status (and that had supposedly placed them under government control) to make new, unprecedented demands. Once they had been an assortment of isolated and politically ineffective groups, but now—as an officially recognized industry—they were able to present an organized resistance to the government and to insist that they be acknowledged as part of the Kenyan polity. Because the bill had been passed, the government was now obliged to negotiate—as best they could—with the matatu owners.

Yet it is doubtful that any negotiations could have changed the ways in which matatus conducted business. Since the Matatu Bill was so poorly implemented, and because the government had no effective means of enforcing its provisions, the matatu owners were able to ignore many—perhaps most—of the changes it mandated. They simply refused to comply with the laws when it was economically expedient. As a matter of fact, routinely breaking the law became for the owners and operators a means of participating in the "legislative" process. To put it another way, the government more or less had to give in to what they could not control. The owners knew this, and so they conveniently dismissed or defied the law whenever it was convenient, or whenever they wanted to force the government's hand. One could say that for the matatu owners, breaking the law had become a way of making the law. And there was little the government could do but acquiesce. If and when it tried to enforce the laws, the owners could merely point to the ensuing chaos caused by the government's attempts at enforcement, and then protest that the government was not adhering to its philosophy of *Nyayo*. Whenever the police tried to crack down, they disrupted the matatu service, and then the government was accused of being insufficiently "mindful of other people." They were damned if they did, and damned if they didn't.

It is no wonder, then, that Moi often felt he was forced to capitulate to the owners' endless demands, and the matatu owners felt they were often forced to criminalize themselves and risk punishment for their resistance. In this regard, the Matatu Bill had succeeded only in forcing all involved to act against their wishes. And yet both sides could also invoke the law whenever it served their interests, especially when it was necessary to influence public opinion or gain advantage in the courts. Unfortunately, the public was too often caught in the middle of this perpetual tug of war, or left stranded on the roadside, unable to get where they needed to go. No one was particularly happy with the way things were working, and all sides were forced to make unwanted concessions. Nevertheless, the outcomes were usually workable, and in some ways even desirable, despite the questionable means and the occasional disruptions that, for a time, left everyone dissatisfied and resentful. Still, the law was not going to go away, even if it had not proven entirely propitious. It had locked the owners and the government into an intricate and sometimes violent dance, and it was never quite clear who was actually leading the dance. Yet unlike typical dancers, these participants managed to do more than simply circle around one another or gyrate in place. These dancers actually propelled the country forward. Although they may not have known it at the time, the interactions that the Matatu Bill initiated—whether good or bad—would eventually benefit both the government and the matatu owners.

SEVEN

"Only Those Who Are Afraid Use Force"

October 13, 1988, marked the tenth anniversary of Moi's rule. At that same time, the Kenyan post office issued a postage stamp commemorating the government-run Nyayo Bus Service (NBS). It pictured smartly dressed men and women accompanied by children in tidy school uniforms; they were all serenely lined up on a spotless platform next to one of the new Nyayo buses as a young, white-coated usher politely welcomed them onto the bus. The stamp also depicted a map of Kenya emblazoned with the number 10, and the words "love, peace, and prosperity" written below, which were presumably meant to celebrate Moi's wonderful achievements over the past ten years as president.

But proclaiming success is not the same as achieving it, and the ideals so brashly pronounced on the stamp remained aspirational at best. The NBS buses had been around since 1986, but in a smaller number, and their commemoration two years later seemed rather premature. Then again, the government had decided, earlier in 1988, to increase the number of Nyayo buses to three hundred, almost as many as KBS (which, incidentally, had also augmented the number of its buses in the previous year). The Nyayo buses were a big deal for the Moi regime. Already ten years into his administration he still felt the need to demonstrate he was in control, and according to his thinking, more buses meant more "love, peace, and prosperity" for the regime. And he may have been at least partly right in this instance: the Nyayo buses charged lower fares than matatus and the KBS, because they received fuel subsidies from the government and free labor from the men and women serving in the National Youth Service (NYS). The NBS had, then, a distinct advantage over its rivals, and naturally Moi took full credit for the low, "patriotic" fares and proudly characterized them as "*mwanainchi*" (that is, fares for the people). Nor did he hesitate to contrast the subsidized NBS with the higher fares charged by the KBS and the matatus.[1]

That Moi was being hypocritical was not lost on anyone in the matatu industry. The introduction of Nyayo buses, coupled with the expansion of KBS and the patriotic posturing, meant the government intended to offer the matatus stiff competition. This was not the first serious challenge matatus had faced, so they were unlikely to be persuaded by the president's "patriotic" appeals.[2] The most immediate effect of the competition was to make it even more difficult for matatu workers to obey the Matatu Bill than it had been before. There was greater pressure on the touts to fill the matatus; owners inevitably had less time and money to keep the vehicles in proper repair; and drivers, who now had several hundred more buses to beat, were forced to race through the streets at ever higher speeds to get first crack at potential passengers. More alarmingly than the pressure on their business was the direct pressure from the government: if the government felt certain matatu owners to be uncooperative they were subjected to Moi's repressive measures—imprisonment without trial and, in some cases, physical torture.[3]

The actual message being sent was quite clear, despite all the harmony portrayed on the commemorative stamps. The government wanted complete control of the transportation industry and was willing to do whatever was necessary. Simply manipulating the law, as Moi had done in the previous years, had not proven enough to subjugate the industry, which was too essential and too unstructured to control by shoving improvised legislation through Parliament. With or without the law, the ease with which matatu strikes could cripple the economy in a matter of few hours revealed to everyone that Moi did not have the control he claimed, and that the nation was not nearly as peaceful and prosperous as proclaimed. Embarrassed by his weakness, unable to tolerate his lack of control or sense of vulnerability, he sometimes resorted to brute force; if he could not squeeze matatu owners out of business he would scare them out. And yet, as is often the case, the use of force only revealed his own precariousness—especially to those he most hoped to frighten. As one imprisoned and tortured matatu owner said to me, "An afraid person has a tendency to use force."[4]

But Kenya was nowhere near as prosperous as Moi wanted it believed, even as he was promoting the Nyayo buses to remind everyone how his regime had spearheaded the country's economy. The country's situation was troubled, to say the least. In the late 1980s Kenya experienced one of its worst economic declines since independence, and it could not afford the relative extravagance of three hundred new Nyayo buses. In fact, Moi's boast that he had been responsible for the new buses was misleading at best; the buses had been donated, rather than bought by Moi's government. The Japanese, Danish, and Dutch had given the Moi government over three hundred bus chassis and engines, and the Italian government had paid for the bodywork to be completed in Kenya. Development aid was also provided by the Japanese, which Moi's government used to build a large center for servicing the buses and for housing the NYS staff.[5]

The new buses, then, were a sign of neither Kenya's prosperity nor Moi's success; they were, more accurately, a telling example of the government's dependency on foreign aid. Still, the Nyayo Bus Service was becoming a big investment, an institution of sorts, and yet the bigger it became the more it indicated that Moi was willing to let foreign aid destroy the only major indigenous business in the country: the matatu industry. So it was difficult for anyone who owned or worked on a matatu to see the introduction of these new buses as anything but a threat to their livelihood. They were certainly not the subject of any kind of patriotic pride, nor could the offer represent "love, peace, and prosperity" to anyone affiliated with the matatu industry.

None of this prevented Moi from introducing the buses, in batches of ten or twenty, at several of the major bus stops in the city. Their launch was meant to be a great celebration. All the businesses and offices in the city center were expected to close for the introduction of the buses, so that the president could be honored with all the pomp and glory the city could muster for the three-hour event.[6] It began as the president's procession of limousines, decked with Kenyan flags, slowly descended upon the bus stop where the brand-new buses were parked, whereupon Moi majestically climbed out of the limousine to be escorted by his bodyguards onto a small platform from which to address the appreciative audience.[7] As they welcomed him, he raised his *rungu* (wooden baton) and then solemnly intoned:

FIGURE 12   Moi inaugurating Nyayo buses. Courtesy of the NMG, Nairobi

"Harambee."

The gathered crowd would echo him: "Harambee."

Moi continued: "Nyayo."

Audience: "Nyayo."

Moi: "Kenya iko wapi?" (How is Kenya doing?)

Audience: "Juu" (Up, high, prosperous, unified, thriving).

Moi: "Kenya iko wapi?" (How is Kenya doing?)

Audience: "Juu" (Up, high, prosperous, unified, thriving).

After the ritual, Moi gave a short speech, about twenty minutes long, in which he reiterated the supposed achievements of his rule, emphasized the peacefulness, unity, and prosperity of Kenya, and proclaimed that the buses would help ease the country's transportation problems. Incidentally, one such speech was delivered on October 10, 1987, a day that Moi had declared to be Moi Day:[8] "With the population of 24 million people, the majority living in the rural areas and many without hope of owning a car, a perfect public transport system is a major factor to the development pace. It is the blood on which the heart of the economy throbs, the axle on which Kenya's development wheel revolves around. Whenever there is a critical need for public transportation, you can be sure of finding an olive green bus with blue registration number by the name of Nyayo Bus coming to people's rescue."[9] Moi's sales pitch was blatant—he could have been delivering advertising copy. But the speech was directed at an audience beyond the potential commuters; he was also addressing the foreign governments who had contributed so generously and, he hoped, would do so in the future. Evidently Moi was worried that his use of development money might be questioned, and that it might eventually be cut off, so he made it a point to reassure investors that the Nyayo Bus Service would be "structured and managed in a way that makes profits while creating employment opportunities and contributing to the nation's transport sector."[10] What could be better for the country than this new and improved bus service? To the president it seemed obvious, and if you did not buy into his sales pitch you could easily find yourself in trouble—straightaway you would be reprimanded and declared an enemy of the nation.[11]

This kind of brazen and coercive salesmanship was fairly typical of Moi's conduct as president. For instance, he would crow at choreographed ceremonies about his generosity and compassion, especially toward primary schoolchildren, by bragging how he had initiated a program to provide a once-a-week allowance of free milk to the kids.[12] And when he boasted of the Nyayo buses, he never failed to point out that they were safer for schoolchildren, and that the fares were cheaper than those of the matatus and KBS. Perhaps more importantly, he argued, they were providing employment for young people straight out of high school. As the ceremonies ended, schoolchildren from nearby schools would sing a song in praise of Moi, always careful to incorporate phrases that flattered their magnanimous leader—*Nyayo, baba wa taifa* (father of the nation), *Mutukufu Raisi* (His Eminent, The Illustrious President). To conclude these events, Moi would raise his baton as if to consecrate the buses, wave them off with ritualistic grandeur, and then the drivers, clad in long white coats, would depart from the bus stop one by one, accompanied by their white-coated conductors and ushers. A few minutes later Moi's limousine would drive off, offices would reopen, shopkeepers would open up their shops again, and the city would resume its normal business—the Nyayo buses having played their part in the political puffery of an ailing, insecure regime.

Initially the buses operated only in Nairobi, but eventually a few were assigned to routes in other major towns such as Kisumu, Kisii, Nakuru, and Mombasa. Unlike matatus or the KBS, the Nyayo buses in the provincial cities did manage to run on schedule. Indeed, many of the people who lived in these towns at the time had only high praise for the buses. "We used to call them DAF," Mark Imbuga told me, referring to the Dutch company that had donated the buses' chassis. "They came on time, three times a day from Nairobi to Nakuru," and he added that "the youth service people were quite courteous."[13] As I spoke to him several other people gathered around, and all of them concurred with his opinion. "It was nice to have the buses, because, you see, they were very clean and there was usually room to sit," recalled Marita Beba from her home in Mombasa.[14]

In Nairobi, on the other hand, the buses ran during the peak hours on already busy roads. They were not exactly welcomed; the routes the buses covered were lucrative and the presence of the buses inevitably caused conflicts with the KBS and the matatus. Their schedules cut directly into the KBS business, which did not welcome the competition, and some commuters preferred the newer, larger buses to the smaller minibuses. In some ways, the matatus were less affected by the additional buses because they were still able to provide their inimitable service; the quick, maneuverable matatu could go more places, more quickly than the buses, and thus remained invaluable to commuters negotiating Nairobi's notorious traffic jams. On the other hand, now that the Nyayo buses could work the same streets, they put the moribund KBS at a distinct disadvantage. And Moi compounded the damage by introducing the "no-standing" rule for the KBS buses in May 1987. Since the KBS buses had always relied on standing passengers to help finance its operations, the company soon began losing money; the prohibition effectively worked to undermine the KBS even further, and as a result the bus company was forced to move to periphery routes and conduct more of its business during the nonrush hours.[15]

FIGURE 13   The languishing KBS, 1987. Courtesy of the NMG, Nairobi

The lower fares the Nyayo Bus Service charged did not help the KBS's situation either. NBS could afford to charge lower fares partly because the company relied on the free labor of the National Youth Service (NYS). It is worth looking at the NYS briefly. The Moi-era NYS traces its roots to the 1960s and the earlier administration.[16] Kenyatta had initiated the organization in the mid-1960s to help provide temporary training and a small stipend to the youth who had worked with him during the decolonization period and had supported his KANU party in the first elections after independence.[17] After working for Kenyatta during the elections, many of the young men found themselves unemployed, and so Kenyatta, fearing that they might regroup to support the opposition KADU party, established the NYS to occupy their time. Members of the NYS worked on infrastructure and other development projects, ostensibly as a way of forging cultural unity and building the nation.[18] However, the plan, which "borrowed heavily from late colonial programs designed to subject young men and women to the authority of the state in the name of self-help," did not last long.[19] By the 1970s the NYS had slowly disintegrated due to lack of funding, and eventually Kenyatta let the program dissolve because he felt his political rule was sufficiently consolidated and he no longer feared that the idle youth would devolve into dissidents.

Moi was not as confident. In the early 1980s he revived the NYS as soon as he began to face political opposition. This time, though, it was the youth who had passed their high school exams and were waiting to attend university who were forced to join NYS. In fact, service in the NYS was made a prerequisite to a university education. (Many of these students would have just finished the recently introduced 8-4-4 curriculum that Moi hastily imposed on the country in 1985; this new curriculum introduced more technical and vocational subjects compared to the previous liberal arts education.)[20] Moi's ostensible purpose was to turn the high school students into young men and women who enjoyed working with their hands and valued technical skills, but just as importantly, he wanted to create youth who were dedicated to the state—that is, dedicated to KANU.[21] He was sometimes successful. Some of these young men trained in the NYS did end up helping out the government by serving as conductors and ushers for the Nyayo Bus Service.

———

Because the government gave the Nyayo Bus Service preferential treatment, the company was able to operate at a significant profit, at least initially. However, in spite of its profits (the NBS boasted profit of nine million shillings in 1990), the project was flawed in ways that determined its early demise.[22] To begin with, by pushing itself into the private sector, the government had broken its own promise not to compete with private entrepreneurs, which in this case meant the matatu owners.[23] Yet angering the matatu owners was not the only problem; there were also logistical complications. Because the main components of the buses were imported, it was difficult to obtain spare parts from local sources—so when buses broke down they stayed broken down. It was equally hard to find mechanics or professional drivers familiar with the operation of the foreign buses, which meant that the government was eventually forced to import spare parts and hire foreign technicians to fix the buses. In the long run, the cost of operating the Nyayo buses became a substantial liability on the government accounts.[24]

Even if that was not enough to bring about the end of the Nyayo Bus Service, one could count on corruption and embezzlement to also play a significant role in its collapse. For instance, Moi, with characteristic nepotism, appointed one Major Koitaba, an army officer from his own Kalenjin tribe, to head the project. The major had no experience running a business, nor had he any training in transportation or economics. He was, however, like many government officials of his type, quite an experienced swindler, and he quickly set about misappropriating funds from the NBS. His stratagems were not particularly original—for example, the major would place large orders for spare parts or fuel, of which only a fraction would actually be delivered, leaving the rest to be shared among the managers and others along the supply chain.[25] Nor did it take much time for him to find help in fleecing the company. Slowly but surely, the drivers and conductors from the National Youth Service got in on the act. Because they were not paid a real salary, they gradually began reimbursing themselves by appropriating shillings from the passengers' daily fares. Given all the graft, the Kenyan Treasury found it increasingly difficult to underwrite the company's costs; likewise, the government found it impossible to find a remedy for the lack of spare parts and qualified drivers, or to undo the ill will that resulted from the irate and embattled competition and the rot of corruption. Like the implementation of the Matatu Bill, the formation of the Nyayo Bus Service quickly began to look like another hasty, makeshift solution to the immensely complicated issue of public transportation in the country.

No wonder, then, that the Nyayo Bus Service crawled along for just five years, leaving fewer and fewer buses on the road each month, until at last it sputtered to a stop at the beginning of 1992. A local newspaper writing of its decline noted that only fifty-five of the three hundred buses introduced countrywide were still operating, and that the rest had either "collapsed or [been] vandalized."[26] This was more attention than it got from most news outlets. Most of the NBS obituaries were written in an offhand manner and seemed oddly disinterested or indifferent, as if describing the death of some minor celebrity.

———

Still, despite its passing, while the Nyayo Bus Service operated, it had provided matatus with some serious competition. Immediately after the first bunch of Nyayo buses—nearly one hundred of them—started operating in Nairobi at the beginning of 1986, it was clear that they could compete with matatus along the more popular routes. Whereas the KBS had decided to move to the peripheral routes rather than compete directly with the Nyayo buses, for the most part matatus stayed on the busy commuter routes and fought. They were not about to surrender their lucrative routes or profitable schedules, and so they continued to run on the main routes during the peak hours, just as they had before the arrival of the NBS. In order to survive, however, they began—as they had in the past—to drive faster and more recklessly to get first chance at winning passengers. And, sure enough, this led yet again to a significant increase in the number of accidents and fatalities. No one was happy. The more the heedless matatus caused accidents, the more impassioned became the debates about the necessity of tightly regulating them. As in previous years, these debates were heard everywhere in Kenya—on the radio and TV, in churches, in public speeches, and in every café. And there was no lack of material to feed the flames. One had only to glance at newspaper headlines to get a sense of outrage. They were despairingly matter of fact: "6 more killed in matatus," "31 claimed by road accidents," "Matatu kills 9 boys," "11 people killed in a horror matatu crash," "10 more killed in a matatu smash," "6 hurt as 9 killed, as matatu rolls," "4-year-old killed by a matatu," "30 pupils hurt in a matatu crash," "Matatu accident claims 4 lives."[27]

These were almost daily occurrences, and proposals for measures that might help reduce the number of matatu accidents filled the newspapers, ranging from personal appeals to nationwide policy requirements. A few of the more extreme suggestions included a prohibition of matatus on the roads after 6:00 p.m. and requiring that all matatus be fitted with radios so that the drivers could receive hortatory messages as they drove. Several letters to the editor reasonably suggested that road safety education be made part of the primary and high school curriculum; they argued that a "greater sense and consciousness of the need for road safety [should be] instilled in young children while still at school," so that they would be turned "into safe motorists and pedestrians when they grow up."[28] The minister of transport and communication even took the drastic measure of passing a new law requiring that all matatus be fitted with speed controls, but the exorbitant costs of these gadgets made their implementation impossible. And Moi, with his customary guarded and apprehensive approach to policy, quietly decided to rescind the law when the matatus threatened to go on strike.[29] In this case, it was probably a wise move.

Several members of the public submitted some of the most useful and economically sensible suggestions. One was quite simple: give matatu owners more time to repay their loans so they would not feel so pressured to race through the streets for passengers (the only downside of the suggestion was, regrettably, that the owners would end up paying more interest).[30] Another obvious suggestion was that all drivers be required to pass an eye exam before being issued a driver's license. It is, of course, surprising that this was not already a prerequisite; one would think that this modest requirement would have been included in the initial Matatu Bill of 1984 (even though it may not have had much effect upon the number of fatal accidents).[31]

Where the law proved insufficient, sometimes satire was employed to discourage matatu drivers from speeding. For instance, some sardonic wit came up with a popular sticker that read:

At 80 kph, God will take care of you
100 kph, Guide me O Thou Great Jehovah
120 kph, Nearer my God to thee
140 kph, This world is not my Home
160 kph, Lord I am coming home
And at over 180 kph, Precious memories[32]

Like all satire it employed irony to encourage reform, and though it may not have had an immediate effect, at least it had an appreciative audience, since, according to one hopeful passenger, "many Kenyans were Christians and God-fearing people."[33] It is perhaps an indication of the matatu's obstinacy that the song's satiric message was co-opted by matatu drivers; it became known as the "speed song" and was placed prominently in the windows or on the seatbacks of almost every vehicle. And its appropriation was plausible; at one level the sticker's critique of careless drivers urges them to drive more carefully, yet, at the same time, it implies that the passengers should simply tolerate— and find humor in—the situation. Even if it was meant to be tongue-in-cheek, the sticker really advocated a kind of passivity since it assured them that death in a matatu accident would earn them a place in heaven. Chance was not in their hands, but God's. Just cram yourself in and pray for the best; either way a matatu would get you where you were meant to go. Everybody wins: the matatu owner makes a profit, and you either reach your destination or get a shot at salvation. The speed song became so popular that it was sold even in tourist shops, giving visitors the impression that tolerating speeding matatus and the risks that came with them was just an offbeat aspect of the Kenyan character, too rooted in the city's way of life to be changed.[34]

There were still other interesting suggestions. One of the motorists in Nairobi believed that while external deterrents were necessary, the key to avoiding accidents existed in the psychic temperament of the individual driver. Matatu drivers, he suggested in a letter to the newspaper, should adopt his own practice: "before I overtake [i.e., pass another car] I take a deep breath and ask myself a question three times: Shall I make it or shall I not, Shall I make it or shall I not, Shall I make it or shall I not?"[35] In other words, if only matatu drivers would chant this calming incantation they might make the journey safely. Or, the implacable laws of physics would provide them with an answer.

———

Be that as it may, a more meditative attitude might have helped do more than just prevent accidents. It might have helped improve the general behavior of matatu operators, which nearly everyone considered disgraceful. And for good reason. Throughout the late 1980s, the drivers, the conductors, and the touts were reliably rowdy and abusive to passengers and to competing matatus, in utter disregard of the tenets of the Matatu Bill, and despite the persistent warnings of MVOA officials. Many of them acted as if the events of August 1, 1984, had never happened, as if the Matatu Bill had never been passed. Take, for instance, the case of Selina Aluso, a mother of thirteen children, who had an encounter with matatu operators on November 2, 1986: "I boarded the KBS bus and sat just behind the driver. Other people also got in, but as the driver was about to take off, a matatu overtook the bus and stopped abruptly in front of it, blocking the way. Both the driver and conductor shouted at the matatu driver and touts, who were calling for passengers to move out of the way."[36] According to Aluso, "the matatu moved a few feet to allow the bus to pass, but further ahead the matatu again blocked the way, making the bus driver slam on the emergency brakes to avoid hitting the rear of the matatu." This, she said, happened a third time. But this time, she told the reporter, "the conductor came to the front door and started yelling at the matatu touts and driver, triggering an exchange of obscenities between the two groups. Four touts came to the bus and started banging its sides, challenging the bus driver to come out and fight. One of the matatu operators rushed back into the matatu, returned with a plastic bottle, and sprayed liquid at us." The liquid, Aluso related, "caught me on the left side of my face, including my eye and chest, the back of my neck and left leg. I felt a terrible burning sensation all over my body and I fell down on the floor of the bus screaming and asking for help. . . . I held on to a nearby passenger and asked him to blow cool air on my eye, which felt like it was burning. The liquid also caught the conductor and other people and there was total confusion in the bus." The touts fled back to the matatu and raced off, fearing capture by bus passengers and the gathering crowd. A "good Samaritan" escorted Aluso to the nearby Kenyatta National Hospital, where, "for nearly an hour before applying medicine," a doctor rinsed acid from her eye. As a result of the acid attack her eyes had become "overly sensitive" to light and her vision permanently blurred.[37]

As horrible as this incident was, it was not all that exceptional—in fact, it was rather symptomatic. The competition posed by the Nyayo Bus Service had aggravated an already tense situation by making matatu workers more anxious about their ability to make a living, and by forcing them to fight for passengers. The inevitable effect was more antagonism, conflict, and hooliganism. Eventually the behavior of operators became so threatening that by mid-1988, many Kenyans were beginning to feel that the task of disciplining matatu operators had become too important and too complicated to be left to the MVOA alone. The whole society—licensing agencies, police, government officials, passengers, elders, parents, and church leaders, all of them—needed to step up and demand change. This message was captured nicely in a cartoon in one of the daily papers that pictured a hapless Nderi at a "MVOA Seminar on Safety and Discipline," placating a group of callous operators, one of them sporting a T-shirt embellished with the word "POWER" across the chest. In the caption, Nderi pacifies them with the helpful reminder: "No, you don't have to throw acid at passengers to instill discipline in them." In the foreground a cat grins sadistically over a dead mouse.

"No, you don't have to throw acid at passengers to instil discipline in them.... Next question please?"

FIGURE 14   Courtesy of Paul Kelemba

To make matters worse, it had become clear by the end of 1987 that the MVOA matatu operators, conductors, and especially touts, had drifted toward political views that were hostile to Moi, and many of them began turning their matatus into political sites where they could openly criticize the government.[38] Even though MVOA officials probably shared many of the operators' sentiments, they knew that in the politically sensitive climate of the late 1980s it was not prudent to air those concerns so publicly. The operators were laying themselves open to the possibility of detention without a hearing. So, again, the MVOA was faced with another delicate challenge: banning political talk in matatus. Its attempts to quiet the operators did not go over well, and almost immediately conductors and drivers began to accuse Nderi of being a "traitor" to their cause, of being "weak" and a "coward."[39]

In time the pressures Nderi experienced became unbearable, and internal feuding within the MVOA caused it to split into competing factions. Besides, there was a general feeling among the association's officials that Nderi had become too dominant, and that he too often spoke with the press without consulting them. Much of what Nderi told the press, they felt, did not reflect what matatu owners really thought, and the resulting estrangement became so destabilizing that several officials resigned. One of the trustees of the Mombasa branch left because of what he called an "unhealthy working climate."[40] At the end of November 1987, the MVOA secretary, Kinyanjui Chau, also resigned and complained that "Mr. Nderi had been giving matatu owners a raw deal." "Of late," he said, Nderi "has been making political statements that are contrary to the MVOA constitution," and he further accused Nderi of making unilateral decisions without the mandate or approval of the executive committee.[41]

In his own defense, Nderi argued that if there had been any failure in his office it had been caused by the lack of cooperation from the various branches of the MVOA, and he had therefore been forced to act autonomously. He also claimed that the association's financial situation was so bad that he was running the office without funds, and he dismissed the specific allegation that he had wined and dined MVOA delegates from all over the country to get elected.[42] But it was not only the MVOA by which he felt persecuted. He had also managed to get into trouble with the law. At a meeting organized by the traffic management committee, he managed to get himself "charged with causing disturbances" for his histrionic behavior. Apparently he had shouted loudly and violently at the meeting, declaring that a certain decision the committee made was "biased," before he flung his files violently on the table and returned to his seat—all in response to a verdict supposedly passed against him.[43] This was enough to put him in jeopardy, and apparently enough to justify police intervention. The atmosphere was that tense.

By the end of 1987 the MVOA officials' hostility toward their chairman, and the increased media criticism of Nderi and the MVOA in general, left the association weakened, and fewer and fewer members wanted to be affiliated with it. Members began to abandon the dysfunctional association. Some of the former members defected to the Matatu Association of Kenya (MAK), a fledgling matatu owners' group led by one Kariuki Mbuthia—who was, by the way, not entirely without scandal.[44] It was clear, however, that by the beginning of 1988 the MVOA was succumbing to internal and external pressures. In the meantime, matatus continued to career recklessly through the streets and alleyways, and the number of serious accidents continued to rise.

––––––

At the end of February 1988 a fatal accident involving three matatus on Nakuru-Elburgon Road, near Molo, left twenty-seven people dead and many injured.[45] This incident had followed close on the heels of other matatu accidents that had taken 165 lives since the New Year. But the Molo accident caused a nationwide outcry. President Moi sent condolences to the families of those killed and commiserated with the victims by lamenting that "matatus had become [more] an agent of death and destruction than an asset."[46] The minister of transport and communications, Arthur Magugu, was similarly appalled; for him, "careless driving and speeding" had been the cause of the accident and the loss of life.[47] Their condolences were surely heartfelt, but both were reiterating the widespread sentiment that something had to be done. The sentiment was echoed in all the major newspapers, where, once again, the letters to the editor were conspicuously negative and even began questioning whether the country really needed matatus.[48] They had a point. In addition to the unconscionable loss of life, the impact of the fatal accidents on the economy made matters even worse. According to Magugu there had been more than 1,800 deaths in road accidents in 1986, and 1,900 in 1987, and these accidents were costing the country over 3.7 billion shillings per year.[49] More than half of these fatal accidents involved matatus.

Three days after the fatal Molo accident, the transport minister called a press conference in which he announced that all the matatus would be required to undergo retesting by special teams made up of officials from the Ministry of Transport and Communication, traffic police, and the National Youth Service.[50] He also insisted that the police carry out a massive crackdown on defective matatus in Nairobi. As a result, close to 150 matatus were impounded at the police headquarters each day and held for at least four days. Naturally, matatu owners did not want anything to do with the crackdown. As usual, Nderi conveyed their resentment to the public, claiming that the new rules were "discriminatory and constituted the harassment of matatu operators," and he went on to say that all Kenyans were bad drivers, and if retesting needed to be carried out then "all drivers in the country should undergo retesting—with the exception, of course, of the President and Vice President."[51] Not satisfied with merely calling out the government and other drivers, Nderi also demanded that Moi sack his minister of transportation and the chief vehicle examiner, Kuria Kanyingi. Still not satisfied, he proceeded to call the first major nationwide matatu strike.[52]

The strike could not have occurred at a worse time in the country. It was scheduled at the beginning of the Easter holiday, which made it more or less impossible for anyone to visit family in the rural areas. Moreover, the strike threw the public transportation system in the whole country into disarray. The few buses that drove people to their homes in the upcountry withdrew from the roads because they were being stoned and harassed by matatu touts. As newspapers reported, "Hundreds of stranded commuters watched helplessly as a convoy of buses were driven past [because they were prevented from stopping], honking continuously and leaving a trail of dust. *Manambas* [touts] cheered them wildly as police watched helplessly."[53] The government was caught completely off guard.

In Nairobi a few raucous conductors patrolled the streets in their matatus making sure that no was breaking the strike. If found, they would be dealt with appropriately. They were also on the lookout for KBS buses. Touts from the matatus carried *rungus* (whips) and stoned the buses, so that many of them were forced to leave the streets.[54] Newspapers also reported that "bus stops at residential areas and on the way into the city resembled public *barazas* [meeting places]" because the residents could do nothing but stand around waiting without knowing what to do.[55] At the usually busy Eastleigh residential area it was reported that touts and conductors passed by passengers taunting them sarcastically—"We don't want your money, we have made enough to live on for now."[56] Some of them reveled in the chaos, gloating that it was "time people realized the importance of matatus." Outside Nairobi the situation was just as bad—in the western town of Kisumu, for example, touts and conductors stoned any vehicle violating the strike, and on at least one occasion overturned a taxi and seriously beat up the driver until the riot police intervened.

The bus drivers were not the only victims of the strike. Because the service provided by the KBS and Nyayo buses was insufficient, there was little either could do to combat the strike's effects, and so commuters were left to fend for themselves. It was not easy; the abrupt disappearance of matatus from the streets paralyzed the city and closed down much of the city's business. Schoolchildren were forced to walk miles to school every day, pregnant women gave birth at bus stops because they had no ride to the hospital, and the sick died at home. Photographs of these "scenes of sheer despair and helplessness" were sensationally displayed in Kenya's daily newspapers.[57] As usual, the headlines did not hesitate to underscore all the suffering: "Thousands stranded in matatu slow-down," "Matatu strike paralyses town," "Transport Crisis as Matatu Strikes." Because the consequences were so crippling, the public was unwilling to see anything but malice in the strike. Like the headlines, the ever-popular letters to the editor were loud and predictably furious; matatu operators are "a lot sent from hell," proclaimed one letter. "Matatus are a curse to mankind," wrote another bitter correspondent.[58] Some of those writing to the editors insisted that the government provide an alternative means of transportation—apparently forgetting about the Nyayo Bus Service buses.[59] Inevitably, class conflicts began to emerge. Many felt that the government should not yield to the pressure and give in to matatu demands; others felt that rich people in high positions did not realize—or refused to realize—that the matatu crisis was an urgent problem and that the lives and livelihoods of ordinary people were at stake. The problems needed to be solved without delay, and yet, as commuters were left abandoned at the roadsides, as the economy suffered and lives were lost, the government seemed unable to do anything.[60]

After having witnessed the chaos in the city for three days, Moi finally relented and revoked Minister Magugu's new regulations; he also asked the police to release the vehicles they had impounded. In a dramatic meeting with the press, Nderi—somewhat disingenuously— thanked the president "profusely" for intervening to bring the matatu crisis to an end.[61] But Nderi's professed gratitude did not help him; this time he had gone too far and angered Moi beyond repair. Addressing the nation during this strike, President Moi publicly accused Nderi and the matatu operators of "plotting to blackmail [extort] the government," and of being responsible for the deterioration of the Kenyan economy.[62] And as if this was not enough, he further accused the matatu operators of performing "callous and anti-social acts," and of refusing to embrace the *Nyayo* philosophy of being "mindful of the welfare of others"—a philosophy that required "that *wanainchi* render services to others without being propelled by lust for money."[63] Clearly, President Moi viewed this strike as an open confrontation with the government on the part of matatu owners and the MVOA, and he warned MVOA officials that if they did not obey him in the future he would dissolve their association.[64] Moi held the grudge for nearly nine months.

The scapegoating of Nderi and of the MVOA was not as easy or as simple as Moi would have liked, however. The country's transportation systems were just too complicated to be pinned to one man. Later that year, on December 3, 1988 (exactly three months after he had consecrated the three hundred new buses in that extravagant ceremony in downtown Nairobi), Moi took a short trip to Arusha, Tanzania. Upon his return he found out that the country buses had increased fares by nearly 113 percent. Apparently they, too, had forgotten the lessons of *Nyayo*. The passengers were angry, and so was Moi, and he reacted as he had before—with a lack of forethought or consideration of the cost: he banned the Kenya Country Bus Owners Association (KCBOA).[65] And while he was at it, he banned the Matatu Association of Kenya (MAK), and of course, the MVOA.[66] Nderi was sent into detention.

Now that all these organizations were officially dead, the accusations started flying. Moi's postmortem of the MVOA is worth considering, in particular, for its out-and-out hypocrisy. According to President Moi, the MVOA had been demanding a 5,000-shilling membership fee and daily fees amounting to 50 shillings per day, but had supposedly done nothing to help the owners maintain their vehicles. The MVOA officials denied these accusations and responded that the fees were used to secure parking lots and to maintain matatus in good order. But the president remained adamant and stuck to his claim that the organization had done absolutely nothing to help matatu owners take care of their vehicles. Moreover, Moi accused the central organization of the MVOA of duplicating the services of the branches so as to increase its income, and he laid the blame for the increase in police persecution and harassment upon the MVOA as well as the increase in traffic accidents. He even insinuated that they were indifferent to the carnage on the streets—"when matatus continue to kill Kenyans . . . the association does nothing," and he seemed to imply that all the mishaps and tragedies could have been averted if the association had simply established requirements for safe driving.[67] He capped all these accusations by spitefully adding that the MVOA had even failed to establish a credit union for matatu operators as it had originally claimed it would do, and then concluded with the rancorous suggestion that that matatu owners were better off on their own, without the MVOA.[68] Accordingly, in his order banning these organizations, Moi declared that from now on each matatu or bus owner would look after his or her own interests individually. Since the MVOA had failed to manage the entirety of the transport system and its economy, the MVOA's existence was obviously unnecessary, and therefore it needed to be abolished. Moi had found his scapegoat.

In the end, then, Moi was content to blame the MVOA, and not his own government, for doing nothing to improve the image of the industry or help the nation. Of course, the president neglected to acknowledge that his own government bore any of the responsibility to regulate the matatu business, nor did he consider that it might be unfair to expect the MVOA to provide solutions to all the social and economic problems associated with city's transport. But Moi had found a culprit—Nderi and his association—and he was not about to let pass the opportunity to assign responsibility to someone outside the government.

One of the most unsettling consequences of Moi's censure was soon made visible to all. When the press was finally able to visit Nderi after his release from detention they confronted a man who was clearly not himself. The usually voluble spokesman looked "visibly shaken," and would only say to reporters' questions that "we have been trying to do a lot to alleviate the problems of both commuters and matatu owners, but since it is a decision from the Head of State, we can only say it is a 'wise decision.'"[69] Nderi's meekness was bewildering, even unnerving. The change in his demeanor, his strangely subdued answer, and his uncharacteristic deference to the wisdom of the president, surely signaled to the observant that Moi's government was becoming so repressive, so despotic, that even a shrewd, hardened fellow like Nderi felt that the only option open to him was to concede to the government's allegations.

———

I spoke with Nderi in June 2004 about the events surrounding the banning of the MVOA.[70] Since my account of events had been drawn largely from newspaper stories and a few interviews, I was particularly interested in what he thought of my interpretation of the events, my portrayal of the various characters, and especially my characterization of him. Was he as stubborn, indomitable, energetic, outspoken, and domineering as the man I had encountered in the interviews and newspapers?

"Aaaaihh!" he roared, "I was very tough then. I was strong and determined. See, I was a young man then and very determined."

Nderi was perhaps in his late seventies when I spoke with him, and he now walked with the help of crutches. When I asked about the crutches, he told me why they were necessary: "See, they did this to me while I was in prison. And now I can't walk, now I am just an old man, a crippled old man."

"Who did this to you?" I asked.

"Hmmmmm!" He patted my hand, looked me directly in the eye, and said, "You don't ask questions like that." Nevertheless, he went on to inform me that he had in fact held a press conference after the banning of the MVOA, and that during the conference the police had stormed into the room, arrested him, and imprisoned him without trial. While in prison, he was tortured and his legs were broken.

Worried that my representation of Moi's government might be unduly harsh, I asked him if it was as insecure and ineffective as it appeared in my account.

"You know if you are comfortable in yourself you have the confidence to talk with people nicely. You don't use force; only those who are afraid use force," he replied.

I reminded Nderi that several groups and publications had been

FIGURE 15   Joseph Nderi and Kenda Mutongi, June 18, 2004.

banned at the same time that Moi had banned the MVOA. I pointed out, for example, that *Beyond* magazine, published by the National Council of Christian Churches of Kenya, had been banned because it had become a forum for criticizing Moi's government.

"Yes," he nodded.

"So when the newspapers reported that you looked 'visibly shaken' after the banning of the MVOA, you were actually afraid?"

Again he looked directly at me and said, "Yes. See, I now knew my life was finished; I was done, because I had been fighting for the rights of matatu owners."

But when I reminded him that matatus were constantly breaking the traffic laws and bribing the police, and that the crews were rowdy and needed discipline, he merely laughed the comment away. But he did go on to tell me how he had tried to "streamline" the industry, and how it was difficult for the MVOA to do it alone, and how the industry is simply difficult to regulate. When I mentioned the rival matatu organization, the Matatu Association of Kenya (MAK), which was also banned by the government, and which might have helped with reform, Nderi looked away, laughed, and exclaimed, "Ahhhhhahhah, Kariuki Mbuthia, don't even remind me of that crook."

He was happy to be reminded, though, of the *Matatu*, the journal that the MVOA published between 1983 and 1985. I had found copies at the University of Nairobi library and had made a few extra copies for him. As he flipped through the pages, he smiled and chuckled, remarking that the journal reminded him of the happy days of the MVOA, and he seemed content to sit lingering in the soft light of nostalgia recalling to himself his old friends and old battles. Eventually I managed to shake him from his reveries and change the subject. I asked him about his final statement to the press, the one in which he had so strangely deferred to the former president's wisdom. I handed him a copy of the newspaper clipping. He took at it eagerly and remarked, "I remember that clipping. Ayayayayayaah. . . . What are you doing to me, Professor Kenda? What are you doing to me?" And then he read it back to me out loud, quietly and slowly: "A visibly shaken Mr. Nderi said: 'We have been trying to do a lot to alleviate the problems of both commuters and matatu owners, but since it is a decision from the Head of State, we can only say it is a 'wise decision.'"[71]

"Did you really believe it was a 'wise decision?'" I asked.

Again he told me, "You don't ask questions like that." But he answered anyway, without embarrassment, even with a note of pride: "That is what I was supposed to say, and at that time you said what you were supposed to say. . . . You see, you said what they wanted to hear, because you had to survive."

PART FIVE

Organized Crime?
1988–2014

EIGHT

KANU Youth Wingers

The banning of the MVOA had left the matatu industry without a sense of direction. Without an organization to steer its political course, or a spokesman to articulate its viewpoint, the matatu workers were left each one to themselves, subject to dictates of the market, the whims of the police, and of course the arbitrary decrees of the government. Divided and disorganized, the matatu workers posed less of a threat to the authorities, though at the same time they had become harder to control and more open to the temptations of resistance. To put it another way, the absence of the MVOA had created a vacuum, the kind of vacuum abhorred by a politician. But it also presented President Moi with an opportunity, one that he smartly filled with a group of mostly young men who became known as KANU Youth Wingers (KYW).[1] Their role was to observe the matatu terminals and to report on those supporting the opposition parties; simply put, they were spies. Their introduction was a preemptive move on Moi's part. In the early 1990s, as Kenyans became frustrated with one-party domination and began agitating for change, the Moi regime was concerned that opposition parties would enlist support from matatu workers—and he could not allow that to happen.

The matatu workers had already been subject to government scrutiny for decades, and most of them—the touts, conductors, and drivers—had become highly politicized, often by the adverse effects that scrutiny had had upon their livelihoods. Many had come to distrust the government, and they became one of the first coalitions to occupy the vanguard of multiparty politics. Since many of them worked in centralized parking lots, particularly in Nairobi, they were highly visible, and the public could not help but notice their numbers and their politics.[2] Finding your way onto a matatu often meant finding your way into a political debate. But members of the KYW were just as visible as the matatu workers, perfectly outfitted, as they were, in black trousers or skirts, red shirts, and green berets—the colors of the Kenyan flag. Dressed in the nation's colors, the KYW proceeded to act more or less as a de facto police force and were tacitly granted the power to mete out instant justice. Or injustice.[3] One of their instructions was to intimidate matatu workers and passengers and to compel them to support KANU. In addition to spying, they were more or less ordered to act as political henchmen, stomping out dissent and safeguarding the esteem of KANU.

But that was not the story Moi told the public. Instead, he argued duplicitously that the youth wingers were high-minded civil servants who had "volunteered to be in the forefront in the war against crime, and that the public should assist them and should not be afraid to go to them when the police are not around."[4] In speech after speech, Moi is reported to have said the youth wingers were working closely with the police to "wipe out crimes in the city."[5] And yet despite the president's advocacy, it soon became evident to everyone that the presence of the KYW had only served to intensify the violence in the matatu parking lots; nor did Moi's deception go unnoticed by the matatu workers and their passengers. The MVOA touts were particularly unconvinced by Moi's rhetoric.[6] Because the youth wingers were given orders to clash with anyone they suspected of supporting the opposition parties, whether operators or passengers, they directly interfered with the work of the touts, and so the touts saw them as a threat to their jobs. When the touts resisted their interference, the youth wingers, equipped with *rungus*, stones, machetes, or iron bars, could be counted on to intimidate or assault their opponent with impunity. In a short time, the matatu parking spaces turned into battlegrounds.

The opposition parties reacted to the presence of the KYW by recruiting their own young henchmen and placing them in the parking lots to retaliate. Moi had clearly expected the matatu owners to submit to the KYW and had not anticipated their resistance, but the KYW's intrusion only provoked the workers into a confrontation, one that became more violent as the weeks passed, until finally it became clear that Moi's attempt at intimidation had failed. Ultimately, he lost control of the lots. And, perhaps even more importantly, the open challenge to KANU by the matatu workers prompted the general public to come to a new realization: opposition was possible, and just maybe an even more legitimate democracy could be achieved. In due course, the newly roused public followed the lead of the matatu workers and began their own persistent demands for democracy, and eventually they forced Moi to set a date for multiparty elections, to be held in late 1992.

For the opposition parties the irony was delicious: Moi had unwittingly enabled the democracy he had been fighting against.[7] His use of the KYW to enforce his political will had only weakened him. An unfortunate side effect, however, was that once again the image of the matatu industry was tainted by the violence. Any political benefit that the country might have realized through the resistance of the matatu workers was obscured by their established reputation for malevolence and violence, and the parking lot battles with the KYW only made that reputation worse. Fair or not, that legacy of ill will became difficult to overcome.

———

Moi began to exert an even firmer grip on his rule in the early 1990s.[8] To enhance the government's ability to keep watch on dissenters he set up KANU offices in rural locations as well as in provincial and district offices. The new offices were shrewdly located near bus stops—almost certainly so he could better monitor matatu workers.[9] As the number of offices began to proliferate in the Kenyan landscape, the offices' influence was quickly felt. Officials in charge of the offices worked closely with local chiefs, rounding up the young and unemployed (mostly men) to join the KYW.[10] Many of the unemployed had a primary- or secondary-level education and were literate, and they were receptive to KANU's entreaties as the prospect of permanent employment in the government was an attractive option. For many, simply the promise of occasional remuneration was convincing enough.[11]

For the jobless, membership in KANU offered an encouraging reprieve from the privations of poverty and unemployment, and for once Moi's government seemed to be giving attention to the destitute it had otherwise ignored. "Back then the government promised us many things," recalled James Kibisu, a former youth winger. "And then because you worked for the government and you wore a nice uniform, you felt special, it was like you had power like a policeman; it was a nice job."[12] Musa Mwaniki, another one-time youth winger, told a similar story: "See, youth winger was a nice job to have. I graduated from secondary school and I was sitting around for many years without a job; it was a job, and you had the power of the government in your hands, so we just did what we were told, and made some money."[13]

By the mid-1990s there were at least thirty KYW working at every major parking lot in Nairobi and other cities, and up to five KYW were installed at each of the smaller metropolitan and rural matatu stops.[14] Overall, KANU's recruitment campaign was a success. The youth wingers stood out vividly in their uniforms—though they sometimes exhibited the comic implausibility of a toddler wearing his father's shoes. Even if the clothes did not quite make the man, Moi reasoned that the uniforms at least gave the KYW recruits a dignified and commanding look and conveyed the impression that they could be trusted and should be listened to when they spoke in support of KANU—especially compared to the ragtag touts working for MVOA.[15]

One of the youth wingers' more aggressive moves was to take over responsibility for organizing and assigning matatu routes, a role previously held by MVOA officials. This sensitive task had always been a potential source of conflict since it was simply impossible for every operator to work a lucrative route, particularly in Nairobi where there were always scores of passengers and a great deal of money to make. However, the KYW officials proved particularly insensitive to this issue, and either out of inexperience or unwillingness, failed to allocate routes carefully or fairly.[16] Since there seemed to be no protocols, or the KYW simply ignored them, it helped to have the KYW in your corner if you wanted to be assigned a profitable route; quite predictably, the best routes were assigned to those the KYW deemed sympathetic to KANU and less profitable routes to those suspected of siding with the opposition parties.[17] This ended up dividing the matatu workers into two opposing camps, each vying for better routes and parking spots and suspicious of the other's motives and politics. Those willing to go along with KANU kept working and making profits, and those who resisted were inevitably considered enemies of KANU. As I was told by Juma Mukiri, who owned a matatu in the early 1990s, "it was not a good time to be in the matatu business because everything at the time was about politics, not [about] making money. . . . It was about whose side you were on. You wondered what the Youth Wingers knew about the matatu business, but then they were supported by Moi, and there was nothing to do."[18] Another operator, Martin Chege, agreed, though his response avoided any direct mention of politics: "In the MVOA days, how much money you paid determined which route you got, so at least then you just knew where you belonged, and that was nice."[19]

Still, this practice also had its problems; it too was inequitable. If the MVOA had made it easy to buy lucrative routes without troubling oneself with politics, it must have unfairly favored the wealthy matatu owners. When I suggested this to Chege, he gave me a pragmatic answer: "yes, but then it was different because you knew that if you could somehow find ways to get more money, you could be guaranteed a better route. It was real business, not politics . . . real business, you see."[20] Better, it seems, that the routes were commodified than politicized.

Even if the violence and favoritism raised the levels of conflict to intolerable levels, the presence of the KANU Youth Wingers in matatu parking stations unquestionably helped the idea of multiparty politics gain ground. Anyone who paid attention could see that KANU's practices had incited opposition, and that it was not going to be easily subjugated.[21] In fact, opposition to their behavior in the parking lots became a regular item of discussion in the Kenyan Parliament.[22] Whenever the Parliament addressed the topic of youth wingers, or the opposition they provoked, KANU members would mechanically begin repeating Moi's talking points—the KYW was performing a valuable service to the country by eliminating crime and maintaining order at matatu stops. Their rehearsed rhetoric made no mention as to how "maintaining order" also meant intimidating supporters of the emerging opposition parties, such as the Democratic Party (DP) or the Forum for the Restoration of Democracy (FORD).[23] Moi merely ignored the opposition MPs' complaints about the KYW's tyranny in the parking lots and bullying of passengers and continued to pay tribute to the valiant efforts of KYW in preventing crime and political hooliganism.

But the opposition wanted answers, and they relentlessly questioned Amin Walji, then assistant minister of local government, about KANU's practices. But they got nowhere with him. Whenever pressed for answers, Walji just claimed to be above mere politics: "If there is a problem between the matatu owners, the business community and the KANU Youth Wingers, that is a 'political problem.'" He insisted, moreover, that "my ministry should not be dragged into the issue."[24] Despite his avowal of innocence, despite his self-effacing claim to be above the trifling "political problem," everyone knew that he spoke for Moi, and that Moi had placed the youth wingers in the lots to help secure his political position. But no one in the government was going to admit this—and besides, it clearly must be something other than political to place in the parking lots young, uniformed men without training and task them with beating up anyone who disputed government policy.

Although the assistant minister may have managed to evade the problem successfully, others were not so fortunate. The more Moi's tactics succeeded, the more they made members of the opposition determined to raise the profile and power of their own parties.[25] They responded to the government's evasions by persisting in their interrogation of KANU, and by making plans to place their own parties' "youth wingers" at the matatu parks. It could be said that wanting their own wingers was tacit acknowledgment of Moi's success, but the more salient point is that the opposition was not afraid to imitate his tough tactics; they were willing to challenge KANU and contest their control over some of the city's most important public spaces. To counteract the power and visibility of KANU, the opposition also began recruiting young, unemployed men to work for them, outfitting them in uniforms that represented their own party colors—green, blue, and orange.[26]

Thus began the colorful and impassioned campaign to establish multiparty politics in Kenya. Young men roamed the parking lots clad in flamboyantly colored uniforms, shouting curses at other touts, and banging on vehicles to persuade passengers to enter *their* matatus, and when not noisily canvassing the lots, they gathered in furtive groups to plot strategies against their rivals, or leaned haughtily against their vehicles, smoking or chewing *khat*. No peace or quiet was to be found anywhere near the parking lots. They had become bedlam. Everywhere the acrid air resounded with the roar of racing engines and blaring horns, and with the din of threats, quarrels and name-calling—though

FIGURE 16 Clashes among touts and KYW in matatu parking lots, 1991. Courtesy of the Standard Group, Nairobi

almost always, amid the confusion, there wandered a scattered group of cowed passengers, full of dread, apprehension, and resentment.[27] And yet at the same time, it was an exciting and transformative period for those interested in multiparty politics. The more passionate and volatile the conflicts, the more people began to see signs of something resembling freedom of speech, and the more they witnessed others openly speaking out and debating, the more they began to see the possibility of political change.

But then change was going to come at a cost. The friction caused by the introduction of the youth wingers and their efforts to discourage political activities in the parking lots had probably been anticipated, and perhaps even planned, though it is unlikely that anyone had expected the conflicts to flame up so quickly or so violently. On June 19, 1991, for example, a violent brawl broke out in the city parking lot between FORD youth wingers and the KYW.[28] Four people were seriously injured and hospitalized. Eyewitness accounts stated that members of each of the different youth winger groups were involved in what amounted to little more than gang warfare.[29] The brawls were eye opening, and part of what was revealed was the possibility of the resistance. The clearly perceptible distinctions between different parties, if not the subtleties of their policies, enabled a public recognition that KANU power was being contested. As some of the witnesses commented, the parking lot brawls between groups of rival youth wingers gave the impression that "multi-party politics had indeed arrived."[30]

———

There was, however, another group vying for power in the parking lots. The touts from the days of the MVOA still haunted these spaces, hoping to eke out an existence despite having been exiled by the infiltration of the KYW and other groups. Although marginalized by the youth wingers, they refused to abandon the relatively decent living they had been enjoying in the matatu industry.[31] Their presence created yet another problem for the government, and the question of what to do with the touts came up repeatedly in Parliament, and a few of the more socially conscious MPs attempted to get the government to provide alternative employment for the touts. On June 23, 1990, a KANU MP from Nakuru West (J. Mungai) spoke up for the touts by insisting they, too, were Kenyans and deserved to be treated as citizens, and he reminded the Parliament that "some of them are KANU members." They had been put out of work because of the actions of the government, and their situation should be of immediate concern to the legislature—"Where do we take them when we remove them from the bus stations?"[32] Also speaking out on the tout's behalf was Mr. Munyi (assistant minister for culture and social services), who argued that the government had an obligation to provide alternative employment for touts, many of whom were supporting families, and because "they are Kenyans who deserve to be looked after." The touts had "started the matatu industry," he reasoned, and therefore "should not be completely eliminated." He also worried that they might resort to violence if ignored. However, the assistant minister's proposed solution was comically impractical: he recommended that the touts be given the opportunity to "mingle with the KYW" and to benefit from their benign influence. The KYW, he said, would "help discipline them."[33]

The former touts had indeed become a problem, but it is unlikely that they would benefit from being "disciplined" by those who had forced them from their jobs. The touts had been unruly and pugnacious since the late 1980s, and it was laughable to think that the KYW could control them; besides, the KYW themselves were hardly models of good behavior and would have benefited from some discipline. Then again, many of the touts did manage to find occasional employment with matatu operators, despite the disruptive presence of the KYW, and despite the fact that the government had banned them from working in the parking lots. Operators preferred the experienced touts who were familiar with the matatu terminals, who could coax passengers into chosen vehicles, and who were willing to carry the passengers' luggage.[34] According to many of the conductors and drivers, the expelled touts were steady workers with whom they had "an established relationship."[35] Juma Mukiri recalled that he had "worked well with them," and he believed it was simply the right thing to do: "some of them were young men from your village, so how could you just fire them? You tried to find some small, small jobs for them, even though the government wanted them out of the parking terminals. You could not just leave them like that."[36]

Understandably, the KYW did not want these former touts anywhere near the parking lots, since they competed for the tips that the KYW counted on and presented a constant threat to their political mission. So conflict between the former touts and the youth wingers was inevitable and, as usual, it turned violent—for instance, on January 19, 1990, hostilities flared up as a KANU youth winger climbed onto a matatu and forced off a tout who was securing luggage on the roof; the tout fell and sustained a fractured leg.[37] Similarly, on May 14, 1990, three KYWs chased and assaulted a tout who had been seen receiving a tip. His fellow touts hurried to the victim's rescue and retaliated, inciting a fight that raged on until the police arrived to break it up, but business in the parking lot was closed for several hours.[38] Truculent exchanges of this kind were fairly common and much publicized by the press—which again, like their recklessness and rudeness, contributed to the taint of the matatu industry's reputation.

————

The troublesome situation in the parking lots was further exacerbated when the government decided to impose a levy on matatu operators in order to pay KYW stipends; each vehicle was to be charged a 20-shilling fee to leave the terminal.[39] Nothing could have been more unwelcomed, and the operators were justifiably outraged and refused to pay, and they also threatened to hold another strike if the government did not rescind the charges. They also argued that the youth wingers were too lazy or too weak to lift heavy goods onto the roofs of the vehicles and were therefore of little use to them. Sooner or later, the operators ended up having to pay the touts to complete tasks the KYW neglected, and they resented paying twice for the same service, especially when the despised levies served only to subsidize the venality and incompetence of government factotums.[40] As former members of the MVOA, the operators were justifiably incensed that they should have to pay fees to the very people who had moved in when their organization was disbanded. Not only were they no longer permitted to govern themselves, now they were forced to pay for that privilege.

Still, what was most offensive to Moi's opponents among the matatu operators was that the youth wingers were KANU employees, and the fees collected propped up the reigning political party. Moi's opponents saw these funds not only as lost income but also as money spent undermining their own political interests. They were, in effect, being taxed to bankroll their own defeat. This was evident to anyone who belonged to a political party other than KANU, and it was especially galling when it was their own former touts who were actually doing the work in the terminals, lifting the heavy loads, cleaning up the vehicles, and recruiting passengers. Matatu owners had good reason to question a levy subsidizing an unwelcome organization that had seized their employees' jobs, neglected their duties, and worked against their political interests. It was a little like paying for your own parasites.

To make things worse, KYW officials were not averse to using aggressive methods to collect the levies since they were confident of government backing. One of their more obvious measures was to block terminal exits with barriers to prevent matatu operators from leaving, a tactic that certainly succeeded in eliciting a reaction. Skirmishes promptly broke out as matatu workers trapped in the terminals tried to force their way out and members of the KYW defended themselves with matching ferocity. Often passengers, who considered themselves unjustly impeded, abandoned their places in line or clambered out of the vehicles to join in the fights or hurl stones at the KYW. Almost invariably each faction suffered casualties—bystanders, workers, and youth wingers alike—until the police would arrive and break up the melee by firing warning shots into the air. In the meantime matatu services were interrupted and most travel in the city halted as long as the brawl lasted.[41]

The matatu industry, as usual, received the preponderance of blame for this pattern of events. As the gruesome details of the battles were published, little attention was paid to the complicated motives of the parties involved, or the injustice of the situation; the spectacle of general lawlessness was too engrossing. What mattered to the public was the disruption to services, rather than the political and economic interests of the matatu workers, or the fact that they were only reacting to provocation. Few outside the industry considered how the new levy might undermine the principles of self-governance and fair taxation. But for the many small-business owners who could ill afford the fees, the levy imposed an unsustainable burden: "We cannot afford to pay gate collections to the KANU branches, pay bus park charges to civil authorities, and at the same time pay toll charges. What profits shall we make?" complained matatu owner Clementine Oboa.[42] He could accept that the Nairobi City Council required tolls, which owned the land occupied by matatu terminals, but he argued that the KANU branches provided no service for their fees.

And the KYW levy was only the tip of the iceberg. Matatu owners had been required by the government to pay a lump sum when they were granted routes, but now the fee was increased—from 5,000 to 7,000 shillings. There was no indication that the government planned to do anything with the new revenues, no plans to maintain or upgrade the country's appalling roads or build new bus stops. Many of the roads were so deeply potholed they were impassable and increased the costs of vehicle maintenance as well as the risk of accidents.[43] In the end, matatu operators simply began to avoid roads they deemed unfit or unsafe, depriving transportation to residents of the affected areas, increasing traffic on already busy streets, and triggering yet more public dissatisfaction.[44]

As a matter of fact, avoidance was becoming an overall strategy—avoid the roads, avoid the terminals, and avoid the levies. One way the drivers found to evade levies was to direct passengers to wait on the roadsides just outside the terminals so that the drivers could avoid the terminals altogether. And passengers were often happy to oblige the drivers, who collected them quickly and drove off before the KYW could stop them.[45] There was little the KYW could do to stop passengers from making surreptitious arrangements with drivers, except deflect their frustrations onto the touts left behind once the matatus had departed.

The drivers' sympathies were with the touts since they still depended on them for much of their business, and the reprisals and beatings touts endured eventually prompted a response from workers in just about every aspect of the business. The most useful, and usual, course of action was to threaten a strike, and this is exactly what they did. However, the KYW officials were contemptuous and scoffed at the threats, claiming a strike would be tantamount to denying the KYW its government-ensured "means of livelihood" and stressing that the dedicated youth workers were merely "earning their living honestly."[46] So the harassment of the touts continued, the matatu operators went on strike, and Nairobi once again came to a standstill.[47] Eventually a compromise would be reached, but before long the same cycle would play itself out again, and again, in the months before the first multiparty election.

Resentment toward the KYW increased as commuters gradually came to the realization that it was the youth wingers who were primarily responsible for the disruption of their lives and livelihoods. But it was not only the commuters who had become dismayed. Eventually KANU started to reap the consequences of their actions as some of its longtime members switched to opposition parties; some even burned their KANU registration cards in protest. As the number of defectors began to increase more rapidly toward election day (December 29), KANU national secretary Joseph Kamotho decided to take matters into his own hands, and he abolished the levy collection indefinitely, in order, he said, to "achieve peace, harmony, and understanding among those involved."[48] Unwilling to admit that the strikes had worked, he spoke instead of canceling the levy since it had caused "public resentment," and he attributed the hasty policy change to KANU's sensitive concern for the public's welfare.[49] President Moi, always ready to capitalize on anything that might enhance his image, insisted straightaway that he be given credit for abolishing the levy and for his kindness toward matatu owners who were "suffering" on account of the charges.[50] This was a classic example of Moi's political style: publicly feigning sympathy for the matatu operators and passengers, while having privately worked to undermine their interests—in this case by having encouraged many of the KYW's hostile activities.[51] Perhaps Moi had no choice but to cover up the KYW interference. If hypocrisy is the homage that vice pays to virtue, Moi had been forced to make a payment. Since he could not afford to suffer the damage to his image that the strikes had occasioned, he had little choice but to keep up appearances, disavow the KYW, and embrace the cause of the matatus. It was a hypocrisy that he was willing to embrace—at least for the time being.

––––––

Despite Moi's elimination of the levy and the end of the strike, the brutality of the KYW's activities became more widespread and flagrant as election day approached. For instance, the government had abolished touting, confidently assuming that the KYW would persuade passengers to line up and board vehicles in an orderly fashion, but the orderly lines did not wondrously appear, nor did the touts disappear; on the contrary, they continued to solicit passengers as lustily as ever. But now they were subject repeatedly to violent attacks. So much so, in fact, that the "illicit" touts were actually starting to earn the public's sympathy, even from those who had considered them a necessary evil that did not deserve any place in a legitimate business.[52] In addition to attacks on the touts, the KYW often made false accusations against the touts—for instance, charging them of robbing commuters of their money or property. And if the police (who often sided with the KYW) deemed the touts sufficiently guilty, the KYW would be allowed to punish them, usually with a whipping.[53] As far as the touts were concerned, they were basically being subjected to mob-style justice; guilt or innocence often depended upon having the talent, or the good fortune, to escape the vindictive allegations of the youth wingers.

The KYW harassment was not just limited to Nairobi, or focused only on the touts. Passengers transiting to other towns could be forced to pay bribes or present identity papers to the KYW.[54] The Moi government, like the previous colonial government, was fearful of dissent, so Kenyans were required to carry *kipande* (identity cards) and to answer officials' questions concerning what business they were about. Anyone unable to produce his or her card, or to give satisfactory answers to interrogators, was typically detained in cells located in the KANU offices. Such surveillance offered the KYW another opportunity to badger or

The way I see it is that the Kanu youth wingers' role in society has to be better defined.

FIGURE 17   Courtesy of Paul Kelemba

persecute anyone they chose: all they had to do was casually denounce someone they considered unreliable or potentially threatening as an "enemy of the state," an "enemy of development," or simply as a "suspicious looking stranger" and their victim could be tossed into jail.[55] If the detainee was considered particularly hostile or subversive, the KYW would not hesitate to resort to torturing their captives by whipping them or burning them with a hot iron bar until a confession was extracted.[56] It was no coincidence that many of the so-called enemies were from the opposition parties.

Anyone advocating multiparty politics could be subjected to such treatment. For instance, on February 12, 1991, the KYW, General Service Unit (GSU), and the police descended upon a combined rally of opposition parties and began whipping any of the participants they could capture, and opening fire on others. Ten people were killed and hundreds injured.[57] A similar incident occurred in Machakos town as a female opposition party member was addressing a group of *Maendeleo ya Wanawake* women. KYW thugs burst in, assaulted and injured several of the women, and hauled others away from the rally.[58] Another horrific example occurred during the trial of Koigi wa Wamwere, a prominent human rights activist and a member of the opposition.[59] In a show of force, the government mobilized hundreds of the KYW to surround the court. Journalists, lawyers, and supporters of Wamwere who tried to pass through the cordon were knocked down and beaten with truncheons, *rungus*, and whips. The victims were left lying wounded and denied assistance while the KYW threw stones at the cars of the Wamwere supporters who tried to assist the injured.[60] It was lost on no one that it was Moi's government that was tacitly employing the KYW as a "police force" to terrorize its opponents.

An even larger-scale demonstration of the government's use of the KYW to terrorize and control common citizens occurred during the demolition of the Muoroto slum in 1990.[61] The shantytown housed an estimated 30,000 people and was located near one of Nairobi's major matatu stops, the Machakos Bus Station. Many Muoroto inhabitants sold goods at the matatu stops, and they had established cooperative relations with the matatu touts. In exchange for discounted goods or food from local women (*mama wa mboga*), the touts would provide protection from Nairobi City Council guards (the *askaris*) who patrolled the bus station and frequently arrested the vegetable vendors for hawking.[62] Whenever the *askaris* approached, touts would hurl stones at them while an allied group of touts hid the hawkers' merchandise. However, hawking was not the real issue. What really provoked the raids upon the vendors was the government's belief that Muoroto harbored "seditious elements," even though there is little evidence to suggest that the residents of Muoroto were guilty of anything more seditious than trying to earn a living.

The issue came to a head on the morning of May 25, 1990, when Nairobi City Council *askaris*, accompanied by the police and hundreds of KYW, descended on Muoroto to root out all the supposedly seditious elements. A circle of bulldozers was set up around the slum and, in a military-style operation, the machines began flattening the residents' homes as the newly destitute looked on in despair.[63] Some 30,000 people were instantly made homeless, their houses and livelihoods destroyed and their belongings scattered like broken china as government forces perpetrated one of the most violent mass evictions in postcolonial Nairobi.[64] Wearing the colors of the Kenyan flag, the members of the KYW served as willing mercenaries in the violent displacement of their fellow Nairobians.[65]

The razing of the slum might have temporarily helped keep Moi's political opponents in check, but no one now could ignore the fact that the KYW were not helping to keep the peace, but were instead harassing innocent people and violently abusing their rights. To the degree that they contributed to the disorder and bloodshed, they no longer had any rationale for their existence. Indeed, the youth wingers' behavior had become so violent that it became a topic of heated discussion in Parliament, despite the fact that the potential for repercussions for speaking out against the wingers. Some of the MPs spoke out despite their fears—for instance, Matu Wamae, the MP from Machakos town, asked the other members of Parliament, "How can *wanainchi* be told to go and report to the KANU youth wingers when they are working to torture citizens?"[66] His criticism was seconded by Dr. Lwali-Oyondi, who argued that it was precisely because the government backed the KYW that they were allowed to "terrorize, rob, and maim innocent people." And, he added: "They do everything under the noses of the police. They can get hold of anyone, torture him until he can't walk and then drag him to the police station and the police have nothing to say. Where are the *wanainchi* expected to go for help?"[67] And yet even against this chorus of accusation, Moi continued to maintain that the KYW were a peaceful organization, devoted to the betterment of a democratic Kenyan society.

_____

Unfortunately for Moi, there was little honor among those working in government service. As the election and the nominations for candidates approached, internal divisions within the KYW started to surface. Certain members of KANU had allowed local or personal interests to supersede their interests in the KYW, and before long interparty conflicts erupted. The most obvious source of conflict was the attempt by certain politicians to use KYW members to further their own political interests; to improve their chances in the election several KANU politicians began hiring members of the KYW to harass their KANU opponents and prevent their nomination. As these personal clashes intensified, splinter groups of youth wingers emerged and refashioned themselves into new "parties," usually under auspices of the politicians who had hired them: Jeshi la Mzee (Fred Gumo), Jeshi la Embakasi (David Mwenje), and Jeshi la Mbela (Darius Mbela), as well as the Kaya Bombo Youth, the Baghdad Boys.[68] These newly organized factions—and there were many others—were little more than private armies prepared to commit violence in the service of the individual politicians they represented. The political conflicts between these private factions essentially became gang wars, and they usually took place in the matatu parking lots, which meant that matatu operators were unavoidably drawn into their pitched battles. So once again, matatu operators were implicated in ugly skirmishes, begun by outside groups, because they took place on their turf.

Although it is easy to lay the blame at the feet of the KYW since they seemed to be at the center of almost all the conflicts in the city, it is important to remember that they were often little more than pawns in a larger game. A few underhanded politicians were using the KYW for their own political gain, with no regard for the disruption often created by their mere presence, let alone their cruel and coercive conduct. And it should also be remembered that the members of the KYW were obliged to follow orders if they were to keep their jobs, and few of them could earn a living other than by hijacking the jobs of the former MVOA touts. And besides, once they had taken the touts' jobs, they had to do the extra work of coercing people to support KANU, in addition to soliciting passengers and handling baggage (which they did actually do sometimes).[69] Although their efforts to influence the public may have been of little avail, few people dared to directly confront them because they understood that the youth wingers' power derived mostly from those who controlled them.[70] To many their red, black, and green uniforms indicated they were mere functionaries, and they were seen by nearly everyone as irrelevant to the actual business of operating a matatu.[71] Nevertheless, most Kenyans understood them to be Moi's henchmen and viewed them with as much respect as that "title" deserved.[72] According to journalist Wahome Mutahi, for instance, "The armies of youth wingers that I see languidly hanging out at bus stops are big eyesores in the city. Their numbers at some bus stops in Nairobi does not justify the work they do. In some instances they look more decorative than functional in their black boots, red shirts, black sweaters, and green berets as they lean on matatus, perhaps just waiting for their cut from fees they collect in the name of helping keep order. They lack training and so they do not know the limits of their powers. They think they are the police."[73] Nearly everyone I interviewed about the role of the KYW in the early 1990s spoke negatively about them. It did not matter whether they lived in the country or the city; their views were the same. "Those men were thugs," said John Kaveya; who at the time lived in Kakamega, in western Kenya. "When you saw them, you ran away. They were a nuisance to the public."[74] According to Ann Mbugua from Nakuru, "they were government spies too . . . aaaahhh . . . we did not like them at all."[75] She had witnessed brawls between KYW and townspeople and remained particularly contemptuous. The sentiments in Nairobi were similar; the KYW were remembered as thugs and crooks by practically everyone and had been subject to ridicule in newspapers and magazines (in satirical columns such as "Masharubu's World," "Whispers," and "Malimoto") where they were often portrayed toadying up to fat, supercilious politicians. Syndicated cartoonists like Gado and Madd depicted KANU Youth Wingers as ignorant dupes serving as politicians' lackeys, or as hooligans feeding off society like "vultures."

The public's perception of them never really improved, and after the first multiparty election in December 1992, the KYW faced even more hostility. Once the election results had been determined in favor of Moi, the reelected president quickly abandoned the KYW. The jobs he promised them never materialized. As a result the unemployed and embittered members of the disbanded KYW responded with predictable lawlessness by forming their own gangs that roamed the parking lots and matatu routes, extorting money from the matatu operators. Of course, this was not so different from what they had done before the 1992 election, though now they had to manage without government sponsorship, and without wearing their patriotic outfits.

The presence of the gangs was all very familiar to the matatu owners. They had been besieged by gangs before, and the disruption caused by the new gangs was more or less like that caused by the former youth wingers. Of course the disorder was just as intolerable to matatu owners as before, especially the wealthy ones. But now at least they could take matters into their own hands without worrying so much about a government crackdown or a stint in prison.

For the time being, political battles had been largely settled by the elections, and most of the owners who had the resources felt it more expedient to co-opt the gangs than to try and defeat them. Rather than oppose the gangs and risk losses, the owners—that is, the wealthy owners—simply decided to employ the gangs themselves. Since they couldn't beat them, they hired them, and so the government gangs were conveniently privatized. Besides, someone had to do the owners' dirty work, and so, just as Moi had used the youth wingers to dominate the political process, the wealthy matatu owners began using the former youth wingers to dominate the matatu market.

The methods were the same, only the objectives were economic rather than political. Once the wealthy owners had recruited the gangs, the gangs set about frightening passengers of the smaller operators onto their bosses' matatus. And even worse, they forced the smaller operators onto less lucrative routes, where they remained stuck until they could appease the gangs and possibly regain access to the profitable routes.[76] But this was unlikely. For start-up operators, the situation was further complicated by the liberalization of the Kenyan economy after the election, which made it easier to import larger vehicles into the country—particularly the Nissan fourteen-seat vans. Wealthy operators launched these new more luxurious vehicles on the lucrative routes, and naturally passengers were drawn to them.

So the path into the matatu business became narrower, riskier, and much more difficult to negotiate. Because the more successful owners were able to employ the former youth wingers, they were no longer subjected to coercion; they were now the ones doing the coercing. In effect, the wheel had come full circle. The young unemployed men of the KYW, who had been hired by Moi to check the power of the matatus, were now being paid by the wealthy operators to increase that power. Fortified by their small armies, the established owners could police the competition and shake down the less prosperous matatu operators. Essentially, the wealthy owners began operating like cartels, making demands much like those of the hirelings who had invaded their turf a few years before. Much like the KYW, they instituted stringent new rules to regulate the entry and operation of new matatus, and they demanded exorbitant goodwill and parking fees. These new rules and regulations, along with the increased fees, also made it next to impossible for new operators to enter the business and survive. And those few who did survive ultimately joined the other wealthy operators to further corner the market—usually by hiring their own gangs.

But soon an even bigger fish swam into the picture, one big enough to swallow up the matatu cartels: the Mungiki. In the mid-1990s the industry was invaded by a larger, stronger, more villainous group of hoodlums than those from the former KYW. This new mega-gang laid siege to the parking lots, seized the profitable routes, infiltrated the highest levels of government, and thereby managed to overturn the industry once again.

NINE

Mungiki: Fighting a Phantom?

On a cool day in October 2001, the Nairobi City Council (NCC) held a seminar on public transportation in their main building on City Hall Way. Ibrahim Ndura Waruinge, the national coordinator of the Mungiki, an organized crime group, decided to attend. He arrived clad in the Mungiki colors of red, yellow, and green, signed his name in the NCC guest book, where he listed himself as a "stakeholder," and sat comfortably in the open, airy room along with thirty or so other participants.[1] When the authorities realized he was present, they confronted him and asked what interest the Mungiki could possibly have in the matatu sector, and why they had suddenly concerned themselves with "security enforcement." The leader of the gang feigned innocence: "Mungiki felt it was its duty to man terminuses such as Dandora's to put order to the route system."[2]

"But the owners and passengers have not asked Mungiki to do so," the meeting's chairman interjected.

"Sometimes," replied the Mungiki boss, "it is good to act without prompting when it comes to the traveling public's best interests."[3]

His composure was extraordinary given the fact that his presence at the city council meeting was a little like having Al Capone attend one of Herbert Hoover's cabinet meetings to announce that he was looking out for the citizens of Chicago.[4] By the early 2000s, it seemed, Mungiki had become so well established in Nairobi that its leaders could openly participate in the public domain. The organization claimed to have nearly one million members, and it unrepentantly reported earning about 1.8 billion shillings per year from its control of matatus in Nairobi alone.[5] The matatu operators could no longer afford to ignore them and, somehow, they needed to find a way to weaken the gang's grip on their business.

Like the KANU Youth Wingers, Mungiki's origins are usually tied to the beginning of multiparty politics in Kenya, and it is true that the gang's existence is partly a result of one of Moi's more unpleasant power plays.[6] Afraid of losing power, Moi instigated a plot that relied upon ethnic violence to disrupt the democracy movement. Essentially, he pitted one tribe against another. In 1991, Moi declared the Rift Valley region to be exclusively reserved for pastoralist tribes, particularly the Masai and (his own tribe) the Kalenjin, and he basically encouraged their militias to move into the Rift Valley and attack the Kikuyu who had settled there.[7] It made no difference that the Kikuyu had lived in the area for decades; they had occupied the valley since the white colonialists had confiscated their land and kicked them out of central Kenya at the turn of the twentieth century.[8] Now it was being done to them again, this time by their countrymen and their president. The result of Moi's policy was horrendous: approximately 1,500 Kikuyus were killed and more than 300,000 were left landless in violent clashes.

However, Moi was not satisfied with the fact that his mercenary "militias" had driven Kikuyu settlers out of the Rift Valley. He was prepared to benefit from the catastrophe by turning the violence into a piece of propaganda: Moi and his officials brazenly argued that, as evidenced by the tribal violence, Kenya was a deeply tribal and fragmented society and was therefore not ready for multiparty elections. And he insisted that Kenya would degenerate into ethnic violence if multiparty elections were to take place—just look at what had just happened in the Rift Valley.[9] Moi's maneuver was no doubt borrowed from the despot's manual of tried and true tactics: cynically incite violence and then justify government oppression by pointing to conflict. The president did not take into account the possible consequences.

Many of the Kikuyu who found themselves landless as a result of the "ethnic conflicts" ended up moving into the neighboring Laikipia area. Once they had relocated, many of the dispossessed responded to their impoverishment by joining together and forming Mungiki, a Kikuyu term that simply means a "big gathering" or "the masses." The initial goal of the movement was to help its members support one another and to assist in cultivating the little land they still had; their intention was to share whatever they were able to produce on the land.[10] In a sense the refugees were trying to revive traditional Kikuyu ideas of communalism. Let down by the secular state and disillusioned with their fortunes since independence, they harkened back to traditional Kikuyu religion, and to the more recent history of resistance rooted in Mau Mau, to find a way forward.[11] But they did more than adopt communalist ideals; like Mau Mau fighters, Mungiki members began growing their hair into long dreadlocks, smoking snuff, and instituting compulsory oath-taking rituals.[12] The men also insisted that the female members of the group be circumcised as they had been in traditional Kikuyu society.[13] In these early days, Mungiki could be roughly characterized as a predominantly Kikuyu social, religious, and political movement whose ideology had been motivated primarily by a desire for social justice.[14] But this relatively innocuous version of Mungiki began to change rapidly in the mid- to late 1990s as it spread its roots throughout central Kenya and into Nairobi and other major cities.[15] The larger it grew, the less communal it became and the more it started to depend on violence to get what it wanted.

––––––

When Mungiki began to infiltrate the matatu terminals in the mid-1990s, many of the gangs of former youth wingers (both from KANU and from opposition parties) simply surrendered to Mungiki. They knew they were outmatched. The feisty, dreadlocked, snuff-smoking Mungiki members, already embittered by months of poverty and idleness and hardened by resentment, quickly overwhelmed the mostly clean-cut, uniformed, and comparatively weak youth wingers who had supposedly been too feeble to lift luggage onto the roof of a matatu.[16] The former youth wingers had no choice when confronted with Mungiki's ultimatum: to either join the movement or leave. For many, leaving was not an option since they had nowhere to go, and trying to stick around without pledging to the gang was impossible and could mean injury or even death—in fact, a few of the former youth wingers who defied the ultimatum were summarily hacked to death.[17] Not many were willing to be murdered by Mungiki and so they simply joined up.

It did not take long for Mungiki to realize that matatus were an easy target for extortion.[18] Ibrahim Ndura Waruinge, the head of Mungiki's Nairobi branch, and effectively the spiritual leader, adviser, and custodian of all Mungiki members in the Nairobi area, was perhaps the first to see that the cash collected from passenger fares was ripe for the picking. There, before his eyes, was the most lucrative—and most vulnerable—business in Nairobi.[19] Soon Mungiki was installing its "collectors" in the Nairobi matatu terminals to demand money from the owners—all, of course, in the name of protection.[20] The owners had no choice but to pay, and in no time at all the matatu industry became Mungiki's main source of revenue: nearly 5 percent of earnings from the matatu industry went to Mungiki in the form of protection money.[21] As it turned out, matatus may well have given Mungiki new life; without the protection money, they might have eventually disbanded and disappeared.

But Mungiki could make extortion pay because it had built for itself an extremely ruthless reputation. It was not unusual for an organization like this to fulfill its self-proclaimed role by initiating exactly the kinds of bloody brawls and murders from which it pledged to protect matatu owners and workers.[22] Interestingly, their violent provocations seemed to mimic Moi's method of creating conflict from which its victims then had to be protected. However, it is important to recognize that Mungiki's involvement in the matatu industry was not simply limited to intimidation and extortion. Their relations with matatu operators were complicated. The gang could play both sides, at times working to undermine the state to the benefit of the matatu operators; at other times it seemed to be collaborating with the Kenyan government and the politicians. Its allegiance shifted easily, usually depending on where power and profits were to be found.[23]

In either case, Mungiki's involvement in the matatu industry put the industry once again at the center of Kenya's contested social, economic, political, and cultural life. The parking lots, even the matatus themselves, became places where debates were waged about what was and was not legal, and who had the right to earn a living off the matatus. It was not quite clear, for example, whether the Mungiki were simply thugs out to extort money from matatu workers or legitimate entrepreneurs offering protection where the police could not, or would not. Its motives were so amorphous, and its methods so unpredictable, that it was not always clear who or what the organization represented. Or if it was an organization at all. It sometimes seemed as if matatu operators were merely fighting a phantom whose shape was always shifting.

In September 2007, one of Kenya's daily newspapers published a gruesome story of a young man by the name of Steve Kamau (not his real name) who was forcefully initiated into the Mungiki mob in the late

1990s. According to the story, Kamau left his village in central Kenya shortly after he finished his secondary schooling in order to look for a job in Nairobi.[24] After several months of unsuccessful job hunting, a friend approached him and asked if he might be interested in working in the matatu industry. The prospect excited Kamau and he eagerly jumped at the opportunity, hoping it would help turn his economic situation around. The next day his friend picked him up at 6:00 a.m. and led him to a shack located in Mathare slum, not far from the banks of the Nairobi River. There they encountered five men, dressed in traditional regalia, who asked Kamau to enter the shack. They locked the door behind him, and one of the men ordered him to take off his clothes and then run round and around the room seven times while chanting Kikuyu phrases. Fearing for his life, he obeyed. When he finished running, one of the men "descended on him with a whip flogging his bare skin mercilessly," and as he shouted in pain, the men ordered him to shut up and then forced him to eat raw meat and drink "some liquid" that he could not identify.[25] Without his consent, he had been initiated into the Mungiki sect.

The men told Kamau that if he divulged any secrets about his initiation he would be killed, and that he should never again drink alcohol or smoke or have sex with a woman who was not a member of Mungiki.[26] Later that night, the five men handed Kamau over to a Mungiki officer who informed him that his job was to collect money from matatu drivers and touts on the Dandora route; this was his job for the next three years. During one of the police crackdowns on Mungiki he was caught and sent to jail; eventually Mungiki bailed him out and he returned to his village. When a *Nation* journalist talked with him in 2007, Kamau was, according to the journalist, "withdrawn and was unwilling to share all his experiences as a member of Mungiki."[27] After nearly ten years, either he was still too frightened to reveal his experience, or it was too painful to talk about.[28]

This kind of violent recruitment was not unusual, at least according to reports in Kenyan newspapers or accounts given in interviews.[29] But not everyone was shanghaied. Many joined Mungiki willingly because they believed the gang offered a solution to their economic troubles.[30] Nor were all of its members refugees from the menacing ethnic conflicts in the Rift Valley; some of them were victims of the government's general mismanagement of the economy, or the structural adjustment programs forced upon Kenya and other developing countries by the World Bank and IMF in the early 1990s. Basically these programs stipulated that markets be opened up for free trade, though this obliged

FIGURE 18   Mungiki members sniff tobacco. Courtesy of the Standard Group, Nairobi

governments to cut back on programs helping the unemployed, building infrastructure, or providing social services.[31] The reasoning behind these programs was that open markets would encourage ordinary
people to become entrepreneurs. But as it turned out, only a few individuals (many of whom were connected to politicians and the government) would benefit from the policies; it particularly benefited those
who managed to create monopolies. More often than not, the policies
resulted in increased exploitation, fewer opportunities, and greater dis-
parities between the rich and the poor.[32]

   Another consequence of these programs was that throughout the
1990s, more people moved to Nairobi to look for work. Often the only
option for them was to settle in the low-income areas of Eastlands, or
in the gritty slums of Kibera, Kawangare, or Mathare. These areas were
expanding faster than ever before, which led to a corresponding expansion in the informal sector of the economy and an especially large
increase in the number of petty traders. Everywhere one looked the
streets teemed with kiosks, shoeshine stands, street hawkers peddling
chapati or roasted maize, newspaper vendors, palm readers, quack doctors, and nearly anything else that could be turned into a few shillings.[33] Also adding to the disorder was the growing number of street

kids and prostitutes.[34] Before long the crowding transformed the low-income areas of Eastlands into a labyrinth of clogged alleys and over-burdened streets crowded with pedestrians dodging dark mounds of indeterminate sludge and zigzagging their way through the sale racks of cheap, tinseled imports.[35] People scuffled with each other to protect the little they had and to keep newcomers from encroaching on their paltry territory. Wherever one looked, the struggle to find a livelihood laid siege to the senses, though it was also evident that the unregulated market had solved the problems of only a lucky few. There were scarcely any real prospects for Nairobi's new arrivals, and the economic promises of neoliberalism seemed little more than fantasy believed only by its few beneficiaries.[36]

––––––

Mungiki entered into this discouraging situation, and at first they seemed to offer a practical alternative. By suggesting a return to tradi-tional Kikuyu culture as a way of redemption, and as a way of provid-ing jobs and creating strong communities, they sounded a note many demoralized young Kikuyu men and women wanted to hear. A large number of them responded.[37] In fact, Mungiki became so successful in its recruitment that by the early 2000s, the sect claimed to have several branches across the country with a total membership of about 2.5 million.[38] With this many members they could pretty much do what they wished. Once the organization had established its presence on matatu routes in low-income areas of Eastlands, and in the slums of Mathare and Kawangware, they began extorting money from matatus. This quickly became Mungiki's main source of livelihood.[39] By the late 1990s, Mungiki was demanding that matatu owners on these routes pay between 20,000 to 50,000 shillings before they could ply their routes, and on top of that they had to fork over 300 shillings per day (about 5 percent of the typical daily income) before they would be al-lowed to operate.[40] Normally Mungiki members worked in pairs at the terminal exits where they stopped the matatus, confronted the drivers, and collected the money—often right in front of the police.[41]

Despite the obvious coercion, Mungiki leaders, such as Ibrahim Ndura Waruinge, generally believed they were providing opportuni-ties for the poor and helping provide for the needs of society. And in some ways they were. "I became a good person," recalled James Njoroge, who joined Mungiki in the late 1990s, and he claimed that Mungiki was responsible for his salvation: "I was a school dropout and used to drink alcohol and sniff glue and take all kinds of drugs, but I became a good person after I joined Mungiki." Immediately after joining Mungiki he was assigned a job as a collector in the matatus that plied the Dandora route.[42] By the time I interviewed him in 2005, he had quit Mungiki because he "was becoming too tired of working in matatus." Nevertheless, while he worked as a collector for Mungiki, he had managed to save enough to buy a kiosk in Dandora where he currently makes a living selling basic provisions. "I would not be here if it were not for Mungiki," he said proudly as he pointed at the soda, bags of tea, and tampons behind the counter. Njoroge was proud of his achievements, and he even invited me to visit his house in Dandora where he lived with his wife and two children. I accepted. The two-room house was immaculately clean and well furnished, and I enjoyed drinking a cup of tea with the family.

Njoroge was hardly the only person to speak highly of Mungiki's willingness to help its members get back on their feet in the tumultuous period of the late 1990s. Mungiki members interviewed by other scholars have also recounted how the organization had helped rescue them from poverty and despair, and especially how it had assisted them with the opening of small businesses; many recalled that it had helped care for the widows of Mungiki members killed by the police or in gang violence.[43] In these and other ways, Mungiki was not just supportive, but necessary—or so its members believed. They were, they insisted, keeping order and providing protection for ordinary citizens by guarding the parking lots and securing routes in the absence of government assistance or an effective police force.[44]

There was some truth to their claims. In the late 1990s the parking lots in particular had become remarkably violent as young, out-of-work idlers preyed upon embattled passengers and pilfered kiosks. According to Eric Maina, the owner of two matatus, "the parking lots were then full of pick-pocketers. But when Mungiki came they ended up taking the youth and recruiting them to work for them, and they gave them the job of collecting money from matatus. Mungiki helped clean up the parking lots *kabisa, kabisa* [very, very much]."[45] Peter Mwaniki, another matatu owner in the late 1990s, added his approval—"Mungiki then was good. . . . It was good for the young people."[46]

I asked what had changed Mungiki, what had turned it from its ideal of community service and social justice into a criminal organization.

"Money, Money, Money, I tell you money is not always a good thing. See, Mungiki started to get a lot of money from politicians and rich matatu owners and that is what turned it into a bad group."

Mwaniki and Maina went on to tell me that rich matatu owners gave Mungiki a lot of money to intimidate their rivals, making it harder for the not-so-rich matatu owners to remain in the industry. They were fortunate to have already entered the business before Mungiki became, as they put it, "greedy," but once the large amounts of money were demanded it began forcing them out. So with the collusion of the wealthy owners, Mungiki more or less controlled who operated a matatu and where they went. When I asked Maina if it was true that Mungiki controlled the competition in the business he answered with an assured "yes."

"That must have been good for those already established in the business?"

"Yes," he answered.

I interviewed several other matatu owners from the mid-1990s, all of whom had entered the business before Mungiki had become so tainted with corruption. They generally agreed with Mwaniki and Maina. Daddy Thengz (not his real name) was one of those whose entry into the industry captures nicely the experience of those who had benefited from the government's neoliberal socioeconomic policies in the 1990s. Daddy Thengz graduated from Kenyatta University in 1994 with a degree in English literature and worked for two years as a reporter for one of the Kenyan daily newspapers. He saved most of the money he earned, and, as he proudly noted, "entered business"—that is, he opened a couple of small businesses: "a little shack selling secondhand clothes on a street corner in posh Westlands" and "a little bar made of plastic and cheap wood leaning over an open drain on a road not far from the clothes stall."[47] As soon as he could manage, he bought a couple of matatus and moved into "a poky office" in one of central Nairobi's then-emptying high-rises. He called the business Berich Limited, and he became a "guerrilla dealer"—that is, he made his money by entering into "small deals" and quickly exiting. He was doing better than many and was able to buy a town house, get married, and raise twin boys.[48]

Daddy Thengz provides a successful example of what might be called "Generation Matatu." This generation came of age in the early 1990s and had been around the matatu culture their whole lives, listening to the stories, watching the workers, and following their successes and failures. Many of them were highly educated and enterprising. For instance, after Daddy Thengz bought his first matatu in 1998, he made enough money in the first two years to go to Dubai and buy a couple more vehicles; he added another vehicle each of the following three years until he had acquired five. He had borrowed part of his initial investment capital from his parents, who themselves had been in the matatu business for nearly two decades. Because of this family backing, he was one of the few people poised to benefit from the economic liberalization of the 1990s, and that had made it easier for him to import the vehicles.[49] He could also afford to pay off Mungiki. To him matatus represented one of Kenya's success stories: "I liked the cash flow from the business because you had money every day," he told me, with a big smile on his face. "It is the one area in Kenya where hard work pays; you see the rewards of your hard work; the people who work in the industry are some of the most hard-working people in Kenya. People are proud to work hard so that they can become self-made."[50]

But even as he made good profits, the money he still had to "dish out" to Mungiki was an aggravation that eventually led to his decision to give up the business. Daddy Thengz told me that he had decided to leave the matatu business in 2004 due to Mungiki demands: "I began to worry a lot about Mungiki violence," he told me, "but also the [Mungiki] guys were taking a lot of money from us." So after nearly ten years of what Daddy Thengz called "exploitation," he became "very tired," and when an opportunity opened up for him to enter a video business on River Road he eagerly accepted.[51]

I also had a series of conversations with Timothy Mwendo, a spirited, broad-chested fellow sporting a goatee. He had been in the matatu business for almost five years and had in his own opinion "done well." But he quit the business in 2002 because "the business was very demanding," and he was losing a lot of money to Mungiki. "Mungiki was the last straw for me. After paying them for two years, I decided I was wasting my money. . . . Working in the industry is a lot of work and a lot of headaches." I asked Mwendo about the claims that Mungiki was offering "protection." He rolled his eyes and added dismissively that any assertions made about protection "did not make any sense because matatu owners need protection from precisely the same people who claim that they are providing protection." The only thing that Mungiki was useful for, he told me, was that they "were able to bring up their families with money 'stolen' and 'robbed' from innocent Kenyans."[52]

His cynicism was shared. Many others, especially matatu owners, expressed a similar sense of frustration with Mungiki, and with the KANU government in general. As was the common practice, they wrote to the editors of the main Kenyan daily newspapers complaining about the government and the police for not protecting them from the gang's exploitation. "Mungiki is like a tick and matatu operators are the cows whom they suck," wrote one exasperated matatu owner to the *Nation*, and he ended his letter by pleading for the government's help—"We appeal that they be dealt with immediately."[53] On the many occasions the matatus went on strike, the operators demanded that the government intervene to protect them from their "protectors." In response, the government officials would turn back to the operators and ask that they help the police identify the individuals who were extorting money from them.[54] Of course, government officials knew that this was impossible since the gangs would—quite literally—hack the operators to death if they revealed the identity of their Mungiki tormentors. On very rare occasions the KANU government would try to appease the operators by carrying out a few raids in search of Mungiki members, only to release the captured hoodlums a few days later.

––––––

By the early 2000s Mungiki's dominance was unprecedented, though there were still conflicting views as to who it was and what it did, and as to whether it was actually serving the community or preying upon it.[55] Its role in the matatu industry had always been ambiguous, or at least it had been until large amounts of money entered into its dealings. In some ways, Mungiki had become more effective than the police at "policing" the city, and many politicians (including Moi) began to notice. They were not about to let an opportunity pass. Eventually the government came to see the organization as a powerful force that could be used to help intimidate the opposition, and it soon began outsourcing its strong-arming to Mungiki. It was a useful arrangement for both parties: Mungiki made friends with those in power, and the government found someone to do its dirty work, thus absolving itself of accountability. Not only did Mungiki supply KANU with the necessary political thuggery, it also provided the government with cover—and therefore with plausible deniability.[56] In 2002, for instance, Moi secretly recruited Mungiki to work with him to win his chosen candidate the presidency of KANU.[57] His candidate, Uhuru Kenyatta, was the son of Kenya's first president and a devoted member of KANU, and he was endorsed without reservation by Mungiki's chairman and spiritual leader, John Njenga Maina. Predictably, the members of Mungiki could be heard hailing Uhuru Kenyatta as *kamwana* (the youth), and as the "liberatory" young man "from the hills."[58] On the day that Uhuru was officially nominated, one commentator wrote that "hundreds of thousands of Mungiki youth came in buses and mini-buses, donkey-carts and on foot, descending on Nairobi streets from all directions, in

FIGURE 19   Courtesy of Godfrey Mwampembwa

a procession that caught many Nairobi residents by surprise. Imagining themselves as the Iregi revolutionaries of Kikuyu mythology, these Mungiki youths wielded machetes, clubs, or sticks, in a dramatic parade that resembled the *interahamwe* in the 1994 Rwanda genocide."[59] Uhuru also solicited Mungiki's support by cunningly representing "Mungiki youth as victims of Kenya's economic meltdown" and making sure that "his staunch Kikuyu supporters like the Nairobi mayor, Dick Waweru, and Juja MP Stephen Ndicho, had no qualms about openly supporting the sect."[60] By the time of the election, Mungiki claimed close to four million members and could hardly be ignored.

Large as the organization was, it still relied on matatus for a significant percentage of its income.[61] But now it had backing from the KANU, making the Mungiki feel they could get away with the elimination of their rivals—as was the case on March 2, 2002, when a group of about three hundred Mungiki armed with machetes, swords, and knives went around to the matatu terminals, shops, and bars in Kariobangi North beating and stabbing local residents.[62] Twenty people were confirmed dead at the scene and thirty-one were admitted to the hospital with serious wounds. The carnage had been triggered by nothing more than a rivalry over control of matatu terminals, and even after the violent murders the KANU government made no effort to eradicate Mungiki or to sever their (unacknowledged) ties.[63] Mungiki remained as powerful as ever. Shortly after its murderous rampage Mungiki increased its cash demands on matatus; every driver registered after May 2002, soon after the murders, had to pay 5,000 shillings to Mungiki, and each conductor 3,000 shillings, before being allowed on the road. Moreover, any new owner of a matatu now had to pay a hefty introductory fee of 60,000 shillings (up from the high of 50,000) before being allowed to operate (and they still had to give the sect 300 shillings each day). The burden was too great for many of the owners, and by the end of that year the government-supported Mungiki had taken over fifteen of the most lucrative routes in Nairobi.[64]

Yet things quickly changed after the election. Luckily for matatu operators, KANU lost the presidential election, despite its underhanded tactics, and the new leader, Mwai Kibaki, carried out what appeared to be the first of a series of major crackdowns on the cartel.[65] As promised in his campaign speeches, he outlawed the sect and imprisoned its main leaders; he also sent army squads around the outskirts of Nairobi to round up the Mungiki who had fled the city.[66] And in order to protect matatu operators from Mungiki's extortion, the minister of transport introduced, in January 2004, what has become known as the Michuki rules (named after the minister). The rules would help, as he put it, "tame matatus."[67] These were perhaps the strictest laws the matatu industry had encountered since 1984, when the government had forced matatu owners to get licenses.[68] The most significant of the new rules ensured that only employees of the two major matatu owners' associations could watch over the parking lots, which meant that Mungiki could no longer claim to be providing protection. The changes were welcomed, the situation at the terminals calmed down, and it seemed as though matatu operators would finally be a little more in control of their own fate. For a while, at least, it appeared that Mungiki had been outlawed, or at least forced underground.

But the calm did not last long. Mysteriously, on May 15, 2005, the operators of all the matatus that ran from the CBD to Eastleigh via Juja Road went on strike for about six hours, paralyzing businesses in the area.[69] Nairobi residents were perplexed by the strike, and the commuters forced to walk through the day's torrential rain wondered what had gone wrong this time.[70] It turns out that Mungiki had organized the strike—with the collusion of their supposed enemy, the matatu owners.

It was not immediately clear why, especially since Mungiki was considered defunct by most of Nairobi's residents. But it had not yet given up the ghost; it was still there, behind the scenes, pulling the strings. "Since Mungiki cannot come out in the open," one of the matatu owners told the *Nation*, "Mungiki mobilized our drivers and conductors to demonstrate against the police."[71] The unexpected collaboration was not without its reasons; it turns out that the police had more or less replaced the "outlawed" Mungiki and begun collecting extortion money from the matatu operators. In response, Mungiki, in yet another of its many mutations, decided to intercede on behalf of the matatu owners to help them combat the venality of the police. It is doubtful that they were stepping in out of goodwill or concern for matatu owners, and far more likely that they were safeguarding their own interests. As reported in the *Standard*, "Mungiki's beef with the police was that the officers were harassing the matatu drivers and touts—their people—to whom they [Mungiki] owe protection, and they are paid handsomely for it."[72] In other words, their own ability to extort the matatu owners had been threatened, and they were determined to defend it. Of course, the irony was that Mungiki was actually earning the protection payments that the matatus had been paying them for so long; remarkably, it had aligned itself with the matatu workers and was, for maybe the first time, actually protecting them instead of simply coercing fees from them. As far as the matatu workers were concerned, however, the police and Mungiki belonged in the same category.[73] They were both plunderers, preying upon matatus without regard for the law, and they did not see much difference between the supposedly legal, state-sanctioned police and the obviously illegal (and sometimes state-supported) Mugiki. The workers had to submit to whichever of the two groups happened to be defrauding them at the time, and neither of these seemingly implacable forces cared much about the law or the livelihoods of the owners, drivers, and touts.

It was not supposed to be like this after Kibaki's violent crackdown on Mungiki in 2003, or the passing of the stringent Michuki rules of January 2004. It was clear that the reforms had had little impact on Mungiki. "Nothing has changed," a matatu owner told the journalists who were covering the strike, and he noted that the powerful Mungiki sect had returned to own and control matatu routes in Dandora, Eastleigh, Githurai, and Kayole. "It is like we were thrown from the frying pan into the fire," he said.[74]

While nothing had changed for the matatu operators who were still dishing out money either to the police or to Mungiki, the Mungiki had taken a few months off to remake itself, physically and ideologically. Its first move after the crackdown was to change its center of operation from Dandora to Mlango Kubwa, the sprawling slum off Juja Road. In this new location Mungiki could continue its operations unabated and yet remain largely unwatched, despite the government's dire warnings. On the whole, it considered itself unassailable—for instance, a Mungiki youth from Mlango Kubwa made the chest-thumping boast to a journalist of one of the daily newspapers, saying that the movement was "here to stay. . . . Some people in the current government thought they could finish us, but they soon realized Mungiki was a force to reckon with." The young man, who spoke on condition of anonymity, bragged that "the sect owns Juja Road."[75] And it was true: Mungiki had taken over the most populous Eastleigh routes of number 6 and number 9, and every matatu on those routes had to pay 200 shillings a day to a group of Mungiki gathered at strategic points. "If you do not pay or if you give the boys a hard time," the young man warned, "you will be taught a lesson."[76]

Another important way in which the Mungiki reformulated itself was to change the physical appearance of its members so that they did not stand out so vividly. The members shaved their dreadlocks and, instead of their usual green, yellow, and red "uniforms," began wearing regular clothes so they looked more like typical commuters in Nairobi. This, of course, made their extortion much easier to hide. The story of thirty-five-year-old Mark Njuguna offers an interesting example of the effects of the makeover.[77] He first encountered the new Mungiki after their makeover, in January 2005, believing that Mungiki had been eradicated by the new government policies. As Njuguna drove happily along the Juja Road in his brand-new twenty-five-seat minibus, he was stopped by a small group of young men a few miles before he arrived in Eastleigh. His driver knew who the men were and warned Njuguna to "cooperate." The men—who, according to Njuguna, looked just like "regular people"—were members of Mungiki and demanded 50,000 shillings from him, calling it the entry fee for his new matatu. After putting together his lifetime savings to buy the brand-new vehicle, Njuguna did not have any money left to pay the lump sum. The bagman was generous enough to let him pay the fee in installments, because he "belonged to the house of Mumbi [the house of Kikuyu]."[78] Fortunately—or perhaps unfortunately—for the matatu owners, the continued strength of the organization allowed this kind of flexibility; they could afford to accommodate their victims and accept the extortion money on installment plans. It was just this kind of financial adaptability that contributed toward Mungiki's continued success. Their actions were criminal, to be sure, but they were handled with such entrepreneurial know-how as to escape outright retaliation, and so they always managed to operate successfully in the interstices between hardened crime and the city's ever-changing popular economy.[79] They knew just when to swerve and when to bend.

In addition to changes in appearance, some of the Mungiki members converted to Islam and changed their names, so instead of James or Mark or Philip, and such, there were now a lot of Mohammeds, Salims, Ibrahims, and Husseins in the movement.[80] In practical terms, these conversions were intended to broaden the diversity of the movement and make it less Kikuyu, and it was indeed rumored that Mungiki had begun to accept non-Kikuyu members. This new inclusiveness also helped the organization extend its tentacles deeper into areas of the population that it had not yet reached. All of these factors—its relocation, its new appearance, and its deeper ties in the communities—were apparent in their organization of the matatu strike on that rainy day in May 2005, and in the manipulative ways in which they claimed to be "friends" of the matatu operators.

The government, however, seemed to be oblivious to all of these changes, and there are still real questions as to how the government could not have known that Mungiki was remaking itself and expanding its reach to become even more effective. After all, Michuki's rules had only been put in place a few months before, and yet already it was clear that they were having little, if any, effect; and President Kibaki had tried—as he had promised during his campaign—to exert some control over Mungiki. But his policies, too, were having little noticeable effect.

It was probably the case that the organization simply could not be controlled since its form was so amorphous and its practices so pliable. Trying to control it was like trying to squeeze, the air out of a balloon—the tighter you squeeze, the more the air simply goes somewhere else. The same was true for Mungiki: the more pressure was applied to one area of its operation, the more the organization would simply relocate and establish itself elsewhere.[81] For instance, when a *Nation* reporter interviewed a police officer from the nearby Pangani police station and asked him questions about the gang's proliferating influence, the officer replied with a shrug—"It is not a secret that Mungiki runs Juja Road. Mungiki collects money from matatu owners; there's nothing new there. The government knows the Mungiki still exists and what can they do?"[82]

To make matters worse, the organization had a tendency to absorb its purported enemies. According to the same officer, the army squad that had been formed in 2003 to eradicate Mungiki followers had in fact ended up partnering with the gang members, and now Mungiki was sharing the money it collected from matatus with members of the squad. One of the Mungiki members confirmed this, asserting that "the police are poorly paid, are greedy and are not interested in their work." They were certainly not to be feared—"When you see the police vehicle in Mlango Kubwa they are here to see our bosses." According to this confident Mungiki member, the organization had "enough money to buy justice and police officers who try to make their life difficult. . . . But if any police officer becomes too much, we deal with him."[83]

More and more, it seemed that Mungiki had effectively undermined state authority, so much so that members of the army squad whom the government had sent out to the streets of Nairobi had decided to ally with the criminal sect. They knew where the real power was. The question now was whether or not Mungiki could even be isolated and identified, or had the sect mutated into something too nebulous and indistinguishable to be tracked down and contained. One matatu owner interviewed by the *Nation* suggested that the police had quit trying to find out: "Mlango Kubwa is Mungiki's territory and no policeman wants to lose his life fighting fearless and dangerous people," and he concluded that the police had simply given up fighting the gang.[84] When *Nation* interviewed a few policemen to see if they concurred, they were met with either indifference or admissions of defeat. "Some police sources say," wrote the *Nation* journalist, "their officers are not ready to shed blood fighting a phantom." "Who are the Mungiki?" one officer asked, and then offered an answer himself: "Those people are dangerous and seem to have some ubiquitous political backing."[85]

The police officer was correct in his belief that the government and politicians had colluded with the gang. One piece of circumstantial evidence was the increase in violence by Mungiki that always seemed to accompany elections. Every election year it seemed as though Mungiki had become more ruthless and more brutal in asserting its prerogatives, and the government did nothing because the violence served its purposes. The lead-up to the bloody 2007 election was no exception.[86] It was rumored that many political candidates from NARC, the party that had taken over from KANU, had hired Mungiki to intimidate members of the opposition parties.[87] Given free rein by the government, Mungiki became particularly ruthless in its interactions with matatus, introducing even harsher measures than in the previous couple of years when they had been working underground. In Eastleigh, for example, the adherents of Mungiki vetted all the matatu crews for opposition and dictated to the matatu owners whom they could employ.[88] For the benefit of that service, each member of a matatu crew was expected to pay a registration fee in order to be allowed to drive or serve as a conductor. Those who complied ended up resigning themselves to a life of servitude and exploitation; those who resisted were routinely killed.[89]

In 2007, Mungiki also took over the slums and low-income neighborhoods in Eastlands and beyond, and by all appearances seemed to be setting itself up as a shadow government. As usual, Mungiki created a sense of insecurity by committing violent muggings and burglaries so they could compel residents to pay for protection. They enriched themselves by tapping electricity from the high-voltage power lines and forcing the customers to buy the stolen power from Mungiki.[90] They also took the law into their own hands by setting up kangaroo courts, which purported to settle disputes—about rents or domestic quarrels or petty thefts—which in reality meted out instant justice (or injustice) that was usually biased in their favor. And when it was deemed necessary, they imposed curfews on the residents.[91]

But these violent and unauthorized actions did not end with the election. Mungiki also exploited the postelection violence by further tightening its grip on the residents of Nairobi, who began to live in constant fear for their lives.[92] After the election when the NARC no longer tolerated their thuggery, the government once again carried out a crackdown on Mungiki. And once again, the group simply moved its operation center, this time to the rural areas of central Kenya. Again, the violence followed them to their new location, reaching a bloody culmination in April 2009. In apparent retaliation for the government's extrajudicial killings of nearly five hundred Mungiki members, and the torture of some eight hundred, the gang hacked twenty-eight people to death.[93] The retaliations were most likely triggered by the government's alleged assassination of Oscar Kamau Kingara, a human rights lawyer who had been investigating the police killing and torture; he was shot by three gunmen in dark suits while sitting in his Mercedes outside the University of Nairobi dormitories.[94]

According to the Kenyan daily newspapers, Mungiki's retaliatory attacks had become much more deadly than the earlier attacks of March 2002. Kenyans were irate and again wrote letters to the editors of the major Kenyan newspapers asking the government to put an end to the vicious cycle of revenge killings by vigilante groups. They condemned the "failed police system" and noted that the "forces of law had abdicated their power."[95] Kenyans in the countryside were beginning to feel unsafe. That year it was reported that fewer people made the customary Christmas visit to their rural homes in central Kenya, but chose rather to stay in Nairobi where they claimed to feel at least a little bit safer.[96] A poll taken at around that time by the major newspapers, by means of text messaging, indicated that about half of the people in Nairobi blamed the existence of Mungiki on politicians.[97] Their conclusion may have been justified, though it could never be conclusively determined if and how the criminal organization was working for or against the government.

Still, if the government was unable to control Mungiki, the blame was partly theirs. Both the Kenyan state and individual politicians had actively enabled the extortion Mungiki practiced. Moreover, the politicians and the Kenyan government had demonstrated a pattern of conveniently hiring Mungiki to intimidate opposition groups during elections. The habit of delegating violence foolishly allowed criminal groups like Mungiki to flourish and made the state an accidental accomplice in their success.[98] Perhaps even worse, the recurrent patronage by the government made Mungiki feel it had been granted certain prerogatives, and its members came to feel that they had license to steal, assault, or even kill, with impunity. But no matter, the government needed mercenaries and, more often than not, it was in the government's best interest to keep Mungiki around as a necessary evil ready to enforce its policies and help win elections.[99] The government's occasional crackdowns on Mungiki were usually intended as ruses meant to calm down the public with the appearance of action. Similarly, Mungiki's periodic attempts to undermine the government served to demonstrate to the state that the group was strong enough to be trusted with the business of intimidating its opponents, and also too strong to eliminate. To the impartial observer it was becoming clear that "organized crime, policing, and the state all belong to the same continuum."[100]

Mungiki's place on that continuum was always changing, but over time it had turned out to be an effective parasite. Regardless of the social or economic conditions, it would carefully calibrate how much it could take from the matatu industry without killing its host.[101] Like most parasites, it demonstrated a high degree of specialization. For instance, the organization did a better job of providing security in the parking lots than the government had ever managed, and the matatu owners often welcomed them for this service. And Mungiki's presence was useful because it helped regulate who would or would not be allowed into the industry (this was a boon to established matatu owners who could pay the gang's fees). But, still, it was a balancing act.[102] Mungiki was a criminal organization, and it was not going to allow the matatu industry to grow beyond its power to control it. It could not allow the industry to become so large that it got out of hand, but it also had to be careful to ensure that the industry remained open enough to prevent the owners from seeking protection from other gangs or the police. It wanted a racket it could keep a grip on.

It was never really evident how matatu owners, or the general public, could possibly have found a way to escape Mungiki's grip. Fighting organized crime, as one scholar has put it, is a "never-ending process, not a battle or a short war that can be expected to end in the near future. It is more like the struggle of the Dutch against the sea—painstakingly building dike after dike before the value in reclaimed land will show, while being prepared to be overwhelmed by freak storm surges, and always taking the long view."[103] But there is a big difference between the struggle by the Dutch against the sea and the struggle of the matatu industry against Mungiki: the laws of physics did not apply. The organization was always changing shape and always changing sides; it could not be contained because it was always moving to new places and adapting to new circumstances and making new demands.[104] In the end it was a losing battle. Matatu owners, it seems, were not fighting a known element; they were fighting a phantom.

PART SIX

Generation Matatu, Politics, and Popular Culture, 1990–2014

TEN

Music, Politics, and Profit

Although Mungiki continued to prey upon the financial
fortunes of matatus, the matatu owners were determined
to retain control over aspects of their business not subject to the gang's influence. The most obvious areas left
to them were the vehicles themselves and the social world
that surrounded them. Mungiki might have control over
parking lots, the routes, and the fees, but it could not control the actual experience of riding in a matatu; that remained the province of the drivers, conductors, and touts,
and they took full advantage of it. By the early 1990s, the
typical matatu ride was jarring and noisy and provocative,
and nothing could be further from the rickety pickups of
the past, laden with wooden benches and cackling fowl.
In a matter of only a few years the owners had managed
to modify new, larger vehicles into mobile discos that
pumped out loud, topical hip-hop into the coaches and
onto the streets; they fashioned the exterior of the buses
into billboards, festooned with snappy slogans and popular portraiture; and the workers transformed the language
of the matatus into something distinctive by adopting
Sheng—a trendy, hybrid patois—as their exclusive language and using it to cajole their customers on board or
to hound them with their politics. The mere necessities
no longer were enough for riders: a new matatu was expected to offer a more alluring and entertaining ride. Passengers wanted amenities, they wanted to enjoy the virtues of comfort, technology, and freedom in a space that
was on the streets, and of the streets, but that remained a
place apart. The more an owner could offer these services,

the more unique they could make the experience of their own matatu, the more successful they became, and the more successful the industry became.

Many of these advances were made possible by the economic liberalization of the early 1990s that had lifted trade barriers and opened the way for imports. Almost immediately the new, well-appointed minibuses were sporting the advanced electronics from Asia and the Middle East that had started to make their way to Kenyan markets, along with music and videos from the West. If they could afford it, owners installed the imported, state-of-the-art electronics—mostly powerful stereos and speakers—to play music as loudly as was tolerable, and even louder, since the latest electronics and the loudest music tended to attract more customers, especially the younger, hipper crowd.[1] Matatus were becoming a cultural gateway of sorts. All kinds of people and every aspect of Nairobi life met in matatus. They provided a place where the newest music could be played, often before it even made its way onto local radio (if anyone needed confirmation that the new matatus were in vogue it was provided by the government, which tried to regulate the loud music by citing health and moral issues). Matatus were also a place where Nairobi youth could enjoy the same delights their Western counterparts might find in a mall, where they could see and be seen, and check out new fashions. Perhaps more importantly, the inside of a matatu was a place where politics could be openly discussed.[2] Altogether the music, the styles, and the feeling of freedom inside the enclosed coach of a matatu imparted to the passengers an exciting sense of transgression.

So by the late 1990s the matatu had become a social and cultural focal point. In many ways, music had been the starting point. Kenya's budding musicians began to compose their own hip-hop for the matatus by borrowing the beats and styles of popular Western music and inserting their own lyrics, in Sheng, the new and somewhat subversive language (used by matatu workers) that combined vocabulary from English, Swahili, and other local languages.[3] Many of the lyrics were the standard fare of the boy-meets-girl kind, though over time many of the songs started to offer social or political commentary that condemned the poor living conditions endured by many in Nairobi or the injustices committed by the Moi government.[4]

As a matter of fact, the music typically played in matatus came to serve an important role in the democratization movements of the 1990s and early 2000s.[5] The combination of the music with the Sheng dialect allowed a matatu operator to transform his or her vehicle into a political space, unlike almost any other public space in Kenya. The introduction of popular culture into the matatus may have begun as a commercial expedient meant to attract passengers, but it quickly became a means of protesting government injustices concerning matatus, and just about everything else—particularly current social, economic, and political frustrations.[6] As operators became more outspoken—and there was no better place for this than the inside of a matatu—they eventually gave rise to a powerful social and political counterculture, popularly known as the "matatu culture." This culture, as one popular song put it, became unstoppable and unbeatable—or, to quote the song, "unbwogable."[7] Ultimately it inspired a critical, combative, and politicized generation like none that Kenya had seen in its recent history.[8] This "Generation Matatu" came of age between the late 1980s and 2000s, as Kenya began to embrace economic neoliberalism, and at the height of the country's struggle for multiparty politics. Most of the young men and women of this generation had at least a high school education and were therefore considered to be of the educated, or at least the literate, class. They had higher expectations. When the Kenyan economy nearly collapsed in the 1990s, many younger people became disillusioned with their corrupt leaders and began to see the government as counterproductive, even as the enemy of economic development. To escape the dead end of government work, or the occasional absurdity of government policies, the younger generation began to look for options in the popular economy. For the many who had lost faith in the traditional paths of progress, the matatu industry provided one of the best options. And it also offered the added cachet of Sheng, music, and subversion.[9]

———

A decade or so earlier, in the 1980s, it was not uncommon for matatu workers to play music in their vehicles, though it was usually played on a radio or on a portable cassette player. Reggae, *lin'gala*, gospel, or *benga* were the most popular genres since Nairobi lacked a vibrant international music scene like those found in other hotbeds of African hip-hop such as Dakar, Kinshasa, and Johannesburg.[10] Besides, the matatus of the previous decades—typically pickup trucks or old minivans— were not sleek enough to show off expensive music systems, nor were the electronics as readily available as they were to become in the 1990s. In any case, the matatu workers of the earlier generation were not really ready to appreciate such luxuries; they were more practical, of necessity, and were typically young men with only a primary school education who felt they needed to dress and behave modestly if they were to get ahead.[11] The matatu then was more functional than trendy or fashionable—though it could even then provide a place for voicing dissatisfaction or dissent.[12]

In the early 1990s, however, as matatus gradually became more modern and comfortable, and the ride became more entertaining, they began to captivate the younger workers in the city. Much of the modernization of the vehicles was enabled by a set of economic reforms, which altogether changed the experience of the matatu owners and passengers. The most visible impact of the reforms was the new, flashier minivans imported from places like Dubai, Doha, China, and Thailand. As the World Bank pushed Kenya and many other countries of the Global South to open up their markets to foreign trade, it became easier for middle-class investors to import cars and join the matatu business.[13] This resulted in matatus that were simply more comfortable and dependable. However, the economic reforms had effects on far more than the conditions of the matatus. Along with opening their markets, the government had been forced by mandate to make structural adjustments to their budget, which resulted in huge cutbacks in government expenditures and massive government layoffs. There were fewer jobs to be had. The decline in job opportunities hurt the whole economy, but it was high school graduates who were hit hardest by the reforms; suddenly it had become more difficult for them to secure steady work. And so, desperate to earn money and strike out on their own, they began drifting into the matatu terminals hoping to find work as conductors or drivers on a magnificent new matatu.

But it was not just desperate young graduates who gravitated toward the matatus. The more fabulously they were transformed from the simple, practical means of transportation, the more young men and women were drawn to the enticing culture emerging around the matatus, so much so that they had even started to prefer them over other means of transport. Well-to-do kids wanted to travel to school in matatus just to listen to the new music—for instance, Josphat Mwangi, a high school student, told me that he could use his parents' car but he preferred to ride in matatus; he called it an "addiction," and his favorite matatu went by the name of "Liquid" (as in DJ Cam). "The entertainment is fantastic," he added, "the seats are also very comfortable, and the lighting gives me the feeling of being in a disco."[14] Another student from a prestigious high school, whose parents owned two cars, said that he preferred riding matatus to hear the music and meet his buddies and maybe some pretty *chillies*—girls—from his neighborhood.

A teenage girl told the *Nation* that she often waited for her favorite matatu, sometimes for over an hour, because, she claimed, "the matatu has a nice music system and color."[15]

The updated matatus were all of a sudden beginning to attract a different kind of worker and passenger. While in the previous decades being young and cool meant having a steady, salaried office job, in the 1990s the definition of *chic* began to take on a different meaning. For one thing, it meant riding the right kind of matatu, a beautiful *motii* (vehicle), otherwise known as a *manyanga*. It meant knowing the hip-hop culture from the United States and adopting its styles and attitudes (it was common to see commuters carefully studying the *Source* magazine for the latest trends in American hip-hop); it meant wearing Nike sneakers and buying stylish clothes—Polo, Hilfiger, Cross Colors, Karl Kani, and other trendy labels—most of which were bought in the flourishing markets in Nairobi that imported used clothing.[16] And it meant sporting a baseball hat worn backward and wearing the right accessories—for instance, a silver pendant with padlocks, or comparable budget facsimiles of bling-bling. For many of the young matatu devotees, social or economic class seemed to be less important than knowing the latest hip-hop hits, or wearing the right kinds of clothes. Ideas of class and respectability were different inside a matatu; they were more open and egalitarian. And to some, more maddening.

If a ride in a matatu had become maddening it was often because the hip-hop music could not be escaped. It had become so important that it was common to read reports about high school kids skipping school to ride in matatus and listen to music the whole day. They immersed themselves in the explosive early rap of MC Hammer, for instance, or Vanilla Ice, until a few years later the deep voice and lewd lyrics of Snoop Dogg made him a big hit.[17] "It used to be like a nightclub," noted one young interviewee in one of the daily newspapers, "disco lights and everything."[18] So desperate were some to get on board that it was not unheard of for conductors to give girls *sares* (free rides) in exchange for sexual favors. "Women would make their way home from work or school," she added, "listening to the sounds of Eminem bellowing, 'You can suck my dick if you do not want my shit,' and not bat an eyelid."[19] A middle-aged woman passenger on one of the Eastlands routes, upset by the explicit sexual nature of the hip-hop lyrics, complained that in one of the songs she had heard a long, high musical note that the singer sustained, and sustained, until it finally reached its longed-for limit, and then fell silent, but for two breathless voices, panting and exhausted. "Only the deaf," she sighed, "are left with any doubt as to what action is taking place."[20]

The debate surrounding the loud matatu music followed predictable generational lines.[21] "Matatu music spoils young girls," claimed Anna Wambui, a thirty-eight-year-old mother of three teenage girls. Other women interviewed by the daily newspapers argued that the loud music was bad for pregnant mothers and young children. "I had a rough time in the matatus when I was pregnant, as the loud music used 'to beat' into my womb," said Jane Wamae, a thirty-seven-year-old resident of Kawangware.[22] Another commuter, Agnes Njuguna, alleged that pickpockets took advantage of the loud music to rob people: "I was robbed when I got confused by the loud music."[23] Likewise, a letter to the editor of the *Standard* newspaper complained that the music was played so loudly that instead of offering entertainment, it had become another form of harassment, though the author was also keen to point out that it was not just matatus that created the unconscionable racket, but also discos and bars and street preachers, and the prayers from the mosques, and noise from construction sites, and from the incessant stream of trucks, cars, buses, and motorbikes that "belched thick clouds of smoke and earsplitting noise from their engines." Noise, the letter concluded, "is most dangerous when it is loud, meaningless, irregular, and unpredictable."[24]

It is true that complaints often went unheeded. Matatu workers insisted that they could not stop playing loud music because it was the music that attracted passengers. "If your matatu did not cause a *marurumi* [thunderstorm] while playing the latest hip-hop music," a conductor told me, "no one would enter it."[25] And no one could complain and expect any change. For instance, James Wafula described to a journalist of one of the daily newspapers what seemed a common experience: he had once taken it upon himself to "openly complain about loud music but . . . I was surprised to see some people saying they really didn't mind." He blamed the public for passively encouraging the "touts to harass them with deafening music because they don't raise a finger against it."[26]

No level of noise was quite loud enough, so it was not unusual to hear commuters complain about the atmosphere created by the din of revving engines, the shouting touts, and the steady boom of amplified hip-hop. The matatu parking stations had a "terrifyingly aggressive air to them."[27] This corresponds with what I saw and heard while visiting various stations in Nairobi in the 1990s. Each one seemed a tower of Babel. All the drivers turned the music to the loudest volume and then amplified the noise by revving their engines and blowing their horns, while the conductors banged on the vehicle's side, whistling and shouting the names of their destinations: *"Esilinabatisajanaga-ramlagokubwasentressasabeyabas!"* (Eastleigh via Ngara, Mlango Kubwa and St. Teresas; same low fare as that of a KBS, bei ya bus).[28] Or *"Gongreskosbulbulkonawaraka!"* (Ngong Race course, Dagoretti Corner). To the uninitiated ear, the conductors made no sense, they seemed to be speaking in tongues, or chanting incantations like the witch doctors exorcising demons, as I had heard as a child in the village. And adding to the deafening noise of the music and motors and carnival barking were the shouts of vendors selling food, used clothing, and supplies out of makeshift stalls, and the cries of beggars and street kids yowling harshly to attract attention of the passersby who had to weave their way around trash heaps and open sewers. Not only were the stations an assault upon the ear, they also offended the nose and insulted the eye.

Finally, in August 1992, the minister of transportation and communications gave the police permission to fine any matatu that played loud music. He worried that Kenya would end up with "a nation of deaf people, that deafness caused by loud music was incurable"; he believed that loud music was "bad for pregnant mothers and little children."[29] So the police were ordered to arrest all the conductors who "play indecent music with the intention of corrupting the morals of their passengers."[30] In support of the minister, the *Nation* carried an article by a Dr. M. Cruz, who was of the opinion that the music was a health risk to the public and commuters, and claimed to have treated many matatu touts who had lost their hearing.[31]

In spite of these arguments, matatu workers refused to heed the order and actually went on strike in protest of the penalties. They justified the strike by claiming that loud music was important to their business, and that the police merely used the law to "harass" them and as an excuse to ask for bribes. Again, the entire city of Nairobi came to a standstill.[32] When the matatu workers went back to work the next day, many of them would remain silent while in the city center, but then turn the loud music on once on the road out of town—there was nothing, then, that the passengers or police could do. If passengers requested that the volume be lowered, the conductors smirked and told them to go buy their own vehicles, or walk, if the music bothered them.[33]

——

The controversy over the loud music became even more intense when Kenyan musicians started composing their own hip-hop music in

Sheng. The first major hip-hop groups in Kenya—Kalamashaka, Mau Mau Camp, and Poxi Presha—dealt with "ghetto life" like many of their counterparts in United States.[34] The privations of poverty, coping with alcohol and drug abuse, and crime provided the content of much of their music.[35] There were, of course, many other artists whose songs did not make so much of a popular impression, but that were still played at the highest volume. Some of them were, frankly speaking, unintelligible. Back in 1998, for example, I boarded a matatu to Buruburu, and the lyrics were: bang, bang, bang, bang . . . "Go to church" . . . bang, bang, bang, bang . . . "But not to pray" . . . bang, bang, bang, bang . . . "And I will be your God" . . . "Let us talk about sex" . . . bang, bang, bang, bang . . . "Let us talk about sex," and so on, interminably. I was baffled by the lyrics, or at least by their mind-numbing stupidity, but when I looked around, I saw several fellow passengers nodding as if by reflex action. Of course, what my uninitiated ear had failed to grasp, I realized later, was that sometimes simple rhythms were all that were required, and also that passengers were in part just responding to the improvements made by the new technology; it was often the much improved sound that had influenced the ways in which passengers reacted to—and appreciated—the music.[36] Very few had stereos at home that could match those in the matatus.

The major concern of Kenyan hip-hop musicians, however, was not the quality of the sound systems but the pirating of their music. Like many countries in Africa, Kenya lacked effective copyright laws, and many of the more popular songs were copied illegally, which of course made it harder for the musicians to earn any income from royalties. When the musicians complained to the Music Copyright Society of Kenya, the society responded by singling out the matatu industry and insisting that matatus pay for the rights to the music, much like radio or TV stations pay for the privilege of broadcasting certain events. Naturally, matatu workers and owners would not hear of this, and so, again, they went on strike. Again the whole city of Nairobi came to a halt for a day so they could make a point; they were not going to pay the musicians anything. The matatu owners even bellyached in a press release that the copyright society was trying to "blackmail" them, and they decided that they would "continue playing music because music is played in restaurants and discos without any complaint by society."[37] They may have had a point, though they continued to be careful not to play music too loudly in the city center where the police were likely to catch them, but as soon as they hit the edge of town they ramped up

The way I see it: Even passengers are forced to abet the matatu law-breaking sub-culture.

FIGURE 20   Courtesy of Paul Kelemba

the pirated tunes—"kaboom, Kaswap Oooh Eheeee!! Zing zag jah glory man."[38]

———

In this instance, as in so many others, it seemed impossible that the government would ever be able to regulate the matatu industry successfully. When it came to the music, however, there may have been more at stake than the nuisance of noisy stereos. There was much more going on than simply playing the music to entertain, or annoy, or even make people deaf. In fact, the government had reason to worry; increasingly the music was starting to contain information airing opposition to Moi's regime and less about sex. Matatu workers were seeking out more songs about social justice and multiparty politics, and then proceeding to bombard the passengers with their political messages as they crisscrossed the city. They had a captive audience. The songs' messages reverberated, and in due course the music's partisan content became a crucial part of the political movement as multiparty politics heated up. It was not long before matatu workers could be seen signaling to one another their opposition to one-party rule (they were the first group to wave two fingers as a symbol for multiparty political systems). Eventually it was matatu workers who began leading organized protests against Moi's blatant violation of human rights in Kenya.[39]

That the protests more or less began with matatus was no coincidence. Matatus went everywhere, and everything could be found out in one. News of any injustice was easy to come by from songs or fellow passengers—often even more so than in the newspapers. And, sadly, there were quite a few instances of injustice to be heard, some of them so extreme as to whip up emotions. For example, in February 1990, Robert Ouko, then Kenya's minister for foreign affairs, was brutally murdered a few miles from his home near Kisumu town. Ouko had been investigating a corruption case in a molasses factory near Kisumu, and it was rumored that Moi himself was deeply involved in the fraud. Ouko had been shot once in the head, his limbs broken, and his body set on fire.[40] The whole country was riveted as the details of the murder emerged and quickly became overwhelmed with shock and anger. The government claimed Ouko had committed suicide, though of course many wondered why a man would break his own limbs and then set himself on fire before putting a bullet in his head. And Ouko was not the only victim. In August that same year, Alexander Muge, the bishop of Eldoret and an outspoken opponent of Moi's regime, was murdered in what was believed to be a road accident staged by the government.[41]

The government was certainly capable of other, less violent abuses. In May 1990, Kenneth Matiba and Charles Rubia, former cabinet ministers, were detained without trial and held at the Kamiti Maximum Security Prison (Matiba was denied medication and suffered a stroke while being held). The ministers were guilty of publicly speaking out against Moi and asking that Section 2A of the current constitution, which had rendered Kenya a de jure one-party state, be repealed. The detentions and murders left many Kenyans incensed. On July 7, 1990, human rights leaders, well-known lawyers, opposition politicians, and others organized a rally at the Kamukunji grounds in Nairobi to pressure Moi into accepting the demands of the prodemocracy forces and to release Matiba and Rubia.[42] Moi refused, arguing that a multiparty system would lead to "fractionalization and violence in Kenya's ethnically heterogeneous society."[43] He then, under the guise of unity, sent paramilitary troops to disperse the rally. They managed to disperse the crowds temporarily, but they did so violently. Some of the demonstrators escaped by running away, others by climbing into nearby matatus to hide; still others grabbed any weapon that came to hand—stones, tree branches—and began throwing them at the police and through storefront windows in central Nairobi. Thus began the week-long series of demonstrations and riots that came to be known as Saba Saba (Seven-Seven, because they took place on July 7). They were some of the most disruptive uprisings independent Kenya had ever experienced.

The main protests took place in densely populated Eastlands, where

FIGURE 21   Saba Saba riots, July 1990. Courtesy of the NMG, Nairobi

hundreds of matatus plied the streets. In Dandora neighborhood, for example, the police confronted a hide-and-seek crowd that kept calling out, "Matiba na Rubia *wawachiliwe; vyama vive viwili!* [Free Matiba and Rubia; let there be two parties!]." Matatus drove around the Eastlands area with their lights on, guiding the crowds, and playing loud songs lamenting the city's poverty, homelessness, and unemployment. As they led the protestors through the main roads in Eastlands drivers had to dodge the remnants of the demonstrators' attack against the police—the stones, broken glass, and tree branches.[44] Residents sat perched on rooftops watching the police patrol the neighborhoods; on the ground, however, the police arrested journalists, confiscated their cameras, and destroyed the film.[45] A *Kenya Times* journalist was told by the police to either hand over his camera, "or get a bullet on the spot."[46] The police clearly did not want witnesses.

On Juja Road, also in the eastern part of Nairobi, a combined force of riot police and members of the paramilitary General Service Unit (GSU) battled with protestors who sheltered behind barricades like French revolutionaries. They fought on through the week, tearing up the streets and smashing vehicles until Juja Road became impassable. A great many matatu workers joined the fight, some by providing transportation to the protestors, others by passing out leaflets or delivering supplies, and there were always several matatus driving the streets packed with people singing songs in praise of Matiba and Rubia, and playing music by Moi's zealous opponent, Joseph Kamaru.[47] As the matatus honked and circled around the various neighborhoods in Nairobi, the passengers would yell out to onlookers, "We want two parties! We want Matiba and Rubia out!" The drivers were also on the lookout for matatus that had refused to participate in the strike.[48]

When Moi finally went on the air to ask that matatu workers return to their jobs, the workers refused, saying they would only do so if the detained politicians and church leaders were released.[49] When nothing was done the rioting became general and residents all over the city joined with the protestors' attacks on the police.[50] They were not to be intimidated; a shot fired at the crowd only triggered louder blasts from matatu music systems. Demonstrators burned a KBS bus that had refused to comply with a temporary rule imposed on matatus that they cease carrying passengers. In the meantime, the police crisscrossed the city arresting any journalists, politicians, and human rights activists whom they accused of being ringleaders.[51]

Church leaders came out strongly against the police violence. "The action of the police was dictatorial, cowardly, and weighs the power of the government against defenseless people," said Bishop F. R. Mwangi of the Anglican Church, and he also argued that unless the government allowed dialogue, the church and the public would continue to oppose the leadership of a one-party state.[52] Other church leaders prayed to God to "touch the hearts of those in power so that they might release Mr. Rubia and Matiba."[53] And they prayed for President Moi to have "patience, grace, and reason to bear with those whose political perspective was at variance with the government."[54] "We need a Joshua," they implored, "to help bring us together." Perhaps their prayers were effective: on the fifth day of the protests, matatus returned to work.

But Nairobi was never the same again. Rubia and Matiba were eventually released and went on to form the Forum for the Restoration of Democracy (FORD) party in 1991. The launching of FORD had officially turned Kenya into a multiparty state. The Saba Saba riots had been instrumental in achieving the reforms. The protests helped popularize the idea of multiparty elections, and in time, the protests came to represent the principle that democracy must include respect for human rights and the basic responsibilities of the government to its citizens. Always at the forefront, matatu workers played a significant role in the protests' success. They knew what it meant to have the power of self-determination and to be frustrated by its denial, and their experiences helped underscore the idea that other voices should be heard and respected.

Not all of the opposition was so dramatic as the riots, or so effective. There were still many unresolved problems in the city of Nairobi and in the rest of the country, despite the success of the protests and the introduction of the multiparty system. Kenyans in the slums and low-income areas of the city still experienced all the social problems linked to poverty. The government's "structural adjustment" programs had improved the economies of only a few and left many in a state of poverty, crime was widespread and murders were frequent, the 8-4-4 education system had been corrupted, land reform was needed, there was little or no health management, no one collected the garbage, no one addressed the question of squatters and the demolition of slums, and the justice system left the injured no recourse since the courts were corrupt and no one expected a fair trial.[55] At one point matatu workers even went on strike because of the impassable roads and their killer potholes.[56]

All of these problems lay behind the Saba Saba rebellions, and all of them were yet to be addressed. But the success of the multiparty reforms were inspiring, and matatu workers were eager to exercise their political clout in other, less spectacular ways, if they could help defeat Moi's coercive policies. They did not always resort to strikes or violence—they were willing, sometimes, to pressure the government to change policy by simply showing support for a cause. In October 1989, for example, Professor Wangari Maathai learned of Moi's plan to construct a sixty-story Kenya Times Media Trust Complex in Uhuru Park, the largest park in Nairobi and the equivalent of Hyde Park in London or Central Park in New York City. Maathai, along with members of the Greenbelt Movement, openly demonstrated in opposition to the plan, though the government quickly arrested and detained them without trial. Although Maathai was eventually released, most of the less famous members of the Greenbelt were kept in detention.

After her release Maathai organized the mothers of those still detained and had them camp out at Uhuru Park for months in a place that came to be known as Freedom Corner. The detainees' mothers stripped in public (an act that expressed extreme violation of the women's rights), and went on a hunger strike.[57] They kept up their vigil in the park for three months. To show their support for the women, matatu drivers made a point of changing their routes so they could pass by Freedom Corner every time they drove in or out of the city; as they drove by the tents they would sound their horns and the conductors would wave two fingers and, of course, raise the volume of the protest songs for all to hear. With the help of the matatus, the Maathai campaign became a public relations nightmare for Moi, and eventually the courage of the women and the pressure from the matatu workers helped force him to withdraw his plans to put skyscrapers in Uhuru Park.[58]

If the matatus' music had helped again, it was no surprise; music was proving an effective means of rousing public pressure on the government and forcing it to enact political, economic, and social reforms.[59] In 2002, Gidi Gidi Maji Maji recorded a single about their struggles with shantytown poverty called "Unbwogable"—a nonce word in Sheng that had recently entered Kenya's lexicon and which means "unbeatable" or "unstoppable." The song's themes of pride and progress made it an immediate hit with the matatu conductors; its lyrics dramatized the shared experiences, memories, and socioeconomic immobility of the majority of Kenyans, and it gave voice to the defiance and determination shared by the downtrodden. The song was blasted in the matatus nonstop during the months before the December election, and it was adopted as the campaign anthem for a coalition of opposition parties that was mobilizing young voters to oust the hardline twenty-five-year-old Moi regime. It certainly seemed to have helped inspire voters since the changes promised by "Unbwogable" had come to pass. The KANU party had been defeated in the general election of 2002, after having been in power for nearly a half century. However, the story of the song's evolution was not over; it was speedily adopted by the victors—the National Rainbow Coalition (NARC), led by Mwai Kibaki—as their anthem, and its message of resistance and invincibility was rewritten to include triumph. The song itself was *unbwogable*— once a popular hit, its supple idioms made it adaptable to other ends, so that with a subtle shift of context it could work as an effective song of political protest or an anthem of party allegiance.[60]

Whatever the song might ultimately mean, the themes of "Unbwogable" had their humble start in the matatus, on the obnoxiously loud stereos that pummeled the passengers with noise. Yet its far-reaching success provided evidence that the loud music in the matatus had in some ways succeeded in becoming a means of political protest. The success was not just due to the music, though. The defiant dialect of Sheng had also played a part. Picked up by the matatu workers, and irreverently flaunted in and around the matatus, Sheng became a powerfully transgressive language—at once private and brazenly public, and ultimately political. Its use could signal allegiance to a special group, and yet when it was spoken in public it was commonly intended to exclude or safeguard the group's territory, or, as we have seen, in the right context Sheng could become a tool of political resistance.

There is no consensus about when Sheng originated in Nairobi. While some scholars date it to as early as the 1930s, others believe that Sheng originated in the 1960s and '70s among working classes in Eastlands, where parents and children shared a single room. In these crowded quarters children, or possibly teens, invented Sheng as a private language so that their parents could not listen in on their secrets; eventually, it made its way into the schools, and from there onto the streets and into the matatus. (In the 1980s and '90s, the number of students was far beyond the system's capacity, and many of the students had only fading knowledge of their mother tongues and a mediocre grasp of the country's two official languages, Swahili and English.)[61] By the mid-1980s Sheng had become the lingua franca among certain groups of Nairobi youth, and particularly among matatu conductors. They began to use it everywhere.[62] For the young it answered a need to create their own mother tongue, and for all its users—especially the matatu workers—Sheng had the aura of insurrection that made its use a form of civil disobedience (much like *Tsootsital* or *Flaaital* in South Africa, urban Wolof, and *Camfranglais* in Senegal and Cameroon).[63] In a sense, the rise of Sheng parallels the rise of the Generation Matatu, a generation whose members were born into poverty and were often at odds with the authority of the government. Speaking Sheng connected you with a young, restive, politically aware cohort of urban sophisticates—about a million strong.

The early forms of Sheng were random and fluid, though it gradually developed more stable, systematic patterns of usage. This streamlining can partially be attributed to matatu workers since they did, after all, need to conduct a business.[64] The more time one spent in a matatu the more one could, with effort, begin to follow their shouts, whispers, and catcalls—Nairobi became *Nai*, then *Nairo* and, finally, *Nairobbery*; the rich women from the gated communities of Westlands, Lavington, Muthaiga, and Karen became *wababis* (feeble Barbie dolls); "mother" became *mathe*, then *masa*, until, finally, the poor woman became *sama* (to choke); and "father" became *fathee* and then *buda* (Gujarati and Hindi for "old man"). Passengers became *choroboa*, *dondoa*, and then, sadly, *kaa square* (squeeze in), and girlfriends or attractive women might be labeled *chillies, atoti, kwara, lalez, mndito, spleng,* and even *jada,* after the beautiful actress Jada Pinkett Smith.[65]

Even radio's keenest observer of the social scene, Leonard Mambo Mbotela, started speaking in Sheng in the late 1980s. He sometimes descended into Sheng in his radio show, *Je Huu Ni Ugwana?* (Hi, Is This Proper?), about social life in Kenya, and his colorful commentary at football games endeared him to thousands of fans in East and Central Africa. Sheng would become a staple of the show's appeal. Mbotela would use it to condemn the *mabosi wanaodimandi chai* (bosses that demand bribes), the *mameidi wanaowapindua mama watoto* (maids who are rude to their employers), and the *mashugadadi wanaopotesha* who preyed upon schoolgirls (that is, the "sugar daddies" who lured innocent schoolgirls). He spoke often of *self-confidensi ni kitu muhimu sana* (self-confidence is important). Of course, some of the more traditional listeners found this use of language inappropriate, particularly because the point of the show was ostensibly to educate the masses, and that meant the use of proper Swahili, and not Sheng. But Mbotela's show featured prominently on the schedule of the Voice of Kenya, the government-run station, and what critics did not realize—or even want to acknowledge—was that Sheng was the new language of the young masses. By speaking Sheng, Mbotela was doing what his job required: he was reaching out to the young people of Nairobi who used this new vernacular.[66]

Despite the controversy surrounding Mbotela's use of Sheng, his was in fact a toned-down version of that spoken by matatu conductors. No one on the radio approached the extremes of linguistic innovation practiced by the conductors. The public was not ready for the onslaught of phrases like, *"Taunitaunikumburikumburi. Nafasikubwakamakanisa. Derebebawengipassengiaingiaubebwe. Nafasimob!* [This matatu is going to town. The fare is five bob, get in, there is plenty of space. Driver, carry them all. Get in everybody. There is lots of space!]." Or, *"Sirikaliikombeleinameni. Watu wakae watatu watatu kwa kiti jameni fanyeni speed, inameni* [The police are ahead, please squeeze in tight, and quickly bend down as low as you can so the police do not see you]."[67] Without objection the passengers would crouch down so the police would not spot them and stop the matatu. But how they understood to do so remained a mystery to many.

Of course, that was the point. The language was meant to be a mystery, and the purpose of the linguistic acrobatics was to prevent the understanding of anyone from outside the community. Sheng was important because it enabled the youth to assert their identity and at the

Nairobi's matatu men have developed a language that is not easily understood by newcomers to the city.

FIGURE 22   Courtesy of Paul Kelemba

same time exclude those who could not speak it.[68] It was one way—along with music and fashion—through which Generation Matatu could define itself and create a culture and could also defiantly fight for it rights, and the rights of other Kenyans.

———

In June 1997, Kenyan writer/activist Binyavanga Wainaina returned to Nairobi after living in South Africa for ten years; upon his return he wrote a poignant memoir about growing up in Nairobi and the changes he had observed.[69] "After the soft light and mellow manners of Cape Town," Wainaina wrote, "Nairobi is a shot of whisky." The shot was rudely served up by matatu culture. It is what he first noticed on his drive from the airport into the city center: "Matatus: those brash, garish Minibus-Taxis, so irritating to every Kenyan except those who own one, or work for one. I can see them as the best example of contemporary Kenyan art. The best of them get new paint jobs every few months. Oprah seems popular right now, and Gidi Gidi Maji Maji, one of the hottest bands in Kenya, and the inevitable Tupak. The colored lights, and fancy horns and the purple interior lighting; the hip-hop blaring out of speakers I will never afford." Wainaina took a long stroll

213

on River Road, and wrote: "This is the main artery of movement to and from Public Transport Vehicles. It is ruled by *Manambas* [matatu conductors] and their image: a cynical, hard demeanor—every laugh is a sneer, the city is a war or a game. It is a useful face to carry, here where humanity invades all the space you do not claim with conviction."

The matatu culture of Nairobi in the 1990s and 2000s that Wainaina writes about so passionately was, for better or worse, Nairobi's version of urban hip-hop culture. It represented the Kenyan version of the modern world, and the music, the clothing, the language, all became symbols of the young Nairobians' defiance of traditional roles. But it was also something more; it also signaled their defiance of traditional politics and was a fervent indication of their desire to succeed on their own terms. It was the youth's urgent need to feel *unbwogable*— "unstoppable" and "unbeatable"—that helped make the new matatu culture a means of bringing about change in Kenya's political system and force reforms upon the socioeconomic and political injustices that had become so rooted in the Moi government.[70] Their aims may have been fairly radical, and perhaps not always understood or articulated, but in the end the youth of Nairobi succeeded in turning the matatu into a source of identity, into a way of life, complete with its own music and language, and its own *unbwogable* worldview.

ELEVEN

"Pimp" My Ride

Buruburu is a large lower-middle-class residential neighborhood in the Eastlands area of Nairobi.[1] The houses there, mostly townhouses with striking orange-tiled roofs, were built in the 1970s and '80s and retain their original urban flavor. In 2006, the neighborhood supported a fitness center, a large supermarket, and a string of pleasant pubs; at the time it was the only area in Eastlands with ATMs. Buruburu also had two major garages, Catskill and Two M Auto Tech, both of which specialized in painting or—as they say in Nairobi—"pimping" matatus. I first visited the garages in June 2009 with my research assistant, Matt Gichuru, an artist who worked at Catskill garage. Although a perfectly nice guy, he goes by the ominous nickname of "Toxic."

When we arrived at the garage, Toxic introduced me to three men—James Macharia, Titus Ouma, and Patrick Kesiyemi—who were waiting for the workers to finish pimping their matatus with all the latest accessories. We shook hands, and Macharia, whose vehicle was nearly finished, showed me what the artists had done so far. The immaculate twenty-four-seater was in the final stages of preparation; ready to be installed were four TVs, a stereo with multiple sets of speakers, and several flashing signs—all this and much more, he assured me, was going to be fitted into the vehicle. The outside of the matatu was even more bewildering; already airbrushed on the bus's exterior were paintings of George Bush and Osama bin Laden together on one side, and on the other Barack Obama kissing his wife, Michelle. The revamp was going to cost him about 200,000 Kenyan shillings, nearly US$3,000, of his own money, in addition to the two million shillings ($17,000) he had borrowed from a local bank and from siblings living in the United States, France, and Dubai. The painting and electronics accounted for at least 15 percent of the cost of the vehicle, and were intended, "to attract passengers" since "passengers like a beautiful-looking, pimped car, that is up-to-date." And Macharia joked that by plying route 9 (the busiest route in Nairobi, running from the central business district to Eastleigh) in a flamboyantly decorated matatu, he could "retire as a prosperous man in less than forty years."[2] The extravagant pimping was a means to a comfortable retirement.

Still, it is not easy to make sense of the excess, even if it might contribute to a leisurely old age. No doubt the electronics, the airbrushed images and inscriptions, and the proliferation of the topical stickers inside the cabins helped establish matatus as an inescapable cultural phenomenon. And, admittedly, it was a common belief among owners that you could "make more money with a *manyanga* [a pimped-up matatu]," because the "young people want to ride a nicely pimped-up matatu."[3] But, practically speaking, none of the pimping up was necessary. Commuters could just as well have taken clean, unadorned vehicles and enjoyed quite a comfortable ride. Nor does the commercial appeal of all the additions seem to justify the effort and expense; after all, the market would seem to dictate that simpler matatus would allow for lower fares, something that passengers would have appreciated.

All the embellishments, then, were meant to do something more than merely attract customers. In some cases, it may have been yet another way of drivers communicating with their passengers; on the simplest level the decorations made their vehicles more easily identified. But there was more to it than this. Just as they exploited hip-hop and Sheng to propagate their political views, the operators, many of them members of "Generation Matatu," also used the vehicles themselves to announce their presence and assert their individuality. In a sense they were staking a claim. By turning their matatus into mobile billboards of opinion, humor, hostility, or even outright absurdity they were also indirectly proclaiming their prerogatives, their indomitable right to exist, or, you might say, their "unbwogableness." This made them more than mere vanity projects. There was an unsettling subtext of politics in whatever they did, and in the very act of embellishment the operators were inevitably putting their political beliefs on display—though it was not always easy to figure out the political intent of the airbrushed artwork on the matatus' exteriors. In many ways, it did not matter whether the messages were expressions of idiosyncratic taste or coded communiqués of political opposition; the "pimping" of vehicles had become another aspect of the business that the government was unable to control. No matter how much the owners were censured or condemned for their garish, overly accessorized matatus, they had nonetheless created moving advertisements of the attitudes, obsessions, and anxieties of Kenyan society.

––––––––

The habit of elaborately adorning vehicles, especially public transportation vehicles, is hardly unique to Kenya. Throughout Africa, South Asia, the Caribbean, and the Middle East, such vehicles have been decked out with elaborate paint jobs and ornaments.[4] Similar decorations could be found on hair salons, barbershops, and kiosks and pushcarts.[5] In all of these places the decorations naturally reflected local traditions and over time exhibited changes in style and taste. But in Kenya in the mid-1990s, especially in Nairobi, the electronics and paintings and slogans achieved a distinctiveness that gave them an unprecedented cultural import and placed them at the forefront of all kinds of pressing social issues.

Prior to the 1990s, the elaborate decoration of matatus was relatively rare. The old minivans and pickups had always featured some sort of slogan inscribed on its exterior, though they tended to be religious (partially in response to the rise of evangelical proselytizing during economic downturns).[6] "May God Bless," "On the Road to New Jerusalem," "Christ is the King," "Exodus," "Yahweh," "I am the Way," and "Psalm 23": all gave the impression that matatus were vehicles of faith, and that all those inside the old and overflowing wrecks would enjoy God's grace and survive their journey.[7] There was also the slight possibility that the biblical slogans were intended as criticism of the government for forcing matatus to comply with certain traffic laws, as, for example, the stringent rules of the Amendment Act of 1984. If God was right with them, protecting them—riding shotgun, so to speak— the government had no business interfering. If the engine of a matatu worked well enough to be on the road, if it served its purpose, the officials had no business involving themselves in the vehicle's lack of windshield wipers, emergency doors, or a new coat of paint. The appeal to a higher power could conceivably be seen as a way of rising above the government's petty bickering, and thus their self-righteousness became a form of subversion.[8]

This may be reading too much into simple protestations of faith, and in any case the popularity of such overtly religious sentiments eventually faded, replaced by a demand for elaborate and topical paintings—so much so that art schools in Nairobi began to train students in the decoration of matatus. One of the most popular schools was Buruburu Institute of Fine Arts (BIFA), where many of the matatu artists I encountered had been trained.[9] The college was started by a Christian organization in 1990 and grew rapidly in the 2000s, training students from across the country, and from abroad, in all the arts: product design, graffiti arts, drawing and painting, fashion, video production, interior design, fabric decoration, and sculpture. Walking through Nairobi in the 1990s one was likely to see the students' works adorning the panels of a matatu. Typical were the airbrushed names or figures of popular culture—"Public Enemy," "Tupac," "Snoop Dogg," "MC Hammer"—that were usually accompanied by some belligerent trademark—"Conqueror," "Subdue," "Dominate," or "Predator"—intended to demonstrate the workers' toughness.[10] Surely anyone operating a vehicle that brandished a graffitied inscription so fearsome should be able to vanquish all obstacles in their way, whether it be the police, the government, or too-rowdy passengers. The identification with the American hip-hop artists was perhaps more innocuous, but even so it was a brash statement of the operators' cosmopolitanism, and maybe something the passengers might hope to absorb by association.[11]

The paintings on the matatus' sides and rear also reflected current interests. For instance, one of the big themes of matatu decor in the early 2000s was the fast-paced development of information technology taking place in Nairobi, especially the advent of the cell phone that was

FIGURE 23   Matatu, 2010. Courtesy of the NMG, Nairobi

now available to most of the middle class. So rather than the names of rappers one might see the words "Internet," "Anti-virus," "Spyware," or "SMS only!" floating over the heads of pedestrians as they ambled down the streets. Or, when the United States elected its first black president, and Kenya's most powerful descendant, the operators were happy to brag about having one of their own lead the world's most powerful country—by Christmas of 2008 almost every matatu had Obama's name as part of its decor: "Daddy Barack," "Bwana Obama," or "Obama Wetu, our Obama."

Most of the more overtly political inscriptions could be interpreted as not-so-subtle comments on the violence of Moi's regime: when one saw "Golan Heights," "Chechnya," or "Bosnia Herzegovina," emblazoned on the side of a matatu, the owner was probably identifying with the victims.[12] Although again, it was nearly impossible to discover any coherent message by the invocation of these war-torn places. They may have been meant to announce political sympathies or draw political analogies between Nairobi and the embattled cities.[13] But some of the juxtapositions defy interpretation—for example, what might we make of the vehicles upon which a name like "Arafat" was written next to a name like "Sweet Baby," or when "Bosnia" was incomprehensibly placed next to "City Heart Winner"? It is possible that these names could be intended as mere provocations, or as a kind of coded indication of belief or ideals, whatever those might be. Also possible is that the nonsensical juxtapositions were an attempt at absurdist humor.[14] And though this itself might seem nonsensical, it was true that a kind of feisty, farcical humor was important in the world of matatus. It was, after all, a tough, combative business, the hours were long and the conditions difficult, and so the industry attracted men who were physically and mentally prepared to go to battle when the occasion demanded.[15] Humor allowed the men to relieve tension, and it might also help lighten the anxiety among passengers who felt that traveling aboard a matatu was a risky proposition.[16]

Finally, the matatus were often inscribed with an indication of the matatu owners' origins, especially those plying route 9 to Eastleigh, where a large number of Somalis and Ethiopians had managed to settle and enter the matatu business after having fled their war-stricken countries—so it was common to see matatus in Eastleigh with names like "Mogadishu," "Abyssinia," or "Red Sea." Whether intended as an affirmation of identity, a nostalgic reminder of home, or even a claim of their right to be in the city, it is hard to tell, but it was the case that the social position of Somalis in Kenya was precarious in the 1990s.[17]

"Many people you talked with in Nairobi hated the fact that the Somalis and Ethiopians were there: Kenyans saw Somalis as thieves. They came with nothing but now they began to run all the businesses in Eastleigh," according to Eric Njuguna.[18] I asked him to explain to me how the Somalis had somehow managed to take over the matatu routes to Eastleigh—his answer was uninhibited: "They don't pay taxes, they simply bribe the government to get out of paying taxes. They are also so united and they do not allow Kenyans there." I let him continue without interruption, and he spoke bitterly of the unwelcome presence of Somalis in Kenya, calling them pirates, drug users, and so on. His resentment was echoed in the magazine and newspaper headlines from the period, which made no attempt to hide their prejudice: "Go Build Somalia," "Somalis in Minneapolis on Handouts," and "Somalia: chaotic, dark-age cesspit of poverty."[19]

Given all the antipathy, the Somalis' practice of emblazoning their matatus with the names of their origins may have been an act of defiance, though mostly it ensured that potential passengers, and especially Somali and Ethiopian passengers, were easily able to identify specific vehicles and use them regularly.[20] It was important for them to be

FIGURE 24 First Avenue, main business area in Eastleigh, 2009. Courtesy of the NMG, Nairobi

able to affirm their ethnic identity, particularly in Nairobi where they were becoming numerically, and financially, a powerful minority—so much so that their financial success was beginning to breed resentment from native Kenyans.[21] And, truth be told, the Somalis and Ethiopians had managed to carve out for themselves a significant niche by the early 1990s. It was clear to anyone familiar with the city that they had managed to turn Eastleigh into "Little Mogadishu" or "Little Addis" and made it into a major trading center.[22]

Eastleigh has always had a history of attracting new immigrants. Initially, it was South Asians who moved into the area, though after Kenya's independence in 1963 most of them left for greener pastures in other parts of Nairobi, and Africans (mostly Kikuyus) began to move in and buy property. Since the late 1980s, however, Eastleigh had become increasingly populated by Somali traders, who, according to Binyavanga Wainaina, "set up shop and brought in all kinds of products— cheap and useful products, along with the shiny and breakable."[23] They had made it the most popular site for trading in Nairobi: "It looks like the whole Somali economy has settled in the place. There are bazaars everywhere, and thousands of people milling about, wheeling and dealing."[24]

Almost all of the owners employed artists trained in graffiti by the art schools established in Nairobi in the 1990s and 2000s. There was great demand for such artists. Buruburu Institute of Fine Arts (BIFA) opened a second branch, and even the elite Nairobi Art Academy introduced a course on graffiti art. The number of graduates from these schools more than doubled since they had opened in the early 1990s.[25] Toxic, my research assistant, was a product of BIFA. He was born in 1979 in Buruburu, the youngest of six children, and was raised there. He admitted to being stubborn and causing "a lot of trouble" in school; he was suspended several times and had to attend a number of different secondary schools before he graduated.[26] Eventually he enrolled at the BIFA, where he earned a diploma in painting after which he did freelance work for a couple of years, decorating kiosks for small bazaar traders in the city center and in upper-class Westlands. He also started reading the *Source* magazine, a trendy American magazine, looking for the latest music and fashion styles to reproduce on T-shirts.[27]

A few years later, in 2007, Toxic and his friends formed a matatu pimping group, the "Cream Team." By working quickly so that owners could get their vehicles back on the road fast, Toxic found that the team could easily earn 80,000 shillings ($1,000) for each job—"So, you see, this is good money."[28] Like his colleagues at Cream Team, he read the newspaper voraciously and was fully aware of current national and international politics and culture. This internationalism was an important Generation Matatu trait; in fact, Toxic regularly drew cartoons for a politically radical weekly newspaper.[29]

———

Artists like Toxic also created stickers that matatu conductors and drivers stuck onto the backside of the seats inside the matatu. As simple as they were, these stickers became an important part of the passengers' experience. They could not be ignored since everyone who entered a matatu was forced to confront them head-on as soon as they sat down.[30] The messages on the stickers, though, were not nearly as ambiguous as the names and slogans painted on the vehicles' exteriors. As a matter of fact, quite a few of them offered unrepentant acts of antagonism aimed directly at the passengers, especially at female passengers. Most of them were outrageously sexist, yet none of the conductors seemed bothered by this, and several even justified themselves by doubling down on their misogyny—women have a tendency "to complain and nag," griped one conductor, and so he placed the stickers on the seatbacks to "teach them a lesson."[31]

This kind of chauvinism surprised no one. Most of the passengers, in fact most of the general public, tended to view matatu drivers and conductors as boorish. For instance, Gitau Warigi, a journalist with the *Nation*, describes their behavior in the most scathing and unforgiving terms: "When you think of a matatu, the worst images crowd your mind. The way it careens about reminds you of a frenzied lunatic. The crew is rude and uncouth, both to their customers and to motorists. The music blaring from within a matatu can split your eardrums, but when you politely ask the crew to lower the decibels, you get rewarded with an impossibly vulgar epithet that leaves you shocked."[32] A number of the people I interviewed had similarly unkind words for matatu workers—the best they could say was that the workers were "a nuisance." "The mouths of matatu men," remarked Mary Kariuki, a University of Nairobi student, "have no brakes. Matatu conductors talk poison."[33] Newspaper headlines were equally caustic in condemning matatus and referred to them as "hellholes," or as the "black hole of Calcutta," and they insisted that matatus are "the bane of Kenya's motor industry."[34]

The matatu workers were not about to let such comments go unnoticed, and they retaliated with stickers celebrating their own insensitivity and sexism: *Ni wewe umechelewa usiharakishe dere* (you are the one who is late, not the driver); *Usikojoe, usikule, orote ndani ya gari* (do not urinate, eat, or fart inside this matatu); *Wasichana ni kama matatu, ukikosa moja ingine inapita unaingia* (women are like matatus; if you miss one you can always find another one). Churlish stickers like these, so pitifully juvenile and misogynistic, made it fairly clear that conductors placed them on the seatback in an attempt to live up to their bad reputations.[35]

In a way, the stickers merely represented another reaction to government intervention. When the government attempted to regulate the industry by instituting strict rules prohibiting what workers could write on the exteriors of their vehicles, the conductors and drivers simply asserted themselves even more aggressively on the stickers *inside* the matatus—though this time the passengers bore the brunt of their anger.[36] Some of the slogans were rather sullen and defensive: *Hakuna ubeshte na dere, lipa gari* (there is no friendship with the driver, pay the fare); *Kazi ni kazi bila nipate unga* (this is a job like any other, it allows me to feed myself). Others rudely admonished riders of their duties as passengers: *Tapika ulipe 200 ya car wash* (if you throw up in this car you must pay 200 shillings for cleaning), or *Songeana ama ununue gari yako* (move your butt and create space for other passengers or else go and buy your own vehicle). As belligerent as these stickers might be, one could make the argument that they were attempts at humor, intended to defuse the animosity that existed between the passengers and conductors. The abuse was general, and so no one felt singled out by the stickers, and, in a sense, the conductors were reminding the passengers of their own frustrations, and even implying that they and the passengers should feel a sense of camaraderie—"We are all in this together." Besides, as Matthew Mwenesi commented, "Matatu men are matatu men . . . there is nothing to do. You do not take what they say as personal."[37] Moreover, the passengers were more or less making themselves complicit with the matatu operators' lewd behavior and language by shrugging off the rude messages. As soon as they conceded that there was nothing to be done, the passengers were implicitly accepting the offenders' rude instructions or their sexist vulgarities. By tolerating bad behavior they came to normalize it.[38]

Nor did passengers show any scruples about using the matatu operators for their own advantage, or manipulating them to make their commuting more convenient. For instance, they routinely forced matatus to make unscheduled stops or tried to skip out of paying the fee. And they could be equally rude. In other words, passengers conveniently tended to turn the matatu operators into scapegoats, and then excused their own negligent behavior by blaming the scapegoats. In this regard, the stickers might be considered a form of protest. If you were going to be blamed for bad behavior you might as well behave badly, so badly that the accusers might reconsider their conduct. Of course, no one was likely to win this kind of dispute, though given the circumstances much of the onus fell upon the matatu workers. In truth, the interdependence that existed between passengers and matatu operators made it impossible to know who was right and who was wrong.[39]

In June 2004 I rode in several matatus specifically with the intention of finding out how the passengers interacted with one another and with the conductors and drivers. I was particularly interested in how passengers responded to the seatback stickers. David Maina, a conductor, was one of my main sources of information. Short and stocky, Maina was in constant motion, running around the matatu station, talking to everybody and cracking jokes; he was also more than willing to talk about himself. Born in a family of nine siblings in Nyeri, a small town in central Kenya, he attended the fairly competitive Nyeri High School and graduated in 2000 with a D average (which is not actually bad since a C average was sufficient for admission to college).[40] After trying unsuccessfully for three years to find an office job in and around Nyeri, he was eventually forced to move to Nairobi and live with his cousin. After a year or so of job hunting, he quit looking for conventional employment and turned to matatus. He did not have any trouble getting a job as a conductor because, as he stated proudly, "Matatu owners prefer to hire people with high school certificates."[41]

I rode along in Maina's matatu several times that month. Named after Memphis Bleek, a famous African American rapper, the vehicle was painted bright green with yellow stripes and had TLC ("tender loving care") signs plastered all over it.[42] The seats inside Memphis Bleek had bright pink plastic covers so that when you sat down it sounded as if some naughty child had slipped a whoopee cushion under your backside. On the back of the front seats, directly facing the passengers, were four stickers placed side by side: "Even if I drive [at] 200 kph, this world is not mine"; "Men are like oxygen, women cannot do without them"; "A woman is like a common maize cob for every man to chew"; and, in obvious contradiction to the others, "Abuse women if you were not born by one."[43]

Memphis Bleek shuttled passengers between Nairobi and Kawangware, one of Nairobi's slums. To get to Kawangware, Memphis Bleek
had to go through some upscale neighborhoods, like Hurlingham and
Yaya. So while most of the passengers in Memphis Bleek were poor
and lived in shantytowns, some were relatively well-to-do professional
men and women. One day I rode Memphis Bleek during the morning
rush hour, at six-thirty. I met Maina at the bus stop and he seemed
more edgy, more fidgety, than usual; he sneezed, greeted me, commented on the chilly morning air—"This job is very difficult in this
cold weather"—and then quickly moved on to solicit passengers.[44] After about ten minutes, eleven of them had gathered in the vehicle, and
Maina shut the door and drove off. Along the way, several resolute passengers flagged the matatu down in areas not designated as bus stops;
nevertheless, Maina ignored the government's strict regulations and
asked the driver to stop.[45]

I asked him why he had disobeyed the law to make the prohibited
stops. He looked at me, laughed, and then remarked, "If you don't stop,
the passengers will mark your car and will never use it; they will be
mad at you."

I then asked him about the purpose of the stickers.

"To amuse the passengers," he replied.

"Even the one about women as a maize cob?"

"I think most women like that sticker," he said, gesturing at the
young lady sitting on my right to respond. The woman smiled, looked
down, and said nothing.

The subject of the stickers had come up several times in my previous conversations with Maina because, like his, most of those in other
matatus were similarly misogynistic. But whenever I brought up the
issue, he deflected my questions with a laugh and again insisted that
they were intended "to amuse passengers," or "to kill boredom," or "to
piss off passengers who don't pay their fares."

We drove on, picking up and dropping off passengers, and at one
point a nicely dressed middle-age woman climbed aboard the matatu.
She looked at me, commented on the frigid morning temperatures, and
then sat down next to me. We started chatting and I asked her opinion of the sticker describing "a woman as a maize cob for everyone to
chew." She laughed and said that the sticker was rubbish. "But," she
said, "what can you do? Matatu men are matatu men; they do whatever
they want."

"Do you believe that matatus can't be controlled?" I asked her.

"No, you can't control these people," she responded. "Even now, with the new regulations, they still drive like crazy people and stop wherever they please."

"But they stop because the passengers wave them down."

Taking no notice of my comment, she rolled her eyes and said matter-of-factly, "These people are dirty and obnoxious."

As we chatted away, three young women in school uniforms climbed into the matatu and Maina started to flirt with them. The young women smiled, giggled, looked down at their shoe tops, and then took their seats. Eventually, after the girls had alighted, Maina looked at me, winked, and said in Sheng (so everyone could hear), "*Cheki Michellini*" (Check out those Michelin tires, referring to the women's legs). I could not help but laugh, along with most of the other passengers, except the middle-age woman with whom I had been talking. She remained silent, shook her head, clicked her tongue and looked at me sternly. I had been chastened.

Throughout the years, I had had similar experiences on matatus.[46] None of them were unique. The obstinate attitude of the passengers who signaled drivers to stop in the middle of the road; the prejudicial labeling of all matatu crews as "dirty and obnoxious"; the misogynistic language; and the cruel laughter—this kind of behavior had been remarked upon over and over again in the mainstream media and by ordinary Kenyans.[47] Kwendo Opanga, one of the leading Kenyan journalists, defended matatu workers by saying that they behaved roughly because commuters refused to pay fares or demanded change when they had not paid any money, and he concluded his editorial rather heavy-handedly by asserting that "the matatu culture is indeed a true reflection of Kenyan public—undisciplined, arrogant, and corrupt."[48] Along the same lines, another leading journalist commented that "matatus represent both the best and the worst of Kenya" and added that their wanton disregard of the rules of the road and lack of consideration for other drivers may derive from the fact that all Kenyans are "atrocious behind the wheel."[49]

Most of the people I interviewed echoed these sentiments. No matter who I talked to about the notorious reputation of Nairobi's matatu workers—young or old, male or female, poor or rich—they all seemed to agree there was a strong connection between the behavior of matatu operators and that of the passengers. Grace Ouma, a fairly well-to-do woman in her thirties, believed that "to regulate matatus you have to regulate the behavior of the whole of the Kenyan population"—and she punctuated her comment with a laugh.[50] In the same vein, Mary Kariuki, a young student at the University of Nairobi, also laughed when I brought up the reputation of matatu operators and said, "Oh yes, I hate and fear matatus all right. But I won't live without them: I refuse to live in a Nairobi without matatus."[51] And one of the older fruit vendors in the matatu parking lots, James Mutive, told me how the city of Nairobi and the general functioning of Nairobi society would fail to exist without matatus, but he insisted that the excesses of a "matatu man" reflected the impatient, aggressive, and youthful qualities of Nairobi. Shaking his head with resignation, he surmised that the obscene literature and art on the matatu was the language of a polluted, poor, and unplanned city.[52]

———

Of course, the matatu operators themselves had much to say about their eternally troubled relationships with passengers. When I traveled to Nairobi during the 2000s I often interviewed Samson Mungai, one of the men employed by the Matatu Welfare Association (MWA) to supervise the parking stations and ensure that matatus lined up in proper turn while loading passengers. In his mid-forties, Mungai belonged to the older generation of matatu workers. Before taking up his new position he had worked as a conductor for at least fifteen years in the 1980s and 1990s. I spent many hours talking leisurely with Samson in the parking station and watching him interact with other matatu operators, street hawkers, and street kids.

Mungai is soft-spoken and gentle in his manners, and I found it difficult to believe that a man as gracious as Samson Mungai could thrive in the matatu industry. So I asked him to tell me why he thought matatu crews had acquired such a terrible a reputation. He insisted that the reputation was unfair, though he admitted there were several "mannerless" matatu workers. "But"—he patted my wrist as he elaborated his point—"if you have three kids and one of them is behaving badly do you beat all of them?" Sometimes passengers encourage matatu men to behave badly, he argued, and offered me the following scenario: "Imagine, for example, a very pregnant woman who leaves home and is mad at her husband who has deserted her and is not supporting her and their kids. She gets into a crowded matatu and a drunk slumps next to her and begins fondling her and touching her belly and squeezing closer to her." Like a good storyteller, Mungai paused here to let me imagine the woman's state of mind. "The woman gets mad. She gets so mad at every man so that even when you ask her for her fare she refuses to pay." He paused again, this time so I could consider the conductor's dilemma. "What do you do? At the end of the day you have to give your boss a certain amount of money."[53] Then thoughtfully, Samson argued that matatu operators are often forced to react to bad circumstances, the behavior of matatu crews has been conditioned by the general behavior of the Kenyan society, and finally that matatus have been blamed unfairly for everything wrong with the city of Nairobi.[54] Kenyans, he said, needed to realize that matatu men are not different from any other Kenyan struggling to feed a family under very difficult economic circumstances, and like others, they occasionally "have to be mean and even break the law in order to achieve this goal."

Mungai was an easy person with whom to sympathize, and he was right about the hardships encountered by workers in the matatu industry.[55] On an average day, matatus make about nine round trips between the residential areas and the city center. Most conductors, like Maina, make about 350 shillings (or US$5) per day, which comes to about US$150 per month if they work every day. Relatively speaking, this is not a bad wage since most people in Kenya with a high school education, working as clerks, make about US$130 per month, and so many of the conductors are better off than the average clerk. But even if they are a little better off, the work on a matatu is much more demanding—the long hours, the harassment from the police and the gangs, and the truculent customers, all take their toll. They are not in it for sport—"it is not that matatu drivers love accidents," he insisted, "they speed to meet deadlines if they are to keep their jobs."[56] As Mungai succinctly put it: "Operating a matatu is not a business for the faint-hearted."

My conversations with other matatu workers revealed similar sentiments: the work was endless and exacting, their shabby behavior was only the symptom of external pressures, and they reiterated how the passengers often forced them to act badly. Wounded and cynical, they sometimes sounded like a pessimistic lot. A few matatu workers told me how "in Kenya you must become a thief if you are to succeed," just look at the politicians who were the real thieves who, "gobbled the fat off the country."[57] Others noted that the politicians had been responsible for frustrating the dreams of young people like themselves—though one conductor irreverently admitted, "I wish I were a politician, I would eat too."[58]

I asked Charity Wanjiru the same questions when I met her in the Kawangware parking station in June 2004. She was the only woman conductor I met, and I think I had wanted to hear that her experience had been better, that passengers had treated her more politely because she was a woman. That was not the case, and in fact, her treatment had often been worse. She appeared calm and confident, but confessed that some passengers had labeled her "a prostitute" because she worked as a conductor—"Look at me,'" she asked indignantly, "look at me, do I look like a prostitute to you?" The money she earned was "clean money" and it was better to "work as a conductor than be on Koinange Street."[59] Wanjiru has a high school diploma and was trained as a food server but, like Maina, she could not find a job. Even now, working in the matatu industry she does not feel she is getting the respect she deserves from passengers, who insult conductors—no matter their gender—for no apparent reason, calling them "jobless," "untidy," "uneducated," and "good for nothing people."[60] "But," she told me, "the male conductors work very nicely with me; they protect me like they would their little sister."[61]

Relations between the matatu workers and passengers has always been fraught with distrust, and in the past couple of decades the atmosphere surrounding matatus has continued to be cynical, and sometimes downright hostile; more often than not commuters look upon the matatu operators with aversion. But the evidence also suggests that commuters have encouraged matatu operators' rude behavior, and encouraged them to break the law. In other words, the passengers are often complicit in the bad behavior. Impatient commuters flag down matatus at undesignated stops and become resentful of drivers who actually obey the rules; commuters will commonly board an already full matatu and then blame the conductors for "squeezing" them in, or cheat the conductors by not paying the fares. And there is sadly little regard for the matatu workers as people struggling to make a living like everybody else in Nairobi. Commuters act as though matatus exist only for their convenience, and it does not matter to them if the operators are forced to break the law because, as everyone knows, matatu operators will get away with it. No one will hold the drivers and conductors accountable, and if they are caught they need only offer a bribe to escape punishment—and anyway, they are already "criminals."

On the other hand, matatu workers enjoy exploiting the outrageous reputation they have been ascribed. They revel in their reputed delinquency; they engage in excessive and sometimes obscene behavior because they know their actions will be tolerated or prudently disregarded no matter how offensive. And regrettably, there are passengers who like to indulge the workers' lewd acts and language so that they can temporarily enjoy the same lack of constraint.[62] A ride on a matatu can offer an escape from the prevalent norms of social behavior; it is a place where passengers can laugh at off-color jokes or gratify their misogyny without guilt or repercussions.

It is not easy—and perhaps not even necessary—to assign blame for this state of affairs. Almost everyone seems to collaborate in it. Matatu operators understandably want to be seen as tough, abrasive, creative, and hip—like many young urbanites. And yet by mounting the provocative stickers inside the cars, by installing lights and televisions and sound systems, one could argue that matatu operators are also trying to earn some positive recognition. The lights, the noise, the slogans and stickers in the typical matatu are offensive to be sure, and they are meant to be, yet they are self-defensive because they are intended to conceal the workers' reliance upon the passengers' trust, and their vulnerability to the economy, to the police, and to the government. Although few matatu workers would admit it, their insolence and impropriety is mostly an effort to hide the fragility of their situations.

But despite all the mistrust and antagonism, some kind of irrevocable connection with passengers exists. The connection is strong enough to permit the workers to act fearlessly and brazenly without fear of reprisals, but also intimate enough that the passengers—if they try—can relate to the workers' problems and commiserate with their poverty, their working conditions, or their future prospects. These are of course the same issues that passengers worry about. Both sides may complain about each other, but all the accessorizing, all the portraits and stickers that so luridly adorn the vehicles, really serves to create a subtle, coded confederacy between the matatu workers and their passengers. Despite their troubled relations, they know their fates are tied together; they understand one another and can even on occasion share a sense of amity—and anyway, they are aware that if they were to get in an accident they would all share the same fate.

PART SEVEN

Self-Regulation, 2003–14

TWELVE

The Michuki Rules

The ambivalence the public felt toward matatus was unlikely to change. Part of the cause was the continued lack
of oversight. It had been a long time, nearly a decade
and half, since the matatu owners had benefited from a
legal organization that represented them. The disbanded
Matatu Vehicle Owners Association (MVOA), outlawed in
1988, was the last officially recognized matatu owners' organization.[1] However, in June 2003 the new government
of Mwai Kibaki registered the Matatu Owners Association
(MOA). Once again the owners had their own official organization, though there still existed the rather optimistic expectation that the matatu owners would be able to
reform the industry from within. This time it was hoped
that the association would work under the auspices of the
Matatu Welfare Association (MWA), an umbrella organization (legalized just three years earlier in 2000) that was
intended to serve as the intermediary between owners
and the government and between the owners and matatu
workers.[2]

Ideally the MWA would be able to provide some balance
and limit some of the excesses of the interested groups,
particularly the owners, who always seemed to have had a
dominant presence.[3] Despite all the government's formal
recognition, the creation of these two new organizations
was more or less a formality; both organizations had been
around in one form or another since the early 1990s and
had been acting informally on the behalf of the various
parties in the industry. (Of course, the government had
tacitly acknowledged their necessity by declining to shut

them down, except when the organizations had called for strikes.)[4] For the owners and operators the government's recognition fulfilled a long-lasting wish. Like MVOA before them, these two organizations had repeatedly asked that the government register them so that they could legally take part in the running of the industry. And now that they had been sanctioned the organization managed to place two very fine men in charge—Simon Kimutai and Dickson Mbugua. They were both elegant, avuncular, and professional, and it was hoped that they would work together, along with government officials, to make the matatu industry work for the good of everyone involved: the workers, passengers, owners, and the general public.[5] Everything seemed in place. And yet no accord was ever reached. Despite the best efforts of these two capable men, the struggles between the three different groups—the government, the MOA, and the MWA—remained contentious and irresolvable, not unlike the struggles between matatu owners, the police, politicians, and Mungiki. In this case the cause of the dissension was easy to identify; more than anything else, it was the implementation of the Michuki rules, the most stringent regulations the industry had faced since the Traffic Amendment Act of 1984. These new rules drove home the severity of the conflicts and the near impossibility of resolving the competing interests.[6]

The Michuki rules, named after their originator, John Njoroge Michuki, then minister of transport and communication, have become something of a legend in the matatu industry, largely because they were so ruthlessly enforced, at least for the first few months, at a time when Kenya was undergoing important socioeconomic and political changes.[7] The rules, passed in mid-September 2003, were intended to restore "order in the matatu industry and reduce the number of accidents."[8] An admirable goal, no doubt, but there were several new, problematic requirements that would have been difficult to satisfy even in the best of times. First, the Michuki rules stipulated that matatus be fitted with speed limiters and that a 50 kilometer per hour speed limit be enforced. Second, the rules banned all standing passengers in transport vehicles and required that all buses and matatus be fitted with safety belts. In addition, matatu workers had to be vetted by police, receive a certificate of good conduct before employment, and the crews had to wear mandatory uniforms and post their names and pictures in the vehicle. All matatu owners were also required to indicate in the buses the routes they worked and the maximum number of passengers the vehicles could carry, and the owners were required to paint a yellow line around the body of the vehicles so that all matatus looked alike.[9] And finally, there was a new rule that obliged the employees of MOA and MWA to watch over the matatu parking lots so that Mungiki and other gangs could be prevented from extorting money from the matatu owners and workers.[10] The deadline for the changes was the end of November—in other words, all of these regulations were to be enacted within a two-month period. Not only were the owners caught off guard by the rules, but they also resented the government's demand that the reforms be implemented on such short notice and in so little time.

Some of the reforms might have been anticipated since they were a part of the major national reforms that Mwai Kibaki had begun to introduce after he was elected in 2002 as Kenya's third president since independence.[11] Kibaki's election marked an important change in Kenya's political history; it signaled the end of one-party politics. The indefatigable KANU, the party of the previous dictatorial presidents Kenyatta and Moi, had finally lost an election. For many it was a sign of hope. During Moi's regime (Moi had been president for nearly twenty-five years) Kenya had faced almost continual economic decline, certainly the worst period of decline since independence, and when Kibaki was elected most Kenyans held on to the hope that the new president would somehow revive the economy. It was also clear to many that the matatu industry was one of the major engines driving the Kenyan economy, and that its health was essential. But the industry was also in constant crisis—or at least was perceived as being so. Unsurprisingly, Kibaki turned his attention to matatus right away, and he made clear his determination with his choice of John Njoroge Michuki to institute the reforms. Michuki was a man reputed to be one of Kenya's most ruthless politicians, and so at the very least everyone concerned would be forced to acknowledge the seriousness of the government's objectives.[12]

John Njoroge Michuki (1932–2012) was an old guard, and an easily recognizable type in Kenyan politics; he was a member of that first generation of wealthy conservative Kikuyu politicians who took over immediately after independence.[13] Many of the men in this particular group of politicians—President Kibaki was one of them—believed Moi, a Kalenjin, had destroyed Kenya's economy by (among other things) failing to tame matatus and bring order to the industry.[14] It is hardly a surprise, then, that Kibaki picked Michuki to do the job. They already knew each other well, and Kibaki no doubt felt he was someone he could understand and who could understand him.

Although Kibaki and his reformer may have shared the same perspective, the people associated with matatus did not. They were the ones who actually had to implement the idealistic changes. The real work fell upon the new official chairman of the MOA, Simon Kimutai, who inevitably became frustrated and resentful—legitimately so—since the Michuki rules had been sprung upon him without warning, and at no point had he been given the opportunity to offer his recommendations. Michuki had decided upon all of the regulations and deadlines without consulting anyone from the MOA or the MWA; and he did this while representing a government that had supposedly wanted to regulate the industry from within, and with the help of Kimutai and Mbugua. That, at least, had been the new government's much-heralded promise.[15]

Given the fact that Michuki had neglected others' interests from the very outset, it seemed unlikely that the leaders of the two matatu organizations would acquiesce to the new rules. And, predictably, both the MOA and the MWA rejected the regulations as soon as they were announced; more specifically, they objected to requirements that would force immediate costs upon them—the safety belts and speed limiters. These regulations were, purportedly, too expensive for matatu owners to afford, especially given the short deadline. Naturally they asked for the opportunity to speak with Michuki and convince him to rescind the rules, but the minister remained adamant: "The regulations will not be changed and those not ready to obey should prepare to be out of business. This is not a game of hide and seek; it is a matter more serious than that." Michuki was not a man to be casually dismissed—he once said of himself that "if you rattle the snake, it will bite you."[16] By refusing to adhere to the regulations, Mbugua and Kimutai were knowingly inviting a nasty bite from the minister, yet they seemed to have little choice.

Michuki was not simply content to play the autocrat, however. Perhaps sensing that he could slink past the objections of the two leaders of matatu organizations, he uncoiled another, more, subtle trick: he agreed to meet with Mbugua (the leader of the Matatu Workers Association) alone, in a private meeting that excluded Kimutai. By meeting with Mbugua, Michuki no doubt hoped he would be seen as magnanimously addressing the concerns of all matatu workers and not just the owners. That, at least, might be the more benevolent interpretation.

More likely, however, was that he intended to instigate a fight by deciding to exclude Kimutai from the meeting; in other words, he was determined to play the politics of divide and conquer by pitting the two matatu organizations against each other. And it worked. Kimutai was upset at having been shut out of the meeting and was especially miffed at Mbugua for agreeing to the meeting without him and therefore seeming to disregard the interests of the owners. He had thought they were all supposed to be in this together. Kimutai did not hesitate to make his disappointment public: "Mr. Mbugua is a man without a following and—even worse—a non-matatu owner. He is working with the government to frustrate the industry."[17]

True or not, the newspapers duly reported the comment and played up the drama between the two leaders, covering it as they would a horse race or a boxing match. Of course they could not inform anyone exactly what was discussed in the closed meeting between Mbugua and Michuki, though judging from the comments afterward it was clear it did not have anything to do with retracting the regulations. There was nothing to indicate that Michuki had changed his mind, or would ever: "I will not back down. It will not be in the interests of Kenyans."[18] However, it was not Michuki's stubborn persistence, or the fact that he prevailed at the meeting (the regulations would remain unchanged) that surprised anyone; what did end up turning heads was the fact that he had also, somehow, behind closed doors, managed to convince Mbugua to take his side. Or at least appear to do so. After the private meeting the MVA chairman suddenly began insisting that matatu owners "negotiate" with the government and not go on strike. "Change can be postponed," he said, "but not avoided."[19]

Once Mbugua had openly argued against the usefulness of a strike, it was obvious that the two leaders could no longer work together and were destined to quarrel.[20] The conflict with Kimutai intensified when, on November 9, 2003, Mbugua called a meeting of all matatu owners to discuss the new rules. From the moment the meeting started it became a battle of wills: "Kimutai made an effort to arrive early and address the meeting before Mbugua could get there," the *Nation* reported. But Mbugua was not about to be one-upped; when he turned up and "heard that Kimutai was addressing the meeting he walked away vowing never to 'meet with him eye to eye to discuss issues concerning the matatu industry.'"[21] It was probably just as well that he left, since Kimutai, during his address to the meeting, made it clear how annoyed he was by Mbugua's "secret" meetings with Michuki and scornfully dismissed him as irrelevant: "Mr. Mbugua represents nobody. He has no matatu on the road." His comments met with a "sharp clapping" of approval from matatu owners.[22]

Kimutai still had plans to call a strike if Michuki refused to back down and either repeal or delay the new rules: "Let us put the record straight; we are not fighting the government," said Kimutai, "we are fighting Mr. John Michuki and his punitive measures which are of no good to us."[23] He was determined that the owners be allowed to regulate themselves. Even when it came to regulating the speed of the matatus Kimutai insisted that the "best speed governor lies in the driver's head and attitude," not in some expensive mechanical device that the owners would have to pay for. These issues were not to be negotiated; they were, in other words, better off doing everything on their own and avoiding outside interference, mechanical or otherwise. Conversely Mbugua, apparently under the sway of Michuki, continued to distance himself from the threat of a strike and pleaded with the members of MWA all over the country to ignore the proposed strike "and continue rendering commuters services until otherwise advised by the national secretariat." He even characterized Kimutai's decision to call a strike as "unpatriotic," "unjustified," and "uncalled for" and argued that matatu owners only needed to have a "dialogue" with Michuki—just as he had—before deciding to take action as drastic as a strike. "Safety," he said, "is important and MWA wants the government to implement regulations."[24]

Kimutai was not to be swayed any more than Michuki, and so he went ahead and authorized a two-day strike for November 19–20, 2003. Matatu owners heeded his call, went on strike, and straightaway the whole country was paralyzed. The few matatu owners and drivers who tried to ignore the strike routinely had their vehicles pelted with stones, and some of the strikers even began pulling commuters from vehicles. Almost immediately the main streets of Kenyan towns were thronged with people walking to their places of work, while those hoping to travel longer distances were left milling about uncertain of what to do. Sometimes commuters took matters into their own hands. Some began fighting each other over whatever available form of transportation was lucky enough to have escaped the strikers' wrath. At one point the police were forced to rescue a Nairobi-bound bus from Mombasa that had been hijacked by passengers; apparently, the hostile commuters had forcibly boarded the bus by climbing through windows and then ordered the driver to take off, leaving those who had made earlier bookings stranded at the bus station. Eventually the police stopped the bus and obliged those who had no tickets to get off.[25] Although such hijackings seem to have been relatively rare, they nevertheless point to the fact that the strike was breeding a new kind of passenger—aggressive, angry, and ruthless—who was willing to do just about anything.

The frustrations the strike aroused seemed to trigger a spell of national anxiety. During the two days of the strike, Kenyans began reflecting more generally on what was happening to their country. "Where are we going as a country?" asked Silvie Oile, a twenty-one-year-old student at the University of Nairobi. "We have to hear both sides out. Laws of the land must be respected, but seat belts and speed governors are expensive. Adequate time must be set for matatu owners to fix them. Lecturers are on strike, City Council workers too. Now it is the matatus." Given the state of perpetual disruption all of these strikes caused, it is no wonder the country's future seemed uncertain; nor was it exactly clear how things had come to this impasse—for instance, Elizabeth Mathu, a schoolteacher, wondered what had caused the conflict: "we have to ask ourselves, how did we get here in the first place?" She remained hopeful: "I think the overall lesson Kenyans will learn from the strike is about sacrifice. Something will have to be given up."[26]

This kind of soul-searching, this hope to find an "overall lesson," may have been shared by others, though few people felt that the strike would be resolved for the good of the whole community. It seemed that whatever lesson was learned was not one likely to please many people. One commuter remarked acerbically, "*Ndume wawili wakipigana huumiza nyasi* [when two bulls fight it is the grass that suffers]," and he complained, legitimately, that most commuters "do not have alternative means of transportation." Ultimately he looked to the government, which "should talk to the matatus as it is the *wanainchi* [citizens], who suffer in the end."[27] Another commuter blamed the matatu owners. Annoyed at their refusal to install the required devices in their cars, he wondered how the matatu owners could justify spending outrageous amounts of money to install the latest TVs or music systems in their vehicles, but somehow could not afford speed limiters or seat belts: "The music systems which reduce the vehicles to mobile discos are priced much higher than the safety gadgets."[28]

By the end of the second day of the strike, it was clear that President Kibaki needed to intervene if he was to prevent Kenya's economy from shutting down. The president went on the airwaves and ordered matatu strikers to go back to work, and, in one of the few instances of compliance, the strikers listened and actually returned to work. At first it appeared that nothing had been accomplished, though for many drivers and conductors the end of the strike was a blessing of sorts since they could once again earn their daily wages: "We can now get food on our plates as usual," said matatu driver Peter Chege.[29] And yet despite the strike's apparent lack of success, it had managed to achieve one surprising result: it forced Minister Michuki to set up a meeting with Kimutai. This was in itself a small victory, but to everyone's surprise the meeting actually resulted in a compromise; the minister reluctantly offered to give matatus an extension of two months with the condition that the matatu owners agree to make the stipulated changes. Kimutai agreed, and the new deadline for the Michuki rules was set for February 1, 2004.[30] Despite the small victory, however, he continued to insist that the government must, in the future, consult matatu owners before making important decisions about the industry. The government, he maintained, needed to avoid "extreme interference and let the owners manage their businesses so that the industry could become self-regulating."[31]

––––––

What most immediately concerned Kimutai, though, were the logistics so crucial to the implementation of the regulations. In part it was simply a problem of supply and demand. Even if the owners could afford the changes, no one knew if there would be enough seat belts and speed limiters for each and every matatu in the country, or if there were enough garages with enough qualified people to fix the gadgets. And who exactly was going to authorize the final inspections? There could not possibly be enough garages to inspect the more than 50,000 vehicles in just two months. Worse still, Michuki had appointed a particular company in Nairobi—and only one company—as the sole agent for installing the equipment (no doubt for certain "economic" reasons). This decision made it both time consuming and expensive, especially for operators based outside Nairobi who would be required to travel all the way to the city, sometimes hundreds and hundreds of miles, to purchase and install the devices. Also, by granting only one company exclusive rights to issue compliance certificates, the minister had usurped the powers of the Kenya Bureau of Standards and the Transport Licensing Board. As a result of these conditions, only 30 percent of matatus in Nairobi had been fitted by the middle of January 2004, just

FIGURE 25   Courtesy of Godfrey Mwampembwa

two weeks before the deadline; an even smaller percentage had been updated in the other cities of Kenya, let alone the rural areas.[32]

In the end, the matatu owners were left with no options, and Kimutai felt compelled to take the matter to the High Court. The case was heard on one of those hot January days in Nairobi, the kind of day when the heat gets so oppressive that people are forced to escape by retreating beneath shade trees, but that did not deter matatu owners from gathering outside the unshaded High Court gate to await the verdict.[33] They had hope for some kind of relief, but when Kimutai exited the courthouse and walked toward them, looking down and shaking his head, they knew exactly what the verdict was.[34]

Once again they had been denied. They had been fighting the new rules since October of the previous year, they had gone on strike and gone to court, and still it appeared that they had no alternative but to adhere unequivocally to the Michuki rules. The outcome of the court decision, and its consequences, were of concern to the whole city; it was, in fact, an important issue to the whole nation and its economy. Throughout the month of January, therefore, the newspapers gave frequent updates on how matatu owners were or were not successful in complying with the rules. Mostly they focused on the long lines of vehicles waiting to be fixed at the various garages in the country, on the

FIGURE 26 Kimutai and matatu owners returning from the High Court, January 28, 2004. Courtesy of the NMG, Nairobi

shortage of seat belts and speed monitors, on the high prices, and on the subsequent smuggling of parts and the large number of fakes purportedly installed.[35]

But the story became more interesting—or, perhaps, more sinister—as rumors began circulating that the owner of the sole company given the mandate to import seat belts into the country was none other than Michuki's son.[36] Michuki denied allegations of favoritism, and he glibly dismissed the accusations: "It is not a crime for anyone to import them [seat belts] because it has to be done anyway."[37] Apparently that "anyone" might as well be his son, and his obvious evasions led many Kenyans to ask whether the minister had indeed passed this very expensive law in order to benefit his son. At the very least, his granting licensing rights to a single company aroused suspicions, and many people began wondering—quite legitimately—why the minister's demands had seemed so urgent. Was he perhaps racing against time so that his fraudulent behavior might not be discovered?

The cost of buying and installing the seat belts and speed limiters was, however, just one of many critical problems that matatu owners were to face. After going to the expense of fixing their vans, many owners found out they had no drivers. It turned out that many matatu drivers had been working with fake driver's licenses. Moreover, a fair number of those drivers and conductors had criminal records. As the newspapers reported, "most drivers have at one time or another been taken to court for traffic offences, robbery, assault, and other crimes and cannot pass the test."[38] Thus few drivers were able to pass the supposedly "moral test" stipulated by Michuki's new regulations.[39] But even those with no criminal record, those who were considered to be morally fit, could not easily get a license and begin work, since it took at least four weeks for their fingerprints to be checked by the police and the Central Intelligence Department, and another two weeks to get the certificate of good conduct. As the deadline to comply with the new rules quickly approached, a spokesman from Michuki's office urged matatu owners to try and employ members of the National Youth Service—an indication of just how desperate the situation had become.[40]

It is no surprise, then, that by the time the deadline of February 1, 2004, came around, only about 50 percent of matatus in Nairobi were on the road, and far fewer in the rest of the country. And now, due to the sudden shortage of transport, the matatu owners unashamedly increased their fares, and the Kenyans who had to contend with the price gouging asked, once again, why the government had not planned ahead. Inevitably, opinion was divided as to who was at fault. Some people felt that matatu owners had been victimized by the government, while others were quite happy with the work Michuki was doing and were willing to be patient.[41] "Even if matatus were given a whole year on the 365th day, they would be asking for an extension," one cynical passenger wrote in a letter to the *Standard*.[42]

In spite of the conflicting perceptions, it was obvious to anyone walking through the streets of Nairobi that the Michuki rules had shaken up the industry quite a bit. For a while, at least during the first six months of 2004, there seemed to be a new kind of order in the transport industry. There was certainly a decrease in the number of accidents reported; also, the matatus' destinations and passenger capacity were now clearly indicated (though it was doubtful many paid much attention to the passenger limits).[43] Still, the streets were strident as many of the vehicles still boasted their graffiti and artwork and played music at ear-splitting levels.

The reforms had another beneficial effect: the insurance companies began to lower their premiums, believing that the drivers had been vetted and could now be deemed responsible. Insurers, along with the Trade and Licensing Board, also began sponsoring seminars on how to get into the matatu industry and make money without breaking the law. Thousands of people attended, and it was reported that new investors were actually venturing into the industry in the belief that the matatu business had now been cleaned up and they would no longer have to deal with the bribery, the extortion, and the lack of safety. Even long-distance companies—such as the notorious and powerful Molo-Line Services, with more than three hundred vehicles—now observed the rules.[44] In general, there seemed a renewed spirit in the industry, like the clean crisp air after the first rains at the end of the dry season.

————

Just after the first four months of the new rules, in early June of 2004, I arrived in Nairobi to start research for this book, and I breathed this air of optimism. I had been anxious, wondering how I was going to carry out research in one of the most dangerous and chaotic industries in Kenya. My first visit was to the offices of the MWA in Nairobi. When I walked into a tall, dilapidated building on the congested end of Moi Avenue, there was a crowd of people waiting for the elevator, and after a twenty-minute wait, we finally reached the MWA office. I walked in and introduced myself to Dickson Mbugua, the organization's chairman.

In distinct contrast to the negative stereotypes that surrounded matatu workers, Mbugua was a quiet, soft-spoken man with gentle manners who appeared to be in his early or mid-fifties. I liked him instinctively and enjoyed talking with him, but I also wondered how such a pleasant person could be the head of a group of men with such a disreputable and belligerent reputation. As we talked at length about the industry I could not help but remain preoccupied with the question of the industry's notorious reputation. After about an hour or so, I told Mbugua that I was interested in doing field work and talking to as many matatu drivers, conductors, and passengers as possible—would he be kind enough to introduce me to some of them? He immediately called up one of the supervisors at the nearest parking lot, who came over and picked me up from Mbugua's office. It seemed that the chairman had been forthcoming about everything during our conversation—everything but his relations with Kimutai. Mbugua never mentioned his rival from the MOA.

The supervisor took me to the Railways matatu parking station, right next to the once-grand Nairobi railway station and across the street from the area that had housed the United States Embassy until the 1998 bombings. While walking around the Nairobi CBD (Central Business District) in the previous few days, I had been impressed by

FIGURE 27   Dickson Mbugua (*left*), June 2004. Photo taken by Kenda Mutongi.

how clean the streets looked compared to my memories of just a couple years before, but I was even more impressed by the changes that had taken place since President Kibaki had taken over. The Railways parking lot, like many other Nairobi parking stations, now had a park with beautiful bougainvillea planted in perfect small circles, and placed at intervals throughout the park were several attractive white benches with the words "A Joint Public Utility Initiative" written on them. Even the employees had been spruced up—maroon shirts and trousers for the conductors, blue shirts and pants for the drivers. They looked like unassuming schoolboys in uniform.

The whole place seemed orderly. Even the passengers lined up before the arriving matatus, rather than surging en masse at the door like livestock at feeding time. There were several supervisors employed by MWA who ensured that the matatus also lined up in orderly fashion, on a first-come, first-served basis. Perhaps most encouraging were the new, ecological Iko toilets at the end of the parking lot—the toilets were a landmark innovation in the city, the brainchild of David Kuria.[45] Kuria was born in Elburgon, Rift Valley, in 1971, and earned a bachelor of architecture degree from Jomo Kenyatta University of Agriculture and Technology in 1992. For many years he worked for an NGO

FIGURE 28   Kenda Mutongi with matatu drivers and conductors, June 2004

making a good salary, but with a combination of funding from organizations like Ashoka and others, he began to think about how he might refurbish the old city council public toilets.[46] He had done so beautifully. The public toilets in the Nairobi central business district, once an eyesore (at the very least), had become a pleasant stop, complete with radio music. One paid only five shillings (about five cents) to use the facilities, which were located at various points in the city. More than 1,200 people were employed by the Iko toilet company. There were now also public shoeshine services in the parking lot as well as outlets for snacks, fruits, water, and other necessities.

Mark Mutori, an employee of the MWA, managed this parking lot and ensured that matatus followed the rules. Tall and slim, with Harry Potter spectacles, Mutori seemed more reserved than many other matatu owners I had met. He had graduated from the prestigious Strathmore Business College (Nairobi) in 1991 and then worked as a clerk at the Kenya Commercial Bank, but he had been laid off the previous year. He invested his severance money in a matatu—a typical Generation Matatu move, I suppose. He bought his vehicle in April after the Michuki rules had been instituted, and, as one of the new investors, he was concerned about making sure that the matatu drivers and conductors obeyed the rules so that he could succeed—and so that he would not be at a disadvantage. "This is a good industry," he told me, "it is the only industry that pays taxes regularly; the city council would go broke were it not for the money it got from the matatus, from parking fees to registration fees."[47] He clearly wanted the matatu industry to receive more respect from the public—most matatu people are nice, he insisted, "they help each other out," and he was proud to be paying taxes and only wished that everybody else with an income would do the same.[48] At the very least, Mutori's confidence was an indication that the reforms were working.

———

I returned to Nairobi in June 2006, and this time I was determined to meet the matatu industry's other mover and shaker, the younger one, Simon Kimutai, the chairman of the Matatu Owners Association. I stopped at one of the matatu parking stations and asked one of drivers where the MOA was located. Curiously, he did not know, but he asked around for me and eventually got directions to Accra Road. I set off walking east through the congested streets of Nairobi central business district, with its copiously provisioned *dukas* selling phones, SIM cards, televisions, furniture, and all kinds of cheap goods from China and Thailand, via Dubai.[49] The scene was chaotic. "Matatus crawled by, bumper to bumper, honking obstinately; a few drivers, tired of waiting in the traffic, decided to 'sort out' their problem the best way they knew how, by inching themselves out of the queues and onto the sidewalks, earning scowls and insults from pedestrians scurrying out of the way and coughing in the clouds of dust in the vehicles' wake."[50] Meanwhile, the conductors and touts of empty matatus sang out discordantly, hoping to attract uncommitted passengers.

I was staggered—what had happened to Michuki rules? This congested, anarchic Nairobi felt very different from the Nairobi of two years before, though it was in many ways a much more familiar place. The Nairobi of June 2004 had been a dream, a city temporarily transformed to reflect the ambitions of Minister Michuki. When I arrived at the supposed home of the MOA, the security officer had never heard of the organization; however, the guard sitting next to him remembered that MOA had been in that building for a year, but it had now moved to another building on Nkrumah Road. He gave directions and I started walking back the way I had come, encountering the same dust, the same crowds in the dukas, and the same disgruntled passengers herding around the matatus. I arrived at the right office, in Tumaini

House, and asked at the reception desk if I could talk with Mr. Kimutai, and once I had explained to the receptionist my mission she gave me permission to enter the office.

The MOA chairman was a man about my age. He was mild-mannered, dressed in a beautiful suit; he was attentive, soft-spoken, and sharp witted. A remarkable fellow. Like Mbugua, he was not what I expected of a matatu man. We greeted each other and I introduced myself and explained my project, and as we chatted he told me he was a Kalenjin, from Moi's tribe.

"So why didn't you get along with Moi?" I asked.

He shook his head and then started to tell me about himself: he was born and raised in Kericho to a Kenyan mother and a white settler farmer who left the family when Kimutai was young. He had grown up poor and wore his first pair of shoes when he went to high school, which he quit in Form 5 to join the Kenya Air Force. Unfortunately, he was expelled from the air force after its attempted coup on Moi's government in 1982. He was arrested and imprisoned for four years.

After his release from prison, he enrolled for a diploma course in supplies management at the Kenya Polytechnic. "I was so anxious to make up for lost time and for my education," he told me, and he expressed deep regrets about dropping out of high school.[51] He managed to finish his diploma in about a year and started making furniture and selling it by the road at Dagoretti Corner in Nairobi, but that was not successful. He then went to work as an interior designer, but that was no more successful than the furniture business. So he borrowed money from Equity Bank and bought his first matatu and started plying the Kangemi route (a densely populated low-income area). To repay the loan quickly he decided to drive the route himself and save the salary of a driver. He was soon able to buy a second matatu and hire a driver; a third matatu soon followed, and he decided to stop driving and focus on supervising the business.

"Matatu is a good business, you can make money . . . good money," he told me when I marveled at his unusual success. As he told me about the many ways economic liberalization of the 1990s helped people like him do well, he was particularly careful to point out the importance of the Equity Bank.[52] Originally established as a small mortgage lender in the mid-1980s (the Equity Building Society), in 1994 the Equity Bank became a microfinance institution, providing low-cost loans to ordinary people to start businesses. For people like Kimutai the results were revolutionary. Prior to the Equity Bank, the realm of banking had been the province of a privileged few, and one needed a letter of introduction simply to open an account. Before microfinance banks came into existence, "one had to spend months making frenzied calls asking . . . his or her second cousin to call so-and-so's uncle. But that is not the case anymore, at least not at Equity Bank. They call you Sir or Madam! They are nice to you! You can see the manager! You can get a small loan in one day!"[53] By the mid-2000s Equity had become Kenya's largest bank and controlled one-third of the country's bank accounts, largely because it had targeted as customers the vast majority of Kenyans who had never opened an account before; it had also invested millions of dollars in building a sophisticated IT system. Equity soon became known as the *mwanainchi* bank, the bank of the people.[54]

Still, getting a loan was not enough to build a successful matatu operation—as Kimutai said repeatedly, "you have to have some experience in order to succeed. Most of the owners had been drivers to begin with, and that is what works." He still believed that matatu work was "the best job in town." For example, "if you go to industrial areas and work the whole day you make 200 shillings, but if you are a conductor you make 600 shillings, and a driver between 800 and 1,000 shillings, so you are doing better in the matatu industry. It is a difficult job at the beginning, and requires very long hours, but once you are used to it you are fine." When I asked him about how the industry was attracting more educated youth he seemed gratified by the question: "Education is the key to success. If an educated person like me joins the matatu industry, then the matatu industry has succeeded. . . . The matatu industry is the only industry that has not been infiltrated by foreign aid workers," he said matter-of-factly; "that is why the industry has survived and thrived for nearly forty-five years. The matatu industry is a seriously Kenyan industry."[55]

Kimutai was more modest when telling his story of becoming the chair of the Matatu Owners Association. "In the early 1990s there were a lot of KANU Youth Wingers at the bus terminus extorting money and harassing drivers. Although I didn't fear these guys, I thought the other owners needed a voice to stop these people who were fleecing us. That's how we started organizing MOA, but we were not legal until 2003. I took charge." Try as he might, he could not quite hide the fact that his efforts had been exceptional: "There was a big leadership vacuum in the sector and something needed to be done to bring sanity in route allocation. Previously, there had been no political will to deal with the problem, after MVOA was banned. My finest hour was when I called for a national strike. With the support of matatu owners, we managed to send a message that the new matatu organization could bring about reform. But I still insist that you do not succeed in bringing about reforms merely by bringing uniforms and badges. Attitudes can only change through training."[56] His task, as he saw it, was to bring some professionalism into the industry's operations and to make sure that matatu owners spoke with one voice through the association. It was probably an impossible goal, though he succeeded better than could have been expected.

About his rival Mbugua, he remained much more reticent. He chuckled briefly, said nothing for a few seconds, and then asked me if I had spoken with him. I had indeed met him two years earlier and thought him a very nice person. Kimutai smiled at my revelation, perhaps a bit sarcastically, and said nothing, except that I should go visit Mbugua again and ask him what he is up to these days.

My experiences with Kimutai and Mbugua had been pleasant. They are both clever fellows who are genuinely eager to rid the matatu industry of its notorious reputation, and to see it recognized as a major part of the Kenyan economy. It remains a mystery why they have not been able to unite and speak with a single, strong voice when their mutual interests have been threatened by the government.[57] Obviously, the two men could not speak with one voice all the time since they represented different groups—the owners and the workers—that often had competing interests, and no doubt they had to give priority to their own organization and the interests of their members. But frequently the interests of the groups overlapped, especially when they had to coordinate policy with the government about routes and regulations.

On the other hand, the motivating interests of the MOA and the MWA were often at odds and could not be easily aligned. In this regard, the government could—and probably should—have played a more constructive role. It could be argued that it was the government's responsibility to ensure that the competing interests of the two groups were resolved so that they could better serve the interests of the rest of the society. It was the government's duty, for example, to meet with the major stakeholders in the matatu industry—together—and discuss how to go about reforming the industry; it was also the government's responsibility to ensure that all the logistics of carrying out the reforms were in place, and carried out fairly, before they began dismantling the system.[58] And the government could have done a much better job of ensuring that the reforms could actually be put into place, and that they did what was intended and were sustainable.

But the political climate of the early years of the Kibaki administration, and the personalities of the government leaders, simply prevented this from happening. When in 2003 the Kibaki government succeeded the invincible Moi, it believed that it needed to pay off political debts, and so it put into office oversized egos like Michuki, whose only desire was to enact reforms that counteracted those of Moi's government. Many such men were waiting in the wings, and when placed in power they governed with little concern for the consequences of the policies. Many were so intent upon avenging past abuses that they rarely attended to repercussions of their plans, and to prove themselves they were simply going to force the needed reforms, by whatever means necessary, without regard to the consequences.

And they were also going to reward themselves as well. Too many were like Michuki in this regard—pompous, scheming fellows who used the reforms as a ruse so they could confer largesse upon their friends and families.[59] To make matters worse, Kibaki, unlike the previous presidents, was a hands-off leader who liked to delegate responsibilities, and this made it that much easier for others to take the reins and abuse their power.[60] So it was no surprise when Michuki cynically tried to divide and conquer the matatu industry by playing off the MWA against the MOA: his efforts prevented them from uniting and becoming strong enough to resist his policies.[61] And he also knew exactly who to pressure since the less powerful MWA had no choice but to collude with Michuki if it wanted to keep its place at the table.[62] In the end, however, the hasty, manipulative, and haphazard ways in which Michuki went about reforming the matatu industry meant that the changes the rules were meant to enact could never be sustained.

In fact, it is hard to say that they actually improved the situation at all. The only real benefit of the reforms was the fact that the number of accidents declined (though in all likelihood the decline was due to the fewer number of passengers in each vehicle, and the fewer number of vehicles on the roads—both consequences of the Michuki rules). The most significant effect was that the slowdown the rules caused forced owners to raise fares so that they could earn the money needed to meet the new regulations. Of course this meant that even fewer people could afford to travel on the matatus.

Yet the higher fares may have encouraged more people to invest in matatus. The number of new vehicles rapidly increased, so quickly that the government actually ran out of registration plates.[63] In any case, by 2006, as the economy recovered and low-cost loans were more readily available, even more people began buying matatus, fares went down to pre-2004 levels, and with more people traveling on matatus the number of accidents and fatalities began rising again. The roads were no safer than before, and so, by the beginning of 2006, there was already indication that Michuki's rules had had little if any effect upon the matatu industry. Little had changed, most likely because the rules had been autocratically imposed from above and did not address the realities on the streets, nor could they be sustained without resorting to economic extortion or brutal force by the government. Of course, none of this mattered to Michuki; by the end of 2005, Michuki had already left his position as the minister of transport and communications for greener pastures in the Kibaki government.[64]

Interestingly, in 2006 MOA and MWA did manage to come together temporarily to try to regulate and rebuild the industry from within. The plan was, ideally, to reach a long-held goal: to make the matatu industry self-regulating so that it could preempt government interference altogether.[65] For the moment, at least, the two organizations reached an agreement to halt the bickering that was wearing them down and put aside the competition that had only served the interests of the government.[66] Together, the two organizations protested that the police had gradually transformed the Michuki rules into instruments of extortion—in other words, compliance with the rules had become more about paying money to the right people than about fixing the vehicles or reforming the business. "We want to merge so that we can speak with one voice and we want to become a professional body with a code of ethics," Mbugua told the press.[67]

And for a while it worked. During their brief period of unity, the MOA and MVA succeeded in making the government upgrade speed requirements for matatus—from 80 km per hour to 100 km per hour—by successfully arguing that the vehicles' strong engines were being strained because 80 km per hour was too low a speed. They also convinced the government that buses should be subjected to the same rules as matatus, and particularly that the buses not be allowed to transport standing passengers. Finally, they demanded that the government spend some of its revenues repairing the roads. Somewhat surprisingly the government agreed to the demands and began using the new revenue to fix the roads.[68]

But this solidarity quickly dissolved in 2007 when MOA bought an insurance company without consulting MWA.[69] It was not an insignificant move. Throughout the 2000s, many insurance companies in

Kenya had filed for bankruptcy because they could not afford the large number of claims (it turns out that many of the claims—mostly those made by matatu owners—were fraudulent).[70] By the end of 2006, there were hardly any insurance companies left through which matatu owners could insure their vehicles, even though they were required by law to do so.[71] Kimutai decided to have the MOA purchase one of these insurance companies, a company called Invesco, so that there would always be insurance available. He believed that by investing in Invesco, matatu owners would be more likely to manage their "risks" with more caution; that is, they would be less likely to make unnecessary or unwarranted claims if the claims were going to cost the MOA's own company. "We own the company," Kimutai told the press, "so we have to manage our own risks."[72]

However, the purchase of Invesco brought Kimutai into direct conflict with Mbugua. Invesco had outstanding claims of about 600 million shillings, most of it owed to matatu owners, passengers, and workers, and Mbugua—quite reasonably—wanted to make sure the claims were paid off before MOA acquired the company.[73] But Kimutai argued vehemently that the decision to pay off outstanding claims was up to the members of the MOA itself, and none of MWA's concern.[74] The two groups have not worked together since.

By and large, the pattern over the past ten years suggests that the two leaders have tended to come into conflict with each other during unstable periods, particularly when Nairobi and the rest of the country were going through especially rapid changes—which, in point of fact, happened quite often. Change triggers uncertainties, and the uncertainties cause the organizations to look after their own interests with added zeal. Whenever they perceived that the size of the pie was changing, or might change, they were determined to compete for the largest slice.[75] On the other hand, during periods of political and economic stability, they seemed to have implicitly—and sometimes explicitly—agreed not to compete. At such times the two associations tended to cooperate, since they then could afford to look at the larger picture and consider together the shared public good and the norms of behavior that were in their own, and the larger society's, best interest. During these brief periods of cooperation they also became less susceptible to the divide-and-conquer tactics that had so often weakened the industry, and their cooperation also gave them stronger bargaining power in their negotiations with the government. But we have yet to see whether or not the two groups are going to handle future challenges together.[76] Or if they will return to the usual antagonisms whenever the stakes are high and the industry's well-being is threatened. The question is really whether or not the self-interested divisions will continue in times of scarcity and change, or, when it is most needed, the various groups will put aside their own interests for the greater good.[77]

———

In May 2014, I returned to Kimutai's office to find out how things were. He had by this time moved to a much nicer office—with carpets and leather sofas—away from the city center. He was not there, but I was given his phone number and when I called he was pleased to speak with me, though he was anxious about studying for final exams—he was in school again, a man of his age and accomplishments. It turns out he had enrolled in a business management degree program at Kabianga University in Kericho: "one should never stop learning; I am always trying to figure out how I can improve myself."[78] When I called back after his exams and Kimutai answered, his voice sounded different, more relaxed, and he began telling me about his family, and especially how important it is to continue going to school so he can keep up with his children studying abroad in the United Kingdom, Japan, and the United States. He now visits his family house in Kericho (about 150 miles from Nairobi) every weekend to see his wife, and because—he now says—he likes the quiet life. He has been chairman of the MOA for over a decade, though it is not his fault, he insists, because he keeps getting elected by matatu owners (he laughed, but said nothing when I joked about his rigging the elections and turning into another autocrat). At the moment Kimutai was preoccupied with introducing *Bebapay*, a card system whereby passengers prepay money on a card and use it instead of cash.[79] He believed some of the main problems in the industry can be fixed with the cashless system. Potentially such a system could eliminate gangs who would be put off by the lack of cash; it would make income easier to tax since drivers and touts would be paid a salary, and it would help regulate the drivers who would have to follow stricter schedules.

I asked him about Mungiki, and whether it was true that the gang had attacked him and beaten him up. He sighed, was silent for a moment, and then said quietly, "The Mungiki are bad, bad people who have ruined the matatu industry." Still, he was optimistic, and had some hope that the recently opened Savings and Credit Cooperation Organizations (SACCO) might be a solution to the gang problem. In 2010, the government, in an attempt to eliminate gangs from the matatu industry, introduced a policy that required all matatu owners to become members of a SACCO. Any industry could form a SACCO; the policy was not exclusive to matatus. In the case of matatus, however, each owner was required to register to become a SACCO member by identifying his/her vehicle with the route where it was operating.[80] This requirement has, so far, been enforced effectively (probably since no one will be issued a Transport License Board permit without first joining an existing SACCO).

Each SACCO has its own rules and regulations. For instance, some charge a fixed fare to passengers at specified times of the day, which means that all the matatu owners in that SACCO have to comply with that particular fare. In addition, the matatu owners are expected to contribute about 500 shillings every day; 200 shillings of that goes to managing the SACCO (paying the employees who collect these monies or run the SACCO activities), and the remaining 300 shillings is often credited to the account of the individual matatu owner. The owner is allowed to withdraw the money whenever he or she needs it, or borrow a loan against it as with a typical bank account. Some of the money collected by the SACCOs was used to hire guards to watch over the matatu parking lots so that Mungiki could not take over and claim to be providing protection.

It looked as though the SACCOs might be a solution to Mungiki's corrupting effect, but in October 2011 matatu operators began to report that gangs demanding protection money had again started harassing them. Their appearance was really no surprise.[81] The gangs often showed up during elections, and owners were predictably angry and disgusted that it should be happening again: "Many of us [matatu owners] are servicing loans and it is hypocritical for the minister to incite an outlawed sect to take our hard-earned money from us. We will pull back our vehicles until the government machinery deals ruthlessly with this cartel," said one of the operators, who requested anonymity. It has been reported that Mungiki was crucial in helping Uhuru Kenyatta win the contested 2012 election. We will have to wait to see if indeed the SACCOs will have a lasting positive impact.[82]

When I finally asked Kimutai again about Mbugua, he paused and said that he does not know anything about him and had no idea where he might be located. The sometime adversary had been relegated to the past, or at least Kimutai was feigning so. In any case, it seemed like Kimutai and his MOA had outlasted everyone—Mbugua, the Nyayo Bus, the long defunct KBS, the KANU Youth Wingers, political competition, and even the Michuki regulations. Matatus were still around, transporting millions and millions of people throughout Nairobi and Kenya. And though the industry was hardly perfect, the matatu owners and workers were determined to keep experimenting with new ways to improve their matatus to better serve the passengers—as long as they could make profits for themselves.

Making It in Nairobi

It is no longer possible for someone with a little ingenuity, a battered pickup, and a few wooden planks to hustle their way into the matatu industry. Those days are long gone. What was once little more than an ad hoc assortment of rebuilt old wrecks shuttling poor passengers from the suburbs to the city has transformed itself into a multi-million-dollar business that employs Kenyans of all backgrounds and abilities. The transformation took a little more than a half century, and it was accomplished despite the dearth of resources, the cutthroat competition, the ill-willed interference of the gangs and the government, and the stifling pollution of corruption. All of these obstructions had to be either dispatched or defeated, and the matatu industry has done so, in addition to providing gainful employment to the thousands of Kenyans who were eager and enterprising enough to meet its tough demands. No matter how poor or uneducated, no matter how remote their village, if they were willing to come to the city and work hard, there was work to be found on board a matatu or in the garages—as drivers, touts, conductors, mechanics, electricians, and even as artists.

Yet the obstacles were many. If you did find work in a matatu you were most likely subject to ferocious competition and shady, sometimes violent, treatment from nearly everyone with whom you came in contact—the other operators, the gangs, the police, the government, even passengers. Everything about the industry was contestable and subject to force. Control over the lucrative routes was monopolized by the cartels of wealthy owners who

FIGURE 29   Central Nairobi, 2016. Courtesy of the Standard Group, Nairobi

excluded struggling newcomers; gangs such as Mungiki extorted the
workers and crippled the business; the police demanded bribes to allow matatus to stay on the roads; even the politicians used the matatu
industry as a battleground for their coercive politics by hiring hooligans to sway elections. Unfortunately, the matatu industry responded
in kind with conduct that was insolent and acrimonious, despite the
damage to its reputation. Almost without exception it has been seen
as ruthless, as aggressively competitive, as a business that is coarse and

careless toward its patrons and violent toward its adversaries. It has been persistently—and justifiably—linked with crime and corruption, and with a streak of recklessness that has made traffic fatalities an ugly inevitability.

On the other hand, it has received almost no aid of any kind. The government, in particular, failed to offer the industry any assistance, even when it would have been in their best interest, and the best interest of the city. Had the government provided stronger regulatory oversight it might have helped guide the industry and eliminated the cartels and the gangs; it might also have helped improve safety by reducing the overcrowding, the indifference to traffic laws, and the high rate of accidents; and it might have also helped mitigate the noise, pollution, and congestion.[1] A better-functioning government might also have distributed the all-too-important matatu routes more equitably and assigned them in a way that helped balance competition.[2] Leveling the playing field by means of antitrust action might have kept the matatu market more open and competitive.[3] As it is, most of these problems still persist, and it could be convincingly argued that a combination of regulated markets and a more representative, democratic government might have provided a way forward.[4] None of this happened. The government, when it was present, seemed only willing to exploit the industry for its own purposes—usually to fill its own coffers or strengthen the power and influence of its officials. The succession of Kenyan governments, especially the government of Daniel Arap Moi, were too compromised and too politically weak to manage the matatus in a way that might have introduced more competition and efficiency. Moi's government tended to assert its presence through bribery, manipulation, corruption, and red tape. Even when the government did try to play a more constructive role, its actions usually ended up demonstrating little more than its own weakness and vulnerability to private influence. More often than not, its self-serving interventions intensified the violence in the industry as it compelled the owners to fight even more fiercely to secure their livelihoods. The Michuki rules provide the most obvious example.

And yet despite all the obstacles and failures, self-imposed or otherwise, the city would be unrecognizable without the matatus nosing their way through the teeming streets, blasting their hip-hop, and proclaiming their power. Not only has this once marginal mode of transportation changed the social and political climate of the entire country, it has also created a generation of its own, a powerful, politically active and business-savvy generation steeped in global cultures and ready to expand its cultural authority. The culture of the matatu is still a work in progress.

———

The progress that the matatu industry made was accomplished on its own. It is important to remember this. If the typical matatu has been transformed from a chugging VW bus to a garish modern coach stuffed with the latest techno-wizardry, it was done independently, and after the country had gained its independence. Once the nation was liberated, the resources of its economy were liberated as well; once workers could actually go into the city to find jobs or start businesses or make investments, a new economy was unleashed.

Just as significant, though less obvious, was the fact that the matatu industry has always operated independent of the good intentions of foreign intervention, particularly the intervention of NGOs. That in itself is an important achievement, especially given the magnitude of the business and its importance to Nairobi. While it is undeniably true that NGOs have been important in the economic development of many parts of Africa, they have certainly not provided remedies for all its economic woes—nor to be fair have they ever pretended to. But then all too often the NGOs have been oversized and aloof; too often they overlook the needs of their constituencies in order to meet the centrally planned expectations of their foreign donors; and too often they ignore the knowledge of local people and the informed, spontaneous solutions they can provide. After all, the staff of a typical NGO is unlikely to know the ins and outs of shantytown alleyways, the politics of the gangs, or how much and how to bribe the police. One does not hear much of the local hip-hop rolling out the windows of NGO Land Cruisers; NGO staffers do not speak Sheng. These things are important. If we want to understand how the average worker in Nairobi makes a living, we cannot continue to focus principally on the foreign aid development model, which asks for measureable returns and clear-cut stories, and which is at once too broad and too blinkered to take in the messy, complicated lives that it hopes to improve. The fact is that most Kenyans trundle on equivocally in the markets and on the matatus, and for the most part their lives exist free from the influence of foreign aid or foreign aid workers.[5] Certainly the matatu industry never needed them; it managed to invent itself and grow on its own.[6] As, I suspect, many other up-and-coming businesses in Africa have, and will.

Yet it is hard to know, since there are very few detailed historical studies of large capital businesses created and owned solely by Africans in postcolonial Africa. I believe that studies of these kinds of businesses are long overdue.[7] We need to know much more about what Africans themselves are doing in their markets and behind their storefronts, about the risks they are taking, the businesses they are creating, and the profits they are making, and especially the problems they are facing in earning their own livings. A microscope can teach us as much as a telescope. For decades now one of the big questions in the economic history of the Global South has centered on which development path its countries might choose, and we can debate in the abstract the relative merits of a state-controlled economy, a free-market economy, or one that welcomes foreign aid. But those debates always seem to ignore the people on the streets. But if we ignore the struggles of these people, we are ignoring much of the truth. At least in Kenya, it was the local businessmen and small investors—like the matatu owners—who possessed the necessary knowledge, who understood the transportation needs of Nairobi's residents, and who created workable solutions. To see the kind of work they accomplished we need to descend to street level and look at the indigenous businesses, at all the young men and women willing to experiment and take risks in an economy that has fewer and fewer traditional opportunities. It is usually the case that the more closely we look, the more complicated and interesting the narratives become, and one could say, the more promising they become. At the very least we need to take seriously what ordinary Africans are making in Africa and how they are making it. Recognizing these efforts requires that we revise our ways of seeing and challenge conventional thinking about the African continent.[8] Despite the sometimes staggering problems that Kenya and other African countries face, many of the men and women I interviewed in Nairobi see Kenya as bursting with promise and opportunity, now more than ever before.

Acknowledgments

Many thanks go to all the people in Kenya—especially to matatu workers, owners, passengers, and many others—who made the time to talk with me about their experiences with the matatu industry (see the bibliography for names).

To the following people who read early drafts of the manuscript, thank you friends: Uwem Akpan, Chuck Ambler, David Anderson, Adam Ashforth, Florence Bernault, Magnus Bernhardsson, Robert Blunt, Timothy Burke, Leslie Brown, Michael Brown, Alison Case, Jessica Chapman, Teju Cole, Nathan Connolly, Julie Crawford, Robert Dalzell, Sara Dubow, Aminatta Forna, Ali Garbarini, Anne Gerristen, Peter Geschiere, Mwangi wa Githinji, Dan Goodwin, Kiaran Honderich, Marc Jaffe, Tony Kihara, Jacqueline M. Klopp, Eric Knibbs, Liesbeth Koenen, Harro Maas, Keguro Macharia, Jim Mahon, James Manigault-Bryant, Karen Merrill, Joseph C. Miller, Ngugi wa Mkoma, Susanne Mueller, Julia Munemo, Ngonidzashe Munemo, Patrick Mutongi, Vincent Mutongi, Mkoma wa Ngugi, Nimu Njoya, Frank Oakley, Paul Ocobock, George Ogola, Paul Park, Jacob Rasmussen, James Robinson, David Rossitter, Merida Rua, Natalie Scholz, Phil Smith, Anand Swamy, Lynn Thomas, Bill Wagner, Binyavanga Wainaina, Luise White, Scott Wong, and James Wood.

This book would not be possible without the careful attention of the following readers: Daniel Branch, Lucy Gardner Carson, Jonathan Conning, Richard Egan, Laura Fair, Alan de Gooyer, Dawn Hall, Gretchen Long, Eiko Maruko Sinaiwer, Evan Mwangi, Derek Peterson, and

Cathy Silber. Extra special thanks to Eiko for pushing me and encouraging me to keep writing. You are a good friend, Eiko.

To friends and family for their moral support—many thanks: Paige Bartels, Heidi Betz, Denise Buell, David Edwards, Theo Davis, Molly Magavern, Margaret McComish, Nicole Mellow, Margaret Opanga, Rene Salemink, Micah Singer, David L. Smith, and Mary Catherine Wimer.

I presented drafts of the manuscript at the African Studies Center at Five Colleges, Amherst; Bard College, Human Rights Program; Columbia University, Committee on Global Thought; Emory University, Conference on Politics and Citizenship in Post-Colonial Africa; Johns Hopkins University, History Department; Kenyatta University; Michigan State University, History Department; Netherlands Institute for Advanced Study in the Humanities and Social Sciences; Northwestern University, Center for Historical Studies Symposium; Princeton University, Institute for Advanced Study; Rutgers University, African Studies; University of Amsterdam; University of Florida, Gainesville; University of Leiden, the Netherlands; University of Michigan, Anthropology and History Workshop; University of Nairobi, Anthropology Department; University of Notre Dame, African Studies Program; University of Warwick, Global History Workshop; University of Wisconsin–Madison; the Williams College Africana Studies Colloquium, Global Studies Colloquium, and History Department Colloquium; Yale University, History Department.

Thanks to the following for much-needed research and writing support: The Institute for Advanced Study, Princeton; The National Endowment for Humanities (NEH); The Netherlands Institute for Advanced Study in the Humanities and Social Sciences/The Royal Netherlands Academy; Williams College, Dean of Faculty Office.

So many thanks to the hard-working team at the University of Chicago Press: Carrie Adams, Ellen Kladky, Renaldo Migaldi, Dylan Joseph Montanari, Priya Nelson, and Ryo Yamaguchi. And T. David Brent is, of course, a brilliant editor.

To my children, Ada and Stefan, and my husband, Alan de Gooyer, I love you dearly.

Abbreviations

BIFA	Buruburu Institute of Fine Arts
CBD	Central Business District
DP	Democratic Party of Kenya
FORD	Forum for the Restoration of Democracy
KANU	Kenya African National Union
KBS	Kenya Bus Service
KCBOA	Kenya Country Bus Owners Association
KENATCO	Taxi Company
KNA	Kenya National Archives
KYW	KANU Youth Wingers
MAK	Matatu Association of Kenya
MOA	Matatu Owners Association
MVOA	Matatu Vehicle Owners Association
MWA	Matatu Welfare Association
NARC	National Rainbow Coalition
NBS	Nyayo Bus Service
NCC	Nairobi City Council
NMG	Nation Media Group
OTC	Overseas Transport Company
PSV	Public Service Vehicle
SACCO	Savings and Credit Cooperation Organization
TLB	Trade and Licensing Board
UTC	United Trading Company

Notes

1. For studies of matatus, see Mbũgua wa Mũngai, *Nairobi's Matatu Men: Portrait of a Sub-Culture* (Nairobi: Contact Zones, 2013); Meleckidzedeck Khayesi, Frederick Muyia Nafukho, and Joyce Kemuma, *Informal Public Transportation: Matatu Entrepreneurship* (Burlington, VT: Ashgate, 2014); Sunita Kapila, Mutsembi Manundu, Davinder Lamba, and Mazingira Institute, *The Matatu Mode of Transportation in Metropolitan Nairobi* (Nairobi: Mazingira Institute, 1982); and Jacqueline Klopp, "Towards a Political Economy of Transport Policy and Practices in Nairobi," *Urban Forum* 23, no. 2 (2012): 1–21. None of these studies offer historical depth.

2. For studies of popular economies in Kenya, see, for example, Kenneth King, *Jua Kali Kenya: Change and Development in an Informal Economy, 1960–1995* (Athens: Ohio University Press, 1996); and Joyce Nyairo, "Jua Kali as a Metaphor for Africa's Urban Ethnicities," Mary Kingsley Zochonis Lecture at SOAS, July 2, 2005.

3. For some recent critiques of development aid in Africa, see William Easterly, *The Tyranny of Experts: Economists, Dictators, and the Forgotten Rights of the Poor* (New York: Basic Books, 2014), and *The White Man's Burden: Why the West's Efforts to Aid the Rest Have Done So Much Harm and So Little Good* (New York: Penguin 2006); Dambisa Moyo, *Dead Aid: Why Aid Is Not Working and Why There Is a Better Way for Africa* (New York: Farrar Strauss and Giroux, 2011); Howard French, *China's Second Continent: How a Million Migrants Are Building a New Empire in Africa* (New York: Knopf, 2014); and

Jagdish Bhagwati and Arvind Panagariya, *Why Growth Matters: How Economic Growth in India Reduced Poverty and the Lessons for Other Developing Countries* (New York: PublicAffairs, 2014).

4. Binyavanga Wainaina, *Discovering Home* (Nairobi: Kwani, 2006), 1.

5. For recent examples of similar historical studies that place a particular business in a broader social, cultural, religious, and political context, see Laura Fair, *Reel Lives* (Athens: Ohio University Press, forthcoming); Bethany Moreton, *To Serve God and Wal-Mart: The Making of Christian Free Enterprise* (Cambridge, MA: Harvard University Press, 2009); and Nathan Connolly, *A World More Concrete: Real Estate and the Remaking of Jim Crow South Florida* (Chicago: University of Chicago Press, 2014).

6. Paul Ocobock, "Joy Rides for Juveniles: Vagrant Youth and Colonial Control in Nairobi, Kenya, 1901–1952," *Social History* 31, no. 1 (2006): 39–59.

7. Eric Randall, letter to the editor, *Nation*, September 9, 1971.

8. Kenda Mutongi, "Thugs or Entrepreneurs: Perceptions of Matatu Operators in Nairobi, 1970 to the Present," *Africa* 76, no. 4 (2006): 549–68.

9. Author's observations and experience growing up in Kenya in the 1970s and early 1980s.

10. See, for example, *The Standard*, January 22, 1978, and *Nation*, May 17, 1980.

11. Meleckidzedeck Khayesi, Frederick Muyia Nafukho, and Joyce Kemuma, *Informal Public Transport in Practice: Matatu Entrepreneurship* (Burlington, VT: Ashgate, 2014), 47–49.

12. Mutongi, "Thugs or Entrepreneurs," 550–53.

13. Ibid., 553–56.

14. Mũngai, *Nairobi's Matatu Men.*

15. The literature on Mungiki is immense. See, for example, Bodil Folke Frederiksen, "Mungiki, Vernacular Organization, and Political Society in Kenya," *Development and Change* 41, no. 6 (2010): 1065–89; Peter Mwangi Kagwanja, "Facing Mount Kenya or Facing Mecca? The Mungiki, Ethnic Violence, and the Politics of the Moi Succession in Kenya, 1987–200," *African Affairs* 102 (2003): 25–49, and his "'Power to *Uhuru*': Youth Identity and Generational Politics in Kenya's 2002 Elections," *African Affairs* 105, no. 418 (2006): 51–76; David Anderson, "Vigilantes, Violence, and the Politics of Public Order in Kenya," *African Affairs* 101, no. 405 (2002): 531–55. Terisa E. Turner and Leigh S. Brownhill, "African Jubilee: Mau Mau Resurgence and the Fight for Fertility in Kenya, 1986–2002," *Canadian Journal of Development Studies / Revue canadienne d'études du développement* 22, no. 4 (2001): 1037–88. Grace Nyatugah Wamue, "Revisiting Our Indigenous Shrines through Mungiki," *African Affairs* 100, no. 400 (2001): 453–79; Jacob Rasmussen, "Outwitting the Professor of Politics? Mungiki Narratives of Political Deception and Their Role in Kenyan Politics," *Journal of Eastern African Studies* 4, no. 3 (2010): 435–49, and his "Mungiki as Youth Movement Revolution: Gender and Generational Politics in Nairobi, Kenya," *Young* 18, no. 3 (2010): 30119. M. Ruteere, *Dilemmas of Crime, Human Rights, and the Politics of Mungiki Violence in Kenya* (Nairobi: Kenya Human Rights Institute, 2008).

16. Kagwanja, "Power to *Uhuru*," 51–60.

17. Angelique Haugerud, *The Culture of Politics in Modern Kenya* (Cambridge: Cambridge University Press, 1997); Klopp, "Towards a Political Economy of Transport Policy and Practices in Nairobi," 19–21.

18. I have borrowed this phrase from Teju Cole's description of the atmosphere around bus stops in Lagos in the early 2000s; see his *Every Day Is for the Thief* (New York: Random House, 2014), 35.

19. Mũngai, *Nairobi's Matatu Men*; and Khayesi, Nafukho, and Kemuma, *Informal Public Transport in Practice*.

20. Mbũgua wa Mũngai and David A. Samper, "'No Mercy, No Remorse': Personal Experience Narratives about Public Passenger Transportation in Nairobi, Kenya," *Africa Today* 52, no. 3 (2006): 51–81.

21. For studies of capitalism and anarchism elsewhere, see Luigi Zingales, *A Capitalism of the People: Recapturing the Lost Genius of American Prosperity* (New York: Basic Books, 2012); Robert Nozick, *Anarchy, State, and Utopia* (New York: Basic Books, 2013); James C. Scott, *Two Cheers for Anarchy: Six Pieces on Autonomy, Dignity, and Meaningful Work and Play* (Princeton, NJ: Princeton University Press, 2014), and *The Art of Not Being Governed: An Anarchist History of Upland Southeast Asia* (New Haven, CT: Yale University Press, 2011).

22. For some examples of large capital indigenous entrepreneurship, see the studies on Nollywood. The literature is extensive and is collected in Elizabeth J. Hester, *Nollywood and Nigerian Cinema: A Selective Bibliography of Dissertations and Theses* (New York: CreateSpace Independent Publishing Platform, 2016). For other examples, see Alusine Jalloh, *African Entrepreneurship: Muslim Fula Merchants in Sierra Leone* (Athens: Ohio University Press 1999); Janet MacGaffey, *Entrepreneurs and Parasites: The Struggle for Indigenous Capitalism in Zaire* (Cambridge: Cambridge University Press, 1988); and Kate Meagher, *Identity Economics: Social Networks and the Informal Economy in Nigeria* (Oxford: James Currey, 2010).

23. A. G. Hopkins, "The New Economic History of Africa," *Journal of African History* 20, no. 2 (2009): 155–77. Robert L. Tignor, "The Business Firm in Africa," *Business History Review* 81, no. 1 (2007): 87–110.

24. For examples, see Bessie House-Soremekun and Totin Falola, *Globalization and Sustainable Development in Africa* (Rochester, NY: University of Rochester Press, 2016); Paul Gifford, *Christianity, Development, and Modernity in Africa* (Oxford: Oxford University Press, 2016); Emmanuel Akyeampong, Robert H. Bates, Nathan Nunn, and James A. Robinson, eds., *African Development in Historical Perspective* (Cambridge: Cambridge University Press, 2014); Nicola Swainson, *The Development of Corporate Capitalism in Kenya, 1918–1977* (Berkeley: University of California Press, 1980); Colin Leys, *Underdevelopment in Kenya: The Political Economy of Neocolonialism, 1964–1971* (Berkeley: University of California Press, 1974); and Josephine Milburn, *British Business and Ghanaian Independence* (Hanover, NH: University Press of New England, 1977).

25. The seminal work is Walter Rodney, *How Europe Underdeveloped Africa* (Baltimore: Black Classic Press, 2011).

26. Sara Berry, *Fathers Work for Their Sons: Accumulation, Mobility, and Class Formation in an Extended Yoruba Community* (Berkeley: University of California Press, 1985); Jane Guyer, *Marginal Gains: Monetary Transactions in Atlantic Africa* (Chicago: University of Chicago Press, 2004); and Gareth Austin, *Labor, Land, and Capital in Ghana: From Slavery to Free Labor in Asante, 1807–1956* (Rochester, NY: University of Rochester Press, 2005).

27. Moyo, *Dead Aid*; and Easterly, *Tyranny of Experts* and *White Man's Burden.*

28. Daron Acemoglu and James Robinson, *Why Nations Fail: The Origins of Power, Prosperity, and Poverty* (New York: Crown Business, 2013); Paul Collier, *The Bottom Billion: Why the Poorest Countries Are Failing and What Can Be Done about It* (Oxford: Oxford University Press, 2008); Robert Bates, *When Things Fell Apart: State Failure in Late-Century Africa* (Cambridge: Cambridge University Press, 2008); and Jeffrey Herbst, *States and Power in Africa: Comparative Lessons in Authority and Control* (Princeton, NJ: Princeton University Press, 2014).

29. For an excellent ethnographic study of contemporary Nairobi, see the essays in Hélène Charton-Bigot and Deyssi Rodriguez-Torres, *Nairobi Today: The Paradox of a Fragmented City* (Nairobi: Mkuki Na Nyota Publishers, 2010).

30. Luise White, *The Comforts of Home: Prostitution in Colonial Nairobi* (Chicago: University of Chicago Press, 1990).

31. For examples of similar methodology, see Suketu Mehta, *Maximum City: Bombay Lost and Found* (New York: Random House, 2004); Katherine Boo, *Behind the Beautiful Forever: Life, Death, and Hope in Mumbai Undercity* (New York: Random House, 2012); and Luc Sante, *The Other Paris* (New York: Farrar Straus, 2015).

32. Raoul J. Granqvist, *The Bulldozer and the Word: Culture at Work in Postcolonial Nairobi* (New York: Peter Lang, 2004), 141–75; Mũngai, *Nairobi's Matatu Men*; and Binyavanga Wainaina, *One Day I Will Write about This Place* (London: Graywolf Press, 2012).

33. Mũngai and Samper, "No Mercy, No Remorse," 51–81.

34. For interesting studies of metaphorical meanings of mass transit elsewhere, see Michael W. Brooks, *Subway City: Riding the Trains, Reading New York* (New Brunswick, NJ: Rutgers University Press, 1997); Randy Kennedy, *Subwayland: Adventures in the Land Beneath New York* (New York: St. Martin's Griffin, 2004); and Julia Solis, *New York Underground: The Anatomy of the City* (New York: Routledge, 2007).

35. For studies of Cosmopolitanism, see, for example, Jacques Derrida, *On Cosmopolitanism and Forgiveness* (New York: Psychology Press, 2001); Kwame Anthony Appiah, *Cosmopolitanism: Ethics in a World of Strangers* (New York: W. W. Norton, 2010); Steven Vertovec and Robin Cohen, eds., *Conceiving Cosmopolitanism: Theory, Context, and Practice* (Oxford: Oxford University

Press, 2002); and Nikos Papastergiadis, *Cosmopolitanism and Culture* (New York: John Wiley and Sons, 2013).

36. https://www.facebook.com/search/top/?q=matatu, and https://wambururu .wordpress.com/, accessed June 2, 2015.

37. For example, Marc Smith, *Communities in Cyberspace* (New York: Routledge, 1999); Laura Gurak, *Cyberliteracy: Navigating the Internet with Awareness* (New Haven, CT: Yale University Press, 2003).

CHAPTER ONE

1. Robert Ruark wrote two books about his experience traveling in Kenya, *Something of Value* (New York: Safari Press, 1955) and *Uhuru* (New York: Buccaneer Books, 1962).

2. Ruark, *Something of Value*, 185.

3. For a study of colonial Nairobi, see Luise White, *The Comforts of Home: Prostitution in Colonial Nairobi* (Chicago: University of Chicago Press, 1990).

4. Godwin Murunga, "Inherently Unhygienic Races: Plague and the Origins of Settler Dominance in Nairobi, 1899–1907," in *African Urban Spaces in Historical Perspectives*, ed. Steven J. Salm and Toyin Falola (Rochester, NY: University of Rochester Press, 2005), 98–130. Godwin Murunga, "Segregationist Town Planning and the Emergence of African Political Protests in Colonial Nairobi, 1899–1939" (PhD diss., Northwestern University, 2006).

5. For studies of slavery in eastern Africa, see Marcia Wright, *Strategies of Slaves and Women: Life Stories from East Central Africa* (London: Lillian Barber, 1993); Frederick Cooper, *From Slaves to Squatters: Plantation Labor and Agriculture in Zanzibar and Coastal Kenya, 1890–1925* (New Haven, CT: Yale University Press, 1987).

6. Ronald Preston, *The Genesis of Kenya* (Nairobi: Colonial Print Works, 1947), 6.

7. James Smart, *A Jubilee History of Nairobi* (Nairobi: East African Standard, 1950), 11.

8. Ronald Hardy, *The Iron Snake* (London: Collins, 1965), 20; J. H. Patterson, *The Man-Eaters of Tsavo and Other East African Adventures* (London: Macmillan, 1907), 32.

9. As quoted in Andrew Hake, *African Metropolis: Nairobi's Self-Help City* (New York: St. Martin's Press, 1977), 23.

10. James Henry Patterson, *The Man-Eaters of Tsavo and Other East African Adventures* (London: Macmillan, 1907), 295.

11. A. R. Cook, *Uganda Memories* (Kampala: Uganda Society, 1945), 56.

12. M. E. Chamberlain, *The Scramble for Africa* (London: Longman, 1999), 21.

13. *Times* (London), June 20, 1907, 4.

14. Ibid., 5.

15. *Daily Telegraph* (London), January 9, 1907, 2.

16. Hake, *African Metropolis*, 57–64.

17. For details, see James Fox, *White Mischief: The Murder of Lord Erroll* (London: Vintage, 1998); Errol Trzebinski, *The Lives of Beryl Markham* (New York: Norton, 1995), *The Kenya Pioneers* (New York: Norton, 1988), and *The Life and Death of Lord Erroll: The Truth Behind the Happy Valley* (London: Fourth Estate, 200); Isak Dinesen, *Out of Africa* (London: Modern Library, 1992).

18. M. E. Chamberlain, *The Scramble for Africa* (London: Longman, 1999), 23.

19. Herbert H. Werlin, *Governing an African City: A Study of Nairobi* (London: Africana Publishing, 1974), 39.

20. Government of Kenya, 1960 Statistical Abstract (Nairobi: Government Printer, 1960).

21. White, *Comforts of Home*, 57–58.

22. Timothy Parsons, "'Kibra Is Our Blood': The Sudanese Military Legacy in Nairobi's Kibera Location, 1902–1968," *International Journal of African Historical Studies* 30 (1997): 87–122.

23. White, *Comforts of Home*, 45–46; Godwin Murunga, "The Cosmopolitan Tradition and Fissures in Segregationist Town Planning in Nairobi, 1915–23," *Journal of Eastern African Studies* 6 (2006): 463–86.

24. Murunga, "Cosmopolitan Tradition and Fissures in Segregationist Town Planning in Nairobi," 465.

25. Janet Bujra, "Women Entrepreneurs of Early Nairobi," *Canadian Journal of African Studies* 9 (1975): 213–34, and "Proletarianization and 'Informal Economy': A Case Study from Nairobi," *African Urban Studies* 3 (1978/79): 47–66; and Claire Robertson, *Trouble Showed the Way: Women, Men, and Trade in the Nairobi Area, 1890–1990* (Bloomington: Indiana University Press, 1997), and her *We Only Come Here to Struggle: Stories from Belinda's Life* (Bloomington: Indiana University Press, 2000).

26. Frank Furedi, "The African Crowd in Nairobi: Popular Movements and Elites Politics," *Journal of African History* 14 (1973): 275–90.

27. Kenda Mutongi, *Worries of the Heart: Widows, Family, and Community in Kenya* (Chicago: University of Chicago Press, 2007), 107–17; and John Lonsdale, "Town Life in Colonial Kenya," *Azania* 36–37 (2012): 206–22.

28. White, *Comforts of Home*, 60–67.

29. Government of Kenya, 1960 Statistical Abstract (Nairobi: Government Printer, 1960).

30. David Anderson, "Corruption at City Hall: African Housing and Urban Development in Colonial Nairobi," *Azania Archaeological Research in Africa* 36–37, no. 1 (2001); Richard Stren, "The Evolution of Housing Policy in Kenya" in *Urban Challenge in East Africa*, ed. John Hutton (Nairobi: East African Publishing House, 1970), 57–96.

31. For histories of Indians in Kenya, see Sana Aiyar, *Indians in Kenya: The Politics of Diaspora* (Cambridge, MA: Harvard University Press 2015); J. S. Mangat, *The History of Asians in East Africa, 1886–1945* (Oxford: Oxford University Press, 1969); Robert G. Gregory, *India and East Africa: A History of Race Relations within the British Empire, 1890–1939* (Oxford:

Oxford University Press, 1971); Donald S. Rothchild, *Racial Bargaining in Independence Kenya: A Study of Minorities and Decolonization* (London: Macmillan, 1973); Michael Cowen and Scott MacWilliams, *Indigenous Capital in Kenya: The "Indian" Dimension of the Debate* (Helsinki: University of Helsinki, 1996). For fictional accounts of south Asians in East Africa, see M. G. Vassanji, *The In-Between World of Vikram Lall* (London: Vintage, 2005), *The Book of Secrets: A Novel* (London: Picador, 1996), *The Gunny Sack* (London: Heinemann, 1990), and *And Home Was Kariakoo* (Toronto: Anchor Canada, 2016).

32. Government of Kenya, 1960 Statistical Abstract.

33. Furedi, "The African Crowd in Nairobi," 280–87; Lonsdale, "Town Life in Colonial Kenya," 34–36; and Frederick Cooper, introduction to *Struggle for the City: Migrant Labor, Capital, and the State in Urban Africa*, ed. Frederick Cooper (New York: Sage, 1983), 1–30.

34. Stren, "Evolution of Housing Policy in Kenya," 67–68.

35. Paul Ocobock, "Joyrides for Juveniles: Vagrant Youth and Colonial Control in Kenya," *Social History* 3, no. 1 (2006): 39–59.

36. Tom Opiyo, "The Metamorphosis of Kenya Bus Services Limited in the Provision of Urban Transportation in Nairobi" (master's thesis, University of Nairobi, Department of Civil Engineering, 2003).

37. Interview, Nairobi, July 1, 2008.

38. Interview, Nairobi, July 1, 2008.

39. Robertson, *We Only Come Here to Struggle*.

40. C. Richard Taylor, "Carrying Load: The Cost of Generating Muscular Force," *Physiology* 55 (October 1986): 153–55.

41. Interview, Kakamega, June 12, 2004.

42. Interview, Kakamega, June 12, 2004.

43. For a study of Kenyan music during this period, see John Roberts, "Kenya's Pop Music," *Transition* 19 (1965): 40–43.

44. Interview, Nairobi, June 17, 2004.

45. Interview, Nairobi, June 17, 2004.

CHAPTER TWO

1. For details about this change, see Andrew Hake, *African Metropolis: Nairobi's Self-Help City* (London: Chatto and Windus for Sussex University Press, 1977).

2. Herbert Werlin, *Governing an African City: A Study of Nairobi* (New York: Africana Publishing, 1974).

3. "The Pirates: A *Nation* Investigation," *Nation*, March 13, 1965, 13.

4. For a detailed study of living conditions of the new migrants, see Hake, *African Metropolis*, 120–45.

5. "Purchase of KBS Shares Will Benefit City," *Nation*, October 7, 1966, 7; "Pioneering for Prosperity in Africa," *Commercial Motor*, May 22, 1958,

110–12. http://archive.commercialmotor.com/article/2nd-may-1958/110/ pioneering-for-prosperity-, accessed March 12, 2014; Tom Opiyo, "The Metamorphosis of Kenya Bus Services Limited in the Provision of Urban Transportation in Nairobi" (master's thesis, University of Nairobi, Department of Civil Engineering, 2003); David Anderson, "Corruption at City Hall: African Housing and Urban Development in Colonial Nairobi," *Azania Archaeological Research in Africa* 36–37, no. 1 (2001): 36–57.

6. Opiyo, "Metamorphosis of Kenya Bus Services Limited," 23; P. A. Thomas, "The Advantages of Being LTD," *Transition*, 1968.

7. "Kenya Bus Services Ltd: Public Passenger Transport Services in Nairobi." Position paper presented to the Ministry of Transport and Communications, Kenya Bus Services Ltd., Nairobi, 1980.

8. Isaiah Gibson Aduwo, "The Role of Efficiency and Quality of Service of the Matatu Mode of Public Transportation in Nairobi, Kenya: A Geographical Analysis." Paper presented at the University of Nairobi, Geography Department, 1990.

9. Aduwo, "Role of Efficiency and Quality," 100–13; B. O. Jarabi, "Intra-Urban Mobility and Urban Transportation: A Case Study of Nairobi City, Kenya" (Master's thesis, Institute of Population Studies, University of Nairobi, 1982).

10. "Mayor Opens New Nairobi Bus Station," *Nation*, January 25, 1967.

11. Ibid., 4.

12. *East African Standard*, January 25, 1967.

13. Aduwo, "Role of Efficiency and Quality," 3.

14. "Kenya Bus Services Ltd: Public Passenger Transport Services in Nairobi," *East African Standard*, March 2, 1967.

15. Hake, *African Metropolis*, 12; Herbert Werlin, *Governing an African City: A Study of Nairobi* (New York: Holmes and Meier, 1975). There were about 86,000 Asians, and the number of Europeans had dropped to 21,000.

16. Tom Mboya, *The Challenge of Nationhood* (Nairobi: Heinemann, 1970), 65; E. S. Atieno Odhiambo, "From the 'English Country Garden' to Makambo Mibale: Popular Culture in Kenya in the Mid-Nineteen Sixties," in *Urban Legends, Colonial Myths: Popular Culture and Literature in East Africa*, ed. James Ogude and Joyce Nyairo (Trenton, NJ: Africa World Press, 2007), 155–72.

17. Herbert Werlin, "Nairobi in the Time of Uhuru," *Africa Today* 10, no. 10 (1963): 7–10; Thomas Dow, "Attitudes toward Family Size and Family Planning in Nairobi," *Demography* 4, no. 2 (1967): 780–97; G. Anthony Atkinson, "African Housing," *African Affairs* 49, no. 4 (1950): 228–37; S. M. Kimani, "The Structure of Land Ownership in Nairobi," *Revue canadienne des études Africaines* 6, no. 3 (1972): 379–402; Joe Wamala Muwonge, "Urban Policy and Patterns of Low-Income Settlement in Nairobi," *Population and Development Review* 6, no. 4 (1980): 595–613; Donald Mead, "The Economics of Population Growth," *Transition* (April–May 1967): 40–42.

18. Interview, Kakamega, June 10, 2004.

19. Ibid.

20. Enid De Silva, "Building Their Homes for the Future," *East African Standard*, January 22, 1965.

21. Werlin, *Governing an African City*, 38–48; Hake, *African Metropolis*, 28.

22. Hake, *African Metropolis*, 45.

23. Atieno Odhiambo, "From the 'English Country Garden' to Makambo Mibale," 162.

24. John Roberts, "Kenya's Pop Music," *Transition* 19 (1965): 40–43.

25. "Hard Work Needed Says President," *East African Standard*, January 1, 1965; "Poverty in the City Can Be Ended by Return to Land," *East African Standard*, January 10, 1965; Peter M. Ngau, "Tensions in Empowerment: The Experience of the 'Harambee' (Self-Help) Movement in Kenya," *Economic Development and Cultural Change* 35, no. 3 (1987): 523–38.

26. A. V. Bhide, "Bootstrap Finance: The Art of Start-Ups," *Harvard Business Review* 70 (1992): 109–17.

27. For an interesting biography of African mechanics in the Horn of Africa, see Stefano Belluci and Massimo Zaccaria, "Engine of Change: A Social History of the Car-Mechanics Sector in the Horn of Africa," in *Transforming Innovations in Africa*, ed. Jan-Bart Gewald, André Leliveld, and Iva Peša (Leiden: Brill, 2012), 237–56.

28. Eric Randall, letter to the editor, *Nation*, September 9, 1971.

29. Daniel Miller, ed., *Car Cultures* (Oxford: Berg, 2001), 4–5.

30. Interview, Nairobi, June 14, 2004.

31. Interview, Nairobi, June 16, 2004.

32. George Klute, "Modern Chariots: Speed and Mobility in Contemporary Small Waras in the Sahara," in *The Speed of Change: Motor Vehicles and People in Africa*," ed. Jan-Bart Gewald, Sabine Luning, and Klaas van Walraven (Leiden: Brill, 2009), 45–69. Also see the essays in Gewald, Leliveld, and Peša, *Transforming Innovations in Africa*.

33. Kurt Beck, "The Art of Truck Modding on the Nile (Sudan): An Attempt to Trace Creativity," in Gewald, Luning, and Walraven, *Speed of Change*, 59–80.

34. M. Di Domenico, H. Haugh, and P. Tracey, "Social Bricolage: Theorizing Social Value Creation in Social Enterprises," *Entrepreneurship Theory and Practice* 34, no. 2 (2010): 681–703; T. Baker and R. Nelson, "Creating Something from Nothing: Resource Construction through Entrepreneurial Bricolage," *Administrative Science Quarterly* 50, no. 2 (2005): 329–66; F. Cleaver, "Reinventing Institutions: Bricolage and the Social Embeddedness of Natural Resource Management," *European Journal of Development Research* 11, no. 1 (2002): 54–73.

35. Ted Baker, Anne S. Miner, and Dale T. Eesley, "Improvising Firms: Bricolage, Account Giving, and Improvisational Competencies in the Founding Process," *Research Policy* 32, no. 2 (2003): 255–76.

36. Johann Graf Lambsdorff, Markus Taube, and Matthias Schramm, eds., *The New Institutional Economics of Corruption* (New York: Routledge, 2005).
37. Interview, Nairobi, July 20, 2004.
38. Interview, Mathew Lukalo and Kevin Mwangi, Nairobi, July 5, 2004.
39. Interview, Nairobi, July 2, 2005.
40. S. D. Sarasvathy, "Causation and Effectuation: Toward a Theoretical Shift from Economic Inevitability to Entrepreneurial Contingency," *Academy of Management Review* 26, no. 3 (2001): 243–63.
41. Interviews with Mary Oneko, Mark Otieno, Catherine Mwangi, and Peter Muliso, Nairobi, November 24, 2012.
42. Interview, Nairobi, November 18, 2012.
43. Parker Shipton, *Credit between Cultures: Farmers, Financiers, and Misunderstanding in Africa* (New Haven, CT: Yale University Press, 2010); Parker Shipton, *The Nature of Entrustment: Intimacy, Exchange, and the Sacred in Africa* (New Haven, CT: Yale University Press, 2007); Kate Meagher, *Identity Economics: Social Networks and the Informal Economy in Nigeria* (Oxford: James Currey, 2010); Jane Guyer, "Wealth in People / Wealth in Things: An Introduction," *Journal of African History* 36, no. 1 (1995): 83–90.
44. R. Dart, "The Legitimacy of Social Enterprise," *Non-Profit Management and Leadership* 14, no. 2 (2004): 411–24.
45. Joe Kadhi, "Why, Asks Joe Kadhi: Post-Mortem of the Tragedy," *Nation*, March 9, 1972.
46. Interview, Nairobi, July 2, 2008.
47. Ibid.
48. C. Borgaza and J. Defourny, *The Emergence of Social Enterprise* (New York: Routledge, 2001); A. M. Peredo and J. J. McLean, "Social Entrepreneurship: A Critical Review of the Concept," *Journal of World Business* 41, no. 2 (2006): 56–65.
49. Shipton, *Credit between Cultures* and *Nature of Entrustment*; and Di Domenico, Haugh, and Tracey, "Social Bricolage," 697.
50. "Pirates: Can They Be Eliminated?" *East African Standard*, June 5, 1967, 2.
51. Ibid., 3.
52. Ibid.
53. "Pirate Laws," *Nation*, December 11, 1968.
54. Ibid.
55. *East African Standard*, January 12, 1968.
56. KNA: NCC Reports: May 5, 16, 1968.
57. *Nation*, February, 3, 1968.
58. "Pirates Ahoy!" *Drum*, March 1965, 5.
59. Jaraba, "Intra-Urban Mobility and Urban Transportation."
60. Interview, Nairobi, June 12, 2008.
61. Interview, Nairobi, July 1, 2009.
62. Interview, Nairobi, July 3, 2009.
63. Interview, Nairobi, July 1, 2010.

64. Interviews with Peter Karimu, Mary Otieno, Matt Oremo, and Priscilla Ngodi, Nairobi, November 2, 2004.
65. "UTC Profits See-Saw," *Commercial Motor*, August 6, 1971, 27.
66. Letter to the editor, "Baabla and Praan," *Nation*, April 15, 1966.
67. Ibid.
68. *Nation*, June 19, 1967.
69. Letter to the editor, "Complaint by Bus Users," *Nation*, August 13, 1967.
70. Letter to the editor, *East African Standard*, June 9, 1967.
71. Letter to the editor, *East African Standard*, June 12, 1967.
72. H. Patel, "Best Wishes to KBS," letter to the editor, *Nation*, October 30, 1964.
73. Ibid.
74. Ibid.
75. "Dragged off Bus, Pregnant Woman Claims," *Nation*, November 19, 1968.
76. Richard Sandbrook, "Patrons, Clients, and Unions: The Labour Movement and Political Conflict in Kenya," *Journal of Commonwealth Political Studies* 10, no. 1 (1972): 2–27; Roger Scott, "Are Trade Unions Still Necessary in Africa?" *Transition* 33, no. 2 (1967): 27–31.
77. "Bus Strike Strands Thousands," *Nation*, April 16, 1968, 3.
78. "Bus Strike Ends after Four Days" *Nation*, February 6, 1966.
79. "Bus Strike Ends as Union Boss Submits," *Nation*, February 8, 1966.
80. "Bus Strike Threat," *Nation*, June 1, 1966, 5.
81. "City Bus Strikers Urged: 'Go Back,'" *Nation*, June 9, 1964, 3. It was common for people to visit Kenyatta at his house in his hometown of Gatundu and ask for favors; see chapter 4 for more details.
82. "Busmen Strike after Insult," *Nation*, June 11, 1964.
83. *Nation*, May 12, 1969.
84. "Pirates Ahoy," *Drum*, May 1965.

CHAPTER THREE

1. See, for example, S. Sian, "Reversing Exclusion: The Africanisation of Accountancy in Kenya, 1963–1970," *Critical Perspectives on Accounting* 18, no. 7 (2007): 831–72; Donald Rothschild, "Kenya's Africanization Program: Priorities of Development and Equity," *American Political Science Review* 64, no. 3 (1970): 737–53; David Himbara, *Kenyan Capitalists, the State, and Development* (London: East African Education Publishers, 1994).
2. The National Assembly: House of Representatives Official Reports (Nairobi: Republic of Kenya, March 4, 1966; April 16, 1967; April 4, 1969).
3. Jennifer Widner, *The Rise of a Party-State in Kenya: From "Harambee" to "Nyayo!"* (Berkeley: University of California Press, 1992); Philip Mbithi and Rasmus Rasmusson, *Self-Reliance in Kenya: The Case of Harambee* (Uppsala: Scandinavian Institute of African Studies, 1977).
4. "Pirate Taxi," *East African Standard*, January 12, 1965.

5. E. S. Atieno Odhiambo, "Kula Raha: Gendered Discourses and the Contours of Leisure in Nairobi," in *The Urban Experience in East Africa, c. 1750–2000*, ed. Andrew Burton (Nairobi: British Institute in Eastern Africa, 2002), 254–64.

6. "Mayor of Nairobi Speaks about Pirate Taxis," KNA: NCC Records, January 14, 1968.

7. Ibid.

8. "Pirate Taxis Anger Union," *Nation*, July 13, 1968.

9. John Kamau, "Some of the Fallen Giants," *Nation*, August 26, 2013.

10. Ibid.

11. "Attack on Matatus," letter to the editor by Joseph Nderi, chairman of Matatu Vehicle Owners Association, *Nation*, December 26, 1969.

12. Ibid. For an interesting study of the strategies of corruption, see Johann Graf Lambsdorff, *The Institutional Economics of Corruption and Reform: Theory and Policy* (Cambridge: Cambridge University Press, 2007).

13. See *Nation* and the *East African Standard*. These were the main newspapers in Kenya in the 1960s.

14. "Pirates Ahoy! Drum's Plan to Solve the Matatu Problem," *Drum* (East African edition), August 1966, 5–6.

15. Ibid., 6.

16. "Stop Pirate Taxis," *Nation*, June 20, 1964, 5.

17. "Taxi Cab By-Laws," *East African Standard*, May 12, 1963.

18. For details on MVOA, see chapter 7.

19. "165 Pounds for Pirate Taxi Drivers," *Nation*, August 26, 1964, 3.

20. Interview, Nairobi, June 16, 2004.

21. For more details on Nderi, see chapters 5–7.

22. "Pirate Taxi Man Fined 800 Shillings," *Nation*, March 1, 1962.

23. *Nation*, November 8, 1963, 3.

24. "Pirate Taxi," *Nation*, March 6, 1965.

25. Philly Karashani, "It's War on the Pirate Fleet," *Nation*, January 21, 1969, 31.

26. See, for example, Rothchild, "Kenya's Africanization Program," 737–53; David Himbara, *Kenyan Capitalists, the State, and Development* (London: East African Education Publishers, 1994).

27. Paul Theroux, "Hating Asians," *Transition* 33 (October–November 1967): 46–51; Shiva Naipaul, *North of South: An African Journey* (London: Penguin, 1977); V. S . Naipaul, *A Bend in the River* (New York: Alfred A Knopf, 1979); Anneeth Kaur Hundle, "The Politics of (In)security: Reconstructing African-Asian Relations, Citizenship, and Community in Post-Expulsion Uganda" (PhD diss., Department of Anthropology, University of Michigan, 2013).

28. For an example of a similar eating metaphor, see Michela Wrong, *It's Our Turn to Eat* (London: Fourth Estate, 2010).

29. P. K Balachandran, "An Embattled Community: Asians in East Africa Today," *African Affairs* 80, no. 320 (1981): 317–25; Vincent Cable, "The Asians of Kenya," *African Affairs* 68, no. 272 (1969): 218–31; Michael Chege, "Introducing Race as a Variable into the Political Economy of Kenya Debate: An Incendiary Idea," *African Affairs* 97, no. 387 (1998): 209–30; Robert G. Gregory, "Cooperation and Collaboration in Colonial East Africa: The Asians Political Role, 1890–1964," *African Affairs* 80, no. 319 (1981): 259–73.

30. Gavin Kitching, *Class and Economic Change in Kenya: The Making of an African Petite Bourgeoisie* (New Haven, CT: Yale University Press, 1980); Nicola Swainson, "The Rise of a National Bourgeoisie in Kenya," *Review of African Political Economy* 4, no. 8 (1977): 39–55, and her *The Development of Corporate Capitalism in Kenya, 1918–77* (Berkeley: University of California Press, 1980).

31. Swainson, *Development of Corporate Capitalism in Kenya*.

32. J. R. Nellis, "Expatriates in the Government of Kenya," *Journal of Commonwealth Political Studies* 11, no. 3 (1977): 251–64; L. S. Wilson, "Technical Expertise and Indigenization," *Foreign Aid: New Perspectives*, Recent Economic Thought Series 68 (1999): 127–45; "Expatriates Needed for Some Time to Come, Says Kibaki," *Nation*, May 22, 1970, 4.

33. Balachandran, "Embattled Community," 317–25.

34. Ibid.

35. Sana Aiyar, "Anticolonial Homelands across the Indian Ocean: The Politics of the Indian Diaspora in Kenya c. 1930–1950," *American Historical Review* 116 (2011); "Empire, Race, and the Indians in Colonial Kenya's Contested Public Political Sphere from 1919–1923," *Africa* 81 (2011); White, *Comforts of Home*, 45–46.

36. Herbert Werlin, "Profile of Nairobi in the Time of Uhuru," *Africa Today* 10, no. 10 (1963): 7–10.

37. Theroux, "Hating Asians"; and Balachandran, "Embattled Community."

38. *Nation*, February 13, 1967.

39. *Nation*, October 21, 1967.

40. For a history of Idi Amin's expulsion of Asians from Uganda, see Mahmood Mamdani, *From Citizen to Refugee: Uganda Asians Come to Britain* (Johannesburg: Pambazuka Press, 2011); and Michael Twaddle, *Expulsion of a Minority: Essays on Uganda Asians* (New York: Continuum, 1975).

41. "Lubembe Criticises Lornho Investment," *Nation*, October 1, 1969. Also see National Assembly debates (Hansard, 1969).

42. *Nation*, January 25, 1967.

43. Letter to the editor, *Nation*, September 5, 1967.

44. Theroux, "Hating Asians"; and Balachandran, "Embattled Community."

45. Aiyar, "Anticolonial Homelands across the Indian Ocean," and "Empire, Race, and the Indians in Colonial Kenya's Contested Public Political Sphere from 1919–1923; Keith Kyle, "Gandhi, Harry Thuku, and Early Ken-

yan Nationalism," *Transition* 27 (1966): 16–22; Bodil Frederiksen, "Print, Newspapers, and Audiences in Colonial Kenya: African and Indian Improvement, Protest and Connections," *Africa* 81, no. 1 (2011): 34–52; and Gregory, "Cooperation and Collaboration in Colonial East Africa," 259–73.

46. *East African Standard*, January 12, 1968.

47. "Pirate Taxi Men," *Nation*, July 30, 1964, 5.

48. Vincent Cable, "The Asians of Kenya," *African Affairs* 68, no. 272 (1969): 218–31; Frank Furedi, "The Development of Anti-Asian Opinion among Africans in Nakuru District, Kenya," *African Affairs* 73, no. 2929 (1974): 347–58; and Theroux, "Hating the Asians."

49. "200 Defendants 'Rebel' Outside Kiambu Court, *Nation*, January 9, 1964.

50. "Pirate Men Protest," *Nation*, February 9, 1968, 9.

51. Rothchild, "Kenya's Africanization Program"; Aristide Zolberg, "The Structure of Political Conflict in the New States of Tropical Africa," *American Political Science Review* 2, no. 3 (1968): 64–83.

52. "Pirate Men Protest," 9.

53. Interview, Nairobi, June 15, 2004.

54. *Siasa* means *politics* in Swahili, and in Kenyan Swahili colloquialism, it is often used when one says something they do not mean just to incite a quarrel. For an interesting use of this term, see E. S. Atieno Adhiambo, *Siasa: Politics and Nationalism in East Africa, 1905–1939* (Nairobi: Kenya Literature Bureau, 1981).

55. Interview, Nairobi, June 15, 2004.

56. Theroux, "Hating Asians."

57. Editorials, *East African Standard*, July 12, 1967; *Nation*, December 3, 1966; James Rukia, letter to the editor, *Nation*, February 7, 1967.

58. "Pirates Ahoy!" 6.

59. Ibid.

60. Ibid.

61. *East African Standard*, January 16, 1969.

62. Ibid., September 19, 1967.

63. Kenda Mutongi, "Thugs or Entrepreneurs? Perceptions of Matatu Operators in Nairobi, 1970 to the Present," *Africa* 76, no. 4 (2006): 549–68.

64. Akin L. Mabogunje, "Urban Planning and the Post-Colonial State: A Research Overview," *African Studies Review* 33, no. 2 (1990): 121–203.

65. Interview, Nairobi, July 1, 2008.

66. Ibid.

67. Interview, Nairobi, June 18, 2004. For interesting analyses and critiques of similar kinds of reinvestments in Africa, see Jane Guyer, *Marginal Gains: Monetary Transactions in Atlantic Africa* (Chicago: University of Chicago Press, 204); David Neves and Andries du Toit, "Money and Sociality in South Africa's Informal Economy," *Africa* 82, no. 1 (2012): 131–49; Elizabeth Hull and Deborah James, "Introduction: Popular Economies in South Africa," *Africa* 82, no. 1 (2012): 1–19; and Sara S. Berry, *Fathers Work*

for Their Sons: Accumulation, Mobility, and Class Formation in an Extended Yoruba Community (Berkeley: University of California Press, 1985).

68. Interview, Nairobi, June 18, 2004.

69. James Smart, *Nairobi: A Jubilee History, 1900–1950* (Nairobi: East African Standard, 1950), 86.

70. For a cogent example of a similar process elsewhere in Africa, see Laura Fair, *Pastimes and Politics: Culture, Community, and Identity in Post-Abolition Zanzibar* (Athens: Ohio University Press, 2001).

71. Atieno Odhiambo, "Kula Raha: Gendered Discourses and the Contours of Leisure in Nairobi," in Burton, *Urban Experience in East Africa*, 255.

72. Ibid., 226.

73. Ibid., 256.

74. For examples of leisure and community formation in colonial Africa, see Fair, *Pastimes and Politics*; Emmanuel Akyeampong, *Drink, Power, and Colonial Change: Social History of Alcohol in Ghana* (Portsmouth, NH: Heinemann, 1996); Phyllis Martin, *Leisure and Society in Colonial Brazzaville* (Cambridge: Cambridge University Press, 1995); and Terence Ranger, *Dance and Society in East Africa, 1890–1970* (Berkeley: University of California Press, 1975).

75. Interview, Nairobi, June 17, 2008. For details on women's movements in Kenya, see Audrey Wipper, "The Maendeleo ya Wanawake Movement: Some Paradoxes and Contradictions," *African Studies Review* 18, no. 3 (1975): 99–120.

76. Bodil Folke Frederiksen, "African Women and Their Colonisation of Nairobi: Representations and Realities," *Azania: Archaeological Research in Africa* 36-37, no. 1 (2001): 229.

77. White, *Comforts of Home*, 200–210.

78. As quoted in Frederiksen, "African Women and Their Colonization of Nairobi," 229.

79. Steven J. Salm, "Popular Music, Identity, and the Lumpen Youth of Nairobi," in *Urbanization and African Cultures*, ed. Toyin Falola and Steven Salm (Durham, NC: Carolina Academic Press, 2005).

80. Atieno-Odhiambo, "Kula Raha," 254–64.

81. For details on *Drum* magazine, see Kenda Mutongi, "Dear Dolly's Advice: Representations of Youth, Courtship, and Sexualities in Africa, 1960–1980," *International Journal of African Historical Studies* 1, no. 2 (2000): 230–52. Reprinted in Jennifer Cole and Lynn Thomas, *Love in Africa* (Chicago: University of Chicago Press, 2009).

82. Mutongi, "Thugs or Entrepreneurs?"

CHAPTER FOUR

1. For interesting studies of the culture of politics in Kenya, see Angelique Haugerud, *The Culture of Politics in Modern Kenya* (Cambridge: Cam-

bridge University Press, 1997); Daniel Branch, *Kenya: Between Hope and Despair, 1963–2011* (New Haven, CT: Yale University Press, 2011); and M. Tamarkin, "The Roots of Political Stability in Kenya," *African Affairs* 77 (1978): 297–320.

2. Interviews with Paul Mwangi, Jane Njeri, and Eric Kamau, Nairobi, June 12, 2008.

3. "MVOA Officials Visit to Gatundu" *The Standard*, January 12, 1971.

4. Interview, Nairobi, June 15, 2004.

5. "Mzee Frees Matatus," *The Standard*, June 2, 1973. This day is called Madaraka Day, the day that Kenya attained self-rule from the British in 1963; Kenya officially attained full independence on December 12, 1963, on Jamhuri Day. Both days are commemorated accordingly.

6. Interview, Nairobi, June 15, 2004.

7. "Mzee Frees Matatus," *The Standard*, June 2, 1973, 1; "Full Protection for Minorities in Kenya—Mzee," *Nation*, June 2, 1973.

8. "Full Protection for Minorities in Kenya—Mzee," *Nation*, June 2, 1973.

9. William R. Ochieng', "The Kenyatta Era: Structural and Political Changes," and Robert Maxon, "Social and Cultural Changes," in *Decolonization and Independence in Kenya* , ed. B. A. Ogot and Williams Ochieng' (Athens: Ohio University Press, 1995), 78–110; John Lonsdale, "Jomo Kenyatta, God, and the Modern World," in *African Modernities: Entangled Meanings in Current Debate*, ed. J.-G. Deutsch, P. Probst, and H. Schmidt (Oxford: James Currey, 2002), 67–89; Tamarkin, "Roots of Political Stability in Kenya," 299–310.

10. Branch, *Kenya*; and Charles Hornsby, *Kenya: A History since Independence* (New York: I. B. Tauris, 2012).

11. KBS and other public transportation buses and lorries were excluded. "Mixed Response for President's Decree on TLB Licenses," *The Standard*, June 2, 1973.

12. Ibid.

13. Ibid.

14. Ibid.

15. Peter Anyang' Nyong'o, ed., *30 Years of Independence in Africa: The Lost Decades?* (Nairobi: Heinemann, 2002); Njenga Karume, *Beyond Expectations: From Charcoal to Gold* (Nairobi: East African Educational Publishers, 2009).

16. "Kenya Road Deaths up by Nearly a Third Last Year," *The Standard*, February 6, 1971.

17. "Editorial: The Pirates," *Nation*, December 5, 1970.

18. Kenya National Assembly Official Record (Hansard), June 13, 1966.

19. Ibid., December 6, 1970.

20. Ibid.; "Editorial: The Pirates," *Nation*, December 5, 1970.

21. Kenya National Assembly Official Record (Hansard), December 6, 1970.

22. Ibid.

23. Ibid.

24. "Avoiding the Crush Hours," *Nation*, April 2, 1971.

25. Kenya National Assembly Official Record (Hansard), March 9, 1971.
26. Kenya National Assembly Official Record (Hansard), March 9, 1971. Phoebe Musandu, "Drawing from the Wells of Culture: Grace Onyango and the Kenyan Political Scene (1964–1983)," *Wagadu: A Journal of Transnational Women's and Gender Studies* 6 (2008): 23–38.
27. Kenya National Assembly Official Record (Hansard), March 9, 1971.
28. Ibid.
29. Ibid.
30. Ibid.; "Life to be Made Tough for Matatus," *Nation*, May 7, 1971.
31. "Veteran Politician Dies," *Nation*, August 12, 2012.
32. Kenya National Assembly Official Record (Hansard), March 9, 1971.
33. Ibid.
34. Ibid.
35. Ibid.
36. Ibid.
37. Ibid.
38. "I Have to Walk," letter to the editor by Aggrieved Mwanainchi (citizen), *Nation*, May 22, 1973, 7.
39. "The Road Pirates," *Nation*, December 5, 1970.
40. Ibid.
41. "Call for Another Nairobi Bus firm," *Nation*, March 21, 1971.
42. "Matatu Group Wants Legal Bus Services," *Nation*, December 17, 1970.
43. "Letter to Editor: Run KBS to Help Commuters," *Nation*, June 3, 1971.
44. "Matatu Owners Refused Licence," *Nation*, January 6, 1971, 28.
45. "Boycott Will Hit Citizens," *Nation*, May 23, 1971.
46. "Editorial: The Transport Crisis," *Nation*, February 16, 1971.
47. "Call for Another Nairobi Bus Firm," *Nation*, March 21, 1971.
48. "Shares Urged for Workers in Transport Firms," *The Standard*, December 22, 1970.
49. Ibid.
50. Ibid.
51. Ibid.
52. Tamarkin, "Roots of Political Stability in Kenya."
53. "Taxi Fares Go Up in Price," *Nation*, March 18, 1973.
54. John K Mohochi, "Journey Is Cut Short," letter to the editor, *The Standard*, January 14, 1973.
55. Robert Bates, *Beyond the Miracle of the Market: The Political Economy of Agrarian Development in Kenya* (Cambridge: Cambridge University Press, 2005); Kenneth King, *Jua Kali Kenya: Change and Development in an Informal Economy, 1970–95* (Athens: Ohio University Press, 1996).
56. See, for example, Katherine Boo, *Behind the Beautiful Forevers: Life, Death, and Hope in a Mumbai Undercity* (New York: Random House, 2012).
57. Andrew Hake, *African Metropolis: Nairobi's Self-Help City* (New York: St Martin's Press, 1977).
58. Ibid., 78–92.

59. Kinuthia Macharia, "Slum Clearance and the Informal Economy in Nairobi," *Journal of Modern African Studies* 30 (1992): 221–36.

60. "Poverty in the City Can Be Ended by Return to Land," *East African Standard*, January 10, 1965.

61. Lars Johansson, *In the Shadow of Neocolonialism: A Study of Meja Mwangi's Novels, 1973–1990* (Umeå, Sweden: University of Umeå, 1992).

62. http://lifesspice.blogspot.com/2010/07/considering-meja-mwangis -cockroach.html, accessed May 6, 2014. Ayo Kehinde, "Post-Independence Disillusionment in Contemporary African Fiction: The Example of Meja Mwangi's *Kill Me Quick*," *Nordic Journal of African Studies* 13 (2004): 228–41; Angus Calder, "Meja Mwangi's Novels," in *The Writing of East and Central Africa*, ed. G. D. Killam (London: Heinemann, 1984), 23–44; Johansson, *In the Shadow of Neocolonialism*.

63. Nici Nelson, "Representations of Men and Women, City and Town in Kenyan Novels of the 1970s and 1980s," *African Languages and Cultures* 9, no. 2 (1996): 148–68; and Neil Lazarus, "Great Expectations and After: The Politics of Postcolonialism in African Fiction," *Social Text* 2, no. 4 (2004): 49–63.

64. Richard Sandbrook, *The Politics of Africa's Economic Stagnation* (Cambridge: Cambridge University Press, 1986); Sandbrook, *The Politics of Basic Needs: Urban Aspects of Assaulting Poverty in Africa* (Toronto: University of Toronto Press, 1982).

65. William R. Ochieng', "The Kenyatta Era: Structural and Political Changes," and Robert Maxon, "Social and Cultural Changes," in *Decolonization and Independence in Kenya*, ed. B. A. Ogot and Williams Ochieng' (Athens: Ohio University Press, 1995).

66. Tamarkin, "Roots of Political Stability in Kenya," 297–302.

67. Jennifer Widner, *The Rise of a Party-State in Kenya: From "Harambee" to "Nyayo!"* (Berkeley: University of California Press, 1992); E. M. Godfrey and G. Mutiso, "The Political Economy of Self-Help: Kenya's *Harambee* Institutes of Technology," *Canadian Journal of African Studies* 8, no. 1 (1974): 109–33.

68. E. S. Atieno Odhiambo, "Democracy and the Ideology of Order in Kenya," in *The Political Economy of Kenya*, ed. Michael G. Schatzberg (New York: Praeger, 1987), 177–202.

69. Lonsdale, "Jomo Kenyatta, God, and the Modern World."

70. Robert Bates, *When Things Fell Apart: State Failure in Late-Century Africa* (Cambridge: Cambridge University Press, 2008); Colin Leys, *Underdevelopment in Kenya: The Political Economy of Neo-Colonialism, 1964–1971* (Nairobi: Longman, 1975); Branch, *Kenya*.

71. "Commentary: A Year of Challenge," *The Standard*, January 1, 1970.

72. Ibid.

73. Ibid.

CHAPTER FIVE

1. "Matatus on the Rise," *The Standard*, December 4, 1973.
2. Ngũgĩ wa Thiong'o, *Devil on the Cross* (London: Heinemann, 1987), 31–32.
3. Ibid., 32–33.
4. "Are Matatus Here to Stay," *Nation*, May 12, 1974.
5. "Rich Men in Matatus," *The Standard*, January 4, 1974.
6. "Council Goes to War with Pirate Taximen," *Nation*, January 30, 1974.
7. "Our Gold Medalist Returns," *The Standard*, January 5, 1975.
8. Interview, Nairobi, July 3, 2009.
9. Interview, Nairobi, July 1, 2009.
10. "Bus Passengers Should Be Careful," *Nation*, January 2, 1974.
11. "Matatu Madness Must Be Stopped," *Nation*, July 9, 1974.
12. "Kenya: We Must All Stand Firm to Defeat This Lunacy," *Nation*, July 12, 1979.
13. "Matatu Madness Must Be Stopped," *Nation*, July 9, 1974, 9.
14. For an interesting study of some of the unintended consequences of anarchic behavior, see James Scott, *Two Cheers for Anarchism: Six Easy Pieces on Autonomy, Dignity, and Meaningful Work and Play* (Princeton, NJ: Princeton University Press, 2014).
15. Fred Ndungu, "There Is Always Room for One More Passenger," *Nation*, July 31, 1977. This behavior was often discussed in "Masharubu's World," and "Whispers," popular humor columns in the *Sunday Nation*.
16. Kwamboka Oyaro, "Women, Booze, and Miraa: That Is Life on the Road," *Nation*, April 27, 2001; "Masharubu's World: A Close Encounter with the Agents of Death," *Nation*, March 6, 1988. For a detailed study of road accidents in Kenya, see George Samuel Agoki, "Characteristics of Road Traffic Accidents in Kenya" (PhD diss., University of Nairobi, 1988). For historical studies of khat, see Ezekiel Gebissa, ed., *Taking the Place of Food: Khat in Ethiopia* (Trenton, NJ: Red Sea Press, 2010); and Gebissa, *The Leaf of Allah: Khat and Agricultural Transformation in Harerge, Ethiopia, 1875–1991* (Columbus: Ohio University Press, 2004).
17. Interviews with Joseph Nderi, Peter Chege, and John Maina, Nairobi, June 12, 2004.
18. For details on the relationship between Shiva and V. S., see Helen Hayward, *The Enigma of V. S. Naipaul: Sources and Contexts* (New York: Palgrave Macmillan, 2002).
19. Shiva Naipaul, *North of South: An African Journey* (London: Vintage, 1979), 126–28.
20. Interviews with Marita Kefa, James Olei, Karen Mutse, and Patrick Mwangi, Kisumu, June 17, 2009.
21. "What Is Matatu Bill?" *Nation*, September 13, 1984.
22. Interview, Nairobi, June 6, 2008.
23. Interview, Nairobi, June 7, 2008.

24. Interviews with Marita Kefa, James Olei, Karen Mutse, and Patrick Mwangi, Kisumu, June 17, 2009.
25. "They Just Stopped into the Office," *Nation*, December 12, 1976.
26. Editorial, "Cutting Down on Road Accidents," *Nation*, October 22, 1975.
27. John Gachanji, "The Harassed Matatu Travellers," letter to the editor, *Nation*, June 6, 1974.
28. Ibid.
29. Interview with John Njenga, Nairobi, June 18, 2008.
30. G. M. Kamanja, "Passengers Are to Blame," *Nation*, September 30, 1974.
31. Interview, Nairobi, June 13, 2009.
32. Interview with Liz Muite, Nairobi, June 7, 2009.
33. Interview with Janet Keya, Nairobi, June 12, 2009.
34. Interview with Peter Siringi, Nairobi July 5, 2009.
35. For some examples of this behavior, see Mbũgua wa Mũngai and David A. Samper, " 'No Mercy, No Remorse': Personal Experience Narratives about Public Passenger Transportation in Nairobi," *Africa Today* 12 (2006): 52–81.
36. Interview with Mary Muite, Nairobi, June 12, 2009.
37. Interview with Truphena Onzere, Nairobi, June 7, 2009.
38. Karen D. Lysaght, "Catholics, Protestants, and Office Workers from the Town: The Experience and Negotiation of Fear in Northern Ireland," In *Mixed Emotions: Anthropological Studies of Feeling*, ed. Kay Milton and Maruska Svasek (Oxford: Berg, 2006), 127–44.
39. Interview with Jane Njenga, Stefano Muliro, and Ephraim Ndeda, Nairobi, June 12, 2009.
40. Much like one has to learn how to ride the subway in order to live more effectively in New York or Paris. See Marc Ange, *In the Metro*, trans. Tom Conley (Minneapolis: University of Minnesota Press, 2002); Michael Brooks, *Subway City: Riding the Trains, Reading New York* (New Brunswick, NJ: Rutgers University Press, 1997). Barbara H. Rosenwein, *Emotional Communities in Early Middle Ages* (Ithaca, NY: Cornell University Press, 2007) is an interesting study of a similar process in the early Middle Ages.
41. "Matatus Out of Control," *The Standard*, June 13, 1976.
42. Interview, Nairobi, June 9, 2004.
43. "Two Years for Matatu Driver Who Caused Death," *Nation*, February 12, 1975.
44. "Big Insurance Shock," *Nation*, December 3, 1974.
45. Interview, Kiambu, June 4, 2010.
46. "Crackdown on Defective Vehicles Launched," *Nation*, January 25, 1979.
47. "Matatu Reprieve: They Must Be in Good Shape," *Weekly Review*, February 1, 1979.
48. Ibid.
49. "End of Road for Matatus," *Nation*, February 9, 1979.
50. "The Bus Crash," *The Standard*, February 9, 1979.

51. Ibid.
52. George Godia, *Understanding Nyayo: Principles and Policies in Contemporary Kenya* (Nairobi: Transafrica, 1984); Angelique Haugerud, *The Culture of Politics in Modern Kenya* (Cambridge: Cambridge University Press, 1997).
53. "The Bus Crash," *The Standard*, February 9, 1979.
54. Ibid.
55. "Easing Traffic; Reviewing Different Options," *Weekly Review*, May 4, 1979.
56. J. C. Clymo, "KBS," letter to the editor, *Weekly Review*, November 21, 1979.
57. Ibid.
58. "KBS vs Matatu," *Nation*, November 26, 1979.
59. "Ways to Improve the KBS," letter to the editor, *Nation*, August 21, 1980.
60. "Easing Traffic; Reviewing Different Options," *Weekly Review*, May 4, 1979.
61. Ibid.
62. "Board Listens to Matatu Case," *The Standard*, August 12, 1980.
63. "Matatu Give Up Bus Fare Protest," *The Standard*, April 12, 1980.
64. "Dangerous Matatu Drivers Warned," *Nation*, October 14, 1980.
65. "Matatu Service Stoppage Threatened," *Nation*, October 13, 1980.
66. "End Road Carnage or Else: Moi Warns Matatu Men," *Nation*, August 6, 1980.
67. "Matatu Owners Unite against 'Harassment,'" *Nation*, November 18, 1980.
68. "Matatus Must Be Roadworthy," *Nation*, November 12, 1980.
69. "Reckless Matatu Men Are Warned," *The Standard*, October 20, 1980.
70. "End of the Road for PSV Groups," *Weekly Review*, December 9, 1982.
71. *Matatu: The Official Journal of MVOA*, Nairobi, June 1983.
72. Ibid.
73. "Matatus: A Threat to Bus Firms," *Nation*, July 31, 1983.
74. "On Broken Down Buses, Matatus, and Traffic Lights That Don't Work," *The Standard*, November 28, 1982.
75. "Matatu Fares Are Too High," *The Standard*, May 2, 1983.
76. "More Buses Set for City Routes," *Nation*, May 12, 1983.
77. "Mzee Frees Matatus," *The Standard*, June 2, 1973.
78. "On the Road to a Transport Boom," editorial, *Nation*, June 5, 1973.
79. Ibid.
80. For Kenyatta's iconic reputation, see Daniel Branch, *Kenya: Between Hope and Despair, 1963–2011* (New Haven, CT: Yale University Press, 2011); John Lonsdale, "Jomo Kenyatta, God, and the Modern World," in *African Modernities: Entangled Meanings in Current Debate*, ed. J.-G. Deutsch, P. Probst, and H. Schmidt (Oxford: James Currey, 2002), 45–67; and Tamarkin, "The Roots of Political Stability in Kenya."

CHAPTER SIX

1. For a detailed list of human rights abuses by Moi's regime, see Africa Watch, *Taking Liberties* (Washington, DC: Africa Watch, 1991); Makau wa

Mutua, "Human Rights and State Despotism in Kenya: Institutional Problems," *Africa Today* 41 (1994): 50–56; and S. Hempstone, *Rogue Ambassador: An African Memoir* (Sewanee, TN: University of the South Press, 1997).

2. "Matatu Bill Becomes Law," *Weekly Review*, September 1, 1984.

3. "Price of Bribery," *Weekly Review*, August 17, 1984.

4. For details on Moi's regime, see Makau Mutua, *Kenya's Quest for Democracy: Taming Leviathan* (Boulder, CO: Lynn Reinner, 2008); Daniel Branch, *Kenya: Between Hope and Despair, 1963–2011* (New Haven, CT: Yale University Press, 2011); Angelique Haugerud, *The Culture of Politics in Modern Kenya* (Cambridge: University of Cambridge Press, 1997); Godwin Murunga, "Urban Violence in Kenya's Transition to Pluralist Politics, 1982–1992," *Africa Development* 26 (1999): 165–97; George Godia, *Understanding Nyayo: Principles and Policies in Contemporary Kenya* (Nairobi: TransAfrica, 1984); David Throup and Charles Hornsby, *Multi-Party Politics in Kenya: The Kenyatta and Moi States and the Triumph of the System in the 1992 Election* (Oxford: James Currey, 1998); and Frank W. Holmquist, Frederick S. Weaver, and Michael D. Ford, "The Structural Development of Kenya's Political Economy," *African Studies Review* 37 (1994): 76–110.

5. Korwa Adar and Isaac Munyae, "Human Rights Abuse in Kenya under Daniel Arap Moi, 1978–2001," *African Studies Quarterly* 5 (2001): 1–14.

6. See, for example, Jennifer Widner, *The Rise of a Party-State in Kenya: From "Harambee!" to "Nyayo!"* (Berkeley: University of California Press, 1993).

7. Haugerud, *Culture of Politics in Modern Kenya*, 60–83; and Adar and Munyae, "Human Rights Abuse in Kenya under Daniel Arap Moi," 3–4.

8. Interview, Nairobi, June 20, 2005.

9. E. S. Atieno Odhiambo, "Democracy and the Ideology of Order in Kenya," in *The Political Economy of Kenya*, ed. Michael G. Schatzberg (New York: Praeger, 1987), 177–202.

10. "What Is the Matatu Bill," *Weekly Review*, August 20, 1984.

11. "Matatu Bill," *Weekly Review*, November 9, 1984.

12. "Workers Stranded as Matatu Control Begins," *Weekly Review*, November 9, 1984; "The Matatu Bill Enforced," *Nation*, November 3, 1984.

13. "Determination: Government Presses on with Matatu Regulations," *Weekly Review*, September 14, 1984.

14. "Determination: Government Presses on with Matatu Regulations," *Weekly Review*, September 14, 1984.

15. Ibid.

16. Haugerud, *Culture of Politics in Modern Kenya*.

17. "Matatu People Are Getting on My Nerves, Says Moi," *Nation*, September 14, 1984.

18. "Matatu Owners Body Should Tell Us More," *Nation*, September 15, 1984.

19. Interviews with James Muteve and Mark Maina, Nairobi, June 4, 2010; and Mary Njonjo and Ann Kasila, Nairobi, June 7, 2010.

20. Interview, Kakamega, June 2, 2004.

21. Ibid.

22. "Matatu Owners Body Should Tell Us More," *Nation*, September 15, 1984.

23. Interview with Joseph Nderi, Nairobi, June 12, 2004.

24. "Workers Stranded as Matatu Control Begins," *Weekly Review*, November 9, 1984; for an interesting example of government attempts to regulate public transportation in Tanzania, see Matteo M. Rizzo, "Being Taken for a Ride: Privatization of Dar es Salaam Transport System, 1983–1998," *Journal of Modern African Studies* 40 (2002): 133–57.

25. "Rush on PSV Licenses," *Nation*, November 13, 1984.

26. Interview, Nairobi, June 12, 2007.

27. Interview, Nairobi, June 12, 2007.

28. Interview with James Siringi, Nakuru, June 19, 2008.

29. "Commentary," *Nation*, October 13, 1984.

30. "Matatu Association Boss Sends SOS," *Nation*, February 27, 1985.

31. "How Rational Is the Vehicle Insurance Hike?" *The Standard*, September 1, 1985; Koma Zosi, "Important Role for Insurance Industry," *Drum*, June 1985, 33.

32. "Matatu Association Boss Sends SOS," *Nation*, February 27, 1985.

33. "A Look at KBS Drivers Also Needed," *Nation*, October 12, 1984.

34. Daniel T. Arap Moi, *Kenya African Nationalism: Nyayo Philosophy and Principles* (London: Macmillan, 1986).

35. Stephen Katz, "The Succession to Power and the Power of Succession: Nyayoism in Kenya," *Journal of African Studies* 12 (1985): 155–61.

36. Judith Abwunza, "*Nyayo*: Cultural Contradictions in Kenya Rural Capitalism," *Anthropologica* 32 (1990): 183–203.

37. The slogan was intended to discourage any form of opposition to Moi's rule. For details, see Godia, *Understanding Nyayo*, 90–96; and Throup and Hornsby, *Multi-Party Politics in Kenya*, 56–59.

38. Godia, *Understanding Nyayo*, 123–34; and Throup and Hornsby, *Multi-Party Politics in Kenya*, 110–24.

39. Interview, Nairobi, June 16, 2004.

40. *Matatu Journal*, 1985, 13–14.

41. Ibid.

42. "Manambas and the Traffic Act," *Nation*, February 10, 1985.

43. "Matatu Terms to Improve," *Nation*, May 15, 1985.

44. For a similar argument, see Frederick Cooper, *On the African Waterfront: Urban Disorder and Transformation of Work in Colonial Mombasa* (New Haven, CT: Yale University Press, 1987); *Decolonization and African Society: The Labor Question in French and British Africa* (Cambridge: Cambridge University Press, 1996).

45. Muiru Mugo, *Matatu: The Official Journal of MVOA* 11, no. 3 (March 1985): 1.

46. Gary Libecap, *Contracting for Property Rights* (Cambridge: Cambridge University Press, 1994); Douglass North, *Institutions, Institutional Change, and Economic Performance* (Cambridge: Cambridge University Press, 1990); Jean

Ensminger, *Making a Market: The Institutional Transformation of an African Society* (Cambridge: Cambridge University Press, 2002).

47. "Thousands Held Up in Vehicle Swoop," *The Standard*, May 15, 1985.
48. "Matatus Are a Disgrace," *Nation*, January 7, 1986.
49. "Thousands Held Up in Vehicle Swoop," *The Standard*, May 16, 1985.
50. Ibid.
51. "Matatus Are a Disgrace," *Nation*, May 16, 1985.
52. "Matatu Operators Claim Harassment," *Nation*, May 17, 1985.
53. "Matatus: Police Acts Anger Moi," *The Standard*, May 17, 1985.
54. Ibid.
55. Anuradha Joshi and Joseph Ayee, "Associational Taxation: A Pathway to Informal Sectors?" in *Taxation and State-Building in Developing Countries*, ed. Deborah Bräutigam, Odd-Helge Fjeldstad, and Mick Moore (Cambridge: Cambridge University Press, 2008); Fredrik Soderbaum, "Blocking Human Potential: How Formal Policies Block the Informal Economy in the Maputo Corridor," in *Linking the Formal and Informal Economy*, ed. Basudeb Guha-Khasnobis, Ravi Kanbur, and Elinor Ostrom, UNU-Wider Studies in Development Economics (Oxford: Oxford Universit Press, 2006).
56. "City Matatu Men Protest at Police," *Nation*, April 15, 1986.
57. Ibid.
58. "City Matatu Men Halt Services," *The Standard*, April 15, 1986.
59. "City Matatu Men Halt Services," *The Standard*, April 15, 1986. When I spoke with Nderi in June 2004, he unfortunately did not remember the details of this particular meeting.
60. "City Matatu Men Protest at Police," *Nation*, April 15, 1986.
61. Daron Acemoglu and James A. Robinson, *Economic Origins of Dictatorship and Democracy* (Cambridge: Cambridge University Press, 2009); and Steven Levitsky and Lucan A. Way, *Competitive Authoritarianism: Hybrid Regimes after the Cold War* (Cambridge: Cambridge University Press, 2010).
62. Interview with Joseph Nderi, Nairobi, June 12, 2004.
63. "Fare Hike Hits Matatu Business," *Nation*, January 28, 1985.
64. Lewis Njore, "The Road to Dusty Death," letter to the editor, *Nation*, March 21, 1985.
65. John Kawore, letter to the editor, *The Standard*, April 12, 1985.
66. Letter to the editor, *Nation*, February 11, 1985.
67. Letter to the editor, *Nation*, March 1, 1985.
68. Interviews with John Magethe and Michael Ogeni, Matatu drivers in the 1980s, Nairobi, June 30, 2004.
69. "Is Improving Matatus an Impossible Dream," *Nation*, February 13, 1985.
70. Ibid.
71. Ibid.
72. Kenda Mutongi, "Thugs or Entrepreneurs? Perceptions of Matatu Operators in Nairobi, 1970 to the Present," *Africa* 74 (2006): 549–68.

73. Philip Ochieng, "Let's Shame the Devil, Mr. Michuki," *Nation*, February 8, 2004.

74. Ibid.

75. "Is Improving Matatus an Impossible Dream," *Nation*, February 13, 1985.

76. Ibid.

77. Ibid.

78. Ibid.

79. See, for example, essays in Jean Comaroff and John Comaroff, eds., *Law and Disorder in the Postcolony* (Chicago: University of Chicago Press, 2006); Jeffrey Herbst, *States and Power in Africa: Comparative Lessons in Authority and Control* (Princeton, NJ: University of Princeton Press, 2000); Crawford Young, *The Postcolonial State in Africa: Fifty Years of Independence, 1960–2010* (Madison: University of Wisconsin Press, 2012); Robert Bates, *When Things Fell Apart: State Failure in Late-Century Africa* (Cambridge: Cambridge University Press, 2008); and James C. Scott, *Seeing Like a State: How Certain Schemes to Improve the Human Condition Have Failed* (New Haven, CT: Yale University Press, 1998).

80. Achille Mbembe, *On the Postcolony* (Berkeley: University of California Press, 2001); and Comaroff and Comaroff, *Law and Disorder in the Postcolony*, 1–23.

CHAPTER SEVEN

1. E. K. Esmailjee, "Internal Controls: The Case of Nyayo Bus Service Corporation" (Master's thesis, University of Nairobi, 1993); Tom Opiyo, "The Metamorphosis of Kenya Bus Services Limited in the Provision of Urban Transportation in Nairobi," paper presented at the Department of Civil Engineering, University of Nairobi, 2001; Kindu Waweru, "The Rise and Fall of Nyayo's Buses Service as Graft Eroded All the Gains," *The Standard*, September 11, 2013; and http://www.kenyabus.net/history.php, accessed January 9, 2012.

2. Waweru, "Rise and Fall of Nyayo's Buses Service as Graft Eroded All the Gains."

3. Korwa Adara and Isaac Munyae, "Human Rights Abuse in Kenya under Daniel Arap Moi," *African Studies Quarterly* 5 (2001): 23–40.

4. Interview with John Muchira, Nairobi, July 1, 2008.

5. Esmailjee, "Internal Controls."

6. Waweru, "Rise and Fall of Nyayo's Buses Service as Graft Eroded All the Gains." For examples of political spectacle in other parts of Africa, see Achille Mbembe, *On the Postcolony* (Berkeley: University of California Press, 2001).

7. As witnessed by the author. See also Angelique Haugerud, *The Culture of Politics in Modern Kenya* (Cambridge: University of Cambridge Press, 1997).

8. Moi Day was abolished in 2010 due to constitutional reasons.

9. Ngugi wa Mbugua, "A Drive towards Commuters Comfort," *Nation*, October 10, 1987.

10. Ibid.

11. For a detailed list of human rights abuses by Moi's regime, see Africa Watch, *Taking Liberties* (Washington, DC: Africa Watch, 1991); Makau wa Mutua, "Human Rights and State Despotism in Kenya: Institutional Problems," *Africa Today* 41 (1994): 50–56; and S. Hempstone, *Rogue Ambassador: An African Memoir* (Sewanee, TN: University of the South Press, 1997).

12. Charles Hornsby, *Kenya: A History since Independence* (New York: I. B Taurus, 2013), 400.

13. Inteview, Nakuru, June 18, 2012.

14. Interview, Mombasa, July 3, 2009.

15. Esmailjee, "Internal Controls"; and Opiyo, "Metamorphosis of Kenya Bus Services Limited in the Provision of Urban Transportation in Nairobi."

16. Paul Ocobock, "'Joy Rides for Juveniles': Vagrant Youth and Colonial Control in Nairobi, Kenya, 1901–52," *Social History* 31, no. 1 (February 2006): 39–59.

17. Paul Ocobock, "Serving *Mzee*: Mobilizing Youths and Enduring Legacies in Kenyatta's Kenya, 1955–78," African Studies Association Conference, San Francisco, 2010; Richard Coe, "The Kenya National Youth Service: A Government Response to Youth Political Activists," Ohio University Center for International Studies, Papers in the International Studies, Africa Series, No. 20, 1973.

18. Ocobock, "Serving *Mzee*"; Coe, "Kenya National Youth Service," 23; Timothy Parsons, *Race, Resistance, and the Boy Scout Movement in British Colonial Africa* (Athens: Ohio University Press, 2004).

19. Ocobock, "Serving *Mzee*," 45.

20. Wanyama Muricho and John Changach, "Education Reforms in Kenya for Innovation," *International Journal of Humanities and Social Science* 3, no. 9 (2013): 134–52.

21. Ocobock, "Serving *Mzee*," 42; George Ogola, "The Idiom of Age in a Popular Kenyan Serial," *Africa* 76 (2006): 569–89.

22. Esmailjee, "Internal Controls"; and Opiyo, "Metamorphosis of Kenya Bus Services Limited in the Provision of Urban Transportation in Nairobi."

23. "Is the Public Transport Going the Right Way," *Nation*, October 26, 1986.

24. Ibid.; Waweru, "Rise and Fall of Nyayo's Buses Service as Graft Eroded All the Gains."

25. Waweru, "The Rise and Fall of Nyayo's Buses Service as Graft Eroded All the Gains."

26. Jennifer Widner, *The Rise of a Party-State in Kenya: From "Harambee!" to "Nyayo!"* (Berkeley: University of California Press, 1993), 182–84.

27. There is a vast literature on car accidents in Africa. See, for example, P. Chilson, *Riding the Demon: On the Road to West Africa* (Athens: University of Georgia Press, 1999); Mark Lamont, "Speed Governors: Road Safety and

Infrastructural Overload in Post-Colonial Kenya, c. 1963–2013," *Africa* 83 (2013): 367–84; Adeline Masquelier, "Road Mythologies: Space, Mobility, and the Historical Imagination in Postcolonial Niger," *American Ethnologist* 29 (2002): 829–55; Subine Luning, "A Chief's Fatal Car Accident: Political History and the Moral Geography in Burkina Faso," in *The Speed of Change: Motor Vehicles and People in Africa, 1890–2000*, ed. Jan-Bart Gewald, Sabine Luning, and Klaas van Walraven (Leiden: Brill, 2009), 180–99; and Gabriel Klaeger, "Religion on the Road: The Spiritual Experience of Road Travel in Ghana," in Gewald, Luning, and Walraven, *Speed of Change*, 232–52.

28. Josphat Michoma, Kisii, Kenya, "Road Accidents Can Be Avoided," letters to the editor, *Nation*, April 11, 1986.

29. "Moi Revokes Speed Governors Order," *Nation*, November 22, 1987. For details on Moi's leadership, see Jennifer Widner, "Two Leadership Styles and Patterns of Political Liberalization," *African Studies Review* 37 (1994): 151–74.

30. Mary Materu, "Long Term to Pay Loans," letter to the editor, *The Standard*, April 4, 1986.

31. Dorothy Kweyu Munyakho, "Eyesight and Road Accidents," letter to the editor, *Nation*, March 9, 1986.

32. Japhetha Gathaka, Nairobi, "Speeding Drivers Should Be Netted," letter to the editor, *Nation*, June 27, 1986.

33. Mark Obote, letter to the editor, *Nation*, May 12, 1987.

34. Mark Lamont, "Speed Governors: Road Safety and Infrastructural Overload in Post-Colonial Kenya, c. 1963–2013," *Africa* 83 (2013): 367–84.

35. David Nthiwa, "Speeding Drivers Should Be Netted," letter to the editor, *Nation*, June 27, 1986.

36. "Matatu Acid Victim Relates Her Ordeal," *Nation*, November 2, 1986.

37. Ibid.

38. J. Wainaina, "The 'Parking Boys' of Nairobi," *African Journal of Sociology* 1 (1981): 7–45.

39. "Who Are They to Ban Political Talk," editorial, *Nation*, March 8, 1987.

40. "Matatu Association Official Resigns," *Nation*, December 7, 1987.

41. "Matatu Owners Body Should Tell Us More," *Nation*, November 25, 1987.

42. "Confusion Reigns at Matatu Meeting," *Nation*, March 25, 1987.

43. "Matatu Boss Awaits Verdict," *Nation*, December 2, 1987.

44. "Matatu Boss Faces Cash Fraud," *Nation*, February 28, 1987.

45. "27 Killed in a Road Crash," *The Standard*, March 1, 1988.

46. "Thousands Held Up in a Swoop," *Nation*, March 4, 1988.

47. "27 Killed in a Road Crash," *The Standard*, March 1, 1988.

48. "Help Us Reduce Death on Roads," *Nation*, March 1, 1988.

49. "New Rules to Curb Accidents," *Nation*, March 4, 1988.

50. Ibid.

51. "Help Reduce Road Accidents," letter signed by twenty-seven Thika residents, *Nation*, March 4, 1988; "Driving Away from Death," letter to the editor, *Nation*, March 6, 1988; "Sack Drivers Aged below 35," letter to the

editor from Concerned Commuters of Molo, *Nation,* March 9, 1988; "Do Matatus Want a License to Kill," letter to the editor, *Nation,* March 16, 1988; "Sustain Crackdowns on Matatus," Amazed Commuters in Nairobi, *The Standard,* March 18, 1988; "Need for Discipline on the Road, Sammy wa Kunga, Nakuru, letter to the editor, *The Standard,* March 17, 1988.

52. "Transport Crisis as Matatu Strike," *Nation,* March 15, 1988.
53. Ibid.
54. "Nderi Gets a King's Ransom," *Weekly Review,* March 18, 1988.
55. "Transport Crisis as Matatu Strike," *Nation,* March 15, 1988.
56. Ibid.
57. Joseph Thuo, "The Helplessness and Despair," *Nation,* March 15, 1988.
58. Ngeso Nene, "Private Motorists Should Assist," letter to the editor, *Nation,* March 15, 1988; Francis Maringa, "Greed to Blame for Accidents," letter to the editor, *Nation,* March 15 1988.
59. Sammy wa Kungu, *The Standard,* March 17, 1988.
60. "Transport Crisis as Matatus Strike," *Nation,* March 15, 1988.
61. Ibid.
62. "End of the Road for PSV Groups," *Weekly Review,* December 9, 1988.
63. "Matatus Get Reprieve," *Nation,* March 15, 1988.
64. "Commuters Stranded as Strike Takes Hold," *Nation,* March 15, 1988.
65. "Matatus: Moi Warns Stone-Throwing Touts," *Nation,* March 16, 1988.
66. Interview with Joseph Nderi, Nairobi, June 13, 2004.
67. "Moi Bans Bus, Matatu Unions," *The Standard,* December 3, 1988.
68. Ibid.
69. Ibid.
70. Interview, Nairobi, June 18, 2004.
71. "Moi Bans Bus, Matatu Unions," *The Standard,* December 3, 1988.

CHAPTER EIGHT

1. Mshai Mwangola, "Leaders of Tomorrow? The Youth and Democratisation in Kenya," in *Kenya: The Struggle for Democracy,* ed. Godwin Murunga and Shadrack Nasong'o (London: Zed Books, 2007), 129–63; Jacqueline M. Klopp, "Remembering the Destruction of Muoroto: Slum Demolitions, Land, and Democratization in Kenya," *African Studies* 67, no. 3 (2008): 295–314; and Makumi Mwangiru, Olang Sana, and Kenneth P. Njau, *Facts about Majeshi ya Wazee* (Nairobi: Freidrich Ebert Stiftung Press, 2002).

2. For examples of youth, politics, and public space in other parts of Africa, see Mamadou Diouf, "Engaging Post-Colonial Cultures: African Youth and Public Space," *African Studies Review* 46, no. 1 (2003): 1–12; Thomas Burgess, "Introduction to Youth and Citizenship in East Africa," *Africa Today* 51, no. 3 (2005): vii–xiiv; and Adrienne LeBas, *From Protest to Parties: Party-Building and Democratization in Africa* (Oxford: Oxford University Press, 2011).

3. Mwangola, "Leaders of Tomorrow?" 147; Godwin Murunga, "Urban Violence in Kenya's Transition to Pluralist Politics, 1982–1992," *Africa Development* 26, no. 1/2 (1999): 165–97; Mwangiru, Sana, and Njau, *Facts about Majeshi*, 4–6; M. Ruteere and M. Pommerolle, "Democratizing Security or Decentralizing Repression: The Ambiguities of Community Policing in Kenya," *African Affairs* 102 (2003): 587–604.

4. Raphael Kahaso, "KANU Tames Matatus," *The Standard*, September 6, 1989.

5. Ibid.

6. Daniel Branch and Nic Cheeseman, "Democratization, Sequencing, and State Failure in Africa: Lessons from Kenya," *African Affairs* 108, no. 430 (2009): 1–26.

7. For details on the first multiparty election on December 29, 1992, see David Throup and Charles Hornsby, *Multi-Party Politics in Kenya: The Kenyatta and Moi States and the Triumph of the System in the 1992 Election* (Oxford: James Currey, 1998); Thomas Carothers, "How Democracies Emerge: The Sequencing Fallacy," *Journal of Democracy* 18, no. 1 (2007): 12–27; Daniel Branch and Nic Cheeseman, "The Politics of Control in Kenya: Understanding the Bureaucratic-Executive State," *Review of African Political Economy* 33, no. 107 (2006): 23–45; Angelique Haugerud, *The Culture of Politics in Modern Kenya* (Cambridge: Cambridge University Press, 1995); and Joel D. Barkan, "Kenya: Lessons from a Flawed Election," *Journal of Democracy* 4, no. 3 (1993): 85–99.

8. Jennifer Widner, *The Rise of a Party-State in Kenya: From "Harambee" to "Nyayo!"* (Berkeley: University of California Press, 1992).

9. Haugerud, *Culture of Politics in Modern Kenya*, 45–67.

10. Wahome Mutahi, "Youth Wingers Often Give Party a Bad Name," *Nation*, May 13, 1991; and Mwangiru, Sana, and Njau, *Facts about Majeshi ya Wazee*, 7.

11. Priscilla Wamucci and Peter Idwasi, "Social Insecurity, Youth, and Development Issues in Kenya," in *Africa in Focus: Governance in the 21st Century*, ed. Kwandiwe Kondlo and Chinenyengozi Ejiogu (Cape Town: HSRC Press, 2011), 102–14.

12. Interview, Kakamega, May 29, 2006.

13. Interview, Nairobi, June 12, 2006.

14. Kenya National Assembly Official Record (Hansard), June 23, 1990, 14–15.

15. Raphael Kahaso, "KANU Tames Matatus," *The Standard*, September 6, 1989.

16. Kenya National Assembly Official Record (Hansard), March 12, 1990, 12–14.

17. Mutahi, "Youth Wingers Often Give Party a Bad Name"; Kenya National Assembly Official Record (Hansard), March 12, 1990, 12–14.

18. Interview, Nairobi, July 2, 2008.

19. Interview, Nairobi, June 3, 2009.

20. Ibid.

21. Interviews with Miriam Muliru, Beatrice, Mwongo, Peter Kodela, and Mark Maina, Nairobi, June 14, 2007.

22. Kenya National Assembly Official Record (Hansard), March 12, 1992.
23. Throup and Hornsby, *Multi-Party Politics in Kenya*, 90–97; Francois Grignon, *Understanding Multi-Partyism in Kenya: The 1990–1992 Years* (Nairobi: French Institute for Research in Africa, 1994).
24. "Minister Refuses to Answer Questions," *Nation*, June 24, 1991.
25. Grignon, *Understanding Multi-Partyism in Kenya*, 56–50.
26. Mwangiru, Sana, and Njau, *Facts about Majeshi ya Wazee*, 8–9.
27. Ibid.
28. "Youth Wingers Brawls," *Nation*, June 20, 1991.
29. Ibid.
30. Interviews with Mark Ogova, Mary Ogova, and Shem Otieno, Nairobi, June 2, 2004.
31. "Touting Still Goes On." *The Standard*, January 14, 1991.
32. Kenya National Assembly Official Record (Hansard), June 23, 1990.
33. Ibid.
34. "Operators Want to Work with Touts," *Nation*, May 24, 1989.
35. Ibid.
36. Interview, Nairobi, May 26, 2009.
37. "Youth Wingers Are the Law, and They Get Away with It," *Nation*, May 18, 1990.
38. Ibid.
39. "Matatus Must Pay a Levy," *The Standard*, August 12, 1990.
40. Ibid.
41. "Youth Wingers Fight with Touts," *The Standard*, May 11, 1991.
42. "Matatu Operators Angry at Charges," *Nation*, August, 9, 1990.
43. Sam Kahiga, "Let Me Lead You through Gomorrah," Malimoto Column, *Drum*, March 25, 1989.
44. Ibid.
45. "Boycott of Bus Terminus over Levy Continues," *Nation*, August 10, 1990.
46. Evans Kanini, "Matatu Operators Reject Charges," *Nation*, August 13, 1990.
47. John Kiama, "Matatu Operators Reject Fee," *Nation*, July 4, 1989, 2.
48. Emman Omari, "KANU Drops Disputed Matatu Levy," *The Standard*, December 18, 1992.
49. Ibid.
50. Ibid.
51. Klopp, "Remembering the Destruction of Muoroto"; Branch and Cheeseman, *Democratization, Sequencing, and State Failure in Africa*; Mwangi wa Githinji and Frank Holmquist, "Kenya's Hopes and Impediments: The Anatomy of a Crisis of Exclusion," *Journal of Eastern African Studies* 2, no. 2 (2008): 344–58.
52. "98 in Court over Touting," *Nation*, May 12, 1992.
53. Enock Anjili, "Police Round Up City Touts," *Nation*, January 16, 1992.
54. "The Almighty Law Enforcers," *Nation*, May 2, 1990.

55. Koigi wa Wamwere, *I Refuse to Die: My Journey for Freedom* (New York: Seven Stories Press, 2003); Klopp, "Remembering the Destruction of Muoroto."

56. "The Almighty Law Enforcers," *Nation*, May 2, 1990.

57. *Nation*, February 13, 1991.

58. Ibid.

59. Koigi wa Wamwere, *I Refuse to Die*.

60. Ibid.

61. Prisca Kamungi, *The Lives and Life-Choices of Dispossessed Women in Kenya*, UNIFEM African Women in Crisis Programme, January 12, 2002.

62. Kenneth King, *Jua Kali, Kenya* (Oxford: James Currey, 1996).

63. Klopp, "Remembering the Destruction of Muoroto."

64. Marjorie Macgoye, *Make It Sing and Other Poems* (Nairobi: East Africa Education Press, 1998); and Shiraz Durrani, *Information and Liberation: Writings on the Politics of Information and Librarianship* (Duluth, MN: Library Juice Press, 2008).

65. Macharia, "Slum Clearance and the Informal Economy in Nairobi," 223–29.

66. Kenya National Assembly Official Record (Hansard), October 2, 1992.

67. Ibid.

68. Eric Masese and Ezekiel Mwenzwa, "The Genesis and Evolution of Sungusungu Vigilante Group among the Ambagusii Ethnic Group of Kenya," *Elixir, Social Science* 42 (2012): 6484–92.

69. Mutahi, "Youth Wingers Often Give Party a Bad Name," *Nation*, April 14, 1992.

70. Mwangola, "Leaders of Tomorrow?"

71. Ibid.

72. "Party Youths: An Abused and Misused Lot," *Nation*, April 18, 1993.

73. Mutahi, "Youth Wingers Often Give Party a Bad Name."

74. Interview, Kakamega, April 16, 2014.

75. Interview, Nakuru, April 16, 2014.

76. M. Khayesi, "Struggle for Socio-Economic Niche and Control in the Matatu Industry in Kenya," *DPMN Bulletin* 2, no. 9 (2002): 1–7.

CHAPTER NINE

1. Gitau Warigi, "Urban Gangsters Are Playing Mother Teresa," *Nation*, October 14, 2001.

2. Ibid.

3. Ibid.

4. For a detailed biography of Al Capone, see Luciano Iorizzo, *Al Capone: A Biography* (Westport, CT: Greenwood Press, 2003).

5. Samuel Siringi, "Showdown over Public Transportation," *Nation*, November 16, 2001.

6. The literature on Mungiki is immense. See, for example, Bodil Folke Frederiksen, "Mungiki: Vernacular Organization and Political Society in Kenya," *Development and Change* 41, no. 6 (2010): 1065–89; Peter Mwangi Kagwanja, "Facing Mount Kenya or Facing Mecca? The Mungiki, Ethnic Violence, and the Politics of the Moi Succession in Kenya, 1987–2002," *African Affairs* 102 (2003): 25–49, and his "'Power to *Uhuru*': Youth Identity and Generational Politics in Kenya's 2002 Elections," *African Affairs* 105, no. 418, (2006): 51–76; David Anderson, "Vigilantes, Violence, and the Politics of Public Order in Kenya," *African Affairs* 101, no. 405 (2002): 531–55. Terisa E. Turner and Leigh S. Brownhill, "African Jubilee: Mau Mau Resurgence and the Fight for Fertility in Kenya, 1986–2002," *Canadian Journal of Development Studies / Revue canadienne d'études du développement* 22, no. 4 (2001): 1037–88. Grace Nyatugah Wamue, "Revisiting Our Indigenous Shrines through Mungiki," *African Affairs* 100, no. 400 (2001): 453–79; Jacob Rasmussen, "Outwitting the Professor of Politics? Mungiki Narratives of Political Deception and Their Role in Kenyan Politics," *Journal of Eastern African Studies* 4, no. 3 (2010): 435–49, and his "Mungiki as Youth Movement Revolution: Gender and Generational Politics in Nairobi, Kenya," *Young* 18, no. 3 (2010): 301–19. M. Ruteere, *Dilemmas of Crime, Human Rights, and the Politics of Mungiki Violence in Kenya* (Nairobi: Kenya Human Rights Institute, 2008).

7. Gabrielle Lynch, *I Say to You: Ethnic Politics and the Kalenjin in Kenya* (Chicago: University of Chicago Press, 2011).

8. Tabitha Kanogo, *Squatters and the Roots of Mau Mau, 1905–63* (Athens: Ohio University Press, 1989); and David Anderson, *Histories of the Hanged: The Dirty War in Kenya at the End of Empire* (New York: Norton, 2005).

9. Lynch, *I Say to You*, 99–102.

10. Wamue, "Revisiting Our Indigenous Shrines through Mungiki"; Sunday *Nation* correspondent, "Back to the Shrine: How a Peasant Farmer and His Sons Created a Violent Cult," *Nation*, June 10, 2007.

11. Kagwanja, "Facing Mount Kenya or Facing Mecca?; Wamue, "Revisiting Our Indigenous Shrines through Mungiki"; Turner and Brownhill, "African Jubilee."

12. Michael Njuguna, "Oathing: 63 Deny Charge," *Nation*, December 23, 1994; Watoro Kamau, "Stripping Inmates Allowed," *Nation*, September 22, 1995; and Lucy Ndichu, "Oathing: 58 Fail to Get Bail," *Nation*, January 7, 1995.

13. For details on the history of female circumcision, see Jomo Kenyatta, *Facing Mount Kenya* (London: Vintage, 1962).

14. Turner and Brownhill, "African Jubilee," 45–47.

15. Anderson, "Vigilantes, Violence, and the Politics of Public Order in Kenya."

16. David Macharia, "Matatu Operators in Protest," *The Standard*, August 25, 1989.

17. Siringi, "Showdown over Public Transportation."

18. Kagwanja, "Facing Mount Kenya or Facing Mecca?," 49.

19. For a discussion of how extortionist gangs infiltrated taxis in South Africa, see two overlapping works by Leslie Bank, "The Making of the QwaQwa Mafia? Patronage and Protection in the Migrant Taxi Business," *African Studies*, 49, no. 1 (1990): 23–41, and "A Culture of Violence: The Migrant Taxi Trade in QwaQwa, 1980–1990," in *South Africa's Informal Economy*, ed. Eleanor Preston-Whyte and Christian Rogerson (Johannesburg: Oxford University Press South Africa, 1992), 78–97; and Jackie Dugard, "From Low Intensity War to Mafia War: Taxi Violence in South Africa, 1987–2000," *Violence and Transition Series* 4 (2001): 1–45. For taxi wars in other parts of Africa, see. K. Meagher, "Hijacking Civil Society: The Inside Story of Bakassi Boys," *Journal of Modern African Studies* 213 (2007); D. J. Smith, "The Bakassi Boys: Vigilantism, Violence, and Political Imagination in Nigeria," *Cultural Anthropology* 2, no. 1 (2004): 34–60; Wole Soyinka, *The Beatification of Area Boy: A Lagosian Kaleidoscope* (London: Methuen Drama, 1995); Vusi Ndima, "The Roots of Violence and Martial Zuluness on the East Rand," in *Zulu Identities: Being Zulu, Past and Present*, ed. Benedict Carton, John Laband, and Jabulani Sithole (New York: Columbia University Press, 2009); and Meshack Khosa, "Routes, Ranks, and Rebels: Feuding in the Taxi Revolution," *Journal of Southern African Studies* 18, no. 1 (1991): 232–51.

20. Sunday *Nation* correspondent, "Back to the Shrine."

21. Ibid.

22. For studies of organized crime in Africa, see, for example, Gary Kynoch, *We Are Fighting the World: A History of Maraesha Gangs in South Africa, 1947–1999* (Athens: Ohio University Press, 2005); Clive Glaser, *Bo-Tsotsi: The Youth Gangs of Soweto, 1935–1976* (Portsmouth, NH: Heinemann, 2000); Tony Roshan, *Cape Town after Apartheid: Crime and Governance in the Divided City* (Minneapolis: University of Minnesota Press, 2010). For other relevant literature, see Diego Gambetta, *The Sicilian Mafia: The Business of Private Protection* (Cambridge, MA: Harvard University Press, 1996); Frederico Varese, *The Russian Mafia: Private Protection in a New Market Economy* (New York: Oxford University Press, 2005); Mancur Olson, *The Logic of Collective Action: Public Goods and the Theory of Groups* (Cambridge, MA: Harvard University Press, 1971); and Eiko Maruko Sinaiwer, *Ruffians, Yakuza, Nationalists: The Violent Politics of Modern Japan* (Ithaca, NY: Cornell University Press, 2008).

23. Daniel Branch and Nic Cheeseman, "Democratization, Sequencing, and State Failure in Africa: Lessons from Kenya," *African Affairs* 108, no. 430 (2008): 1–26.

24. "My Trials and Tribulations in Mungiki," *Nation*, June 10, 2007.

25. Ibid.

26. Jacob Rasmussen, "Mungiki as Youth Movement: Revolution, Gender, and Generation Politics in Nairobi, Kenya," *Young: Nordic Journal of Youth*

Research 18, no. 3 (2010): 301–19; and Erik Henningsen and Peris Jones, "'What Kind of Hell Is This!' Understanding the Mungiki Movements' Power of Mobilization," *Journal of Eastern African Studies* 7, no. 3 (2013): 371–88.

27. "My Trials and Tribulations in Mungiki." For an interesting example in other parts of Africa, see Misty Bastian, "'Diabolical Realities': Narratives of Conspiracy, Transparency, and 'Ritual Murder' in the Nigerian Popular Print and Electronic Media," in *Transparency and Conspiracy: Ethnographies of Suspicion in the New World Order*, ed. Harry G. West and Todd Sanders (Durham, NC: Duke University Press, 2003), 65–91.

28. "My Trials and Tribulation in Mungiki."

29. "Forced Oathing in Kawagware," *Nation*, January 12, 1998.

30. Fredericksen, "Mungiki, Vernacular Organization, and Political Society in Kenya"; and Rasmussen, "Mungiki as Youth Movement"; and Henningsen and Jones, "What Kind of Hell Is This!"

31. David Harvey, *A Brief History of Neoliberalism* (Oxford: Oxford University Press, 2007); James Ferguson, *Global Shadows: Africa in the Neo-Liberal World Order* (Durham, NC: Duke University Press, 2006).

32. For a cogent discussion of the effects of the programs on African countries, see Ferguson, *Global Shadows*; and Michel-Rolph Trouillot, *Global Transformations: Anthropology and the Modern World* (New York: Palgrave, 2003).

33. Kinuthia Macharia, "Slum Clearance and Informal Economy in Nairobi," *Journal of Modern Africa Studies* 30, no. 2 (1992): 221–36; and Achille Mbembe and Janet Roitman, "Figures of the Subject in Times of Crisis," *Public Culture* 7 (1995): 323–52.

34. Uwem Akpan, *Say You Are One of Them* (New York: Norton, 2008); Philip Kilbride, Collette Suda, and Enos Njeru, *Street Children in Kenya: Voices of Children in Search of a Childhood* (Westport, CT: Berginand Garvey, 2000).

35. For satirized examples of these conditions in newspaper and magazine columns in Kenya, see "Whispers," "Rural Scene," and "Masharubu's World," in *Nation*; and "Malimoto" in *Drum*.

36. For similar observations of the impact of neoliberal economic policies in India, see Suketu Mehta, *Maximum City: Bombay Lost and Found* (New York: Knopf, 2004); Katherine Boo, *Behind the Beautiful Forevers: Life, Death, and Hope in a Mumbai Undercity* (New York: Random House, 2014).

37. Fredericksen, "Mungiki, Vernacular Organization, and Political Society in Kenya"; Rasmussen, "Mungiki as Youth Movement"; and Henningsen and Jones, "What Kind of Hell Is This!"

38. "Sect Claims 2.5 Million Members," *Nation*, November 25, 1998. For more details, see Henningsen and Jones, "What Kind of Hell Is This!"; Frederiksen, "Mungiki, Vernacular Organization, and Political Society in Kenya"; and Rasmussen, "Mungiki as Youth Movement."

39. Musambayi Katumanga, "A City under Siege: Banditry and Modes of Accumulation in Nairobi, 1991–2004," *Review of African Political Economy* 32, no. 106 (2005): 505–20.
40. "Sect Claims 2.5 Million Members," *Nation*, November 25, 1998.
41. Ibid.
42. Interview, Nairobi, March 6, 2005.
43. Henningsen and Jones, "What Kind of Hell Is This!"; Frederiksen, "Mungiki, Vernacular Organization, and Political Society in Kenya"; and Rasmussen, "Mungiki as Youth Movement."
44. For studies on the privatizing of security as part of economic liberalization, see Alice Hills, *Policing Africa: Internal Security and the Limits of Liberalization* (Boulder, CO: Lynne Rienner, 2000); Bruce Baker, "Living with Nonstate Policing in South Africa: The Issues and Dilemmas," *Journal of Modern African Studies* 40, no. 1 (2002): 29–53; Les Johnston, *The Rebirth of Private Policing* (London: Routledge, 1992).
45. Interview, Nairobi, July 28, 2009.
46. Ibid.
47. Binyavanga Wainaina, "Generation Kenya," *Vanity Fair*, July 2007, 3.
48. Interview, July 29, 2008. For more on Daddy Thengz, see Binyavanga Wainaina, "Generation Kenya," 1–8.
49. Interview with Daddy Thengz, Nairobi, July 29, 2008.
50. Ibid.
51. For details on the video industry, see Mbũgua wa Mũngai, "Made in Riverwood: Dislocating Identities and Power through Kenyan Pop Music," *Journal of African Cultural Studies* 20, no. 8 (2008): 57–80.
52. Interview, Nairobi, June 20, 2008.
53. Waikwa Maina, "Matatu Lose 10 Million Shillings to Cartels," letter to the editor, *Nation*, May 12, 2001.
54. Stephen Muiruri, "70 Arrested in City Crackdown," *Nation*, November 17, 2001.
55. *Nation*, February 20, 2002; Katumanga, "A City under Siege."
56. Daniel Branch and Nic Cheeseman, "Democratization, Sequencing, and State Failure in Africa: Lessons from Kenya," *African Affairs* 108, no. 430 (2009): 1–26.
57. Kagwanja, 'Power to *Uhuru*."
58. Ibid.
59. Anderson, "Vigilantes, Violence, and the Politics of Public Order in Kenya."
60. Ibid.
61. Ibid.
62. Anderson, "Vigilantes, Violence, and the Politics of Public Order in Kenya."
63. Ibid.

64. Stephen Muiruri, "Mungiki A Security Worry for Kibaki," *Nation*, January 8, 2003.
65. Ibid.
66. Michela Wrong, *It's Our Turn to Eat* (London: Fourth Estate, 2010).
67. See chapter 12 of this book for more details on the Michuki rules.
68. Ibid.
69. Hahura, "Mungiki Hit Matatu Trade," *The Standard*, May 16, 2005.
70. Ibid.
71. Ibid.
72. Ibid.
73. For an interesting discussion on organized crime and the state, see Charles Tilly, "War Making and State Making as Organized Crime," in *Bringing the State Back In*, ed. Peter B. Evans, Dietrich Reuschemeyer, and Theda Skocpol (Cambridge: Cambridge University Press, 1985), 170–89.
74. Hahura, "Mungiki Hit Matatu Trade."
75. Ibid.
76. Ibid.
77. This is not his real name.
78. Hahura, "Mungiki Hit Matatu Trade."
79. For a similar argument, see Catherine Cole, "Wole Soyinka's *The Beatification of Area Boy* as Neoliberal Kaleidoscope," in *Neoliberalism and Global Theatres: Performance Permutations*, ed. Lara Nielsen and Patricia Ybarra (London: Palgrave Macmillan, 2012), 189–208.
80. Michael Njuguna, "Mungiki Men in Bid Join Islam," *Nation*, June 1, 2005.
81. Branch and Cheeseman, "Democratization, Sequencing, and State Failure in Africa."
82. Hahura, "Mungiki Hit Matatu Trade."
83. Ibid.
84. Ibid.
85. Ibid.
86. Stefan Dercon, "Triggers and Characteristics of the 2007 Kenyan Electoral Violence," *World Development* 40, no. 4 (2012): 731–44.
87. Nici Cheeseman, "The Kenyan Election of 2007: An Introduction"; Susanne D. Muller, "The Political Economy of Kenya's Crisis"; Michael Bratton and Mwangi Kimenyi, "Voting in Kenya: Putting Ethnicity in Perspective"; David Anderson, "Violence and Exodus in Kenya's Rift Valley," all in *Journal of East African Studies* 2, no. 2, special issue (2008).
88. "Mungiki's Mafia-Style Take-Over of City," *Nation*, February, 4, 2007.
89. Sunday *Nation* team, "The Mungiki Government," *Nation*, February 4, 2007. For more analysis of the government-Mungiki relationship, see Jacob Rasmussen, "Inside the System, Outside the Law: Operating the Matatu Sector in Nairobi," *Urban Forum* 23 (2012): 415–32.
90. Sunday *Nation* team, "The Mungiki Government."

91. "Mungiki's Mafia-Style Take-Over of City"; Wilfried Schärf and Baba Ngcokoto, "Images of Punishment in the People's Courts of Cape Town, 1985–7: From Pre-Figurative Justice to Populist Justice," in *Political Violence and the Struggle in South Africa*, ed. N. Chabani Manganyi and André du Toit (New York: St. Martin's Press, 1990), 341–72. See also Nancy Scheper-Hughes, "Unpopular Justice on Trial," and Wilfried Schärf, "Knitting Necessary Knots," *Democracy in Action* 8, no. 4 (1994): 16–20; and Sufian Hemed Bukurura, "The Maintenance of Order in Rural Tanzania," *Journal of Legal Pluralism and Unofficial Law* 34 (1994): 1–29.

92. "Industry Paralysed with Fear as Threats Continue," *Nation*, August 19, 2008.

93. Patrick Nzioka and John Njagi, "Mungiki Kill Villagers in Night Raid," *Nation*, April 22, 2009.

94. Robert M. Press, "Kenya's Political 'Transition' through the Eyes of Its 'Foot Soldiers' for Democracy and Human Rights (1997–2012)," *Journal of Contemporary African Studies* 30 (2012): 441–60.

95. Ibid.

96. *Nation* team, "Crime Keeps Urbanites Away from Home," *Nation*, December 25, 2009.

97. Mungiki, "Who Is to Blame?" *The Standard*, June 10, 2009.

98. Béatrice Hibou, "Economic Crime and Neoliberal Modes of Government," *Journal of Social History* 45, no. 3 (2012): 643–60; Eiko Maruko Siniawer, "Befitting Bedfellows: Yakuza and the State in Modern Japan," *Journal of Social History* 45, no. 3 (2012): 623–41.

99. Renate Bridenthal, "The Hidden History of Crime, Corruption, and States: An Introduction," *Journal of Social History* 45, no. 3, special issue (2012): 575–81.

100. Tilly, "War Making and State Making as Organized Crime."

101. Kagwanja, "Facing Mount Kenya or Facing Mecca?" 29; "Power to *Uhuru*," 418; Anderson, "Vigilantes, Violence, and the Politics of Public Order in Kenya."

102. For a similar argument, see Diego Gambetta and Peter Reuter, "Conspiracy among the Many: The Mafia in Legitimate Industries," in *The Economics of Organized Crime*, ed. Gianluca Fiorentini and Sam Peltzman (Cambridge: Cambridge University Press, 1995), 116–36.

103. Stergios Skaperdas, "The Political Economy of Organized Crime: Providing Protection When the State Does Not," *Economics of Governance* 2 (2001): 189.

104. Ibid. See also G. Fiorentini and S. Peltzman, eds., *The Economics of Organized Crime* (Cambridge: Cambridge University Press, 1995), 1–26.

CHAPTER TEN

1. Angela Mapendo and John Koigi, "The Matatu Attraction," *Nation*, September 14, 2003; Rukenya Nicholas, "Matatus: Some Hate Them, Others Just Love Them," *Nation*, September 29, 1996; Martha Mbuggus, "Discos on Wheels and Their Hidden Messages," *Nation*, November 12, 1995.

2. http://www.thesource.com/, accessed September 10, 2006.

3. For studies of Sheng, see David Samper, "Talking Sheng: The Role of a Hybrid Language in the Construction of Identity and Youth Culture in Nairobi, Kenya" (PhD diss., Anthropology Department, University of Pennsylvania, 2001). Ali Mazrui, "Slang and Code-Switching: The Case of Sheng in Kenya," *Afrikanistische Arbeitspapier* 42 (1995): 168–79; K. Osinde, "Sheng: An Investigation into the Social and Structural Aspects of an Evolving Language" (unpublished bachelor's thesis, University of Nairobi, 1986); M. Abdulazii and K. Osinde, "Sheng and English in Nairobi," *International Journal of the Sociology of Language* 125 (1997): 1–21; Mary Spyropoulos, "Sheng: Some Preliminary Investigations into a Recently Emerged Nairobi Street Language," *Journal of Anthropological Society of Oxford* 18, no. 2 (1987): 132–35.

4. Mwenda Ntarangwi, "African Hip Hop and Politics of Change in an Era of Rapid Globalization," *History Compass*, 2010; Joy Kibarabara, "From Nyayo Era to Unbwogable Era: A Comparative Content Analysis Study of Three Kenyan Dailies in Their Coverage of the 2002 Presidential Elections" (Shippensburg University of Pennsylvania, Department of Communication Studies, 2003); Joyce Nyairo and James Ogude, "Specificities: Popular Music and the Negotiation of Contemporary Kenyan Identity: The Example of Nairobi City Ensemble," *Social Identities* 9, no. 3 (2003): 383–400; Joyce Nyairo, "Popular Music, Popular Politics: Unbwogable and the Idiom of Freedom in Kenyan Popular Music," *African Affairs* 104, no. 415 (2005): 225–49; James Ogude, "Popular Music and the Negotiation of Contemporary Kenyan Identity: The Example of Nairobi City Ensemble," *Social Identities* 9, no. 3 (2003): 383–400; Wolfgang Bender, "Le hip-hop au Kenya: Créateur d'identité ou nouvelle 'musique nationale'? L'exemple d' 'Unbwogable' de GidiGidi MajiMaji," *Cahiers d'ethnomusicologie* 20, no. 1 (2007): 107–31.

5. Mbūgua wa Mūngai, "Made in Riverwood: (Dis)locating Identities and Power through Kenyan Pop Music," *Journal of African Cultural Studies* 20, no. 1 (2008): 57–70; Chris Wasike, "Jua cali, Genge Rap Music and the Anxieties of Living in a Glocalized Nairobi," *Journal of Music Research in Africa* 8, no. 1 (2011): 18–33.

6. Marissa Moorman, *Intonations: A Social History of Music and Nation in Luanda, Angola, from 1945 to Recent Times* (Bloomington: Indiana University Press, 2008); Frederick Moehn, "Music, Citizenship, and Violence in

Postdictatorship Brazil," *Latin American Music Review* (Fall–Winter 2007): 181–219.

7. "Unbwogable" was the name of the song. For details, see Kibarabara, "From Nyayo Era to Unbwogable Era"; Isabel Hofmeyr, Joyce Nyairo, and James Ogude, "Who Can Bwogo Me? Popular Culture in Kenya," *Social Identities* 9, no. 3 (2003): 373–83; Joyce Nyairo, "Popular Music, Popular Politics: Unbwogable and the Idiom of Freedom in Kenyan Popular Music," *African Affairs* 104, no. 415 (2005): 225–49; James Ogude, "Popular Music and the Negotiation of Contemporary Kenyan Identity: The Example of Nairobi City Ensemble," *Social Identities* 9, no. 3 (2003): 383–400; Bender, "Le hip-hop au Kenya," 107–31; Andrew J. Eisenberg, "Hip-Hop and Cultural Citizenship on Kenya's Swahili Coast," *Africa* 82, no. 4 (2012): 556–78.

8. Ntarangwi, "African Hip Hop and Politics of Change in an Era of Rapid Globalization"; Kibarabara, "From Nyayo Era to Unbwogable Era"; Hofmeyr, Nyairo, and Ogude, "Who Can Bwogo Me? Popular Culture in Kenya," 373–83; Joyce Nyairo, "Popular Music, Popular Politics," 225–49; Ogude, "Popular Music and the Negotiation of Contemporary Kenyan Identity," 383–400; Bender, "Le hip-hop au Kenya," 107–131; Andrew J. Eisenberg, "Hip-Hop and Cultural Citizenship on Kenya's Swahili Coast," *Africa* 82, no. 4 (2012): 556–78.

9. For details on the informal economic sector in Kenya, see Kenneth King, *Jua Kali Kenya: Change and Development in an Informal Economy, 1970–95* (Athens: Ohio University Press, 1996).

10. Tom Michael Mboya, "Young Man, You Keep Insisting That This Is Your Thing, and What Should Your Fellow Men Seduce? Sex, HIV/AIDS, and Tribal Politics in the Benga of Okatch Biggy," *Postcolonial Text* 5, no. 3 (2009): 4–23; Nyairo and Ogude, "Specificities," 383–400.

11. Mutongi, "Thugs or Entrepreneurs."

12. Ngũgĩ wa Thiong'o, *Devil on the Cross* (London: Heinemann, 1981).

13. Matunda Nyanchama, "A Nation Asleep at the Wheel," *Weekly Review*, February 9, 1996.

14. Interview, Nairobi, June 16, 2008.

15. Mapendo and Koigi, "Matatu Attraction."

16. Karen Tranberg Hansen, *Salaula: The World of Secondhand Clothing and Zambia* (Chicago: University of Chicago Press, 2000).

17. Dorian Lynskey, "Straight Outta Africa," *Guardian*, November 5, 2004; Mwenda Ntarangwi, *East African Hip Hop: Youth Culture and Globalization* (Urbana: University of Illinois Press, 2009); Tricia Rose, *Black Noise: Rap Music and Black Culture in Contemporary America* (Hanover, NH: University Press of New England, 1994); Marcyliena Morgan, *The Real Hiphop: Battling for Knowledge, Power, and Respect in the LA Underground* (Durham, NC: Duke University Press, 2009).

18. *Nation*, May 15, 2001.
19. Lynskey, "Straight Outta Africa."
20. Mathenge wa Kigui, "Obscene Song Must Be Banned," letter to the editor, *Nation*, June 15, 1995.
21. Wamahiu Muya, "A Ride into an Unwanted Baby," *The Standard*, May 2, 1992; Fatuma Chege, Zipporah Rimbui, and Waveney Olembo, "Girls and the Painful Matatu Ride," Report by Federation of Women Educationalist, Nairobi 1991.
22. Peter Oriare and Gordon Ondiek, "Crackdown on Loud Music to Continue," *Nation*, August 8, 1992.
23. Ibid.
24. Mironga Momanyi, "The Dangers of Loud 'Music,'" *The Standard*, April 23, 1998.
25. Interview with Samuel Njuguna, Nairobi, June 23, 2004.
26. Chege wa Gachamba, "'Manamba' Madness," *Nation*, September 7, 1994.
27. Interview with Priscilla Ngochi, Nairobi, June 11, 2006.
28. Steve Otieno, "The Crafty Tongues of Nairobi's Matatu Operators," *Nation*, January 11, 1989.
29. Martha Mbugguss, "Discos on Wheels and Their Hidden Messages," *Nation*, November 12, 1995.
30. Ibid.
31. Peter Oriare and Gordon Ondiek, "Crackdown on Loud Music to Continue," *Nation*, August 8, 1992.
32. Ibid.
33. Ibid.
34. Aurelia Ferrari, "Hip-Hop in Nairobi: Recognition of an International Movement and the Main Means of Expression for Urban Youths," in *Song and Politics in East Africa*, ed. Kimani Njogu and Hervé Maupeu (Dar es Salaam: Mkuki na Nyota Publishers, 2007), 107–24.
35. Ibid.
36. Ann Overbergh, "New Technology, New Media, and Emerging Audiovisual Formats and Genres in Kenya," *Culture and Media in Africa* (2012); Mark Katz, *Groove Music: The Art and Culture of the Hip-Hop DJ* (Oxford: Oxford University Press, 2012); Katz, *Capturing Sound: How Technology Has Changed Music* (Berkeley: University of California Press, 2004); Peter Manuel, *Cassette Culture: Popular Music and Technology in North India* (Chicago: Universty of Chicago Press, 1993); David Suisman, *Selling Sounds: The Commercial Revolution in American Music* (Cambridge, MA: Harvard University Press, 2009); Emily Thompson, *The Soundscape of Modernity: Architectural Acoustics and the Culture of Listening in America, 1900–1933* (Cambridge, MA: MIT Press, 2002); Martin Jay, *Downcast Eyes: The Denigration of Vision in French Political Thought* (Berkeley: University of California Press, 1993).
37. Press Release of the Transporters Association of Kenya, August 7, 1992.
38. Wahome Mutahi, "This Matatu Subculture Thrives on Sheer Greed," *Nation*, May 6, 1991.

39. S. Hempstone, *Rogue Ambassador: An African Memoir* (Sewanee, TN: University of the South Press, 1997).

40. David William Cohen and E. S. Atieno Odhiambo, *Risks of Knowledge* (Athens: Ohio University Press, 2004); Edwin A. Gimode, "The Role of the Police in Kenya's Democratisation Process," in *Kenya: The Struggle for Democracy*, ed. G. R. Murunga and S. W. Nasong'o (Dakar: Codesria Books, 2007), 227–60.

41. Cohen and Atieno Odhiambo, *Risks of Knowledge*; Gimode, "Role of the Police in Kenya's Democratisation Process."

42. Timothy Njoya, James Orengo, Paul Muite, Gitobu Imanyara, and Martin Shikuku were also detained.

43. Gimode, "Role of the Police in Kenya's Democratisation Process; Cohen and Atieno Odhiambo, *Risks of Knowledge*.

44. "Three Killed in City Violence," *Nation*, July 9, 1990.

45. Ibid.

46. Ibid.

47. http://web.archive.org/web/20030227150822/http://www.nationaudio.com/News/EastAfrican/03022003/Features/PA6.html, accessed June 19, 2010.

48. "Bus, Matatu Boycott Bites," *Nation*, July 10, 1990.

49. Ibid.

50. David Rogoncho, "Dandora Residents Fight It Out with the Police," *Nation*, July 10, 1990.

51. They included Timothy Njoya, James Orengo, Paul Muite, Gitobu Imanyara, and Martin Shikuku. *Nation*, July 12, 1990.

52. "Church Leaders Pray for Peace in Kenya," *Nation*, July 9, 1990.

53. Ibid.

54. Ibid.

55. Emman Omari, "Koigi, Kathangu Speak Out," *Nation*, January 16, 1992.

56. "Matatus Protest Potholes," *The Standard*, May 8, 1990.

57. A tactic used by women before in other contexts in Kenya. See Andrew Wipper, "Kikuyu Women and the Harry Thuku Disturbances: Some Uniformities of Female Militancy," *Africa* 59, no. 3 (1989): 300–337.

58. Wangari Maathai, *Unbowed: A Memoir* (New York: Anchor, 2007), 80–91; and *The Green Belt Movement: Sharing the Approach and the Experience* (New York: Lantern Books, 2003).

59. Kibarabara, "From Nyayo Era to Unbwogable Era"; Hofmeyr, Nyairo, and Ogude, "Who Can Bwogo Me?; Nyairo, "Popular Music, Popular Politics."

60. Nyairo, "Popular Music, Popular Politics," 37–45.

61. Ali Mazrui, "Slang and Code-Switching: The Case of Sheng in Kenya," *Afrikanistische Arbeitspapier* 42 (1995): 168–79; K. Osinde, "Sheng: An Investigation into the Social and Structural Aspects of an Evolving Language" (bachelor's thesis, University of Nairobi, 1986); M. Abdulazi and K. Osinde, "Sheng and English in Nairobi," *International Journal of the Sociology of Language* 125 (1997): 1–21.

62. Mary Spyropoulos, "Sheng: Some Preliminary Investigations into a Recently Emerged Nairobi Street Language," *Journal of Anthropological Society of Oxford* 18, no. 2 (1987): 132–35.

63. Peter Githinji, "Ambivalent Attitudes: Perception of Sheng and Its Speakers," *Nordic Journal of African Studies* 17, no. 2 (2008): 113–36.

64. Raoul J. Granqvist, *The Bulldozer and the Word: Culture at Work in Post-Colonial Nairobi* (New York: Peter Lang, 2004).

65. Mbũgua wa Mũngai, *Nairobi Matatu Men: Portrait of a Sub-Culture* (Nairobi: Contact Zone, 2013).

66. Nyamira Oduori Radoli, "Kiswahili Is Being Adulterated," letter to the editor, *The Standard*, February 19, 1989.

67. Wahome Mutahi, "This Matatu Subculture Thrives on Sheet Greed," *Nation*, May 6, 1991.

68. Clara Momanyi, "The Effects of Sheng in the Teaching of Kiswahili in Kenyan Schools," *Journal of Pan African Studies* 2, no. 8 (2009): 127–38.

69. Binyavanga Wainaina, *Discovering Home* (Nairobi: Kwani, 2006).

70. Marcyliena Morgan and Dione Bennett, "Hip Hop and the Global Imprint of a Black Cultural Form," *Daedalus* 140, no. 2 (2011): 176–96, at 196.

CHAPTER ELEVEN

1. Most of Eastlands, areas like Umoja, Dandora, Kayole, and Kariobangi South, are working class. Buruburu is considered the main lower-middle-class area in the region. For more details on Buruburu, see Billy Kahora, "Buru Buru," *Chimurenga*, September 23, 2014.

2. Interview with John Macharia, Nairobi, June 9, 2009.

3. Interview with Titus Ouma, Nairobi, June 9, 2009.

4. For Africa, see Sjaak van der Geest, "'Anyway!' Lorry Inscriptions in Ghana," in *The Speed of Change: Motor Vehicles and People in Africa, 1890–2000*, ed. Jan-Bart Gewald, Sabine Luning, and Klaas van Walraven (Leiden: Brill, 2009); E. Date-Bah, "The Inscriptions of the Vehicles of Ghanaian Commercial Drivers: A Sociological Analysis," *Journal of Modern African Studies* 18, no. 3 (1980): 525–31; R. Van Eijk, *Car Slogans in Ghana* (Amsterdam: Cadier en Keer, 2003); G. H. Lewis, "The Philosophy of the Street in Ghana: Mammy Wagons and Their Mottos: A Research Agenda," *Journal of Popular Culture* 32, no. 1 (1999): 165–69; O. B. Lawuyi, "The World of the Yoruba Taxi Driver: An interpretive Approach to Vehicle Slogans," *Africa* 58, no. 1 (1988): 1–13; J. Pritchett, "Nigerian Truck Art," *African Arts* 12, no. 2 (1979); Kojo Kyei and Hannah Schreckenbach, *No Time to Die* (Accra: Catholic Press, 1976); and J. W. Jordan, "The Role of Segregation for Fun and Profit: The Daily Behaviour of the West African Lorry Driver," *Africa* 48, no. 1 (1978): 30–46. For South Asia, see Jamal Elias, *On Wings of Diesel: Trucks, Identity, and Culture in Pakistan* (New York:

Oneworld, 2011); Elias, "On Wings of Diesel: Spiritual Space and Religious Imagination in Pakistani Truck Decoration," *RES: Anthropology and Aesthetics* 43 (Spring 2003): 187–202, and Elias, "Truck Decoration and Religious Identity: Material Culture and Social Function in Pakistan," *Material Religion: The Journal of Objects, Art, and Beliefs* (March 2005). For the Caribbean and Latin America, see R. F. Thompson, "Tap-Tap, Fula-Fula, Kia-Kia: The Haitian Bus in the Atlantic Context," *African Arts* 30 (1996): 36–45; Paul Gilroy, "Driving While Black," in *Car Cultures*, ed. Daniel Miller (New York: Berg, 2001).

5. Brad Weiss, *Street Dreams and Hip Hop Barbershops: Global Fantasy in Urban Tanzania* (Bloomington: Indiana University Press, 2009); R. M. Beck, "Texts on Textiles: Proverbiality as Characteristic of Equivocal Communication at the East African Coast," *Journal of African Cultural Studies* (2005); Elisabeth Linnebuhr, *"Kanga:* Popular Cloths with Messages," in *Sokomoko: Popular Culture in East Africa*, ed. Werner Graeber (Amsterdam: Rodopi, 1992); Sheryl McCurdy, "Fashioning Sexuality: Desire, Manyema Ethnicity, and the Creation of Kanga, ca 1880–1900," *International Journal of African Historical Studies* (2006).

6. The 1980s saw the rise of evangelical churches and Pentecostals, which was in part a response to one of the worst economic declines Kenya had faced in the twentieth century. People sought "salvation," so to speak, in religion. For examples, see Birgit Meyer, "Christianity in Africa: From African Independent to Pentecostal-Charismatic Churches," *Annual Review of Anthropology* 33 (2004): 447–74.

7. Mbũgua wa Mũngai, "Identity Politics in Matatu Folklore" (PhD diss., Hebrew University of Jerusalem, 2003), 40–49; Mbũgua wa Mũngai, *Nairobi's Matatu Men: Portrait of a Sub-Culture* (Nairobi: Contact Zones, 2014).

8. Mũngai, *Nairobi's Matatu Men*; Jamal Elias, *On Wings of Diesel: Trucks, Identity, and Culture in Pakistan.*

9. http://www.bifa.ac.ke/, accessed June 10, 2010.

10. Kwame Anthony Appiah, *Cosmopolitanism: Ethics in a World of Strangers* (New York: Norton, 2006); Andre Gingrich and Richard G. Fox, *Anthropology, by Comparison* (New York: Routledge, 2002); K. Sivaramakrishnan and Arun Agrawal, eds., *Regional Modernities: The Cultural Politics of Development in India* (Stanford, CA: Stanford University Press, 2003); Engseng Ho, *The Graves of Tarim: Genealogy and Mobility across the Indian Ocean* (Berkeley: University of California Press, 2006); and Jennifer S. Hirsch, Holly Wardlow, Daniel Jordan Smith, Harriet M. Phinney, Shanti Parikh, and Constance A. Nathanson, *The Secret: Love, Marriage, and HIV* (Nashville: Vanderbilt University Press, 2009).

11. Appiah, *Cosmopolitanism*; Carol Symes, "When We Talk about Modernity," *American Historical Review* 116, no. 3 (2011): 715–26.

12. Aniel Njoka, "The Coarse, the Crass, the Cranky," *Nation*, April 27, 2001.

13. Ulf Hannerz, "Sophiatown: The View from Afar," *Journal of South African Studies* 20, no. 2 (1994).

14. Njoka, "The Coarse, the Crass, the Cranky"; Mbũgua wa Mũngai, "Hidden $ Centz: Rolling the Wheels of Nairobi Matatu," in *Nairobi Today: The Paradox of a Fragmented City*, ed. Hélène Charton-Bigot and Deyssii Rodriguez-Torres (Nairobi: IFRA, 2010), 351–64.

15. Interview with Nancy Gichuru, Nairobi, June 15, 2009.

16. For example, *Nation*, May 12, 1997; *The Standard*, January 8, 1993, and October 4, 1997; Lawuyi, "The World of the Yoruba Taxi Driver."

17. Interviews with Mohammed Abludahi, Musa Abed, and Ruth Zewde, Nairobi, June 12, 2004. For a detailed and analytical examination of the rise of Somali capital in Nairobi, see Parselelo Kantai, "The Rise of Somali Capital," *Chimurenga*, March 1, 2013.

18. Interview, Nairobi, June 11, 2009.

19. *Nation*, May 10, 1993; *The Standard*, July 12, 1996.

20. Elizabeth H. Campbell, "Urban Refugees in Nairobi: Problems of Protection, Mechanisms of Survival, and Possibilities for Integration," *Journal of Refugee Studies* 19, no. 3 (2006): 396–413; Godwin Murunga, "Refugees at Home? Coping with Somalia Conflict in Nairobi, Kenya," *in African Studies in Geography from Below*, ed. Michel Ben Arrous and Lazare Ki-Zerbo (Dakar: Codesria, 2009); Josylene Chebichi, "The Legality of 'Illegal' Somali Migrants in Eastleigh Estate in Nairobi, Kenya," http://hdl.handle .net/10539/8194, accessed December 14, 2011; Reginald Herbold Green, "*Khat* and the Realities of Somalis: Historic, Social, Household, Political, and Economic," *Review of African Political Economy* 26, no. 79 (1999): 33–49.

21. Parselelo Kantai, "The Rise of Somali Capital," *Chimurenga*, March 1, 2013; Chebichi, "The Legality of 'Illegal' Somali Migrants in Eastleigh Estate in Nairobi, Kenya"; and Green, "*Khat* and the Realities of Somalis."

22. See, for example, Neil Carrier, *Little Mogadishu: Eastleigh, Nairobi's Global Somali Hub* (Oxford, UK: Oxford University Press, 2015).

23. Binyavanga Wainaina, "Generation Kenya," *Vanity Fair*, July 2007, 4.

24. Wainaina, "Generation Kenya," 4–5.

25. *Nation*, January 13, 2006.

26. Interview, Nairobi, June 17, 2009.

27. http://www.thesource.com/, accessed December 14, 2011.

28. Interview, Nairobi, June 15, 2009.

29. Toxic wrote for *The Star* newspaper, established in 2007.

30. Gitau Warigi, *Nation*, May 12, 1998.

31. Nairobi, June 12, 2008.

32. Gitau Warigi, *Nation*, May 12, 1998.

33. Interview, Nairobi, June 8, 2004.

34. For example, Gavin Bennett, "Matauism Is the Bane of Kenya's Motor Industry," *Sunday Nation*, May 3, 1992; Michael Njuguna, "The Day Death

Came to Molo," *"Sunday Nation,* March 13, 1988; and *Nation* correspondent, "Kenya: We Must Stand Firm to Defeat This Lunacy," *Daily Nation,* July 12, 1999.

35. Other equally caustic examples of stickers include *Heri uchawi kuliko fitua* (I would rather have witchcraft than an argument); *Kazi ni kazi, usiogope kazi* (Work is just work, don't be afraid of work, implying that people should not be judged by the kinds of jobs they do; i.e., Matatu conductors should not be looked down upon); *Usilete noma kwa gari* (Don't bring your own private problems to this matatu); *Dere ni wazimu konda ni moto* (The driver is crazy, the conductor is good/fired up); *Karao alipe gari* (The police must pay fare too); *Makosa ya marehemu, hakutumia juala* (The problem of the deceased is that he didn't use a condom); *Unaringa umepimwa?* (You are showing off, are you tested? insinuating HIV status).

36. This refers to Michuki rules. For details, see chapter 12.

37. Interview, Nairobi, June 9, 2008.

38. Mbũgua wa Mũngai, "Identity Politics in Matatu Folklore," 49.

39. Mutongi, "Thugs or Entrepreneurs," 549–50.

40. Somewhat similar to the A-level exam in Britain, the high school exam requires more than a year-long study; usually grade C is the cutoff for university admission in Kenya.

41. Interview, Nairobi, June 19, 2004.

42. Mutongi, "Thugs or Entrepreneurs."

43. Ibid.

44. June 19, 2004.

45. Mutongi, "Thugs or Entrepreneurs." For Michuki rules, see chapter 12.

46. I was born and raised in Kenya, and I rode matatus all the time; I continue to do so during my visits to Kenya.

47. Chege wa Gachamba, "Manamba Madness," *Daily Nation,* September 7, 1994.

48. *Daily Nation,* January 29, 2004.

49. John Githongo, *The East African Standard,* November 2–8, 1998.

50. Interview, Nairobi, June 14, 2004.

51. Interview, Nairobi, June 18, 2004.

52. Interview, Nairobi, June 15, 2004.

53. Interview, Nairobi, June 14, 2004.

54. Interview, Nairobi, June 19, 2004.

55. Ibid.

56. Ibid.

57. Interview with Jane Musira, Nairobi, June 18, 2005.

58. Interview with Mark Mutisya, June 19, 2008.

59. Koinange is the red-light street in Nairobi.

60. Mbũgua wa Mũngai, "Identity Politics in Matatu Folklore," 50–53.

61. Interview, Nairobi, June 18, 2004.

62. Mbũgua wa Mũngai, "Identity Politics in Matatu Folklore," 49.

CHAPTER TWELVE

1. See chapter 7.
2. Samuel Siringi, "Mbugua Finds Himself in the Firing Line," *Nation*, November 20, 2003.
3. Interview with Dickson Mbugua, Nairobi, June 2, 2004.
4. "Matatu Organization Official!" *The Standard*, June 5, 2003.
5. Ibid.
6. For analysis of the competing interests between the two organizations, I have drawn largely from Avinash K. Dixit and Barry Nalebuff, *The Art of Strategy: A Game Theorist's Guide to Success in Business and Life* (New York: W. W. Norton, 2010), and Alvin Roth, *Who Gets What—and Why: The New Economics of Matchmaking and Market Design* (Boston: Eamon Dolan/Houghton Mifflin Harcourt, 2015).
7. Some of the supposed changes included a crackdown on corruption, rapid economic growth and the creation of 500,000 jobs, constitutional reform, and free primary education for all. For details, see Joel Barkan, "Kenya after Moi," *Foreign Affairs* 83 (2004): 87–100; and Jeffrey Steeves, "Presidential Succession in Kenya: The Transition from Moi to Kibaki," *Commonwealth and Comparative Politics* 44 (2006): 211–33. For an excellent overview and analysis of the Moi and Kibaki regimes, see Daniel Branch, *Kenya: Between Hope and Despair, 1963–2011* (New Haven, CT: Yale University Press, 2011).
8. "Michuki Rules," *Nation*, September 15, 2003; "What Are the Michuki Rules?" *The Standard*, September 15, 2003.
9. "Michuki Rules," *Nation*, September 15, 2003; "What Are the Michuki Rules?" *The Standard*, September 15, 2003; and Preston O. Chitere and Thomas N. Kibua, "Efforts to Improve Road Safety in Kenya: Achievements and Limitations of Reforms in the Matatu Industry," *Institute of Policy Analysis and Research (IPAR)*, 2005.
10. Chitere and Kibua, "Efforts to Improve Road Safety in Kenya." For details on Mungiki, see chapter 9.
11. Branch, *Kenya*, 210–30.
12. James Habyarimana and William Jack, "State vs. Consumer Regulation: An Evaluation of Two Road Safety Interventions in Kenya," National Bureau of Economic Research Working Paper No. 18378, September 2012, Cambridge, MA.; M. Khayesi, "Partnership and Dialogue for Implementation of New Road Safety Rules in Kenya: Short Research Report," *African Safety Promotion* 2 (2004): 35–41; and Mark Lamont, "Speed Governors: Road Safety and Infrastructural Overload in Post Colonial Kenya, 1963–2013," *Africa* 83 (2013): 367–84.
13. Daniel Branch and Nicholas Cheeseman, "The Politics of Control in Kenya: Understanding the Bureaucratic-Executive State, 1952–78," *Review of African Political Economy* 33 (2006): 72–99; and Miatta Fahnbulleh,

"In Search of Economic Development in Kenya: Colonial Legacies and Post-Independence Realities," *Review of African Political Economy* 33 (2006): 34–51.

14. For Kalenjin politics, see Gabrielle Lynch, *I Say to You: Ethnic Politics and the Kalenjin in Kenya* (Chicago: University of Chicago Press, 2011).

15. "Matatu Organization Official!" *The Standard*, June 5, 2003; Habyarimana and Jack, "State vs Consumer Regulation," 4.

16. Daniel Kamau and Philip Mwaniki, "Rival Matatu Groups Clash over Strategy," *Nation*, November 10, 2003.

17. Samuel Siringi, "Mbugua Finds Himself in the Firing Line," *Nation*, October 20, 2003.

18. "I Won't Back Down, Says Michuki," *Nation*, October 2, 2003.

19. Siringi, "Mbugua Finds Himself in the Firing Line."

20. Daniel Kamau and Philip Mwaniki, "Rival Matatu Group Clash over Strategy," *Nation*, November 10, 2003, and "What Is the Strategy," *The Standard*, November 11, 2003.

21. Kamau and Mwaniki, "Rival Matatu Group Clash over Strategy."

22. Kamau and Mwaniki, "Rival Matatu Group Clash over Strategy," and "What Is the Strategy," *The Standard*, November 11, 2003.

23. Lucas Barasa, "Matatu Rival Groups," *Nation*, October 25, 2003.

24. Ibid.

25. "Police Rescues Bus Hijacked by Travelers," *The Standard*, November 20, 2003.

26. "Matatu Strike: What Commuters Say," *Nation*, November 20, 2003.

27. Ibid.

28. David Okwembah, "Matatu Men Have Never Backed Order," *Nation*, November 21, 2003.

29. "Matatu Strike: What Commuters say," *Nation*, November 20, 2003.

30. "Matatus Threaten to Double Fares," *Nation*, November 22, 2003.

31. Ibid.

32. Catherine Riungu, "Crunch Time for Matatus," Nation, January 12, 2004.

33. "High Court Rejects Plea to Block Implementation of new Safety Rules," *Nation*, January 29, 2004.

34. Ibid.

35. "Matatu Deadline Approaching," *The Standard*, January 12, 2004; "Can the Matatu Be Fixed," *The Standard*, January 20, 2004; "Michuki Rules," *Nation*, January 13, 2004; "High Court Denies Matatu," *Nation*, January 18, 2004.

36. "Slowdown on Matatu Seatbelt," *Nation*, January 23, 2003.

37. Ibid.

38. Stephen Muiruri, "Matatu Owner's Dilemma as Police Block Fake Drivers," *The Standard*, February 11, 2004.

39. Ibid.

40. "NYS to Rescue Matatu," *Nation*, February 2, 2004.

41. "Matatu vs. Michuki," *The Standard*, February 1, 2004.
42. Ibid.
43. "Are Michuki Rules Working?" *Nation*, March 30, 2004; "Matatu Cleaned Up," *The Standard*, April 7, 2004.
44. Jennifer Graeff, "The Organization and Future of the Matatu Industry in Nairobi, Kenya," Center for Sustainable Urban Development—Earth Institute, Columbia University, 2005; Preston O. Chitere and Thomas N. Kibua, "Efforts to Improve Road Safety in Kenya: Achievements and limitations of Reforms in the Matatu Industry," *Institute of Policy Analysis and Research (IPAR)*, 2005.
45. See chapters 10 and 11 for details on Generation Matatu.
46. http://www.ashoka.org/, accessed January 18, 2009.
47. Interview, Nairobi, June 7, 2004.
48. Ibid.
49. For details on the prevalence of the mobile phone in Kenya, see June Arunga and Billy Kahora, "The Cell Phone Revolution in Kenya," *International Policy Network*, 2007.
50. Wainaina, *Discovering Home*.
51. Interview, Nairobi, June 11, 2006.
52. For an interesting assessment of neoliberalism, see Jeremy Gilbert, "What Kind of Thing Is Neoliberalism?" *New Formations* 80–81, special issue (2013).
53. Binyavanga Wainaina, "Generation Kenya," *Vanity Fair*, June 2007, 3–10.
54. Ibid.
55. Interview, Nairobi, June 11, 2006.
56. Ibid.
57. Avinash Dixit and Barry Nalebuff, *Thinking Strategically*; Michael P. Todaro and Stephen C. Smith, *Economic Development*, 10th ed. (Boston: Pearson Addison Wesley, 2009); Shaun Hargreaves Heap and Yanis Varoufakis, *Game Theory: A Critical Introduction* (London: Routledge, 1995).
58. "Michuki Rules Thrown to the Back Seat," *Nation*, September 5, 2006.
59. Bruce Wydick, *Games in Economic Development* (Cambridge: Cambridge University Press, 2008), 13–16.
60. Branch, *Kenya*, 260–73.
61. Daron Acemoglu, James A. Robinson, and Thierry Verdier, "Kleptocracy and Divide-and-Rule: A Model of Personal Rule," Alfred Marshall Lecture, Massachusetts Institute of Technology 2004; John McMillan, *Reinventing the Bazaar: A Natural History of Markets* (New York: Norton, 2003).
62. Robert Axelrod, *The Evolution of Cooperation* (New York: Basic Books, 1984); Avinash Dixit and Barry Nalebuff, *Thinking Strategically: A Competitive Edge in Business, Politics, and Everyday Life* (New York: W. W. Norton, 1991); Douglas Hofstader, "Mathamagical Themas," *Scientific American* (May 1983): 16–26; William Poundstone, *Prisoner's Dilemma: John von Neumann, Game Theory, and the Puzzle of the Bomb* (New York: Doubleday,

1992); Anatol Rapoport and A. M. Chammah, *Prisoners Dilemma* (Ann Arbor: University of Michigan Press, 1965); David Kreps, Robert Wilson, Paul Milgrom, and John Roberts, "Rational Cooperation in the Finitely Repeated Prisoners' Dilemma," *Journal of Economic Theory* 27 (August 1982): 245–52; Paul Milgrom, "Axelrod's *The Evolution of Cooperation*," *Rand Journal of Economics* 15, no. 2 (1984): 305–9.

63. "Shortage of Registration Plates," *The Standard*, January 9, 2006.

64. Michuki became the minister for internal security and provincial administration, and in 2008 was made the minister of environment and mineral resources.

65. "Matatu Owners Want Bigger Role in Safety Campaign," *Nation*, September 5, 2006.

66. Ngumbao Kithi, "Plan for One Matatu Club," *Nation*, December 1, 2006.

67. Ibid.

68. Ibid.

69. Mancur Olson, *The Logic of Collective Action* or *Power and Prosperity: Public Goods and the Theory of Groups* (Cambridge, MA: Harvard University Press, 1971); Robert H. Porter, "A Study of Cartel Stability: The Joint Executive Committee, 1880–1886," *Bell Journal of Economics* 14 (1983): 301–14.

70. Wangui Maina, "Minister Spells Out Tougher Road Rules," *Nation*, December 14, 2007.

71. Mwaniki Wahome, "For Buses, Policy Shift Reverses," *Nation*, April 10, 2007.

72. Ibid.

73. Lucas Barasa, "Passengers Face Seat Belt Fine," *Nation*, November 26, 2007.

74. Abdulsamad Ali and Mazera Ndurya, "Matatu Groups Split on Increase in Fares," *Daily Nation*, August 20, 2005.

75. Heap and Varoufakis, *Game Theory*; Dixit and Nalebuff, *Thinking Strategically: A Competitive Edge in Business, Politics, and Everyday Life*.

76. Elinor Ostrom, *Governing the Commons: The Evolution of Institutions for Collective Action* (Cambridge: Cambridge University Press, 1990).

77. Nesmith Ankeny, *Poker Strategy: Winning with Game Theory* (New York: Basic Books, 1981); Steven Brams, *Game Theory and Politics* (New York: Free Press, 1979); Acemoglu, Robinson, and Verdier, "Kleptocracy and Divide-and-Rule"; McMillan, *Reinventing the Bazaar*; Avinash Dixit and Susan Skeath, *Games of Strategy*, 2nd ed. (New York: W. W. Norton, 2004); William Riker, *The Art of Political Manipulation* (New Haven, CT: Yale University Press, 1986).

78. Telephone conversation, May 18, 2014.

79. http://www.standardmedia.co.ke/business/article/2000105373/matatu -operators-opposed-bebapay, accessed May 2, 2013.

80. For details on SACCO, see http://www.sasra.go.ke/, accessed July 23, 2013.

81. John Wekesa, "Is Mungiki Back?" *Nation*, March 10, 2012.

82. Ibid.

CONCLUSION

1. Robert Nozick, *Anarchy, State, and Utopia* (New York: Basic Books, 2013).

2. For the importance of property rights to the growth of sophisticated business, see Jonathan Conning and J. A. Robinson, "Property Rights and the Political Organization of Agriculture," *Journal of Development Economics* 82 (March 2007): 416–47; Marcel Fafchamps, *Rural Poverty, Risk, and Development* (New York: Edward Elgar, 2004); and Fafchamps, *Market Institutions in Sub-Saharan Africa: Theory and Evidence* (Cambridge, MA: MIT Press, 2004); Jean-Philippe Platteau, *Institutions, Social Norms, and Economic Development* (Amsterdam: Harwood Academic, 2000); Joseph E. Stiglitz, *Globalization and Its Discontents* (New York: W. W. Norton, 2003); China Scherz, *Having People, Having Heart: Charity, Sustainable Development, and Problems of Dependence in Central Uganda* (Chicago: University of Chicago Press, 2014); Jennifer Graeff, "The Organization and Future of the Matatu Industry in Nairobi, Kenya," Center for Sustainable Urban Development—Earth Institute, Columbia University, New York, 2009.

3. Albert O. Hirschman, *The Passions and the Interests: Political Arguments for Capitalism before Its Triumph* (Princeton, NJ: Princeton University Press, 1997); Albert O. Hirschman and Jeremy Adelman, *The Essential Hirschman* (Princeton, NJ: Princeton University Press, 2013); Joseph E. Stiglitz, *Making Globalization Work* (New York: W. W. Norton, 2007).

4. Deborah Salon and Eric M. Aligula, "Urban Travel in Nairobi, Kenya: Analysis, Insights, and Opportunities," *Journal of Transport Geography* 22 (May 2012): 65–76; C. M. Rogerson, "In Search of the African Miracle: Debates on Successful Small Enterprise Development in Africa," *Habitat International* 25 (2001): 115–42; Graeff, "Organization and Future of the Matatu Industry in Nairobi, Kenya."

5. Amartya Sen, *Development as Freedom* (New York: Anchor, 2000); Easterly, *White Man's Burden* and *Tyranny of Experts*; Colin Leys, *The Rise and Fall of Development Theory* (Bloomington: Indiana University Press, 2009); Gilbert Rist, *The History of Development: From Western Origins to Global Faith*, 3rd ed. (London: Zed, 2009).

6. Hernando de Soto, *The Mystery of Capital: Why Capitalism Triumphs in the West and Fails Everywhere Else* (New York: Basic Books, 2003); Easterly, *Tyranny of Experts* and *White Man's Burden*; Dambisa Moyo, *Dead Aid: Why Aid Is Not Working and Why There Is a Better Way for Africa* (New York: Farrar Strauss and Giroux, 2011).

7. For the few available studies on this topic, see the literature on Nollywood: Elizabeth J. Hester, *Nollywood and Nigerian Cinema: A Selective Bibliography of Dissertations and Theses* (New York: CreateSpace Independent Publishing Platform, 2016). Also see Alusine Jalloh, *African Entrepreneurship: Muslim Fula Merchants in Sierra Leone* (Athens: Ohio University Press, 1999); and Laura Fair's study of the cinema industry in Zanzibar,

Reel Pleasures (Ohio University Press, forthcoming). A majority of economic or business history on Africa tends to focus on agriculture production, slavery, mining, and commodity export, with special focus on the precolonial or colonial periods. See, for example, Gareth Austin, *Labour, Land, and Capital in Ghana: From Slavery to Free Labour in Asante, 1807–1956* (Rochester, NY: University of Rochester Press, 2005); Sara Berry, *Fathers Work for Their Sons: Accumulation, Mobility, and Class Formation in an Extended Yoruba Community* (Berkeley: University of California Press, 1985); Patrick Harries, *Work, Culture, and Identity: Migrant Laborers in Mozambique and South Africa, 1860–1910* (Portsmouth, NH: Heinemann, 1994).

8. Robert Bates, *When Things Fell Apart: State Failure in Late-Century Africa* (Cambridge: Cambridge University Press, 2008), and Bates, *Prosperity and Violence: The Political Economy of Development* (New York: Norton, 2009); Paul Collier, *The Bottom Billion: Why the Poorest Countries Are Failing and What Can Be Done about It* (New York: Oxford University Press, 2008); Daron Acemoglu and James Robinson, *Why Nations Fail: The Origins of Power, Prosperity, and Poverty* (New York: Crown Business, 2013); and Thomas Piketty, *Capital in the Twenty-First Century* (Cambridge, MA: Belknap Press of Harvard University Press, 2014).

Bibliography

Interviews and Conversations

Abed, Musa, Nairobi, June 12, 2004
Abludahi, Mohammed, Nairobi, June 12, 2004
Atieno, Priscilla, Nairobi, July 1, 2008
Beba, Marita, Mombasa, July 3, 2009
Chege, Peter, Nairobi, June 12, 2004, and Kiambu, June 4, 2010
Gichuru, Mathew ("Toxic"), Nairobi, June 11, 13, 14, 15, 2009
Gichuru, Nancy, Nairobi, June 15, 2009
Imbuga, Mark, Nakuru, June 18, 2012
Kamali, Elizabeth, Kakamega, June 12, 2004
Kamau, Innocent, Nairobi, June 9, 2004
Kamau, James, Nairobi, July 2, 2005
Kamau, Joseph, Nairobi, July 3, 2009
Kamau, Moses, Nairobi, June 17, 2004
Karimu, Peter, Nairobi, November 2, 2004
Kariuki, Mary, Nairobi, June 8, 2004
Kariuki, Peter, Nairobi, July 2, 2008
Kasila, Ann, Nairobi, June 7, 2010
Kavitsa, Elena, Nairobi, April 10, 2014
Kefa, Marita, Kisumu, June 17, 2009
Keya, Janet, Nairobi, June 12, 13, 2009
Kimutai, Simon, Nairobi, June 11, 16, 2006, and phone conversation, May 12, 2014
Lukalo, Mathew, Nairobi, July 5, 2004
Lukova, Martin, Nairobi, June 12, 2008
Macharia, John, Nairobi, June 4, 9, 2009
Macharia, Philip, Nairobi, June 12, 2007
Maina, Eric, Nairobi, July 28, 2009
Maina, John, Nairobi, June 12, 2004; April 10, 2014

Maina, Mark, Nairobi, June 4, 2010
Makau, Henry, Nairobi, July 1, 3, 7, 2008
Mbugua, Dickson, Nairobi, June 7, 8, 2004
Muchira, John, Nairobi, July 1, 2008
Muite, Mary, Nairobi, June 7, 2009
Mungai, Samson, Nairobi, June 14, 19, 20, 2004
Mungai, Shem, Nairobi, June 12, 2007
Musira, Jane, Nairobi, June 18, 2005
Muteve, James, Nairobi, June 4, 6, 8, 2010
Muteve, Mariko, Nairobi, April 10, 2014
Mutisya, Mark, Nairobi, June 19, 2008
Mutiva, James, Nairobi, June 15, 2004
Mutori, Mark, Nairobi, June 7, 2004
Mutse, Karen, Kisumu, June 17, 2009
Mwangi, Kevin, Nairobi, July 5, 2004
Mwangi, Patrick, Kisumu, June 17, 2009
Mwaniki, Peter, Nairobi, July 28, 2009
Mwelesa, Peter, Kakamega, June 10, 2004
Mwendo, Timothy, Nairobi, June 20, 2008
Mweneka, Mary, Kakamega, June 12, 2004
Mwisha, Petronella, Kakamega, June 2, 2004
Nderi, Joseph Mwaura, Nairobi, June 12, 14, 15, 16, 18, and July 20, 2004
Ndoro, Jane, Kakamega, June 2, 2004
Ngochi, Priscilla, Nairobi, June 11, 13, 2006
Ngodi, Priscilla, Nairobi, November 2, 2004
Njenga, Jane, Nairobi, June 12, 2009
Njenga, John, Nairobi, June 6, 2008
Njenga, Mary, Kiambu, June 10, 2009
Njeri, Jane, Nairobi, July 3, 2009
Njonjo, Mary, Nairobi, June 7, 2010
Njoroge, James, Nairobi, March 6, 2005
Njuguna, Eric, Nairobi, June 2, 2008
Njuguna, Mary, Nairobi, June 18 and July 1, 2009
Njuguna, Samuel, Nairobi, June 23, 2004
Okwaro, Jasphat, Nairobi, June 20, 2005
Olei, James, Kisumu, June 17, 2009
Oremo, Matt, Nairobi, November 2, 2004
Otieno, Mary, Nairobi, November 2, 2004
Ouma, Grace, Nairobi, June 14, 2004
Ouma, Titus, Nairobi, June 9, 2009
Siringi, Peter, Nairobi, July 5, 2009
Thengz, Daddy, Nairobi, July 28, 29, 2008
Vurigwa, Melissa, Nairobi, November 18, 2012

Wanjiru, Charity, Nairobi, June 13, 15, 2004
Zewde, Ruth, Nairobi, June 12, 2004

Newspapers and Periodicals

Citizen
Commercial Motor
Drum
East African
The Guardian
Kenya Buzz
Nation
The Standard
The Star
True Love
VIVA
Weekly Review

Government Reports at the Kenya National Archives (KNA)

The National Assembly: House of Representatives Official Reports (Nairobi: Republic of Kenya, 1966, March 4–April 30; and 1967, 1969, 1970, September 27–October 24).
Republic of Kenya. *Development Plan 1989–1993*. Nairobi: Government Printer, 1989.
———. *Economic Survey*. Nairobi: Government Printer, 2008.
———. "Kenya Bus Services Ltd: Public Passenger Transport Services in Nairobi." Position paper presented to the Ministry of Transport and Communications, Kenya Bus Services Ltd., Nairobi, 1980.
———. *Kenya Government Economic Recovery Strategy for Wealth and Employment Creation 2003–2007*. Nairobi: Government Printer, 2003.
———. *Kenya Population Census 1989, Volume 1*. Nairobi: Government Printer, 1994.
———. *Laws of Kenya: The Employment Act, Chapter 226*. Nairobi: Government Printer, 1984.
———. *Laws of Kenya: The National Hospital Insurance Act, Chapter 255*. Nairobi: Government Printer, 1977.
———. *Laws of Kenya: The Regulation of Wages and Conditions of Employment Act, Chapter 229*. Nairobi: Government Printer, 1989.
———. *Laws of Kenya: The Trade Disputes Act, Chapter 234*. Nairobi: Government Printer, 1989.

———. *Laws of Kenya: The Trade Unions Act, Chapter 233*. Nairobi: Government Printer, 1984.

———. *Laws of Kenya: The Workmen's Compensation Act, Chapter 236*. Nairobi: Government Printer, 1988.

———. *National Development Plan, 1997–2001*. Nairobi: Government Printer, 1997.

———. *Report of the National Task Force on Police Reforms* (also known as the Ransley Report). Nairobi: Government Printer, 2009.

———. *Survey of Rural Non-Agricultural Enterprises*. Nairobi: Central Bureau of Statistics, 1985.

Theses and Dissertations

Agoki, George Samuel. "Characteristics of Road Traffic Accidents in Kenya." PhD diss., University of Nairobi, 1988.

Chebichi, Joselyne. "The 'Legality' of Illegal Somali Migrants in Eastleigh Estate in Nairobi, Kenya." PhD diss., Kenyatta University, 2010.

Hundle, Anneeth Kaur. "The Politics of (In)security: Reconstructing African-Asian Relations, Citizenship, and Community in Post-Expulsion Uganda." PhD diss., Department of Anthropology, University of Michigan, 2013.

Jarabi, B. O. "Intra-Urban Mobility and Urban Transportation: A Case Study of Nairobi City, Kenya." Master's thesis, Institute of Population Studies, University of Nairobi, 1982.

Mbugua, Catherine Wangeci. "A Sociological Study on Commuters' Compliance to the new Traffic Regulations." Master's diss., University of Nairobi, 2009.

Muchilwa, Z. A. "Matatu Operators' Responses to Changing Government Regulations." MBA thesis, University of Nairobi, 2004.

Mumenya, A. T. "Perception by Stakeholders of New Traffic Regulations in Kenya." MBA thesis, University of Nairobi, 2005.

Mũngai, Mbũgua wa. "Identity Politics in Matatu Folklore." PhD diss., Hebrew University of Jerusalem, 2003.

Ng'ang'a, H. Nyaki. "Determinants of Demand for Insurance Services in the Matatu Industry: A Case Study of ENK SACCO." MBA thesis, University of Nairobi, 2012.

Ogonda, R. Timothy. "The Development of Road System in Kenya." PhD diss., University of Nairobi, 1986.

Onchiri, Haron Oganda. "Graffiti Perspective on Matatus in Kenya: A Lexico-Pragmatic Theory." Master's thesis, University of Nairobi, 2010.

Opiyo, Tom. "The Metamorphosis of Kenya Bus Services Limited in the Provision of Urban Transportation in Nairobi." Master's thesis, University of Nairobi, Department of Civil Engineering, 2003.

Orang'i, Amos. "Factors Hindering the Performance of Matatu Business: A Case of Matatu Owner in Nairobi." Master's diss., Jomo Kenyatta University of Agriculture and Technology, 2006.

Osende, K. "*Sheng*: An Investigation into the Social and Structural Aspects of an Evolving Language." Bachelor's thesis, University of Nairobi, 1986.

Samper, David. "Talking Sheng: The Role of a Hybrid Language in the Construction of Identity and Youth Culture in Nairobi, Kenya." PhD diss., Anthropology Department, University of Pennsylvania, 2001.

Books and Articles

Abdulazizi, M., and K. Osinde. "*Sheng and* English in Nairobi." *International Journal of the Sociology of Language* 125 (1997): 1–21.

Acemoglu, Daron, and James Robinson. *Why Nations Fail: The Origins of Power, Prosperity, and Poverty.* New York: Crown Business, 2012.

Acemoglu, Daron, James A. Robinson, and Thierry Verdier. "Kleptocracy and Divide-and-Rule: A Model of Personal Rule." Alfred Marshall Lecture, Massachusetts Institute of Technology, 2004.

Aduwo, G. O. "The Role, Efficiency, and Quality of Service of the Matatu Mode of Public Transportation in Nairobi, Kenya." *A Geographical Analysis* (1990): 1–8.

———. "Urban Transport System: A Case of the Matatu Mode of Transport in the City of Nairobi, Kenya." *African Urban Quarterly* 7, nos. 1–2 (1992): 120–29.

Agadjanian, V. "Men Doing 'Women's Work': Masculinity and Gender Relations among Street Vendors in Maputo, Mozambique." *Journal of Men's Studies* 10 (2002): 329–42.

Aiyar, Sana. "Anticolonial Homelands across the Indian Ocean: The Politics of the Indian Diaspora in Kenya c. 1930–1950." *American Historical Review* 116, no. 4 (2011): 987–1013.

———. "Empire, Race, and the Indians in Colonial Kenya's Contested Public Political Sphere from 1919–1923." *Africa* 81, no. 1 (2011): 132–54.

———. *Indians in Kenya: The Politics of Diaspora.* Cambridge, MA: Harvard University Press, 2015.

Akyeampong, Emmanuel. *Drink, Power, and Colonial Change: A Social History of Alcohol in Ghana.* Portsmouth, NH: Heinemann, 1996.

Akyeampong, Emmanuel, Robert H. Bates, Nathan Nunn, and James A. Robinson, eds. *Africa's Development in Historical Perspective.* Cambridge: Cambridge University Press, 2014.

Anderson, David. "Corruption at City Hall: African Housing and Urban Development in Colonial Nairobi." *Azania Archaeological Research in Africa* 36–37, no. 1 (2001): 36–57.

——. *Histories of the Hanged: The Dirty War in Kenya and the End of the Empire.* New York: Norton, 2005.

——. "Vigilantes, Violence, and the Politics of Public Order in Kenya." *African Affairs* 101, no. 405 (2002): 531–55.

Ange, Marc. *In the Metro.* Translated by Tom Conley. Minneapolis: University of Minnesota Press, 2002.

Angus, Calder. "Meja Mwangi's Novels." In *The Writing of East and Central Africa*, edited by G. D. Killam, 23–44. London: Heinemann, 1984.

Ankeny, Nesmith. *Poker Strategy: Winning with Game Theory.* New York: Basic Books, 1981.

Appiah, Kwame Anthony. *Cosmopolitanism: Ethics in a World of Strangers.* New York: Norton, 2006.

Arunga, June, and Billy Kahora. "The Cell Phone Revolution in Kenya." London: International Policy Network, 2007.

Atieno Odhiambo, E. S. "Democracy and the Ideology of Order in Kenya." In *The Political Economy of Kenya*, edited by Michael G. Schatzberg, 177–201. New York: Praeger, 1987.

——. "From the 'English Country Garden' to Makambo Mibale: Popular Culture in Kenya in the Mid-Nineteen Sixties." In *Urban Legends, Colonial Myths: Popular Culture and Literature in East Africa*, edited by James Ogude and Joyce Nyairo, 155–72. Trenton, NJ: Africa World Press, 2007.

——. "Kula Raha: Gendered Discourses and the Contours of Leisure in Nairobi." In *The Urban Experience in Eastern Africa, c. 1750–2000*, edited by Andrew Burton, 254–64. Nairobi: British Institute in Eastern Africa, 2002.

——. *Siasa: Politics and Nationalism in East Africa, 1905–1939.* Nairobi: Kenya Literature Bureau, 1981.

Atkinson, G. Anthony. "African Housing." *African Affairs* 49, no. 4 (1950): 228–37.

Austin, Gareth. *Labor, Land, and Capital in Ghana: From Slavery to Free Labor in Asante, 1807–1956.* Rochester, NY: University of Rochester Press, 2005.

Avinash K. Dixit, and Barry Nalebuff. *The Art of Strategy: A Game Theorist's Guide to Success in Business and Life.* New York: W. W. Norton, 2010.

Axelrod, Robert. *The Evolution of Cooperation.* New York: Basic Books, 1984.

Baker, T., and R. Nelson. "Creating Something from Nothing: Resource Construction through Entrepreneurial Bricolage." *Administrative Science Quarterly* 50, no. 2 (2005): 329–66.

Baker, Ted., Anne S. Miner, and Dale T. Eesley. "Improvising Firms: Bricolage, Account Giving, and Improvisational Competencies in the Founding Process." *Research Policy* 32, no. 2 (2003): 255–76.

Balachandran, P. K. "An Embattled Community: Asians in East Africa Today." *African Affairs* 80, no. 320 (1981): 317–25.

Banerjee, Abhijit. *Poor Economics: A Radical Rethinking of the Way to Fight Global Poverty.* New York: PublicAffairs, 2011.

Barkan, Joel. "Kenya after Moi." *Foreign Affairs* 83 (2004): 87–100.

Bates, Robert. *Beyond the Miracle of Market: The Political Economy of Agrarian Development in Kenya*. Cambridge: Cambridge University Press, 2005.

———. *Markets and State in Tropical Africa: The Political Basis of Agricultural Policies*. Berkeley: University of California Press, 2014.

———. *Prosperity and Violence: The Political Economy of Development*. New York: Norton, 2008.

———. *When Things Fell Apart: State Failure in Late-Century Africa*. Cambridge: Cambridge University Press, 2008.

Bayart, Jean-François. *The State in Africa: Politics of the Belly*. 2nd ed. Cambridge: Polity, 2009.

Beck, K. "The Art of Truck Modding on the Nile (Sudan): An Attempt to Trace Creativity." In *The Speed of Change: Motor Vehicles and People in Africa, 1890–2000*, edited by Jan-Bart Gewald, Sabine Luning, and Klaas van Walraven, 151–73. Leiden: Brill, 2009.

Beck, Rose M. "Texts on Textiles: Proverbiality as Characteristic of Equivocal Communication at the East African Coast (Swahili)." *Journal of African Cultural Studies* 9 (2005): 132–60.

Belluci, Stefano, and Massimo Zaccaria. "Engine of Change: A Social History of Car-Mechanics Sector in the Horn of Africa." In *Transforming Innovations in Africa*, edited by Jan-Bart Gewald, André Leliveld, and Iva Peša, 237–56. Leiden: Brill, 2012.

Berman, Jonathan. *Success in Africa: CEO Insights from a Continent*. New York: Bibliomotion, 2013.

Berry, Sara S. *Fathers Work for Their Sons: Accumulation, Mobility, and Class Formation in an Extended Yoruba Community*. Berkeley: University of California Press, 1985.

Beuving, J. "Cotonou's Klondike: African Traders and Second-Hand Car Markets in Bénin." *Journal of Modern African Studies* 42 (2004): 511–37.

———. "Lebanese Traders in Cotonou: A Socio-Cultural Analysis of Economic Mobility and Capital Accumulation." *Africa* 76 (2006): 324–51.

———. "Nigerien Second-Hand Car Traders in Cotonou: A Sociocultural Analysis of Economic Decision-Making." *African Affairs* 105 (2006): 353–73.

———. "Playing Pool along the Shores of Lake Victoria: Fishermen, Careers and Capital Accumulation in the Ugandan Nile Perch Busines." *Africa* 80 (2010): 224–48.

———. "Striking Gold in Cotonou? Three Cases of Entrepreneurship in the Euro-West African Second-Hand Car Trade in Benin." In *The Speed of Change: Motor Vehicles and People in Africa, 1890–2000*, edited by Jan-Bart Gewald, Sabine Luning, and Klaas van Walraven, 127–47. Leiden: Brill, 2009.

Bhagwati, Jagdish, and Arvind Panagariya. *Why Growth Matters: How Economic Growth in India Reduced Poverty and the Lessons for Other Developing Countries*. New York: PublicAffairs, 2014.

Bhide, A. V. "Bootstrap Finance: The Art of Start-Ups." *Harvard Business Review* 70 (1992): 109–17.

Bickford-Smith, Vivian. *The Emergence of the South African Metropolis: Cities and Identities in the Twentieth Century.* Cambridge: Cambridge University Press, 2016.

Bierwirth, C. "The Lebanese Communities of Côte d'Ivoire." *African Affairs* 98 (1999): 79–99.

Boo, Katherine. *Behind the Beautiful Forevers: Life, Death, and Hope in Mumbai Undercity.* New York: Random House, 2012.

Borgaza, C., and J. Defourny. *The Emergence of Social Enterprise.* New York: Routledge, 2001.

Bourdieu, Pierre. *The Logic of Practice.* Translated by Richard Nice. Stanford, CA: Stanford University Press, 1990.

Brams, Steven. *Game Theory and Politics.* New York: Free Press, 1979.

Branch, Daniel. *Kenya: Between Hope and Despair, 1963–2011.* New Haven, CT: Yale University Press, 2011.

Branch, Daniel, and Nicholas Cheeseman. "The Politics of Control in Kenya: Understanding the Bureaucratic-Executive State, 1952–78." *Review of African Political Economy* 33 (2006): 72–99.

Bridenthal, Renate. "The Hidden History of Crime, Corruption, and States: An Introduction." *Journal of Social History* 45, no. 3, special issue (2012): 575–81.

Brooks, Michael. *Subway City: Riding the Trains, Reading New York.* New Brunswick, NJ: Rutgers University Press, 1997.

Brown, A., M. Lyons, and I. Dankoco. "Street Traders and the Emerging Spaces for Urban Voice and Citizenship in African Cities." *Urban Studies* 47 (2010): 666–83.

Brownhill, L. S., and T. E. Turner. "Feminism in the Mau Mau Resurgence." *Journal of Asian and African Studies* 23 (2004): 95–117.

Bujra, J. M. "'Women Entrepreneurs' of Early Nairobi." *Canadian Journal of African Studies* 9 (1975): 213–34.

Bwisa, H. M., and F. M. Nafukho. *Learning Entrepreneurship through Indigenous Knowledge.* Oakville, ON: Nsemia Publishers, 2012.

Cable, Vincent. "The Asians of Kenya." *African Affairs* 68, no. 272 (1969): 218–31.

Campbell, Elizabeth H. "Urban Refugees in Nairobi: Problems of Protection, Mechanisms of Survival, and Possibilities for Integration." *Journal of Refugee Studies* 19 (2006): 396–413.

Carrier, Neil. "The Hilux and the 'Body Thrower' *Khat* Transporters in Kenya." In *The Speed of Change: Motor Vehicles and People in Africa, 1890–2000,* edited by Jan-Bart Gewald, Sabine Luning, and Klaas van Walraven, 175–90. Leiden: Brill, 2009.

———. *Little Mogadishu: Eastleigh, Nairobi's Global Somali Hub.* Oxford: Oxford University Press, 2016.

———. "The Need for Speed: Contrasting Time Frames in the Social Life of Kenyan of *Miraa.*" *Africa* 75 (2005): 539–58.

Carrier, Neil, and Emma Lochery. "Missing States? Somali Trade Networks and the Eastleigh Transformation." *Journal of Eastern African Studies* 7, no. 2 (2013): 334–52.

Certeau, Michel de. *The Practice of Everyday Life*. Translated by Steven Rendall. Berkeley: University of California Press, 2011.

Cervero, Robert. *Suburban Gridlock*. Washington, DC: Transaction, 2013.

———. *The Transit Metropolis: A Global Inquiry*. Washington, DC: Island Press, 1998.

Chabal, Patrick, and Jean-Pascal Daloz. *Africa Works: Disorder as a Political Instrument*. Bloomington: Indiana University Press, 1999.

Charton-Bigot, Hélène, and Deyssi Rodriguez-Torres, eds. *Nairobi Today: The Paradox of a Fragmented City*. Nairobi: Mkuki na Nyota Publishers, 2010.

Chege, Michael. "Introducing Race as a Variable into the Political Economy of Kenya Debate: An Incendiary Idea." *African Affairs* 97, no. 387 (1998): 209–30.

Chitere, Preston O., and Thomas N. Kibua. "Efforts to Improve Road Safety in Kenya: Achievements and Limitations of Reforms in the Matatu Industry." Institute of Policy Analysis and Research (IPAR), 2005.

Churchill, Winston Spenser. *My African Journey*. London: Hodder and Stoughton, 1908.

Clark, Gracia. *African Market Women: Seven Life Stories from Ghana*. Bloomington: Indiana University Press, 2010.

———. *Onions Are My Husband: Survival and Accumulation by West African Women*. Chicago: University of Chicago Press, 1994.

Cleaver, F. "Reinventing Institutions: Bricolage and the Social Embeddedness of Natural Resource Management." *European Journal of Development Research* 11, no. 1 (2002): 65–91.

Cole, Teju. *Every Day Is for the Thief*. New York: Random House, 2014.

Collier, Paul. *The Bottom Billion: Why the Poorest Countries Are Failing and What Can Be Done about It*. Oxford: Oxford University Press, 2008.

———. *Exodus: Immigration and Multiculturalism in the 21st Century*. London: Allen Lane, 2009.

Comaroff, Jean, and John Comaroff. "Law and Disorder in the Post-Colony: An Introduction." In *Law and Disorder in the Postcolony*, edited by J. Comaroff and J. Comaroff, 1–56. Chicago: University of Chicago Press, 2009.

Conning, Jonathan, and J. A. Robinson. "Property Rights and the Political Organization of Agriculture." *Journal of Development Economics* 82 (2007): 416–47.

Connolly, Nathan. *A World More Concrete: Real Estate and the Remaking of Jim Crow South Florida*. Chicago: University of Chicago Press, 2014.

Cooper, Frederick. *On the African Waterfront: Urban Disorder and Transformation of Work in Colonial Mombasa*. New Haven, CT: Yale University Press, 1987.

———. *Struggle for the City: Migrant Labor, Capital, and the State in Urban Africa*. London: Sage, 1989.

Dart, R. "The Legitimacy of Social Enterprise." *Non-Profit Management and Leadership* 14, no. 2 (2004): 411–24.

Date-Bah, E. "The Inscriptions of the Vehicles of Ghanaian Commercial Drivers: A Sociological Analysis." *Journal of Modern African Studies* 18 (1980): 525–31.

Dickens, Charles. *Night Walk*. London: Penguin Classics, 2010.

Di Domenico M., H. Haugh, and P. Tracey. "Social Bricolage: Theorizing Social Value Creation in Social Enterprises." *Entrepreneurship Theory and Practice* 34, no. 2 (2010): 681–703.

Dixit, Avinash K., and Barry Nalebuff. *The Art of Strategy: A Game Theorist's Guide to Success in Business and Life*. New York: W. W. Norton, 2010.

———. *Thinking Strategically: A Competitive Edge in Business, Politics, and Everyday Life*. New York: W. W. Norton, 1991.

Dixit, Avinash, and Susan Skeath. *Games of Strategy*. New York: W. W. Norton, 2004.

Dow, Thomas. "Attitudes toward Family Size and Family Planning in Nairobi." *Demography* 4, no. 2 (1967): 780–97.

Easterly, William. *The Tyranny of Experts: Economists, Dictators, and the Forgotten Rights of the Poor*. New York: Basic Books, 2014.

———. *The White Man's Burden: Why the West's Efforts to Aid the Rest Have Done So Much Harm and So Little Good*. New York: Penguin 2006.

Eggers, William D. *The Solution Revolution: How Business, Government, and Social Enterprises Are Teaming Up to Solve Society's Toughest Problems*. Cambridge, MA: Harvard Business Review Press, 2013.

Eley, Geoff. *Crooked Line: From Cultural History to the History of Society*. Ann Arbor: University of Michigan Press, 2005.

Elias, Jamal. *On Wings of Diesel: Trucks, Identity, and Culture in Pakistan*. New York: Oneworld, 2011.

———. "Truck Decoration and Religious Identity: Material Culture and Social Function in Pakistan." *Material Religion: The Journal of Objects, Art, and Beliefs* 3 (2005): 17–38.

Ensminger, Jean. *Making a Market: The Institutional Transformation of an African Society*. Cambridge: Cambridge University Press, 1992.

Fafchamps, Marcel. *Market Institutions in Sub-Saharan Africa: Theory and Evidence*. Cambridge, MA: MIT Press, 2004.

———. *Rural Poverty, Risk, and Development*. New York: Edward Elgar, 2004.

Fahnbulleh, Miatta. "In Search of Economic Development in Kenya: Colonial Legacies and Post-Independence Realities." *Review of African Political Economy* 33 (2006): 34–51.

Fair, Laura. *Pastimes and Politics: Culture, Community, and Identity in Post-Abolition Zanzibar*. Oxford: James Currey, 2001.

———. *Reel Pleasures: The Business and Pleasures of Movie-Going in Twentieth-Century Urban Tanzania*. Athens: Ohio University Press, forthcoming.

Ferguson, James. *Expectations of Modernity: Myths and Meanings of Urban Life on the Zambian Copperbelt*. Berkeley: University of California Press, 1997.

———. *Give a Man a Fish: Reflections on the New Politics of Distribution*. Durham, NC: Duke University Press, 2015.

Fox, James. *White Mischief: The Murder of Lord Erroll*. London: Vintage, 1998.

Frederiksen, Bodil Folke. "African Women and Their Colonisation of Nairobi: Representations and Realities," *Azania: Archaeological Research in Africa* 36–37, no. 1 (2001): 229.

———. "Joe: The Sweetest Reading in Africa; Documentation and Discussion of a Popular Magazine in Kenya." *African Languages and Cultures* 4 (1991): 135–55.

———. "Mungiki, Vernacular Organization, and Political Society in Kenya." *Development and Change* 41, no. 6 (2010): 1065–89.

———. "Print, Newspapers, and Audiences in Colonial Kenya: African and Indian Improvement, Protest and Connections." *Africa* 81, no. 1 (2011): 34–52.

Freedman, Alisa. "Commuting Gazes: Schoolgirls, Salary Men, and Electric Trains in Tokyo." *Journal of Transport History* 23 (2001): 23–36.

French, Howard. *China's Second Continent: How a Million Migrants Are Building a New Empire in Africa*. New York: Knopf, 2014.

Furedi, Frank. "The Development of Anti-Asian Opinion among Africans in Nakuru District, Kenya," *African Affairs* 73, no. 2929 (1974): 347–58.

Gambetta, Diego. *The Sicilian Mafia: The Business of Private Protection*. Cambridge, MA: Harvard University Press, 1996.

Gebissa, Ezekiel. *The Leaf of Allah: Khat and Agricultural Transformation in Hararge, Ethiopia, 1875–1991*. Athens: Ohio University Press, 2004.

Gebissa, Ezekiel, ed. *Taking the Place of Food: Khat in Ethiopia*. Trenton, NJ: Red Sea Press, 2010.

Gecaga, M. G. "Religious Movements and Democratisation in Kenya: Between the Sacred and the Profane." In *Kenya: The Struggle for Democracy*, edited by G. R. Murunga and S. W. Nasong'o, 58–89. Dakar: Codesria Books, 2007.

Geertz, Clifford. "Thick Description: Toward an Interpretive Theory of Culture." In *The Interpretation of Cultures: Selected Essays*, 3–30. New York: Basic Books, 1973.

Geest, Sjaak van der. "'Anyway!' Lorry Inscriptions in Ghana." In *The Speed of Change: Motor Vehicles and People in Africa, 1890–2000*, edited by Jan-Bart Gewald, Sabine Luning, and Klaas van Walraven. Leiden: Brill, 2009.

———. "Between Death and Funeral: Mortuaries and the Exploitation of Liminality in Kwahu, Ghana." *Africa* 76 (2006): 485–501.

Gerber, Alan, Donald Green, and Christopher W. Larimer. "Social Pressure and Voter Turnout: Evidence from a Large-Scale Field Experiment." *American Political Science Review* 102 (2008): 33–48.

Gifford, Paul. *Christianity, Development, and Modernity in Africa*. Oxford: Oxford University Press, 2016.

Gilbert, Jeremy. "What Kind of Thing Is Neoliberalism?" *New Formations* 80/81 (2013): 7–22.

Gilroy, Paul. "Driving While Black." In *Car Cultures*, edited by Daniel Miller, 67–89. New York: Berg, 2001.

Gimode, E. A. "An Anatomy of Violent Crime and Insecurity in Kenya: The Case of Nairobi, 1985–1999." *Africa Development* 26, no. 1/2 (2001): 295–335.

Gingrich, Andre, and Richard G. Fox. *Anthropology, by Comparison*. New York: Routledge, 2002.

Girard, René. *The Scapegoat*. Translated by Yvonne Freccero. Baltimore: Johns Hopkins University Press, 1986.

Glaser, Clive. *Bo-Tsotsi: The Youth Gangs of Soweto, 1935–1976*. Portsmouth, NH: Heinemann, 2000.

Godia, George. *Understanding Nyayo: Principles and Policies in Contemporary Kenya*. Nairobi: Transafrica, 1984.

Goodale, Greg. *Sonic Persuasion: Reading Sound in the Recorded Age*. Urbana: University of Illinois Press, 2011.

Gough, K. V., A. G. Tipple, and M. Napier. "Making a Living in African Cities: The Role of Home-Based Enterprises in Accra and Pretoria." *International Planning Studies* 8 (2003): 253–77.

Graebner, Werner. Introduction to *Sokomoko: Popular Culture in East Africa*. Amsterdam: Rodopi, 1992.

Graeff, Jennifer. "The Organization and Future of the Matatu Industry in Nairobi, Kenya." Center for Sustainable Urban Development—Earth Institute, Columbia University, New York, 2009.

Granqvist, Raoul J. *The Bulldozer and the Word: Culture at Work in Postcolonial Nairobi*. Washington, DC: Peter Lang, 2004.

Green, Reginald Herbold. "*Khatt* and the Realities of Somalis: Historic, Social, Household, Political, and Economic." *Review of African Political Economy* 79 (1999): 33–49.

Gupta, A. "Blurred Boundaries: The Discourse of Corruption, the Culture of Politics and the Imagined State." *American Ethnologist* 22 (1995): 375–402.

Gurak, Laura. *Cyberliteracy: Navigating the Internet with Awareness*. New Haven, CT: Yale University Press, 2003.

Guyer, Jane. *Legacies, Logics, Logistics: Essays in the Anthropology of the Platform Economy*. Chicago: University of Chicago Press, 2016.

———. *Marginal Gains: Monetary Transactions in Atlantic Africa*. Chicago: University of Chicago Press, 2004.

———. "Wealth in People / Wealth in Things: An Introduction." *Journal of African History* 36, no. 1 (1995): 83–90.

Habyarimana, James, and William Jack. "Heckle and Chide: Results of a Randomized Road Safety Intervention in Kenya." Center for Global Development, Working Paper No. 169, April 2009, Washington, DC.

———. "State vs. Consumer Regulation: An Evaluation of Two Road Safety Interventions in Kenya." National Bureau of Economic Research Working Paper No. 18378, September 2012, Cambridge, MA.

Hagedorn, J. *A World of Gangs: Armed Young Men and Gangsta Culture*. Minneapolis: University of Minnesota Press, 2008.

Hake, Andrew. *African Metropolis: Nairobi's Self-Help City*. New York: St. Martin's Press, 1977.

Hannerz, Ulf. "Sophiatown: The View from Afar." *Journal of South African Studies* 20, no. 2 (1994): 181–93.

Hansen, K. T. *Salaula: The World of Secondhand Clothing and Zambia*. Chicago: University of Chicago Press, 2000.

———. "Who Rules the Streets? The Politics of Vending Space in Lusaka." In *Reconsidering Informality: Perspectives from Urban Africa*, edited by K. T. Hansen and M. Vaa, 62–80. Uppsala: Nordiska Afrikainstitute, 2004.

Hansen, T. B., and O. Verkaaik. "Urban Charisma: On Everyday Mythologies in the City." *Critique of Anthropology* 29 (2009): 5–26.

Hardy, Ronald. *The Iron Snake*. London: Collins, 1965.

Harries, Patrick. *Work, Culture, and Identity: Migrant Laborers in Mozambique and South Africa, 1860–1910*. Portsmouth, NH: Heinemann, 1994.

Harrington, Ralph. "Beyond the Bathing Belle: Images of Women in Interwar Railway Publicity." *Journal of Transport History* 25 (2007): 22–45.

Haugerud, Angelique. *The Culture of Politics in Modern Kenya*. Cambridge: Cambridge University Press, 1995.

Hayward, Helen. *The Enigma of V. S. Naipaul: Sources and Contexts*. New York: Palgrave Macmillan, 2002.

Heap, Shaun Hargreaves, and Yanis Varoufakis. *Game Theory: A Critical Introduction*. London: Routledge, 1995.

Hester, Elizabeth J. *Nollywood and Nigerian Cinema: A Selective Bibliography of Dissertations and Theses*. New York: CreateSpace Independent Publishing Platform, 2016.

Hill, Mervyn. *Permanent Way: The Story of the Kenya and Uganda Railway*. Nairobi: Longman, 1948.

Himbara, David. *Kenyan Capitalists, the State, and Development*. London: East African Education Publishers, 1994.

Hirsch, Jennifer S., Holly Wardlow, Daniel Jordan Smith, Harriet M. Phinney, Shanti Parikh, and Constance A. Nathanson. *The Secret: Love, Marriage, and HIV*. Nashville: Vanderbilt University Press, 2009.

Hirschman, Albert O. *The Passions and the Interests: Political Arguments for Capitalism before Its Triumph*. Princeton, NJ: Princeton University Press 1997.

Hirschman Albert O., and Jeremy Adelman. *The Essential Hirschman*. Princeton, NJ: Princeton University Press, 2013.

Hirst, Terry, with Davinder Lamba. *The Struggle for Nairobi*. Nairobi: Mazingira Institute, 1994.

Ho, Engseng. *The Graves of Tarim: Genealogy and Mobility across the Indian Ocean*. Berkeley: University of California Press, 2006.

Hofstader, Douglas. "Mathamagical Themas." *Scientific American* (May 1983): 16–26.

Holmquist, F. W., F. S. Weaver, and M. D. Ford. "The Structural Development of Kenya's Political Economy." *African Studies Review* 37 (1994): 69–105.

Holness, S., E. Louis Nel, and J. A. Binns. "The Changing Nature of Informal Street Trading in Post-Apartheid South Africa: The Case of East London's Central Business District." *Urban Forum* 10 (1999): 284–302.

Hopkins, A. G. "The New Economic History of Africa." *Journal of African History* 20, no. 2 (2009): 155–77.

Hornsby, Charles. *Kenya: A History since Independence.* New York: I. B. Tauris, 2012.

House-Soremekun, Bessie, and Toyin Falola. *Globalization and Sustainable Development in Africa.* Rochester, NY: University of Rochester Press, 2016.

Hull, Elizabeth, and Deborah James. "Introduction: Popular Economies in South Africa." *Africa* 82, no. 1 (2012): 1–19.

Jalloh, Alusine. *African Entrepreneurship: Muslim Fula Merchants in Sierra Leone.* Athens: Ohio University Center for International Studies, 1999.

———. "Muslim Fula Business Elites and Politics in Sierra Leone." *African Economic History* 35 (2006): 89–104.

Jalloh, Alusine, and Toyin Falola. *Black Business and Economic Power.* Rochester, NY: University of Rochester Press, 2002.

Jan-Knighton, B. "Mungiki Madness." In *Religion and Politics in Kenya: Essays in Honor of a Meddlesome Priest*, edited by B. Knighton, 223–51. New York: Palgrave Macmillan, 2009.

Jensen, Steffen. *Gangs, Politics, and Dignity in Cape Town.* Oxford: James Currey, 2008.

Johansson, Lars. *In the Shadow of Neocolonialism: A Study of Meja Mwangi's Novels, 1973–1990.* Umeå, Sweden: University of Umeå, 1990.

Johnston, Les. *The Rebirth of Private Policing.* London: Routledge, 1992.

Jordan, J. W. "The Role of Segregation for Fun and Profit: The Daily Behaviour of the West African Lorry Driver." *Africa* 48 (1978): 30–46.

Kagwanja, Peter Mwangi. "Facing Mount Kenya or Facing Mecca? The Mungiki, Ethnic Violence, and the Politics of the Moi Succession in Kenya, 1987–2002." *African Affairs* 102 (2003): 25–49.

———. "Investing in Asylum: Ethiopian Forced Migrants and the Matatu Industry in Nairobi." *Les Cahiers de l'IFRA* 10 (1998): 51–69.

———. "'Power to *Uhuru*': Youth Identity and Generational Politics in Kenya's 2002 Elections." *African Affairs* 105, no. 418 (2006): 51–76.

Kahora, Billy. "Buru Buru." *Chimurenga* (September 23, 2014): 5–10.

Kanneworff, Anna Betsy. "'These Dreadlocked Gangsters': The Mungiki as Dramatic Actors in Kenya's Public Arena; From Protest to Political Action?" In *Dilemmas of Development*, edited by Jon Abbink and Andre van Dokkum, 115–30. Leiden: African Studies Center, 2008.

Kanogo, Tabitha. *Squatters and the Roots of Mau Mau, 1905–63.* Athens: Ohio University Press, 1989.

Kantai, Parselelo. "The Rise of Somali Capital." *Chimurenga* 1 (2013): 1–19.

Karume, Njenga. *Beyond Expectations: From Charcoal to Gold.* Nairobi: Kenway Publications, 2009.

Kayongo-Male, D. "Slum and Squatter Settlements in Kenya." In *Slum and Squatters Settlements in Sub-Saharan Africa*, edited by R. A. Obudho and C. C. Mhlanga. New York: Praeger, 1988.

Kehinde, Ayo. "Post-Independence Disillusionment in Contemporary African Fiction: The Example of Meja Mwangi's *Kill Me Quick*." *Nordic Journal of African Studies* 13 (2004): 228–41.

Kennedy, Randy. *Subwayland: Adventures in the Land Beneath New York*. New York: St. Martin's Griffin, 2004.

Keynes, John Maynard. *The General Theory of Employment, Interest, and Money*. New York: CreateSpace Independent Publishing Platform, 2011.

Khayesi, M. "Rural Household Travel Characteristics: The Case of Kakamega District." *Journal of Eastern African Research and Development* 23 (1993): 88–105.

———. "Struggle for Socio-Economic Niche and Control in the Matatu Industry in Kenya." *DPMN Bulletin* 9, no. 2 (2002): 1–6.

Khayesi, M., H. Monheim, and J. M. Nebe. 2010. "Negotiating 'Streets for All' in Urban Transport Planning: The Case for Pedestrians, Cyclists, and Street Vendors in Nairobi, Kenya." *Antipode* 42 (2010):103–26.

Khayesi, Meleckidzedeck, Frederick Muyia Nafukho, and Joyce Kemuma. *Informal Public Transport in Practice: Matatu Entrepreneurship*. Burlington, VT: Ashgate, 2014.

Khosa, M. M. "Routes, Ranks, and Rebels: Feuding in the Taxi Revolution." *Journal of South African Studies* 18 (1991): 232–51.

———. "Sisters on Slippery Wheels: Women Taxi Drivers in South Africa." *Transformations* 33 (1997): 18–33.

———. "Transport and Popular Struggles in South Africa." *Antipode* 27 (1995): 167–88.

———. "Transport and the 'Taxi Mafia' in South Africa." *Urban Age* 2 (1993): 8–9.

Kilbride, Philip, Collette Suda, and Enos Njeru. *Street Children in Kenya: Voices of Children in Search of a Childhood*. Westport, CT: Bergin and Garvey, 2000.

Kimani, S. M. "The Structure of Land Ownership in Nairobi." *Revue Canadienne des Études Africaines* 6, no. 3 (1972): 379–402.

King, Kenneth. *Jua Kali Kenya: Change and Development in an Informal Economy, 1960–1995*. Athens: Ohio University Press, 1996.

Kioy, Deborah. *Matatu Entrepreneurs: A Study on Investors in Kenya's Informal Transport Business*. Saarbrücken, Germany: Lambert Academic Publishing, 2011.

Klaeger, Gabriel. "Ethnographies of the Road." *Africa* 83 (2013).

———. "Religion on the Road: The Spiritual Experience of Road Travel in Ghana." In *The Speed of Change: Motor Vehicles and People in Africa, 1890–2000*, edited by Jan-Bart Gewald, Sabine Luning, and Klaas van Walraven, 212–31. Leiden: Brill, 2009.

Klopp, Jacqueline. "Remembering the Muoroto Uprising: Slum Demolitions, Land, and Democratization in Kenya." *African Studies* 67 (2008): 295–314.
———. "Towards a Political Economy of Transport Policy and Practice in Nairobi." *Urban Forum* 23 (2012): 1–12.
Klute, George. "Modern Chariots: Speed and Mobility in Contemporary Small Waras in the Sahara." In *The Speed of Change: Motor Vehicles and People in Africa, 1890–2000*, edited by Jan-Bart Gewald, Sabine Luning, and Klaas van Walraven, 65–91. Leiden: Brill, 2009.
Krause, Monika. *The Good Project: Humanitarian Relief NGOs and the Fragmentation of Reason.* Chicago: University of Chicago Press, 2014.
Kreps, David, Robert Wilson, Paul Milgrom, and John Roberts. "Rational Cooperation in the Finitely Repeated Prisoners' Dilemma." *Journal of Economic Theory* 27 (August 1982): 245–52.
Kyei, Kojo, and Hannah Schreckenbach. *No Time to Die.* Accra: Catholic Press, 1976.
Kyle, Keith. "Gandhi, Harry Thuku, and Early Kenyan Nationalism." *Transition* 27 (1966): 16–22.
Kynoch, Gary. *We Are Fighting the World: A History of Maraesha Gangs in South Africa, 1947–1999.* Athens: Ohio University Press, 2005.
Lambsdorff, Johann Graf. *The Institutional Economics of Corruption and Reform: Theory and Policy.* Cambridge: Cambridge University Press, 2007.
Lawuyi, O. B. "The World of the Yoruba Taxi Driver: An Interpretive Approach to Vehicle Slogans." *Africa* 58 (1988): 1–13.
Lazarus, Neil. "Great Expectations and After: The Politics of Postcolonialism in African Fiction." *Social Text* 2, no. 4 (2004): 49–63.
Lee, Rebecca. "Death 'On the Move': Funerals, Entrepreneurs, and the Rural-Urban Nexus in South Africa." *Africa* 81 (2011): 226–47.
Lee-Smith, D. "Urban Management in Nairobi: A Case Study of the Matatu Mode of Public Transport." In *African Cities in Crisis: Managing Rapid Urban Growth*, edited by R. Stren and R. White, 276–304. Boulder, CO: Westview Press, 1989.
Lewis, G. H. "The Philosophy of the Street in Ghana: Mammy Wagons and Their Mottos: A Research Agenda." *Journal of Popular Culture* 32 (1999): 165–69.
Leys, Colin. *Underdevelopment in Kenya: The Political Economy of Neocolonialism, 1964–1971.* Berkeley: University of California Press, 1975.
Libecap, Gary. *Contracting for Property Rights.* Cambridge: Cambridge University Press, 1994.
Lindell, I. *Africa's Informal Workers: Collective Agency, Alliances, and Transnational Organizing in Urban Africa.* London: Zed Books, 2010.
Linnebuhr, Elisabeth. "*Kanga*: Popular Cloths with Messages." *Matatu: Journal of African Culture and Society* 9 (1992): 89–93.
Lipartito, Kenneth. "Reassembling the Economic: New Departures in Historical Materialism." *American Historical Review* 121, no. 1 (2016): 101–39.

Lonsdale, John. "Jomo Kenyatta, God, and the Modern World." In *African Modernities: Entangled Meanings in Current Debate*, edited by J.-G. Deutsch, P. Probst, and H. Schmidt, 67–89. Oxford: James Currey, 2002.

———. "Town Life in Colonial Kenya." In *Nairobi Today: The Paradox of a Fragmented City*, edited by Hélène Charton-Bigot and Deyssi Rodriguez-Torres, 3–21. Paris: Karthala, 2006.

Lopes, C. M. "Hug Me, Hold Me Tight! The Evolution of Passenger Transport in Luanda and Huambo (Angola), 1975–2000." In *The Speed of Change: Motor Vehicles and People in Africa, 1890–2000*, edited by Jan-Bart Gewald, Sabine Luning, and Klaas van Walraven, 107–27. Leiden: Brill, 2009.

Lynch, Gabrielle. *I Say to You: Ethnic Politics and the Kalenjin in Kenya*. Chicago: University of Chicago Press, 2011.

Lysaght, Karen D. "Catholics, Protestants, and Office Workers from the Town: The Experience and Negotiation of Fear in Northern Ireland." In *Mixed Emotions: Anthropological Studies of Feeling*, edited by Kay Milton and Maruska Svasek, 127–44. New York: Berg, 2006.

Maathai, Wangari. *Unbowed: A Memoir*. New York: Alfred Knopf, 2013.

Mabogunje, Akin L. "Urban Planning and the Post-Colonial State: A Research Overview." *African Studies Review* 33, no. 2 (1990): 121–203.

MacGaffey, J. "Creatively Coping with Crisis: Entrepreneurs in the Second Economy of Zaire (the Democratic Republic of the Congo)." In *African Entrepreneurship: Theory and Reality*, edited by A. Spring and B. E. McDade, 37–50. Gainesville: University Press of Florida, 1998.

———. *Entrepreneurs and Parasites: The Struggle for Indigenous Capitalism in Zaire*. Cambridge: Cambridge University Press, 1987.

———. *The Real Economy of Zaire: The Contribution of Smuggling and Other Unofficial Activities to National Wealth*. London: James Currey, 1991.

MacGaffey, J., and R. Bazenguissa. *Congo-Paris: Transnational Traders on the Margins of the Law*. Oxford: James Currey, 2000.

Macharia, Kinuthia. "Slum Clearance and the Informal Economy in Nairobi." *Journal of Modern African Studies* 30 (1992): 221–36.

Mahajan, Vijay. *Africa Rising: How 900 Million African Consumers Offer More Than You Think*. Upper Saddle River, NJ: Wharton, 2009.

Makura, M. *Africa's Greatest Entrepreneurs*. Johannesburg: Penguin Books, 2011.

Malkki, Liisa. *The Need to Help: The Domestic Arts of International Humanitarianism*. Durham, NC: Duke University Press, 2015.

Mamdani, Mahmood. *From Citizen to Refugee: Uganda Asians Come to Britain*. Johannesburg: Pambazuka Press, 2011.

Mangat, J. S. *The History of Asians in East Africa, c. 1886–1945*. Oxford: Oxford University Press, 1969.

Mann, Gregory. *From Empires to NGOs in the West African Sahel: The Road to Nongovernmentality*. Cambridge: Cambridge University Press, 2014.

Martin, Phyllis. *Leisure and Society in Colonial Brazzaville*. Cambridge: Cambridge University Press.

Marx, Karl. *Das Kapital*. New York: CreateSpace Independent Publishing Platform, 2011.

Masquelier, Adeline. "Road Mythologies: Space, Mobility, and the Historical Imagination in Postcolonial Niger." *American Ethnologist* 29 (2002): 829–55.

Mavhunga, Clapperton C. *Transient Workspaces: Technologies of Everyday Innovation in Zimbabwe*. Cambridge, MA: MIT Press, 2014.

Maxon, Robert. "Social and Cultural Changes." In *Decolonization and Independence in Kenya: 1949–93*, edited by B. A. Ogot and Williams Ochieng', 78–110. Athens: Ohio University Press, 1995.

Mbembe, Achille, and Janet Roitman. "Figures of the Subject in Times of Crisis." *Public Culture* 23 (1996): 26–47.

Mboya, Tom. *The Challenge of Nationhood*. Nairobi: Heinemann, 1970.

McCormick, D., P. Chitere, R. Orero, W. Mitullah, and M. Ommeh. "Paratransit Operations and Regulation in Nairobi: Matatu Business Strategies and the Regulatory Regime." Pretoria, South Africa, 31st Southern African Transport Conference (SATC 2012), July 9–12, 2012.

McCurdy, Sheryl. "Fashioning Sexuality: Desire, Manyema Ethnicity, and the Creation of the 'Kanga,' ca. 1880–1900." *International Journal of African Historical Studies* 39, no. 3 (2006): 441–69.

McDade, B. E., and A. Spring. "The 'New Generation of African Entrepreneurs': Networking to Change the Climate for Business and Private Sector-Led Development." *Entrepreneurship and Regional Development* 17 (2005):17–42.

McMillan, John. *Reinventing the Bazaar: A Natural History of Markets*. New York: Norton, 2003.

Mead, Donald. "The Economics of Population Growth." *Transition* (April–May 1967): 40–42.

Meagher, K. "A Back Door to Globalisation? Structural Adjustment, Globalisation, and Transborder Trade in West Africa." *Review of African Political Economy* 95 (2003): 57–75.

———. "Hijacking Civil Society: The Inside Story of Bakassi Boys." *Journal of Modern African Studies* 213 (2007): 120–45.

———. *Identity Economics: Social Networks and the Informal Economy in Nigeria*. Oxford: James Currey, 2010.

Médard, Claire. "City Planning in Nairobi: The Stakes, the People, the Side-tracking." In *Nairobi Today: The Paradox of a Fragmented City*, edited by Hélène Charton-Bigot and Deyssi Rodriguez-Torres, 25–60. Paris: Karthala, 2006.

Mehta, Suketu. *Maximum City: Bombay Lost and Found*. New York: Vintage, 2005.

Meredith, M. *The Fate of Africa: A History of Fifty Years of Independence*. New York: PublicAffairs, 2005.

Meyer, Birgit. "Christianity in Africa: From African Independent to

Pentecostal-Charismatic Churches." *Annual Review of Anthropology* 33 (2004): 447–74.

———. *Sensational Movies: Video, Vision, and Christianity in Ghana.* Berkeley: University of California Press, 2015.

———. "'There Is a Spirit in That Image': Mass-Produced Jesus Pictures and Protestant-Pentecostal Animation in Ghana." *Comparative Studies in Society and History* 52 (2010): 100–124.

Meyer, Birgit, and Jojada Verrips. "Kwaku's Car: The Struggles and Stories of a Ghanaian Long-Distance Taxi-Driver." In *Car Cultures*, edited by Daniel Miller, 153–84. Oxford: Berg, 2001.

Middleton, J. *African Merchants of the Indian Ocean: Swahili of the East African Coast.* Wesport, CT: Waveland Press, 2004.

Miguel, Edward. *Africa's Turn?* Boston: Boston Review Books, 2009.

Miguel, Edward, and Mary Kay Gugerty. "Ethnic Diversity, Social Sanctions, and Public Goods in Kenya." *Journal of Public Economics* 89 (2005): 2325–68.

Milburn, Josephine. *British Business and Ghanaian Independence.* London: C. Hurst, 1977.

Milgrom, Paul. "Axelrod's *The Evolution of Cooperation.*" *Rand Journal of Economics* 15, no. 2 (1984): 305–9.

Miller, Charles. *The Lunatic Express.* New York: Macmillan, 1971.

Miller, Daniel, ed. *Car Cultures.* Oxford: Berg, 2001.

Milliken, J., and K. Krause. "State Failure, State Collapse, and State Reconstruction: Concepts, Lessons, and Strategies." *Development and Change* 33 (2002): 753–74.

Moreton, Bethany. *To Serve God and Wal-Mart: The Making of Christian Free Enterprise.* Cambridge, MA: Harvard University Press, 2009.

Moyo, Dambisa. *Dead Aid: Why Aid Is Not Working and Why There Is a Better Way for Africa.* New York: Farrar Strauss and Giroux, 2011.

Mumford, Lewis. "The Culture of Cities." In *Metropolis: Center and Symbol of Our Times*, edited by Philip Kasinitz, 20–42. New York: New York University Press, 1995.

Mũngai, Mbũgua wa. "Hidden $ Centz: Rolling the Wheels of Nairobi Matatu." In *Nairobi Today: The Paradox of a Fragmented City*, edited by Hélène Charton-Bigot and Deyssi Rodriguez-Torres, 351–64. Nairobi: IFRA, 2010.

———. "Kaa Masaa, 'Grapple with Spiders': The Myriad Threads of Nairobi Matatu Discourse." In *Urban Legends, Colonial Myths: Popular Culture and Literature in East Africa*, edited by J. Ogude and J. Nyairo, 25–58. Asmara: Africa World Press, 2006.

———. *Nairobi's Matatu Men: Portrait of a Sub-Culture.* Nairobi: Contact Zones, 2013.

Mũngai, Mbũgua wa, and D. A. Samper. "'No Mercy, No Remorse': Personal Experience Narratives about Public Passenger Transportation in Nairobi, Kenya." *Africa Today* 52 (2006): 51–81.

Muriuki, Godfrey, and G. Mutiso. "The Political Economy of Self-Help: Kenya's *Harambee* Institutes of Technology." *Canadian Journal of African Studies* 8, no. 1 (1974): 109–33.

Murunga, Godwin. "Refugees at Home? Coping with Somalia Conflict in Nairobi, Kenya." In *African Studies in Geography from Below*, edited by Michel Ben Arrous and Lazare Ki-Zerbo. Dakar: Codesria, 2009.

———. "Urban Violence in Kenya's Transition to Pluralist Politics, 1982–1992." *Africa Development* 24, no. 1/2 (1999): 165–98.

Musambayi, Katumanga. "A City under Siege: Banditry and Modes of Accumulation in Nairobi, 1991–2004." *Journal of African Political Economy* 106 (2005): 505–20.

Musandu, Phoebe. "Drawing from the Wells of Culture: Grace Onyango and the Kenyan Political Scene (1964–1983)." *Wagadu: A Journal of Transnational Women's and Gender Studies* 6 (2008): 23–38.

Mutongi, Kenda. "Dear Dolly's Advice: Representations of Youth, Courtship, and Sexualities in Africa, 1960–1980." *International Journal of African Historical Studies* 1, no. 2 (2000): 230–52. Reprinted in Jennifer Cole and Lynn Thomas, *Love in Africa*. Chicago: University of Chicago Press, 2009.

———. "Thugs or Entrepreneurs: Perceptions of Matatu Operators in Nairobi, 1970 to the Present." *Africa* (2006): 549–68.

———. *Worries of the Heart: Widows, Family, and Community in Kenya*. Chicago: University of Chicago Press, 2007.

Muwonge, Joe Wamala. "Urban Policy and Patterns of Low-Income Settlement in Nairobi." *Population and Development Review* 6, no. 4 (1980): 595–613.

Nafukho, F. M. "Consensus Building, Dialogue, and Spirituality Principles of the Learning Organisation Paradigm: Implications for Kenya's Public Service Reform Agenda." *Journal of Third World Studies* 34 (2008): 153–75.

———. "Education through Self-Help: The Case of Kenyan University Students with the Introduction of University Fees Payment." *Journal of Eastern African Research and Development* 24 (1994): 42–53.

———. *The Forgotten Workers: The Case of Public Service Vehicle Drivers in Eldoret, Kenya*. Addis Ababa: Organization of Social Science Research in Eastern and Southern Africa (OSSREA), 2001.

Naipaul, Shiva. *North of South: An African Journey*. London: Vintage, 1979.

Nasong'o, S. W. "Negotiating New Rules of the Game: Social Movements, Civil Society, and the Kenyan Transition." In *Kenya: The Struggle for Democracy*, edited by G. R. Murunga and S. W. Nasong'o, 19–57. Dakar: Codesria Books, 2007.

Nelson, Nici. "Representations of Men and Women, City and Town in Kenyan Novels of the 1970s and 1980s." *African Languages and Cultures* 9, no. 2 (1996): 148–68.

Nevanlinna, Anja Kervanto. *Interpreting Nairobi: The Cultural Study of Built Forms*. Helsinki: Suomen Historiallinen Seura, 1996.

Neves, David, and Andries du Toit. "Money and Sociality in South Africa's Informal Economy." *Africa* 82, no. 1 (2012): 131–49.

Ngau, Peter M. "Tensions in Empowerment: The Experience of the 'Harambee' (Self-Help) Movement in Kenya." *Economic Development and Cultural Change* 35, no. 3 (1987): 523–38.

North, Douglass. *Institutions, Institutional Change, and Economic Performance.* Cambridge: Cambridge University Press, 1990.

Nozick, Robert. *Anarchy, State, and Utopia.* New York: Basic Books, 2013.

Nyairo, Joyce. "Jua Kali as a Metaphor for Africa's Urban Ethnicities." Mary Kingsley Zochonis Lecture at SOAS, July 2, 2005.

Nyatugah, Grace. "Revisiting Our Indigenous Shrines through Mungiki." *African Affairs* 400 (2001): 453–67.

Obama, Barack. *Dreams from My Father: A Story of Race and Inheritance.* New York: Three Rivers Press, 2004.

Obudho, Rose A., and G. O. Aduwo. "The Nature of the Urbanization Process and Urbanism in the City of Nairobi Kenya." *African Urban Quarterly* 7, nos. 1–2 (1992): 50–62.

Ochieng', William R. "The Kenyatta Era: Structural and Political Changes." In *Decolonization and Independence in Kenya*, edited by B. A. Ogot and William R. Ochieng'. Athens: Ohio University Press, 1995.

Ocobock, Paul. "Joy Rides for Juveniles: Vagrant Youth and Colonial Control in Nairobi, Kenya, 1901–1952." *Social History* 31, no. 1 (2006): 39–59.

Odero, W., M. Khayesi, and P. Heda. "Road Traffic Injuries in Kenya: Magnitude, Causes, and Status of Intervention." *Injury Control and Safety Promotion* 10 (2003): 53–61.

Odhiambo, W., and W. Mitullah. "Policies and Regulations for Business Development." In *Business in Kenya: Institutions and Interactions*, edited by D. McCormick, P. O. Alila, and M. Omosa, 40–63. Nairobi: University of Nairobi Press, 2007.

Ogude, James. *Ngugi's Novels and African History: Narrating the Nation.* New York: Pluto Press, 1999.

Ogude, James, and Joyce Nyairo. *Urban Legends, Colonial Myths: Popular Culture and Literature in East Africa.* Trenton, NJ: African World Press, 2007.

Olopade, Dayo. *The Bright Continent: Breaking Rules and Making Change in Modern Africa.* Boston: Houghton Mifflin Harcourt, 2014.

Olson, Mancur. *The Logic of Collective Action: Public Goods and the Theory of Groups.* Cambridge, MA: Harvard University Press, 1971.

Opiyo, Tom. "The Metamorphosis of the Kenya Bus Service Limited in the Provision of Urban Transport in Nairobi." SSATO/World Bank Urban Mobility Component 12th Steering Committee Meeting, Maputo, July 1–5, 2002.

Ostrom, Elinor. *Governing the Commons: The Evolution of Institutions for Collective Action.* Cambridge: Cambridge University Press, 1990

Otiso, K. M. "Colonial Urbanisation and Urban Management in Kenya." In

African Urban Spaces in Historical Perspective, edited by S. J. Salm and T. Falola, 73–95. Rochester, NY: University of Rochester Press, 2005.

Patterson, J. H. *The Man-Eaters of Tsavo and Other East African Adventures*. London: Macmillan, 1907.

Peredo, A. M., and J. J. McLean. "Social Entrepreneurship: A Critical Review of the Concept." *Journal of World Business* 41, no. 2 (2006): 56–65.

Pierce, Steven. *Moral Economies of Corruption: State Formation and Political Culture in Nigeria*. Durham, NC: Duke University Press, 2016.

Piketty, Thomas. *Capital in the Twenty-First Century*. Cambridge, MA: Belknap Press of Harvard University Press, 2014.

Platteau, Jean-Philippe. *Institutions, Social Norms, and Economic Development*. Amsterdam: Harwood Academic, 2000.

Porter, Robert H. "A Study of Cartel Stability: The Joint Executive Committee, 1880–1886." *Bell Journal of Economics* 14 (1983): 301–14.

Poundstone, William. *Prisoner's Dilemma: John von Neumann, Game Theory, and the Puzzle of the Bomb*. New York: Doubleday, 1992.

Prakash, Gyan. *Mumbai Fables*. Princeton, NJ: Princeton University Press, 2010.

Preston, Ronald. *The Genesis of Kenya Colony*. Oxford: Oxford University Press, 1937.

Pritchett, J. "Nigerian Truck Art." *African Arts* 12 (1979): 4–8.

Quayson, Ato. *Oxford Street, Accra: City Life and the Itineraries of Transnationalism*. Durham, NC: Duke University Press, 2014.

Radelet, Steven. *Emerging Africa: How 17 Countries Are Leading the Way*. New York: Center for Global Development, 2010.

Ranger, Terence. *Dance and Society in East Africa, 1890–1970*. Berkeley: University of California Press, 1975.

Rapoport, Anatol, and A. M. Chammah. *Prisoner's Dilemma*. Ann Arbor: University of Michigan Press, 1965.

Rasmussen, J. "Inside the System, Outside the Law: Operating the Matatu Sector in Nairobi." *Urban Forum* 23 (2012): 415–32.

———. "Mungiki as Youth Movement: Revolution, Gender, and Generational Politics in Nairobi, Kenya." *Young: Nordic Journal of Youth Research* 18 (2010): 301–19.

———. "Outwitting the Professor of Politics? Mungiki Narratives of Political Deception and Their Role in Kenyan Politics." *Journal of Eastern African Studies* 4, no. 3 (2010): 435–49.

Riker, William. *The Art of Political Manipulation*. New Haven, CT: Yale University Press, 1986.

Rist, Gilbert. *The History of Development: From Western Origins to Global Faith*. London: Zed, 1997.

Rizzo, Matteo. "Being Taken for a Ride: Privatization of the Dar es Salaam Transport System 1983–1998." *Journal of Modern African Studies* 40 (2002): 133–57.

Robertson, C. C. "Women Entrepreneurs? Trade and the Gender Division of Labor in Nairobi." In *Africa Entrepreneurship: Theory and Reality*, edited by A. Spring and B. E. McDade, 109–27. Gainesville: University Press of Florida, 1998.

Rodney, Walter. *How Europe Underdeveloped Africa*. Baltimore: Black Classic Press, 2011.

Roger, Scott. "Are Trade Unions Still Necessary in Africa?" *Transition* 33, no. 2 (1967): 27–31.

Rogerson, C. M. "In Search of the African Miracle: Debates on Successful Small Enterprise Development in Africa." *Habitat International* 25 (2001): 115–42.

Rosenwein, Barbara H. *Emotional Communities in Early Middle Ages*. Ithaca, NY: Cornell University Press, 2007.

Roth, Alvin. *Who Gets What—and Why: The New Economics of Matchmaking and Market Design*. Boston: Eamon Dolan / Houghton Mifflin Harcourt, 2015.

Ruteere, M. *Dilemmas of Crime, Human Rights, and the Politics of Mungiki Violence in Kenya*. Nairobi: Kenya Human Rights Institute, 2008.

Ruteere, M., and M. E. Pommerolle. "Democratizing Security or Decentralizing Repression? The Ambiguities of Community Policing in Kenya." *African Affairs* 102 (2003): 587–604.

Sachs, Jeffrey. *The End of Poverty: Economic Possibilities for Our Time*. New York: Penguin Press, 2005.

Salm, Steven J. "Popular Music, Identity, and the Lumpen Youth of Nairobi." In *Urbanization and African Cultures*, edited by Toyin Falola and Steven Salm. Durham, NC: Carolina Academic Press, 2005.

Salon, Deborah, and Eric M. Aligula. "Urban Travel in Nairobi, Kenya: Analysis, Insights, and Opportunities." *Journal of Transport Geography* 22 (May 2012): 65–76.

Sandbrook, Richard. "Patrons, Clients, and Unions: The Labour Movement and Political Conflict in Kenya." *Journal of Commonwealth Political Studies* 10, no. 1 (1972): 2–27.

———. *The Politics of Africa's Economic Stagnation*. Cambridge: Cambridge University Press, 1986.

———. *The Politics of Basic Needs: Urban Aspects of Assaulting Poverty in Africa*. Toronto: University of Toronto Press, 1982.

Sante, Luc. *The Other Paris*. New York: Farrar Straus, 2015.

Sarasvathy, S. D. "Causation and Effectuation: Toward a Theoretical Shift from Economic Inevitability to Entrepreneurial Contingency." *Academy of Management Review* 26, no. 3 (2001): 243–63.

Scherz, China. *Having People, Having Heart: Charity, Sustainable Development, and Problems of Dependence in Central Uganda*. Chicago: University of Chicago Press, 2014.

Schumpeter, J. A. *Capitalism, Socialism, and Democracy*. New York: Harper Perennial, 2008.

Scott, James C. *The Art of Not Being Governed: An Anarchist History of Upland Southeast Asia.* New Haven, CT: Yale University Press, 2011.

———. *Two Cheers for Anarchy: Six Pieces on Autonomy, Dignity, and Meaningful Work and Play.* Princeton, NJ: Princeton University Press, 2014.

Sen, Amartya. *Development as Freedom.* New York: Anchor, 2000.

Shane, S. *A General Theory of Entrepreneurship: The Individual-Opportunity Nexus.* Cheltenham: Edward Elgar, 2003.

Sheldon, K. *Courtyards, Markets, City Streets: Urban Women in Africa.* Boulder, CO: Westview Press, 1996.

Shepler, S. "Child Labour and Youth Enterprise: Post-War Urban Infrastructure and the 'Bearing Boys' of Freetown." *Anthropology Today* 26 (2010): 19–22.

Shipton, Parker. *Credit between Cultures: Farmers, Financiers, and Misunderstanding in Africa.* New Haven, CT: Yale University Press, 2010.

———. *The Nature of Entrustment: Intimacy, Exchange, and the Sacred in Africa.* New Haven, CT: Yale University Press, 2007.

Simone, A. "Introduction: Urban Processes and Change." In *Urban Africa: Changing Contours of Survival in the City,* edited by A. Simone and A. Abouhani, 1–28. Dakar: Codesria, 2005.

———. "Pirate Towns: Reworking Social and Symbolic Infrastructures in Johannesburg and Douala." *Urban Studies* 43 (2006): 357–70.

Situma, Lan. "The Matatus: Public Transportation in Nairobi." Nairobi: Nairobi City Council, 1977.

Sivaramakrishnan, K., and Arun Agrawal, eds. *Regional Modernities: The Cultural Politics of Development in India.* Stanford, CA: Stanford University Press, 2003.

Smith, Adam. *Wealth of Nations.* New York: Bantam Classics, 2003.

Smith, D. J. "The Bakassi Boys: Vigilantism, Violence, and Political Imagination in Nigeria." *Cultural Anthropology* 122 (2004): 23–46.

Smith, Marc. *Communities in Cyberspace.* New York: Routledge, 1999.

Solis, Julia. *New York Underground: The Anatomy of the City.* New York: Routledge, 2007.

Soto, Hernando de. *The Mystery of Capital: Why Capitalism Triumphs in the West and Fails Everywhere Else.* New York: Basic Books, 2003.

Soyinka, Wole. *The Beatification of Area Boy: A Lagosian Kaleidoscope.* London: Methuen Drama, 1995.

Steeves, Jeffrey. "Presidential Succession in Kenya: The Transition from Moi to Kibaki." *Commonwealth and Comparative Politics* 44 (2006): 211–33.

Stiglitz, Joseph E. *Globalization and Its Discontents.* New York: W. W. Norton, 2003.

———. *Making Globalization Work.* New York: W. W. Norton, 2007.

Stitchter, Sharon. "The Formation of a Working Class in Kenya." In *The Development of a Working Class Formation and Action,* edited by Richard Sandbrook and Robin Cohen, 34–69. London: Longman, 1975.

Stoller, Paul. *Money Has No Smell: The Africanization of New York City.* Chicago: University of Chicago Press, 2002.

Stren, Richard, and Rodney White. *African Cities in Crisis: Managing Rapid Urban Growth*. Boulder, CO: Westview Press, 1988.

Swainson, Nicola. *The Development of Corporate Capitalism in Kenya, 1918–1977*. Berkeley: University of California Press, 1980.

Swidler, Ann, and Susan Cotts Watkins. "'Teach a Man to Fish': The Sustainability Doctrine and Its Social Consequences." *World Development 7* (2009): 1182–96.

Symes, Carol. "When We Talk about Modernity." *American Historical Review* 116, no. 3 (2011): 715–26.

Tamarkin, M. "The Roots of Political Stability in Kenya." *African Affairs 77* (1978): 297–320.

Taylor, Scott D. *Globalization and the Cultures of Business in Africa: From Patrimonialism to Profit*. Bloomington: Indiana University Press, 2012.

Theroux, Paul. "Hating Asians." *Transition 33* (1967): 46–51.

Thiong'o Ngũgĩ wa, *Devil on the Cross*. London: Heinemann, 1982.

———. *A Grain of Wheat*. Nairobi: Heinemann, 1977.

Thompson, R. F. "Tap-Tap, Fula-Fula, Kia-Kia: The Haitian Bus in the Atlantic Context." *African Arts 30* (1996): 36–45.

Throup, David, and Charles Hornsby. *Multi-Party Politics in Kenya: The Kenyatta and Moi States and the Triumph of the System in the 1992 Election*. Oxford: James Currey, 1998.

Tignor, Robert L. "The Business Firm in Africa." *Business History Review 81*, no. 1 (2007): 87–110.

Tripp, A. M. *Changing the Rules: The Politics of Liberalization and the Urban Informal Economy in Tanzania*. Berkeley: University of California Press, 1997.

Turner, Terisa E., and Leigh S. Brownhill. "African Jubilee: Mau Mau Resurgence and the Fight for Fertility in Kenya, 1986–2002." *Canadian Journal of Development Studies* 22, special issue (2001): 1037–88.

Twaddle, Michael. *Expulsion of a Minority: Essays on Uganda Asians*. New York: Continuum, 1975.

Van Eijk, R. *Car Slogans in Ghana*. Amsterdam: Cadier en Keer, 2003.

Vassanji, M. G. *The Book of Secrets: A Novel*. London: Picador, 1996.

———. *The Gunny Sack*. London: Heinemann, 1990.

———. *The In-Between World of Vikram Lall*. London: Vintage, 2005.

Verese, Frederico. *The Russian Mafia: Private Protection in the New Market Economy*. Oxford: Oxford University Press, 2005.

Wainaina, Binyavanga. *Discovering Home*. Nairobi: Kwani, 2006.

———. "Generation Kenya." *Vanity Fair*, July 2007, 1–8.

———. *One Day I Will Write about This Place: A Memoir*. London: Graywolf Press, 2011.

Wainaina, J. "The 'Parking Boys' of Nairobi." *African Journal of Sociology 2* (1981): 7–45.

Walton, John K. "Power, Speed, and Glamour: The Naming of Express Steam

Locomotives in Inter-War Britain." *Journal of Transport History* 23 (2005): 12–34.

Wamue, Grace Nyatugah. "Revisiting Our Indigenous Shrines through Mungiki." *African Affairs* 100, no. 400 (2001): 453–79.

Wan, M. Y. "Secrets of Success: Uncertainty, Profits, and Prosperity in the Gari Economy of Ibadan, 1992–94." *Africa* 72 (2001): 225–52.

Weiss, Brad. *Street Dreams and Hip Hop Barbershops: Global Fantasy in Urban Tanzania*. Bloomington: Indiana University Press, 2009.

Werlin, Herbert H. *Governing an African City: A Study of Nairobi*. London: Africana Publishing, 1974.

———. "Nairobi in the Time of Uhuru." *Africa Today* 10, no. 10 (1963): 7–10.

White, Luise. *The Comforts of Home: Prostitution in Colonial Nairobi*. Chicago: University of Chicago Press, 1990.

Widner, Jennifer. *The Rise of a Party State in Kenya: From Harambee to Nyayo*. Berkeley: University of California Press, 1992.

Williams, Eric. *Capitalism and Slavery*. Chapel Hill: University of North Carolina Press, 1994.

Wilson, L. S. "Technical Expertise and Indigenization." In *Foreign Aid: New Perspectives*, edited by Kanhaya L. Gupta, 127–45. Recent Economic Thought Series 68 (1999).

Wirth, G. "Transportation Policy in Mexico City: The Politics and Impacts of Privatization." *Urban Affairs Review* 33 (1987): 155–81.

Wrong, Michela. *It's Our Turn to Eat*. London: Fourth Estate, 2010.

Wydick, Bruce. *Games in Economic Development*. Cambridge: Cambridge University Press, 2008.

Zingales, Luigi. *A Capitalism of the People: Recapturing the Lost Genius of American Prosperity*. New York: Basic Books, 2012.

Zolberg, Aristide. "The Structure of Political Conflict in the New States of Tropical Africa." *American Political Science Review* 62, no. 1 (1968): 70–87.

Index